HARRIMAN ALASKA SERIES
VOLUME V

CRYPTOGAMIC BOTANY

BY

J. CARDOT, CLARA E. CUMMINGS,
ALEXANDER W. EVANS, C. H. PECK,
P. A. SACCARDO, De ALTON SAUNDERS,
I. THÉRIOT, and WILLIAM TRELEASE

(Publication 1994)

CITY OF WASHINGTON
PUBLISHED BY THE SMITHSONIAN INSTITUTION
1910

CONTENTS

	PAGE
PREFACE	v
LIST OF ILLUSTRATIONS	ix
INTRODUCTION. By William Trelease.	1
FUNGI. By P. A. Saccardo and William Trelease	11
LICHENS. By Clara E. Cummings	65
ALGÆ. By De Alton Saunders	153
MOSSES. By J. Cardot and I. Thériot	251
SPHAGNUMS. By William Trelease	329
LIVERWORTS (HEPATICÆ) By Alexander W. Evans	339
FERNS AND FERN ALLIES (PTERIDOPHYTES). By William Trelease	373
INDEX	399

ILLUSTRATIONS

PLATES

		PAGE
Plate I.	Moss-draped tree, Southeastern Alaska	Frontispiece
II–VII.	Fungi	54–64
VIII–IX	Lichens	150–152
X–XXIX.	Algæ	212–250
XXX–XL.	Mosses	308–328
XLI–XLIII.	Hepaticæ	368–372
XLIV.	Pteridophytes (*Dryopteris aquilonaris*)	398

TEXT FIGURE

Fig. 1. *Botrychium lunaria incisum* 377

CRYPTOGAMIC BOTANY OF ALASKA

INTRODUCTION

BY WILLIAM TRELEASE

In the organization of the scientific corps of the Harriman Alaska Expedition the phanerogams were assigned to Mr. Frederick V. Coville, of the United States Department of Agriculture, with Mr. T. H. Kearney, Jr., as assistant, and the cryptogams to Prof. William Trelease, of the Missouri Botanical Garden, with Prof. de Alton Saunders as assistant. While their ultimate responsibility for the treatment of their particular groups was not lost sight of, each of these gentlemen, though giving principal attention to his own group, collected all other botanical material which could be cared for; and Prof. W. H. Brewer, of Yale University, and Prof. B. E. Fernow, of Cornell University, both accomplished botanists, as well as other members of the party whose immediate interests were in other fields, made large additions to the collections in both departments of botany. In the results of the Expedition recorded in this volume, all of these collections are taken into account, and credit is given to the respective collectors in the chapters treating of the several groups of plants.

It was evident that the proper examination of the cryptogamic material required the care of specialists, and too much can not be said in acknowledgment of the service rendered by Professors P. A. Saccardo and C. H. Peck, who appear as joint authors of the chapter on Fungi, of Messrs. J. Cardot and I. Thériot, to whom is due the treatment of the mosses, exclusive of *Sphagnum;* of Dr. C. Warnstorf, without whose study the species of the latter genus could scarcely have been named; and of Prof. A. W. Evans and Miss Clara E. Cummings, who contributed the chapters on Liverworts and Lichens, respectively. From the first Professor Saunders devoted his attention almost exclusively to the algæ, and his chapter contains numerous references to the assistance of special authorities on some of the included groups. In the preparation of my own chapter on the Pteridophytes I have received the benefit of similar criticism and suggestion, which is duly acknowledged.

The present volume, therefore, represents not only the aggregate information on flowerless plants obtained by the Expedition as a whole, but the added knowledge of what has been learned of these plants by others — a knowledge which only experts could contribute; and I am sure that I am warranted in expressing to all of the collectors, and to the contributors to the volume, not only my personal gratitude, but that of Mr. Harriman and the editor of the publications of the Expedition, Dr. C. Hart Merriam.

The plants that first catch the eye in a region seen for the first time are usually flowers and trees; still the ferns and their allies do not occupy a greatly subordinate position in the general impression produced by the flora, and, in proportion as either of these more conspicuous elements fails in any region, the flowerless plants in one or another of their groups assume accentuated prominence.

The coast region of Alaska is marked in the southern district by the grandeur of its forests, reaching to approximately the middle of Kadiak Island and the corresponding part of the adjacent peninsula; and, in common with other regions of high latitude or altitude, by the brilliancy of its flowers beyond the forest area. The smaller and more brightly colored plants are usually overtopped and suppressed, except on the mountains, where toward and above the timber line the usual alpine conditions are reached. And yet, a second glance at even the forest region reveals a wealth of cryptogamic vegetation, which gives to the flora a character it would lack were this element removed. No small part of the charm of the brilliantly colored mountain tops and prairies is due to the setting of their flowers in beds of fern and moss, decaying skeletons may be the nidus of conspicuous tufts of *Tetraplodon* or some related genus; and otherwise naked cliffs are everywhere colored in soft but pleasing shades by their own lichen flora.

Landing at almost any point in the forest region, one is so fully occupied with the task of clambering over or under fallen trunks and picking a precarious way through the undergrowth of devil's club and other shrubbery, that it is not until he has forced his way some distance from the shore that he pauses to admire the immense trunks which surround him; and later still comes the realization that the ground is ankle-deep with mosses of the most luxuriant growth, which, saturated from the frequent rains, cover every moldering log, tapestry the living trunks, and hang in festoons from the branches, often so densely as to have smothered the less vigorous outer trees exposed to the wind and to occasional spray from the sea, in this respect recalling the effect sometimes produced in subtropical regions by the trailing *Tillandsia*, on our New England coast, as in Alaska, by species of *Usnea*, and in California by *Ramalina*, of similar growth. In Alaska, however, the true mosses also produce this effect; and the most striking among them are two large species of *Hylocomium* (*H. splendens* and *H. loreum*). Nestling among the carpeting mosses and liverworts are many of the smaller and more delicate flowering plants of this region, as well as a few of the more tender fernworts; and it is here that a large part of the fleshy fungi find the most favorable conditions for their growth.

Whenever an opening occurs in the forest, the bogs of lower latitudes are reproduced, and the peat mosses (*Sphagnum*), in considerable variety, assume their characteristic appearance and afford a nidus for the delicate cranberries, sundews, and butterworts. With the ceasing of the forest begins a continuous wet prairie and bog region, which passes into the true tundra of the high north, frozen to a great depth and thawing for only a foot or two in the short summer, during which, however, its mossy covering is enlivened by a blaze of flowers scarcely to be surpassed.

In these open places ferns appear in greatest luxuriance, and a clamber up the mountain side at Sturgeon River Bay, on Kadiak Island, through wet lady-fern nearly waist-deep, is an experience not soon to be forgotten. Next to this, perhaps the most striking fern is *Blechnum*, the broad sterile fronds of which, pressed to the ground, are in marked contrast with the narrower, erect, fertile ones — a dimorphism again seen in the cliff-brake, *Allosorus*. As in alpine bogs of lower latitudes, the addertongue (*Ophioglossum*) and moonworts (*Botrychium*) are found interestingly associated with true ferns, mosses, and the smaller flowering plants, and the moonworts in particular are represented by a goodly number of the more interesting species. One of the characteristic features of the moraine flora in Glacier Bay and elsewhere is the abundance of a loosely straggling scouring-rush, referable to *Equisetum variegatum* but quite unlike the type of that species; while the common horsetail, *E. arvense*, which is everywhere abundant, assumes, under the influence of environment, a variety of forms and sizes, puzzling alike in the fixity of certain characters (as the triquetrous twigs of the common boreal type) and in the pliability of others.

The authors of the chapters dealing with the several groups of cryptogams have so fully analyzed their respective branches of the Alaskan flora, both as to their components and their relations to the floras of other parts of the world, as to make it unnecessary to do more here than summarize their statements, showing that a total of 1,616 species of cryptogams may now be ascribed to Alaska, of which 240 are fungi, 459 algæ, 400 lichens, 460 Bryophytes, and 57 Pteridophytes.

In a land marked by a long winter, with an abundance of fish and game within easy reach, it is not surprising that the natives of Alaska have given little attention to agriculture, and it is interesting to note, as a consequence of this failure to cultivate plants, that the greatest possible use is made of spontaneous vegetable products. While the most valuable of these are derived from flowering plants, the cryptogams are put to many, if not very important, uses.

To a seaside people, cut off from the interior by high and abrupt mountains with few and remote practicable passes, the sea offers not only the most used highway, but it yields a large part of their subsistence. Though few of the marine plants, which are chiefly algæ, are of much importance as articles of diet,

Mertens[1] found that the Indians ate, both raw and cooked, the lower part of the stipe of a rock weed which he referred to *Fucus vesiculosus* (probably what in this volume is called *F. evanescens macrocephala*), and which, or some related species, is doubtless what Dr. Grinnell[2] notes as being eaten fresh. Mertens also mentions that *Fucus esculentus* (*Alaria* sp), *F. saccharinus* (*Laminaria saccharina*), and '*F. edulis*' are eaten. Professor Saunders observed, on the Harriman Expedition, that the Indians make extensive use of one of the red seaweeds, *Rhodymenia palmata* (the dulse, or dillesk, which is also eaten on the Atlantic coasts, and is said to be used in Kamchatka as the basis of a fermented beverage). He saw them gathering this by the basketful at Orca and in Yakutat Bay, and packing it away, when sun-dried, for the winter, when, as he was given to understand, it is broken up by pounding, moistened with water, and made into a sort of pudding. Mr. M. W. Gorman, who has probably made a more thorough study of the food plants of Alaska Indians than any other person, informs me that another of the Florideæ — a laver — *Porphyra perforata*, is gathered in quantity, washed in fresh water, and pressed into cakes nearly a foot square and about an inch thick, which are dried for future use. Cut into small fragments, these cakes furnish the basis for a decoction used as a remedy for colds and bronchial affections; they are also sprinkled over food as a condiment; and Mr. Gorman adds that before the advent of the white man this was the only source of salt possessed by the natives. It may be this species that Dr. Grinnell[3] refers to as being dried, pressed into cakes, and used as an ingredient of soups and stews; and which Mr. Coville, on the Harriman Expedition, observed in Reid Inlet, made into purple cakes about a foot long, six inches wide, and an inch and a half thick, which the Indians chewed with evident relish. On Douglas Island Mr. Coville also found that the Indians had dried algæ — a form of *Fucus evanescens*, judging from his description — covered with minute fish eggs and called tiyéti. Aside from this occasional

---

[1] Linnæa, 4: 46; Hooker's Bot. Miscellany, 3: 3. 1829
[2] Harriman Alaska Expedition, 1: 139. 1901
[3] Harriman Alaska Expedition, 1: 139. 1901

use as food, the Alaskan algæ are recorded as having formerly furnished fish-lines, for which knotted stipes of the giant kelp, *Nereocystis priapus*, are said by Grinnell[1] and Mertens[2] to have been used, the species being referred to by Mertens under the name *Fucus lutkeanus*. The latter writer also speaks of the hollow stems of the same kelp as used for siphoning water out of a bidarka, a trick no doubt learned from or practiced by the Russians.

Few observations have been recorded on the use of fungi by the natives of Alaska, and no very important use appears to be made by them of any plant of this group. Though the damp woods and fern-covered hillsides of the southern and eastern part of the country afford good conditions for the growth of pileate species, the larger or more fleshy of which are usually called mushrooms or toadstools, no evidence is at hand showing that they are used for food by the aborigines. Though it is probable that, as in their own country, the Russians eat a variety of these plants, only one reference has been found to such use being made by them of the Alaskan species, namely, a statement by Kellogg[3] showing that he found the greatest luxury of one of the Russian villages to be pickled mushrooms, which he determined as '*Agaricus mutabilis*.' Mr. Coville observed one of the bracket fungi, *Fomes tinctorius*, in use by the Tlinkits of Sitka, especially the women, under the name tsakwât, for blackening their faces as a protection against sunburn, the fungus being charred on one side and used as a burnt cork is used in making up for the stage, the resulting color containing often a shade of red from the unburnt part of the fungus. Another species of the same genus, since determined as *F. igniarius*, is mentioned by Nelson[4] as used in the Yukon region for the production of ashes which are mixed with shredded tobacco for chewing. In the manuscript of a paper by Mr. M. W. Gorman, on the natives of the Lake Iliamna region and the plants

[1] Harriman Alaska Expedition, 1: 138–139. 1901.
[2] Linnæa, 4: 48. 1829.
[3] A. Kellogg, Report of the botany of the voyage of the United States steamer *Lincoln*, etc., U. S. State and Treasury Departments, House Ex. Doc. No. 177, Second Session, Fortieth Congress, Russian America, 218. 1868.
[4] Ann. Rept. Bureau Amer. Ethnology, 18: 271. *fig* 93. 1899.

used by them, further reference is made to the same use of this species (so determined by Professor Peck), which is said to be not uncommon on birch in that region.

Scarcely any record can be found of the use of lichens by the people of Alaska, though it would appear probable that in times of famine the abundant Iceland moss, *Cetraria islandica*, and various forms of rock tripe, *Umbilicaria*, might be used as human food. Mosses and lichens, without further specification, are noted by Murdoch[1] as furnishing winter food for reindeer at Point Barrow, and no doubt the abundant and well-known reindeer moss, *Cladonia rangiferina*, is one of the most important of the species referred to. Many of the lichens are elsewhere used as dye-stuffs, but no evidence of such use of any of them in Alaska has been found, though Mr. Coville informs me that one of the Alaskan tree species, *Evernia vulpina*, is the basis of a yellow dye used for basket materials on the coast farther south.

Mosses, referred to above as serving for part of the food of reindeer, are also mentioned by Murdoch[2] under the name múnik, as being employed for lamp wicks, a use to which we observed the bog mosses, *Sphagnum*, to be put at Plover Bay, Siberia. Dr. Hough[3] also mentions that wicks are made of *Sphagnum*, willow catkins, or peat, rolled between the hands with a little fat. Mr. Coville notes the use of moss in making beds for young children as generally prevalent in Alaska as well as in other parts of the United States; and in his manuscript on the Iliamna region, already referred to, Mr. Gorman states that under the name uroveet, *Sphagnum* is used by the natives as a padding or cushion for the baskets of birch-bark or willow in which infants are carried, and that moss saturated with water and placed before the fire is used as a means of inducing copious perspiration after childbirth, as, he believes, a long-established tribal custom, rather than from any good that results. Dry *Sphagnum* is also said by Dr. Merriam to be of frequent domestic use as an absorbent. Aside from this, no

[1] Ann. Rept. Bureau Amer. Ethnology, 9: 59. 1892.
[2] Ann. Rept. Bureau Amer. Ethnology, 9: 59, 106.
[3] Rept. U. S. Nat. Museum, 1896. 1033.

utilization of any of the mosses appears to be known, and no record exists of any use whatever being made of the related liverworts.

The Pteridophytes appear to be used more than any of the lower cryptogams, though, as compared with the flowering plants, they, too, are of but little direct economic value. Gorman[1] states that the natives of the southern part of Alaska cook and eat, under the name of ahh, the rootstock or caudex of *Aspidium spinulosum dilatatum*, which furnishes the first vegetable food obtained by them in spring In his manuscript on the Lake Iliamna region he states that, under the name of uh-ton-àh, the roots of what has been determined as *Athyrium cyclosorum*, and possibly one or two other ferns, are similarly used in the more northern country, and that, when boiled and the decoction sweetened with sugar or molasses, they furnish the basis of a fermented beverage, which, with the addition of flour, is further used in the preparation of a distilled liquor, hoochinoo. The same gentleman informs me that in southeastern Alaska a cough medicine is made from a decoction of the rootstocks of *Polypodium falcatum*, and he has further recorded[2] that in the same district one of the club mosses, *Lycopodium selago*, is chewed and the juice swallowed as a means of producing intoxication. Walpole notes on the label of another species of club moss, *L. annotinum*, collected in 1901 at Mary's Igloo, on the Kuzitrin River, that it is used as a wick for lamps in which seal-oil is burned; and, on the authority of Lieutenant Emmons, Mr. Coville tells me that the dark rootstocks of one of the horsetails, *Equisetum palustre*, are used by the coast Indians as basket material, a use also mentioned by Mr. Gorman for an *Equisetum* called chī-chī-yuĺ-kuth-ā, in his manuscript on the Lake Iliamna region, his collection (242) representing *E. palustre* and *E. sylvaticum*.

The direct utilization of the lower groups of plants as here recorded is relatively unimportant, and it is improbable that any very important uses of these plants remain to be ascertained by white men, though a traveler associating with the natives at any

[1] Pittonia, 3: 78. 1896.—See also Clute, Our Ferns, 146. 1901
[2] Pittonia, 3 80. 1896

point for a sufficient length of time to win their confidence might add much to the information here brought together; but it should be borne in mind that indirectly they possess the highest value, since lichens, Bryophytes, and the fern allies are the earliest soil formers, while the marine algæ furnish food for fish, and thus, ultimately, for man.

THE FUNGI OF ALASKA

BY P. A. SACCARDO, C. H. PECK, AND WILLIAM TRELEASE

INTRODUCTION

IN a very helpful little bibliography arranged according to geographic regions, a recent writer on fungi states that no representatives of this group are known from Alaska. This, however, is not quite true, for Hooker and Arnott many years ago recorded a *Dothidea* and a pseudo-fungus, *Erineum*, from Alaska; Professor Douglas H. Campbell, a few years since, noted the occurrence there of what he doubtfully named *Exobasidium vaccinii;* Professor T. H. Macbride more recently gives Alaska as a locality for five species of Myxomycetes; one rust, at least, is accredited to Alaska; and in his recent account of the vegetation of the Seal Islands, Mr. J. M. Macoun includes seven pileate fungi.[1] The fact remains, however, after taking note of even these recent publications, that almost nothing is known of the fungus flora of Alaska. And yet conditions are favorable for the development there of a large representation of this group of plants, for over the lower coast region fre-

---

[1] It is well known that the Krause brothers, some years since, made important botanical collections about the head of Lynn Canal, and some of their material has been examined and made the basis of published reports by Kurtz, Müller and Stephani; but inquiry made of Dr. Arthur Krause by my friend Dr. Buchenau shows that the collectors paid little attention to this group of plants, and that their collections now contain no Alaskan fungi.

quent rainfall favors the development of moulds, mildews, pileate fungi, and other moisture-loving forms, while the fogs and mists of parts of the upper coast are no less favorable to their growth, and the vast amount of putrescible vegetable material in these districts affords them abundant food. The phanerogamic vegetation of Alaska, moreover, is large and varied, notwithstanding the high latitude of the country, and as there appears little *a priori* reason to expect these higher plants to be much less liable to the attacks of parasites here than elsewhere, a large number of parasitic species is to be looked for.

Occasional collections of fungi were made by several members of the Harriman Alaska Expedition, and in addition to the material so gathered, the phanerogamic collections were subsequently examined for parasitized leaves and other organs, and such earlier material as exists in the herbarium of the Missouri Botanical Garden was also similarly gone over. The result was the accumulation of some hundreds of specimens, representing everything from bulky bracket fungi to sterile leaf spots. As was to be expected, much of this material was either valueless or indeterminable, but it has all been subjected to examination, and on it, with reference to the earlier literature concerning Alaska, the following catalogue is based.

At first a list of the Uredineæ, some few of which Professor J. C. Arthur subsequently examined, and some other things, was prepared by the writer, then a considerable number of pileate species, determined by Professor C. H. Peck, were included. Professor T. H. Macbride determined the only Myxomycete collected, and Professor P. A. Dangeard added determinations of three forms parasitic in *Spirogyra*. The residue, a large and very heterogeneous mass, was then submitted to Professor Saccardo, who, with the assistance of Abbe G. Bresadola for Hymenomycetes, and Dr. G. Scalia for many of the microscopic forms, succeeded in determining from it something over 150 species or varieties, a considerable number of which, as well as a few of those studied by Professor Peck or the writer, are described as new. The responsibility for the present list is, therefore, so divided as to suggest the authorship indicated at its head, though if the entire material had passed through Professor Saccardo's hands, so that he could have been held responsible for all of the entries in the catalogue, it would most fittingly have been ascribed to him.

Where no indication is given, the determinations are those of Saccardo and Scalia, in other cases signs [1] indicate by whom the determinations were made, the annotation or description accompanying each species being attributable to the person who identified it, unless otherwise noted. The collector is indicated for each specimen recorded in the list.

Professor Saccardo's diagnoses are published in Latin, as written, in order that shades of meaning might not be lost in the process of translation, and for uniformity the explanation of his plates is given in the same language.

WILLIAM TRELEASE.

CATALOGUE.

Family TUBERCULARIACEÆ.

Microcera brachyspora Saccardo & Scalia, sp. nov. (pl. VI, fig. 28.)

Sporodochiis sparsis, erumpentibus, carnoso-ceraceis, pulvinatis, 1–1.5 mm. diam., carneis v. fulvellis; hyphis filiformibus, inæqualibus, flexuosis, laxe fasciculatis, 2 μ cr., continuis, minute guttulatis, non v. vix ramosis, intermixtis crassioribus brevioribus, 4 μ cr. conidiis anguste falcatis, utrinque acutatis, 30–40 × 3 μ, guttulatis v. spurie septatis, hyalinis.

New Metlakatla (Trelease, 685, on the bark of some tree, associated with *Nectria sanguinea*).

Fusarium illosporioides Saccardo, sp. nov. (pl. III. fig. 10.)

Sporodochiis gregariis, erumpenti-superficialibus. depresse pulvinatis, .5–1 mm. diam., laxe contextis, superficie subvelutinis, dilutissime roseis, hyphis fasciculato-intricatis, sporophoris variis, modo simplicibus, modo furcatis, interdum opposito-ramosis. usque 50–70 × 5 μ, parce septatis; conidiis fusoideis, sæpius rectis, raro curvulis, utrinque acutiusculis (junioribus obtusulis). 1–2—typice vero 3-septatis, ad septa non constrictis, 20–22 × 4–5 μ.

Sitka (Trelease, 728, on decaying corticated branches of *Ribes*).

[1] Through the catalogue * indicates that the determination was made by Wm Trelease, †that it was made by Professor Peck, ‡by Abbe Bresadola, and §by Professor Dangeard.

Habitu et sporophoris fere illosporioideis species distinguenda videtur.

Family DEMATIACEÆ.

Speira effusa (Peck) Saccardo.

Yakutat Bay (Brewer & Coe, 689c, on corticated branches, associated with *Diaporthe anisomera*).

Speira minor Saccardo.

Yakutat Bay (Trelease, 684, on dead branches, associated with an immature *Cyphella*).

Cercospora apii selini-gmelini Saccardo & Scalia, var. nov.

Hyphis 36–42 × 5–8 μ, fuscidulis, apice leviter tortuoso-torulosis; conidiis bacillari-obclavatis, 1–3-septatis, 52–70 × 6.5–7 μ, hyalinis.

Cape Phipps, Yakutat Bay (Funston, on leaves of *Selinum gmelini*).

Cercospora apii angelicæ Saccardo & Scalia, var. nov.

Hyphis brevioribus, sursum obsolete tortuosis. 20 × 4 μ, demum fuscidulis; conidiis bacillari-obclavatis, usque 80–90 × 3.5–5 μ, obsolete septatis, hyalinis.

St Paul Island, Bering Sea (Trelease, 761, on leaves of *Angelica?*).

Ab hac var. forte non differt *C. polytæniæ* Ell. & Everh.

Scolecotrichum graminis Fuckel

St. Paul Island, Bering Sea (Trelease, 780, on grass leaves).

Coniosporium atratum Karsten & Malbr.‡

Yakutat (Trelease, 824, on dead wood).

Family MUCEDINACEÆ.

Ramularia cercosporoides Ellis & Everhart.

Kadiak (Trelease, 766, 767, on leaves of *Epilobium spicatum*).

Ramularia punctiformis Saccardo, sp. nov. (Pl. III, fig. 8.)

Maculis epiphyllis, brunneis, non marginatis, ovato-oblongis, dein ampliatis; cæspitulis in his maculis dense gregariis, erumpentibus, punctiformibus, albis, epiphyllis; hyphis e nodulo stromatico celluloso pallido oriundis, fasciculatis, cylindraceis, sursum attenuatis, vix denticulatis, hyalinis, 25–30 × 2–3 μ, conidiis fusoideis, rectiusculis, utrinque obtusulis, 16–18 × 2–3 μ, hyalinis.

Yakutat Bay (Trelease, 756, on dying leaves of *Potentilla anserina*).

A *R. anserina* cæspitulis epiphyllis, vere punctiformibus etc. distinguenda.

Ramularia macrospora Fresenius.

Alaska (Fischer, 1880, on leaves of *Campanula linifolia*).

Ramularia heraclei (Oudemans) Saccardo.

Cape Fox (Trelease, 757, on leaves of *Heracleum*).

Ramularia æquivoca Cesati.

Long Island, Kadiak (Trelease, 744); Unalaska (Trelease, 743). On leaves of *Ranunculus*, of the set of *R. montanus*.

Ramularia pratensis Saccardo.

Glacier Bay (Coville, 743); Yakutat (Trelease, 773), Virgin Bay Trelease, 772); Popof Island (Saunders, 775). On leaves of *Rumex occidentalis*.

Ramularia ? arnicalis Ellis & Everhart.

Kadiak (Kellogg in 1867, on leaves of *Arnica chamissonis* — a defective, doubtful specimen).

Bostrichonema alpestre Cesati.

Glacier Bay (Trelease, 762); Yakutat (Trelease, 763). On leaves of *Polygonum viviparum*.

Ovularia bulbigera (Fuckel) Saccardo.

Maculæ arescendo ochraceæ, orbiculari-angulosæ, atro-purpureo-cinctæ, in pag. inf. dilutiores, cæspituli hypophylli, griseoli, punctiformes, hyphæ fasciculatæ, basi in stroma dilute chlorinum bulbiforme coalitæ, 70–100 × 3.5–4 μ, subhyalinæ, obsolete septatæ, sursum leviter tortuoso-denticulatæ; conidia obovata, continua, 16–22 × 10–13 μ, granuloso-farcta, hyalina.

Kadiak (Coville & Kearney, 2361, Trelease, 752, 753); Popof Island (Saunders, 755); Unalaska (Trelease, 754). On living leaves of *Sanguisorba*.

Ovularia sommeri (Eichelbaum) Saccardo.*

Kadiak (Trelease, 721, 722). On twigs of *Myrica gale*.

Ovularia trientalis Berkeley.

See *Tuburcinia trientalis* B. & Br.

Botrytis vulgaris Fries.

Cape Fox (Trelease, 704, on decaying leaves of *Lonicera involucrata*); Yakutat Bay (Trelease, 733a, on decaying stems).

Glomerularia corni Peck.

Orca (Trelease, 823, on still living leaves of *Cornus canadensis*). Hyphæ manifestæ, 1–2-septulatæ, usque 50 μ longæ.

Family EXCIPULACEÆ.

Sporonema strobilinum Desmazières.

Orca (Trelease, 741, on cones of *Tsuga mertensiana;* Trelease, 742, on cones of *Picea sitchensis*).

Family LEPTOSTROMACEÆ.

Leptothyrium vulgare (Fries) Saccardo.

Yakutat Bay (Funston, on branches of *Rubus stellatus*).

Leptothyrium vulgare f. parryæ Saccardo.

Shumagin Islands (Harrington in 1871-2, on scales at base of stem of *Parrya macrocarpa*).

Sporulis rectiusculis, 4-5 × 1.5 μ.

Leptothyrium clypeosphærioides Saccardo.

Unalaska (Harrington in 1871-2, on dead branches of *Rubus chamæmorus*).

Forte *Phoma ruborum* West huc spectat.

Family SPHÆRIOIDACEÆ.

Sphærographium abditum Saccardo & Scalia. sp. nov. (pl. VI, fig. 27.)

Perithecus sparsis, mox superficialibus, globoso-conicis, sæpius longiuscule rostellatis, circ. 500 μ diam., nigris, lenio depressis, contextu parenchymatico, fuligineo, sporulis filiformibus, rectis, raro subcurvis, 50-72 × 1-1 5 μ, continuis guttulatis, hyalinis

Kadiak (Trelease, 737, within dead stems of *Heracleum*, associated with *Leptosphæria doliolum*)

Rhabdospora camptospora Saccardo & Scalia, sp. nov. (pl. VI, fig. 26.)

Perithecus sparsis, subcutaneo-erumpentibus, minutis, atro-nitidis, depresse globulosis, 200 μ diam.; contextu parenchymatico, fuligineo; sporulis bacillari-fusoideis, falcatis, raro rectiusculis, utrinque acutatis, tenuiter 3-septatis, 30-40 × 1-2 μ, minute guttulatis, hyalinis.

Yes Bay (Howell, on dead stems of *Anemone narcissiflora*, 1601).

Nonnullis notis ad *Stagonosporæ pulsatillæ*, sed sporulæ obsoletius septatæ, multo angustiores et acutiores.

Septoria rubi Westendorp.

Cape Fox (Trelease, 751, on still living leaves of *Rubus*).

Septoria canadensis Peck.

Sitka (Trelease, 726); Yakutat Bay (Trelease, 725); Virgin Bay (Trelease, 724). In fading leaves of *Cornus canadensis*.

Septoria dearnesii Ellis & Everhart.

Virgin Bay (Trelease, 759); Yakutat (Trelease, 760). On still living leaves of *Angelica?*.

Differt paululum sporulis sæpe aliquanto longioribus.

Septoria petroselini treleaseana Saccardo & Scalia, subsp. nov. (pl. vi, fig. 23.)

Maculis minutis, amphigenis, angulosis, 1–1.5 mm. lat., diu atro-brunneis; peritheciis sparsis, punctiformibus, hypophyllis; sporulis filiformibus, 40–60 × .5 μ, continuis, non v. indistincte guttulatis, hyalinis.

Virgin Bay (Trelease, 758, in still living leaves of *Conioselinum?*).
A typo maculis et sporulis longioribus et tenuioribus sat differt.

Septoria grylli Saccardo.

Yes Bay (Howell, on leaves of *Agrostis exarata*); Nagai (Harrington in 1871–72, on leaves of *Agrostis geminata*).

Sporulæ variant, in prima 75–90 × 1–1.2 μ, in altera 60 × 1 μ.

Septoria chamissonis Saccardo & Scalia, sp. nov. (pl. vi, fig. 25.)

Maculis nullis v. obsoletis; peritheciis minutissimis, atris, gregariis, innato-prominulis, 65–70 μ diam., globulosis, poro pertusis; contextu membranaceo, tenui, parenchymatico, fuscidulo; sporulis cylindraceis utrinque rotundatis, 3-septatis, eguttulatis, hyalinis, 46–52 × 3.5–4 μ.

Point Barrow (Murdoch, on leaves of *Eriophorum chamissonis*).

Affinis *Septoriæ scirpi* Sacc.; a sequente differt peritheciis multo minoribus, sporulis brevioribus et crassioribus.

Septoria eriophorella Saccardo & Scalia, sp. nov. (pl. vi, fig. 24.)

Maculis nullis; peritheciis sparsis, globulosis, 275 μ diam., profunde immersis, epidermide non atrata tectis, poro pertusis; contextu parenchymatico e cellulis difformibus, minutis, fuligineis composito; sporulis cylindraceo-filiformibus, 70–90 × 2.5–3 μ, minute guttulatis, obsolete septulatis, hyalinis.

Point Barrow (Murdoch, on leaves of *Eriophorum chamissonis*, with the preceding).

A *Septoria eriophori* differt præcteris peritheciis quadruple majoribus.

Stagonospora pulsatillæ Vestergr.

Kadiak; Kukak Bay. In dead stems of *Anemone*.
Probabiliter est forma *S. anemones* Pat.

Stagonospora heleocharidis caricina Saccardo & Scalia, subsp. nov. (pl. VI, fig. 21.)

Perithecia 90–120 μ diam.; basidia subnulla; sporulæ 5–6-septatæ, ad septa non-constrictæ.

Yakutat Bay (Funston in 1892, on dead leaves of a form of *Carex festiva*).

A typo differt sporulis paulo brevioribus, utrinque rotundatis, rarius acutiusculis, 27–34 × 6.5–7.5 μ, omnino hyalinis.

Stagonospora aquatica luzulicola Saccardo & Scalia, subsp. nov. (pl. VI, fig. 20.)

Peritheciis hinc inde gregariis, punctiformibus, globulosis, 150–160 μ diam., poro pertusis, atris, subcutaneis; contextu parenchymatico, fusco; sporulis oblongo-teretiusculis, utrinque rotundatis, rarius acutiusculis et sæpe basi truncatulis, 3-septatis, non constrictis, 23–28 × 3.5–4 μ, e chlorino hyalinis.

Point Barrow (Murdoch in 1883, on leaves of *Luzula arcuata*).

A typo recedit sporulis paullo angustioribus, qua nota ad ejus var. *lacustrem* accedit.

Stagonospora graminum Saccardo & Scalia, sp. nov. (pl. VI, fig. 22.)

Peritheciis laxe gregariis, subcutaneis, e globoso horizontaliter oblongis, atris, poro pertusis, 275–380 × 160–200 μ; contextu parenchymatico, castaneo-fusco; sporulis oblongis, sæpe inæquilateris, 23–28 × 6.5–8 μ, utrinque tenuato-obtusulis, 5–7-septatis, non constrictis, e chlorino hyalinis.

Iliuliuk (Harrington in 1871–2, on dead leaves of *Aira atropurpurea*).

Affinis *S. subseriatæ* (Desm.) Sacc. et præcipue ejus var. *moliniæ* Trail, sed sporulæ 5–7-septatæ (nec 4–5-septatæ), et perithecia oblonga.

Rhynchophoma raduloides Saccardo & Scalia, sp. nov. (pl. V, fig. 17.)

Peritheciis gregariis e basi innata parum incrassata erumpentibus, longe corniculatis, rectis, sursum tenuatis, aterrimis, fragilibus, 1.5 mm. altis, 300 μ cr., apice pertusis globuloque sporularum pallide roseo sæpius coronatis; contextu prosenchymatico, atro; sporulis oblongis, utrinque rotundatis, 7–9 × 2.5–3 μ, uniseptatis, non constrictis, hyalinis; basidiis fasciculatis bacillaribus simplicibus v. furcatis, 20–30 × 2 μ, hyalinis.

Sitka (Trelease, 708, 709, in corticated branches of *Ribes laxiflorum*, associated with *Godronia urceolus*).

Affinis *R. radula* præbet sporulas 12–15 × 4–5 µ.

Phoma complanata (Tode) Desmazieres.

St. Paul Island, Bering Sea (Trelease, 738, on dead stems of *Heracleum*).

Phoma oleracea Saccardo.

St. Paul Island, Bering Sea (Macoun, on dead stems of *Cardamine bellidifolia*).

Phyllosticta helleboricola coptidis Saccardo & Scalia, var. nov. (pl. vi, fig 19.)

Unalaska (Harrington in 1871–2, on leaves of *Coptis trifoliata*).

A typo differt sporulis angustioribus, nempe recte cylindraceis, utrinque submcrassatis, rotundatis, 5 × .5 µ.

Phyllosticta caricicola Saccardo & Scalia, sp. nov. (pl. vi, fig. 18.)

Maculis arescentibus, indeterminatis, plerumque hypophyllis; perithecus minutissimis, atris, globoso-depressis, 50–80 µ diam., poro pertusis, laxiuscule seriatim dispositis; contextu fusco e cellulis polyhedricis 6–8 µ diam. composito; sporulis oblongo-bacillaribus, 4–5 × .5 µ; basidiis minimis.

Orca (Trelease, 628, on leaves of *Carex*).

A *P. caricis* differt defectu maculæ fuscæ et perithecus seriatis.

Family MYXOMYCETACEÆ.

Ceratiomyxa fruticulosa (Muller) Macbride.

MACBRIDE, N. A. Slime-Moulds, 19

Stikine River (Wickham).[1]

Trichia scabra Rostafinski.

MACBRIDE, N. A. Slime-Moulds, 213.

Stikine River (Wickham).

Arcyria denudata (Linnæus) Sheldon.

MACBRIDE, N. A. Slime-Moulds, 196

Stikine River (Wickham).

Arcyria cinerea (Bulliard) Persoon.

MACBRIDE, N. A. Slime-Moulds, 196.

Stikine River (Wickham).

[1] These localities are given by Professor T. H. Macbride, who further determined the single species collected by the members of the Harriman Expedition

Stemonitis smithii Macbride.
MACBRIDE, N A Slime-Moulds, 122.
Stikine River (Wickham).

Tubifera ferruginosa (Batsch) Macbride.
MACBRIDE, N A Slime-Moulds, 156
Stikine River (Wickham)

Diderma niveum (Rostafinski) Macbride.

Yakutat Bay: Hidden Glacier (Trelease, 782); Disenchantment Bay (Brewer, 783), Aguadulce River, Yakutat Bay (Trelease, 784); Orca (Trelease, 785). On mosses, fallen leaves, etc., maturing close to the retreating snow.

Family LABOULBENIACEÆ.

Laboulbenia nebriæ Peyritsch.
THAXTER, Monogr. Laboulbeniaceæ, 320. *pl. 13*
Aleutian Islands, on *Nebria gregaria*.

Family MONADINACEÆ.

Vampyrella spirogyræ Cienkowski §
Popof Island (Saunders, 401*a*, in *Spirogyra porticalis*).

Family PATELLARIACEÆ.

Heterosphæria patella (Tode) Greville
Alaska (Evans, 114*a*); Yakutat Bay (Trelease, 736). On dead stems of *Heracleum*.

Patinella aloysii-sabaudiæ Saccardo, sp nov.[1] (pl. II, fig 6)

Ascomatibus gregariis, majusculis, plano-patellatis, orbicularibus, sessilibus, matrici adpressis sed omnino superficialibus, puncto centrali adfixis, usque 2 mm. diam., ubique nigris, opacis, margine attenuato non prominente, disco minutissime granuloso; ascis cylindraceis, apice rotundatis, basi acutatis breve stipitatis, 84–90 × 10–11 μ, octosporis; paraphysibus stipatis, bacillari-clavulatis, sursum atratis, conidiaque perfecte globosa, atrofuliginea, 11–12 μ diam exerentibus, sporidiis oblique monostichis v. subdistichis, ovato-oblongis rectis curvulisve, 14–15 × 5.5–6 μ, hyalinis

Yakutat Bay (Trelease, 689, on blackened decaying stems); Orca (Trelease, 730, on stem of *Veratrum* — appears to be a young stage of the same).

[1] Dixi in honorem Aloysii Sabaudiæ, Apratiorum ducis, qui anno 1897 summa cacumina Mtis S Eliæ Alaskæ primus conscendit

Eximia species, ob paraphyses conidia magna atra gerentes prædistincta. Excipuli margo cellulis tereti-clavatis, 20–25 × 7 µ, brunneis, liberis præditus est.

Family PHACIDIACEÆ.
Rhytisma? rhododendri Fries.

Unalaska (Macoun, on leaves of *Rhododendron kamtschaticum*).

Forte huc pertinat forma hæc spermogonica. stromatibus amphigenis maculiformibus atris insidis, intus pallidioribus, sporulis ellipsoideis minutis, 2.5–3 × .5 µ, hyalinis, basidiis filiformibus usque 26 × .5 µ fasciculatis suffultis.

Rhytisma salicinum (Persoon) Fries.

Kadiak (Trelease, 698, on leaves of *Salix*).

Fabræa cincta Saccardo & Scalia, sp. nov. (pl. v, fig. 16.)

Maculis suborbicularibus v. irregularibus, 1–2 mm. lat., raro latioribus, in hypophyllo subumbrinis, in epiphyllo expallentibus annuloque atro-purpureo cinctis; ascomatibus epiphyllis, innato-erumpentibus, depressis, 300–400 µ diam., sparsis v. confluentibus, fuscis, disco madore aperto, vix pallidiore, ascis tereti-clavatis, apice rotundatis, jodo cærulescentibus, breve stipitatis, 70–90 × 18–20 µ, octosporis, paraphysibus simplicibus v. parce ramosis, filiformibus apice capitulatis; sporidiis ovato-oblongis, utrinque obtusulis, distichis v. oblique monostichis, 15–20 × 5–6.5 µ, primo continuis, dein ut plurimum 1-septatis, non constrictis, loculo supero quam infero fere duplo majore, hyalinis, guttulato-farctis.

Yakutat Bay (Trelease, 750); Orca (Trelease, 747). On fading leaves of *Rubus*.

Pseudopeziza (Pseudorhytisma) bistortæ (Libert) Fuckel.

Unalaska (Coville & Kearney, 1752; Trelease, 765). On leaves of *Polygonum viviparum*.

Pseudopeziza cerastiorum arenariæ Saccardo, var. nov.

Yakutat Bay (Funston, on dead leaves of *Arenaria lateriflora*, 18, 19).

A typo differt sporidiis paullo majoribus, nempe 14–16 × 4–4.5 µ.

Phacidium diminuens Karsten.

Yes Bay (Howell, in fading or dead leaves of *Carex canescens*, 1709).

Family DERMATEACEÆ.

Godronia urceolus (Albertini & Schweinitz) Saccardo.

Sitka (Trelease, 708a, on dead branches of *Ribes*, associated with *Rhynchophoma raduloides*).

Scleroderris treleasei Saccardo, sp. nov. (pl. III, fig. 7.)

Dense gregaria v. hinc inde cæspitulosa e basi innata punctiformi omnino superficialis, bicolor; ascomatibus initio urceolatis, clausis, mox laciniato-dehiscentibus, majusculis, 2.5–3 mm. diam., scutellatis, extus margineque lacero aterrimis, carbonaceis, rugosis, disco plano-concavo, levissimo isabellino-carneo, ceraceo; ascis clavatis, apice obtuse acutatis, deorsum tenuato-stipitatis, 140×12–14μ, octosporis; paraphysibus filiformibus, apice interdum incurvis furcatisque, totis hyalinis; sporidiis in asci parte superiore fasciculatis, cylindraceo-clavatis, deorsum acutatis, 50–$60 \times 2 \mu$, continuis, hyalinis, interdum curvatis.

Sitka (Kincaid, 693; Trelease, 845). On coniferous bark.

Eximia fungus, quem miror nullam mycologum observavisse. Affinitas non parum dubia, hinc ad *Clithrem*, illinc ad *Coccophacidium nutans* et tunc forte novi generis typus. A *Scleroderri* sporidiis continuis, et paraphysum natura differt. Obturaculum ascorum jodi ope non tingitur. Contextus excipuli indistincte cellulosus, subcarbonaceus, fragilis. Ascomata, cum secedunt, areolam albam in cortice matricis relinquunt.

Family PEZIZACEÆ.

Dasyscypha bicolor (Bulliard) Fuckel.†

Muir Glacier (Trelease, 586, 587, 588); Yakutat Bay (Trelease, 585).

Trichopeziza hamata Saccardo.

Yakutat Bay (Trelease, 584, on twigs).

A typo vix differt pilis minus arcte hamatis, sporidiis (forte non omnino maturis) paullo angustioribus. Cetera eadem.

Trichopeziza relicina (Fries) Fuckel.

Yakutat Bay (Trelease, 735, on decaying stems of large herbaceous plants).

Trichopeziza earoleuca (Berkeley & Broome) Saccardo. (pl. II, fig. 5.)

Disenchantment Bay (Trelease, 732a, on decayed stems of *Lupinus*).

Etsi species Berkeleyana sit brevissime descripta et ex insula Ceylon, tamen nostra videtur eadem. Ascomata urceolata, minutissima, rosea, niveo-villosa. Pili rigiduli, cuspidati, 200–250 × 7–8 μ, continui. Asci fusoidei, 40–50 × 5–5.5 μ, octospori. Paraphyses aciculares, asco paullo longiores. Sporidia allantoidea, 5–6 × 1.5–2 μ, hyalina.

Pirottæa yakutatiana Saccardo, sp nov. (Pl. II, fig. 4.)

Ascomatibus gregariis, urceolatis, basi-contracta superficialibus, majusculis, extus setulosis, siccis nigris, 1 mm. latis et altis, disco (madore tantum conspicuo) concavo cinereo-cæsio; excipuli contextu rigidulo, atro-fuligineo, ad marginem pallidiorem pilis filiformibus, pallide fuligineis, septatis, 40–70 × 5 μ, in fimbrias subtriangulares laxe coalescentibus; ascis tereti-fusoideis, utrinque obtusiusculis, 40–45 × 5.5–6 μ, octosporis, paraphysibus lanceolatis, crassiusculis, ascos superantibus; sporidiis oblique monostichis, fusoideis, rectis, 9 × 2–2.5 μ, hyalinis.

Yakutat Bay (Trelease, 734, on dry decorticated fallen twigs).

A *P. gallica* mox recedit quia quadruplo major, basi coarctata, pilis marginalibus fimbriato-fasciculatis.

Phialea carneala Saccardo, sp. nov. (Pl. II, fig. 2.)

Sparsa, minuta, ubique (in sicco) carnea, glabra; cupula initio minuta, subglobosa, dein ampliata, subhemisphærica v. obconica, .7–1 mm. diam., stipite cylindraceo subtili, 1–1.3 mm. longo, leniter longitrorsum striatulo basique vix incrassata asperulo; disco concavo, levi, roseo, margine extimo pallidiore; ascis tereti-clavatis, deorsum tenuato-stipitatis, 80–90 × 7 μ, octosporis; paraphysibus filiformi-bacillaribus; sporidiis distichis, tereti-oblongis, utrinque obtusulis, rectiusculis, 11–14 × 3–3.5 μ, intus granulosis, hyalinis.

Yakutat Bay (Trelease, 595, on decaying fallen leaves and stipules).

Affinis *P. albidæ, cyathoideæ et broomei*, sed vel colore v. proportione partium satis diversa.

Helotium alaskæ Saccardo, sp. nov. (Pl. II, fig. 3.)

Gregarium, minutum, ubique (in sicco) croceo-aureum, glabrum; cupula initio punctiformi-pertusa dein ampliata plano-scutellata, brevi marginata, vix 1 mm. lata; stipite cylindraceo, crassiusculo, 1 mm. alto, .3 mm. cr., levi, dilutius colorato; ascis tereti-clavatis, apice obtusis, deorsum tenuato-stipitatis, 60 × 5.5–6 μ, octosporis; paraphysibus copiosis, bacillaribus; sporidiis cylindraceo-fusoideis, leniter curvis, 8–11 × 2–2.7 μ, distichis, hyalinis.

Yakutat Bay (Trelease, 597, on decaying decorticated wood).

Ab affinibus speciebus flavis lignicolis stipites sporidiorumque notis satis diversum.

Helotium fumigatum Saccardo & Spegazzini

Yakutat Bay (Trelease, 733, on decaying herbaceous stems, associated with *Botrytis vulgaris*).

Helotium lenticulare (Bulliard) Fries.

Juneau (Trelease, 692, on decaying wood).

Ciboria sp.

Yakutat Bay (Trelease, 686, on *Tsuga*).
Videtur affinis *Ciboriæ strobilinæ* (A. & S.) Sacc.

Ciboria sp.

Yakutat Bay (Trelease, 702).
Accedit ad *Ciboriam rufo-fuscam* (Web.) Sacc. Sunt tamen exempl. unica, non perfecta, hinc determinatio dubia.

Lachnea scutellata (Linnæus) Gill.

Juneau (Trelease, 690, 690a, 690b, 690c, on decaying fallen bark and wood).

Family HELVELLACEÆ.

Vibrissea truncorum (Albertini & Schweinitz) Fries †

Kadiak (Trelease, 596a); Yakutat Bay (Trelease, 596). On wood in water.

Cudonia circinans (Persoon) Fries.

Orca (Trelease, 694, on fragments of wood).

Family HYSTERIACEÆ.

Lophodermium oxycocci (Fries) Karsten.

Kadiak (Trelease, 713, on drying leaves of *Vaccinium oxycoccus*, immature).

Lophodermium maculare (Fries) De Notaris.

Glacier Bay (Trelease, 697, on leaves of *Salix*).

Family MICROTHYRIACEÆ.

Microthyrium harrimani Saccardo, sp. nov. (pl. II, fig. 1.)

Perithecis densiuscule gregariis, superficialibus, dimidiatis, omnino applanatis, orbicularibus, 350–450 μ diam., subinde binato-approximatis, ostiolo centrali pertusis, margine fimbriatis, contextu distincte parenchymatico, radiato; ascis tereti-fusoideis, utrinque obtusulis, 80–100 × 9–10 μ, octosporis, paraphysibus paucis, sæpe furcatis, sporidiis 2–3-stichis, clavato-fusiformibus, utrinque acutiusculis, infra medium 1-septatis, non constrictis, hyalinis.

Orca (Trelease, 739, 740, on fading scales of cones of *Tsuga heterophylla*).

Affine *M. abietis* Mont.

Family DOTHIDEACEÆ.

Dothidella betulina (Fries) Saccardo.

Dothidea betulina β HOOKER and ARNOTT, Bot Beechey 134 — ROTHROCK, Smithsonian Rept. 1867 463 — TURNER, Nat Hist Alaska 85.

Port Clarence (Trelease, 699, on leaves of *Betula glandulosa*, associated with *Sphærella harthensis*).

Dothidella betulina yakutatiana Saccardo & Scalia, subsp. nov. (Pl. v, fig. 15'.)

Stromatibus innato-erumpentibus, pulvinato-applanatis, subtilissime punctulatis, atris, .5 mm. diam., loculis minutissimis, globulosis, 50 µ diam., ostiolo pertusis, ascis oblongo-cylindraceis, apice rotundatis, deorsum nonnunquam incrassatulis, subsessilibus, 40–48 × 10–12 µ, octosporis; sporidiis subdistichis v. polystichis, obovato-cuneatis, apice rotundatis, basi acutatis, 1-septatis, non constrictis, eguttulatis, 10–12 × 3–4 µ, e chlorino hyalinis

Yakutat Bay (Trelease, 703, on dead leaves of some undetermined tree).

Phyllachora filicina Saccardo & Scalia, sp nov. (Pl. v, fig. 15)

Stromatibus epiphyllis, maculiformibus, atris, applanatis, parum emergentibus, ambitu e circulari angulosis, superficie regularis, contextu atro-brunneo, parenchymatico; loculis numerosis, immersis, globosis, 70–80 µ diam, pallidioribus; ascis tereti-clavatis, brevissime stipitatis, 70 × 10–11 5 µ, apice rotundatis, octosporis; sporidiis elliptico-oblongis, utrinque rotundatis, rectis, 14–15 × 5–6 µ, continuis, hyalinis, intus granuloso farctis.

Unalaska (Evermann, 6, on living leaves of *Aspidium lonchitis*). Pulchella species, omnino distincta.

Phyllachora? heraclei (Fries) Fuckel.

Unga Island (Harrington in 1871–2, on living leaves of *Heracleum lanatum*).

More solito sterilis.

Family HYPOCREACEÆ.

Cordyceps militaris (Linnæus) Link.

Orca (Trelease, 695, on pupæ of some insect).

Specimen immaturum, sed videtur hujus species.

Nectria sanguinea (Sibthorpe) Fries.

New Metlakatla (Trelease, 685*a*, on dead bark, associated with *Microcera brachyspora*); Yakutat Bay (Trelease, 684*a*).

Nectria episphæria (Tode) Fries.

Sitka (Trelease, 683, on stromata of some sphæriaceous fungus on branches apparently of *Alnus*).

Family SPHÆRIACEÆ.

Pyrenophora chrysospora (Niessl) Saccardo.

Kukak Bay (Coville & Kearney, 1552*a*, on dead petioles and stipules of *Oxytropis*).

Pyrenophora comata (Niessl) Saccardo.

Port Clarence (Brewer & Coe, 1953*a*); St Paul Island, Bering Sea (Macoun in 1891). On dead leaves and stems of *Arenaria verna* and *A. macrocarpa*.

Pyrenophora polyphragmoides Saccardo & Scalia, sp. nov. (pl. v, fig. 13.)

Peritheciis erumpentibus, sparsis, punctiformibus, nigris, globulosis, 190–220 μ diam., setis rigidis, fuscis, septatis, 160–190 $\times$ 7.5 μ, vertice vestitis, contextu parenchymatico, fuligineo; ascis cylindraceis, rectis curvulisve, apice rotundatis, brevissime oblique stipitatis, octosporis; sporidiis distichis, oblongo-fusoideis, utrinque obtusulis, initio 3-septatis, dein sub-7-septatis, melleis, tandem 9–12-septatis, murali-divisis, medio vix v. non constrictis, 36–56 $\times$ 18 μ, fulgineis.

Popof Island (Harrington in 1871–2, on decayed stems and leaves of *Polemonium humile*).

Affinis *P. phæosporæ* et *P. polyphragmiæ* sed rite distincta.

Pleospora media Niessl

Unalaska (Harrington in 1871–2, in decayed leaves of *Draba vernalis*)

Est forma sporidiis latioribus (26–28 $\times$ 13–14 μ), ut var. *limonum* Penzig.

Pleospora pentamera Karsten.

Walden Island (Hb. Thiel., on leaves and stems of *Dupontia fischeri*).

Sporidia plerumque 5-septata.

Pleospora infectoria Fuckel.

Nagai (Harrington in 1871–2, in dead culms of *Poa cæsia*?).

Pleospora herbarum (Persoon) Rabenhorst.

Point Barrow (Murdoch, 15682, on decaying leaves of *Ranunculus nivalis*), Nagai (Harrington in 1871-2, on decayed leaves of *Oxytropis uralensis arctica*).

Prima est forma macrospora (sp. 44–54 × 20–23 μ), postrema est microspora (sp. 32–36 × 15–16 μ).

Metasphæria empetri (Fries) Saccardo.

Port Clarence (Trelease, 700, on leaves of *Empetrum nigrum*, the specimen not entirely mature).

Massarina dryadis Rostrup.

Point Barrow (Murdoch in 1883, on leaves of *Dryas octopetala integrifolia*, the specimen not entirely mature).

Pseudovalsa ribesia Saccardo & Scalia, sp. nov. (pl. v, fig. 14.)

Stromatibus corticolis tectis, dein erumpentibus, nigris, e peritheciis 4–6 connatis compositis, vix 1 mm. diam., ostiolis obtusiulis breviter emergentibus; ascis crasse cylindraceis, brevissime abrupte stipitatis, apice late rotundatis, 110–130 × 24–26 μ, filiformi-paraphysatis, octosporis; sporidiis distichis, oblongo-fusoideis, primo hyalinis, didymis, strato mucoso hyalino obductis, dein 3-septatis, medio parum constrictis, 38–41 × 16–20 μ, fuscidulis.

Sitka (Trelease, 709a, on dead corticated branches of *Ribes laxiflorum*, associated with *Rhynchophoma*, *Godronia*, *Diaporthe*, etc.).

Sporormia ambigua Niessl.

Kadiak (Trelease, 707, on dung—of ptarmigan?).

Leptosphæria ophiopogonis graminum Saccardo.

Yes Bay (Howell, on dead leaves of *Festuca rubra*, 1722).

Leptosphæria leersiana Saccardo.

Yes Bay (Howell, on leaves of *Agrostis*, 1711, associated with *Sphærella californica*).

Leptosphæria doliolum (Persoon) De Notaris.

Kadiak (Trelease, 737a, on dead stems of *Heracleum*, associated with *Sphærographium abditum*).

Leptosphæria fœniculacea lupina Saccardo & Scalia, subsp. nov. (pl. v, fig. 12.)

Peritheciis globoso-depressis, diu tectis, dein nudatis, sparsis v. subgregariis, minutissime papillatis, 350–420 μ diam., glabris, nigris; contextu parenchymatico, fuligineo; ascis longe clavatis, stipitatis, 100–120 × 13.5–15.5 μ, octosporis, paraphysibus filiformibus septulatis obvallatis; sporidiis subdistichis, fusiformibus, 3–4-septatis, non constrictis, sæpe inæqualibus v. curvulis, dilute olivaceis.

Disenchantment Bay (Trelease, 732, on decaying stems of *Lupinus*, associated with *Phoma*).

Leptosphæria agnita labens Saccardo & Scalia, subsp. nov. (pl. v, fig. 11.)

A typo differt peritheciis in macula flavida paullo majoribus (5 mm. diam.) facile collabentibus; sporidiis non diversis

Unalaska (Trelease, 731, on dead herbaceous stems).

Leptosphæria silenes-acaulis De Notaris

Unalaska (Harrington in 1871–2, on dead petioles and leaves of *Silene acaulis*).

Leptosphæria marginata Niessl

Yakutat Bay (Funston, on leaves of *Pyrola secunda*).

In maculis atris epiphyllis, rarius hypophyllis.

Leptosphæria juncicola Rehm.

Shumagin Islands (Harrington in 1871–2, on stems of *Scirpus cæspitosus*).

Amphisphæria applanata (Fries) Cesati & De Notaris

Yakutat Bay (Trelease, 734*a*, on dry twigs, accompanying *Pirottæa yakutatiana*).

Asci 105–115 × 14–15 μ; sporidia 22–25 × 8–8.5; loculo super. (!) majori et acutiori. Perithecia .5–.6 mm. diam.

Didymosphæria nana Rostrup.

Port Wells (Trelease 910*a*, on leaves of *Alnus*.)

A typo differt sporidiis paullo brevioribus, nempe 18–20 × 6.5–7.5 μ, nec 25 × 7–8 μ.

Didymosphæria arenaria macrospora Saccardo & Scalia, subsp. nov. (pl. iv, fig. 9.)

Sporidiis 40 × 13.5 μ (nec 30 × 14 μ), fuscellis

Shumagin Islands (Harrington in 1871–2, in culms of *Aira cæspitosa brevifolia*).

Diaporthe (Chorostate) strumella (Fries) Fuckel

Sitka (Trelease, 709*b*, on branches of *Ribes laxiflorum*).

Forma *oligocarpa*.

Diaporthe (Chorostate) anisomera Saccardo & Scalia, sp. nov. (pl. v, fig. 10.)

Stromatibus gregariis, corticolis, erumpentibus, ambitu suborbicularibus, convexis, 1.3–1.5 mm. diam , intus ligneo-pallidis; peritheciis 10–20, globosis v. mutua pressione irregularibus, 200–250 μ diam., monostichis, ostiolis breve cylindraceis, parum emergentibus, apice rotundatis; ascis fusoideo-clavatis, apice obtusis, deorsum tenuatis, 80–90 × 11–13 μ, octosporis; sporidiis distichis, obovatis, 14–17 × 5–5.5 μ, infra medium septatis, non constrictis, farctis, hyalinis et initio strato mucoso inæquali obductis, articulo superiore fere duplo majore.

Yakutat Bay (Trelease, 684*b*, on decorticated dead branches of *Corylus?*).

Etsi matrix non certa, species videtur distinguenda ob sporidia eximie anisomera.

Diaporthe (Tetrastaga) pungens Nitschke.

Sitka (Trelease, 728*a*, on twigs of *Ribes*, associated with *Rhynchophoma*).

Forma ostiolis brevius exertis.

Venturia circinans (Fries) Saccardo.

Virgin Bay (Trelease, 746, on living leaves of *Geranium erianthum*, immature).

Venturia kunzei Saccardo.
Coleroa chætomium

Prince William Sound (Trelease, 748); Yakutat Bay (Trelease, 749). On leaves of *Rubus*.

Venturia kunzei ramicola Saccardo & Scalia, var. nov. (Pl. IV, fig. 8.)

A typo differt peritheciis ramicolis in crusta stromatica (propria?) nascentibus.

Unalaska (Harrington in 1871–2, on branches of *Rubus stellatus*).

Sphærella leptospora Saccardo & Scalia, sp. nov. (Pl. IV, fig. 7.)

Peritheciis sparsis, globulosis, primo immersis dein liberis, 220–275 μ diam., poro pertusis, contextu parenchymatico, fuligineo; ascis cylindraceis, rectis v. curvulis, brevissime stipitatis, 50–60 × 7.5–9 μ; sporidiis octonis, distichis, fusiformibus, rectis, medio 1-septatis, non constrictis, 13–15.5 × 2.5–3 μ, hyalinis, sæpe guttulatis.

Yes Bay (Howell, on leaves of *Carex mertensiana*, 1693).

Affinis *S. perexiguæ*, sed perithecia multo ampliora, asci longiores et angustiores.

Sphærella eriophila Niessl.

St. Lawrence Bay (Lutk. Exped., on dead leaves of *Artemisia glomerata* or *A. heterophylla*).

A typo differt (an ab ætate?) ascis sporidiisque paullo angustioribus.

Sphærella graminum Saccardo & Scalia, sp. nov. (pl. IV, fig. 5.)

Peritheciis sparsis, punctiformibus, globulosis, 150–200 μ diam., innato-prominulis, epidermide non atrata tectis, brevissime papillato-pertusis, contextu membranaceo-fuligineo, parenchymatico; ascis cylindraceis, subsessilibus, apice rotundatis, 65–70 × 10–12 μ, rectiusculis, 8-sporis; sporidiis distichis, elliptico-fusoideis, rectis, 13–16.5 × 3.5–4 μ, uniseptatis, non constrictis, plasmate granuloso v. minute guttulato farctis, hyalinis.

Shumagin Islands (Harrington in 1871–2, on dead leaves of *Poa stenantha*).

Affinis *S. cruris-galli*, præcipue distinguenda peritheciis majusculis ratione fructificatione.

Sphærella wichuriana Schroeter.

Yes Bay (Howell, on leaves of *Carex*, 1694).

Sphærella ootheca Saccardo.

Nagai (Harrington in 1871–2, on leaves of *Dryas octopetala*).

Verisimiliter *S. octopetalæ* Oud. non satis differt.

Sphærella stellarinearum (Rabenhorst) Karsten.

Russell Fiord (Coville & Kearney, 987*a*, on old leaves of *Alsine longipes*).

Sphærella harthensis Auerswald.

Port Clarence (Trelease, 699, on living leaves of *Betula glandulosa*, associated with *Dothidella betulina*).

Sphærella alni-viridis De Notaris.

Port Wells (Trelease, 710*a*, 910, on leaves of *Alnus*, associated with *Didymosphæria nana* and *Gnomoniella tubiformis*).

Sphærella californica Cooke & Harkness.

Yes Bay (Howell, on leaves of *Agrostis*, 1711, associated with *Leptosphæria leersiana*).

Sphærella grossulariæ salicella Saccardo & Scalia, var. nov. (pl. IV, fig. 6.)

Peritheciis sparsim gregariis, punctiformibus, 100–130 μ diam.; ascis tereti-oblongis, 52–70 × 13–15.5 μ, brevissime stipitatis, octosporis; sporidiis polystichis, fusoideo-bacillaribus, rectis, 32–34 × 1.5–2.5 μ, uniseptatis, non constrictis, hyalinis.

Kadiak (Trelease, 698, on leaves of *Salix*, associated with *Rhytisma salicinum*).

Sphærella ignobilis Auerswald.

Nagai (Harrington in 1871-2, on leaves of *Agrostis geminata*).
Sporidia 9–10 × 3–3.5 μ, ovato-oblonga, non exacte cuneata; asci paullo breviores, 30–34 × 9–10 μ.

Sphærella adusta Fuckel.

Yakutat (Trelease, 620, on *Epilobium* sp.; Brewer & Coe, 4475, on *E. bongardi*); Orca (Trelease, 619, on *Epilobium* sp.); Unalaska (Brewer & Coe, 2189, on *E. boreale*).

Sphærella pachyasca Rostrup.

Point Barrow (Murdoch, on dead leaves of *Draba alpina*, 15686).

Sphærella rumicis (Desmazières) Cooke.

Juneau (Trelease, 774); Kadiak (Trelease, 771). On leaves of *Rumex occidentalis*.

Physalospora crepiniana (Saccardo & March.).

P. alpina crepiniana.

Alaska (Harrington in 1871-2; Coville & Kearney, 1598, on leaves of *Empetrum nigrum*).

Physalospora borealis Saccardo, sp. nov. (pl. IV, fig. 4.)

Peritheciis laxe gregariis, subcutaneis, dein erumpentibus, globulosis, papillatis, nigris, .3–.5 mm. diam., contextu parenchymatico, duriusculo, fuligineo, ascis cylindraceis, basi tenuatis brevissimeque stipitatis, apice obtusis, 70–75 × 5–6 μ, octosporis, paraphysibus parcis, brevibus; sporidiis oblique monostichis, oblongo-ovoideis, lenissime inæquilateris, 9–10 × 4.5 μ, utrinque obtusulis, intus granulosis, hyalinis.

Kukak Bay (Saunders, on decaying stems of *Anemone*, associated with *Stagonospora pulsatillæ*).

Læstadia saxifragæ Saccardo & Scalia, sp. nov. (pl. IV, fig. 3.)

Peritheciis epiphyllis, punctiformibus, in partibus marginalibus arescentibus foliorum sparsis, globosis, 100–130 μ diam., poro pertusis; contextu parenchymatico fuscello, ascis cylindraceis v. cylindraceo-clavulatis, brevissime stipitatis, apice rotundatis, 60–80 × 10–13 μ, aparaphysatis, octosporis; sporidiis distichis, oblongo-ellipsoideis, utrinque acutulis, 10–13 × 4.5–5.5 μ, continuis, hyalinis.

Unalaska (one of the early Russian collectors in Hb. Bernhardi, on living leaves of *Saxifraga parviflora*).

Pluribus affinis, sed videtur satis distincta. Asci tantum e basi perithecii oriundi.

Guignardia alaskana Reed. (pl. vii.)

REED, Univ Cal Publ, Bot 1, 154, 161 *pl 15, 16.*

Hot Springs, Baranof Island (Trelease, 970); Kadiak; Unalaska Parasitic in *Prasiola borealis*.— Cogeneric with the preceding, but the name *Læstadia* abandoned by the author of the species because preoccupied among the flowering plants

Gnomoniella tubiformis (Tode) Saccardo.

Port Wells (Trelease, 710, on leaves of *Alnus*).

Hypoxylon majusculum Cooke.

Yakutat Bay (Trelease, 786, on dead bark of *Alnus sitchensis*). Sporidia 14–16 × 5.5–6 μ.

Hypoxylon ohiense Ellis & Everhart. (pl. iv, fig 2.)

Sitka (Trelease, on trunks of *Picea*).

Asci clavati tenuiter stipitati, 68–80 × 7–8 μ; sporidia oblique monosticha, oblongo-ellipsoidea, 5.5–7.5 × 2.5–3.5 μ, fuliginea; stroma 2–4 cm. longa et lata, perithecia 1.5–1.7 mm. longa.

Family PERISPORIACEÆ.

Antennaria rectangularis Saccardo, sp. nov. (pl. iii, fig. 9.)

Cæspitulosa v. effusa, superficialis, atro-fuliginea, laxiuscule intricata; hyphis ascendentibus, tortuosis, v subrectis, longissimis, filiformibus, 1.5–2 mm. long., 12–15 μ cr., parce ramosis, multiarticulatis, articulis 22–28 × 12–15 μ, ad septa non v. leniter constrictis, sæpe 1-guttatis; ramis simplicibus, subalternis, angulo perfecte recto patentibus, 70–80 raro usque 400 μ longis, apicibus acutiusculis v. obtusis; perithecus. . .

Sitka (Howell, on shoots and leaves of *Phyllodoce glanduliflora*, 1597).

Certe affinis *Antennariæ robinsonii* B & M., differt tamen hyphis omnibus æqualibus, nec partim torulosis, ramis angulo perfecte recto oriundis, etc.

Limacinia? alaskensis Saccardo & Scalia, sp. nov. (pl. iv, fig. 1.)

Effusa, superficialis, densa, opace atra, subpannosa, 2–4 cm longa, .5–.75 mm. cr.; hyphis mycelii hormiscioideis, filiformibus, simplicibus v. furcatis, 400–500 × 16–18 μ, crebre septatis, ad septa constrictis, articulis globoso-cuboideis, 15–20 × 13–15 μ, subinde latioribus quam longis, fuligineis, plerumque parietali-1-guttatis; conidiis oblongofusoideis, 28–30 × 10 μ, 3-septatis, vix constrictis, fuligineis; peritheciis in mycelio gregariis et subasconditis globulosis, obtusis v.

depressis, 180-200 µ lat., hyphis consimilibus laxe vestitis; ascis (immaturis) clavatis, 90-120 × 15-18 µ, aparaphysatis, subsessilibus; sporidiis. . . .

Glacier Bay (Trelease, 712, on still living bark of *Alnus*).

Mycelium sistit *Hormiscii* v. *Antennariæ* formam; forte *Hormiscio alto* Ehreub. accedit.

Eurotium herbariorum (Wigg.) Link.

Yes Bay (Howell, on *Geum*, 1618).

Family CHYTRIDIACEÆ.

Physoderma menyanthis De Bary.

Kukak Bay (Saunders, 769, on *Menyanthes trifoliata*).

Family SAPROLEGNIACEÆ.

Lagenidium entophytum (Pringsheim) Zopf.§

Popof Island (Saunders, 401c, in zygospores of *Spirogyra porticalis*).

Pythium gracile Schenk.§

Popof Island (Saunders, 401b, in vegetative cells of *Spirogyra porticalis*).

Family PERONOSPORACEÆ.

Peronospora parasitica (Persoon) De Bary.

Yakutat (Saunders, 677, on *Arabis hirsuta*).

Peronospora ficariæ Tulasne.

Glacier Bay (Coville & Kearney, 743, on leaves of *Ranunculus*).

Family USTILAGINACEÆ.

Tuburcinia trientalis Berkeley & Broome.

Kadiak (Trelease, 720); Unalaska (Trelease, 719). On living leaves of *Trientalis*.

The conidial stage, known as *Ovularia trientalis* Berk.

Ustilago vinosa (Berkeley) Tulasne.*

Point Barrow (Murdoch in 1883, in *Oxyria digyna*).

Ustilago bistortarum (De Candolle) Körnicke.

Port Wells (Trelease, 764, in leaves of *Polygonum viviparum*).

Ustilago bistortarum inflorescentiæ Trelease, var. nov.*

Spores very abundant, brownish-purple, subglobose or slightly elongated, 9-14 µ, usually 11-13 µ, almost perfectly smooth.

Kadiak (Trelease, 675); Yakutat (Trelease, 674); Unalaska (Trelease, 676). In the inflorescence of *Polygonum viviparum*.

This differs from var *glabra* in the part of the host plant in which the spores appear, and from the typical form of the species further in its smoother spores.

Family UREDINACEÆ.

Cæoma saxifragarum (De Candolle) Schlechtendal *

St. Lawrence Island, Bering Sea (Trelease, 660, on *Saxifraga bracteata*).

Uredo ledicola Peck.*

Virgin Bay (Trelease, 641); Kadiak (Trelease, 642). On *Ledum palustre*.

Uredo nootkatensis Trelease, sp. nov.*

Sori subhemispherical, about 5 mm. in diameter, deep orange, the affected leaf yellowish. Spores globose to shortly obovoid, the rather thin wall colorless, radiately striate and slightly roughened, 28–31 μ; pedicel colorless, very slender, breaking a short distance from the spore.

Hot Springs, Baranof Island (Trelease, 668, on leaves of *Chamæcyparis nootkatensis*).

Peridermium cerebrum Peck.*

New Metlakatla (Trelease, 667, on *Pinus contorta*).

Æcidium ranunculacearum De Candolle.*

Unalaska (Harrington in 1871–2; Trelease, 663—both on *Anemone richardsonii*, Trelease, 662, on *Ranunculus*).

Held to be a stage of *Uromyces dactylidis*, which has not yet been observed as Alaskan.

Æcidium grossulariæ De Candolle.*

Wrangell (Evans, 95), Juneau (Trelease, 644); Sitka (Trelease, 643); Yakutat (Saunders, 646; Trelease, 645). On *Ribes*.

Æcidium fraseræ Trelease, sp nov *

Spots yellowish, round or sometimes elongated on the petiole or midvein, measuring 2–5 mm. Spermogonia and æcidia amphigenous but most numerous on the lower surface, the former at length brown; peridia not crowded, irregularly or subcircinately placed, about .25 mm. in diameter, cylindrical, without spreading border; spores polygonally subglobose to ellipsoid, nearly smooth, 16–22 μ.

Kadiak (Trelease, 647, 648, 649, on leaves of *Frasera*).

Chiefly differs from the æcidial form of *Puccinia gentianæ* in the grouping of the spermogonia and the form of the peridia.

Æcidium alaskanum Trelease, sp. nov. *

Spots pale, mostly elliptical, about 5×5–10 mm. Spermogonia wanting; æcidia amphigenous, but most abundant on the lower surface, about .25 mm. in diameter, with multifid recurving border. peridial cells about 28 μ broad; spores little longer than broad, nearly smooth, 16–20 μ.

Kadiak (Trelease, 652, on *Habenaria bracteata*, 652a, on *H. hyperborea*, 653, 654, 655, 656, 657, on *H. dilatata*, Trelease, 650, on *Orchis aristata*); Popof Island (Kincaid; Saunders, 658, 659—all on *Habenaria dilatata*); Unalaska (Trelease, 651, on *Orchis aristata*); near Ocean Cape, Yakutat Bay (Funston, on *Habenaria dilatata*, 52); Bering Island (Macoun, on *Habenaria bracteata*, 144).

Of the general appearance of *A orchidearum*, now held to be the æcidial stage of *Puccinia moliniæ*, but differing in the absence of spermogonia and in its larger peridial cells and smaller, less sculptured spores.

Æcidium epilobii De Candolle.*

Glacier Bay (Coville & Kearney, 952); Kadiak (Trelease, 659a). On leaves of *Epilobium*.

Æcidium violascens Trelease, sp. nov.*

Spots large, irregular, effuse, violet especially on the upper surface of the leaf, frequently following the veins which are then thickened. Sori hypophyllous, scarcely .5 mm in diameter, hemispherical, crowded irregularly or along the veins; peridia included, borderless, the irregularly oblong cells about 20×30–40 μ, sinuously and rugosely roughened; spores variously and often polygonally rounded to ellipsoidal, minutely verruculose, 22–28×22–35 μ.

Kadiak (Trelease, 634); Kukak Bay (Saunders, 636, on a leaf with *Puccinia geranii-silvatici*). On leaves of *Geranium erianthum*.

From *A. geranii* this differs in the color of the spots, the frequent thickening of the veins, fewer peridia neither regularly arranged nor with spreading border, and much larger spores.

Æcidium asterum Schweinitz.*

Kadiak (Trelease, 624, on *Aster foliaceus*).

Æcidium parnassiæ (Schlechtendal) Grav.*

Kadiak (Trelease, 665, on *Parnassia palustris*).
See, further, *Puccinia caricis*.

Æcidium claytonianum (Schweinitz) Clinton.
St. Paul Island, Bering Sea (Trelease, 664, on *Claytonia arctica*).

Æcidium circinans Eriksson f. **aconiti-delphinifolii**.
St. Paul Island, Bering Sea (Trelease, 661, on *Aconitum*).

Æcidium astragali-alpini Eriksson.[1]
Muir Glacier (Trelease, 632, on *Astragalus*).

Thecopsora vacciniorum (Link) Karsten.*
Sitka (Trelease, 614, on *Vaccinium*).

Chrysomyxa pirolæ (De Candolle) Rostrup.*
Glacier Bay (Trelease, 771); Disenchantment Bay (Coville & Kearney, 1025). Both on *Pyrola*. Yes Bay (Howell, on *Moneses grandiflora*, 1632). The uredo stage only.

Phragmidium subcorticium (Schrank) Winter.*
Sitka (Evans, 204); Kadiak (Cole; Trelease, 638, 639, 640). On *Rosa cinnamomea*. The æcidial stage only.

Phragmidium rubi (Persoon) Winter?*
Disenchantment Bay, (Trelease, 670); Unalaska (Hb Bernhardi). On *Rubus stellatus*. The uredo only.

Phragmidium rubi-idæi (De Candolle) Karsten? *
Kadiak (Trelease, 671, 672, 673, on *Rubus chamæmorus*). The uredo stage only, forming small sori on the under surface of the leaves.

Puccinia bullata (Persoon) Schroeter.*
Popof Island (Saunders, 617, on *Cœlopleurum gmelini*); St. Paul Island, Bering Sea (Trelease, 618, on *Conioselinum gmelini*).

Puccinia circææ Persoon.*
Juneau (Setchell, 1250, on *Circæa alpina* or *C. pacifica*).

Puccinia laurentiana Trelease, sp. nov.*
Sori hypophyllous, chestnut-brown, round, about 1 mm. in diameter; spores brown, somewhat constricted, about $20 \times 50 \mu$, the apex thickened and with pallescent apiculus, the rather thick walls neither striate nor verrucose; pedicel hyaline, breaking short.

St. Lawrence Island, Bering Sea (Macoun, on *Saxifraga neglecta stolonifera*, 60).

Agreeing more closely with the description of *P. saxifragæ-ciliatæ* than with other described species on genera of Saxifragaceæ.

[1] Determined by Professor J. C. Arthur.

Puccinia saxifragæ Schlechtendal.
SACCARDO, Sylloge Fungorum, 12¹ 641.
Alaska. On *Saxifraga*.

Puccinia prenanthis (Persoon) Fuckel.*
Sitka (Trelease, 623); Kadiak (Trelease, 622, 622a). On *Prenanthes alata*.
The æcidial and teleutosporic stages.

Puccinia fergussoni Berkeley & Broome.*
Kadiak (Trelease, 625, on *Viola blanda*).

Puccinia heucheræ (Schweinitz) Dietel.*
Juneau (Setchell, 1251, on *Heuchera glabra*; Trelease, 615, on *Saxifraga nelsoniana*); Disenchantment Bay (Funston, on *Tellima grandiflora*, 83).

Puccinia tiarellæ Berkeley & Curtis.¹
Head of Russell Fiord (Coville & Kearney, 958a, on *Heuchera glabra*).

Puccinia thlaspeos Schubert.*
Disenchantment Bay (Coville & Kearney, 1112); Kukak Bay (Saunders, 631). On *Arabis ambigua*.

Puccinia porphyrogenita Curtis.*
Douglas Island (Trelease, 616); Sitka (Setchell, 1270). On *Cornus canadensis*. Yes Bay (Howell, on *Cornus suecica*, 1630).

Puccinia asteris Duby.*
Kadiak (Trelease, 624a, on *Aster foliaceus*).

Puccinia valerianæ Carest.*
St. Paul Island, Bering Sea (Brewer, 637, on *Valeriana capitata*).
Uredo and teleutospores are present.

Puccinia geranii-silvatici Karsten.*
Kukak Bay (Saunders, 636a); Popof Island (Saunders, 635). On leaves of *Geranium erianthum*.
Globose and obovoid mesospores, and 3-celled teleutospores, occur occasionally with the normal 2-celled spores. — See further *Æcidium violascens*.

Puccinia procera D. & H.¹
Revillagigedo Island (Howell, on *Elymus dahuricus*, 1723 ?).

¹Determined by Professor J. C. Arthur.

Puccinia caricis (Schumann) Reber?*

New Metlakatla (Trelease, 630); Sitka (Trelease, 629, on *Carex tolmiei*?; Wright, on *Carex*, 1575).

III. Sori oblong, bordered but not covered by the epidermis, when dry fissuring transversely at intervals, dark brown, less black than usual with *P. caricis*, spores brown, 17–20 × about 50 μ, the often somewhat truncated apex much thickened.

Dr. Juel, who was kind enough to examine the specimens in comparison with his *P. uliginosa* (the æcidial stage of which is held to be *A. parnassiæ*), considers it impossible to determine the species of this group without experimental knowledge of their æcidia. — See further *Æcidium parnassiæ*.

Melampsora farinosa (Persoon) Schroeter?*

On *Salix stolonifera*: Disenchantment Bay (Coville & Kearney, 1025a — not producing discolored spots on the leaves; sori mostly hypophyllous but also found on the upper surface and occasionally on the twigs; spores 16–23 μ, paraphyses 15–20 μ in diameter at top, either clavate or capitate).

On *Salix pulchra*: Popof Island (Saunders, 611 — causing small yellow or brown leaf-spots; sori most abundant on the lower surface; spores 16–20 μ; paraphyses about 20 μ in diameter at top).

On *Salix alaxensis*: Muir Glacier (Trelease, 612, 613 — causing distinct often large yellow leaf-spots; sori on both surfaces but most abundant below; spores 16–23 μ; paraphyses 16–20 or occasionally 27 μ in diameter at top).

On *Salix reticulata*: Kukak Bay (Saunders, 608 — not producing spots; the distinct sori scattered over the lower surface of the leaf and a few on the upper surface near the base; spores 16–20 μ; paraphyses 13–20 μ). *M. reticulatæ* Blytt differs markedly in its much larger and usually thicker-walled paraphyses.

On *Salix fuscescens*: St. Lawrence Island, Bering Sea (Trelease, 609 — not causing spots; sori hypophyllous; spores 16–23 μ).

Melampsora alpina Juel?*

Port Clarence (Trelease, 610, on *Salix polaris*).

Producing at most small brown spots; sori amphigenous; spores 16–20 μ; paraphyses 20–27 μ at apex.

Only the uredo form of these doubtfully determined species of *Melampsora* was observed.

Hyalospora polypodii-dryopteridis (Moug. & Nestl.) Magnus.*

Juneau (Trelease, 669, on *Phegopteris dryopteris*).

Only the uredo stage, *Uredo aspidiotus* Pk., was observed.

Uromyces lapponicus Lagerheim.[1]

Unga Island (Saunders, 633, 633*a*, on *Astragalus*).

Uromyces erythronii (De Candolle) Passerini.*

Kadiak (Trelease, 626); Kukak Bay (Saunders, 627). On *Fritillaria kamtschatcensis*.

Family LYCOPERDACEÆ.

Lycoperdon piriforme Schaeffer.*

Cape Fox (Trelease, 607).

Lycoperdon sp.*

Muir Glacier (Trelease, 605).

A minute species, apparently of the bovistoid group, but immature.

Lycoperdon saccatum Vahl.*

Virgin Bay (Kincaid).

Lycoperdon sp.*

Port Clarence (Trelease, 604).

A species apparently of the proteid group — now frequently referred to the genus *Calvatia* — but too immature for naming.

Family NIDULARIACEÆ.

Nidularia candida Peck.†

Fariagut Bay (Trelease, 603), Sitka (Trelease, 599); Orca (Trelease, 602); Yakutat (Trelease, 600). Also collected on Lowe Inlet, B. C. (Trelease, 601), and occurs from Alaska without further designation of locality in the National Herbarium (Evans, 139).

The specimens indicate considerable variation in the species. In some the peridium is much larger than in others, it being 12 mm. long and 10 mm. broad at the mouth in the large specimens. The tomentum of the external surface varies in color from white to gray, and the inner surface from pure white to dingy white, often becoming brown toward the base of the cup, in the smaller cups it is glabrous, but in the larger it is often floccose or downy near the margin. The peridiola, which are about 1 mm. broad, also vary much in color. They are sometimes white on one side and brown on the other, or white with a brown margin, but they are usually brown on both sides, their surfaces may be even or wrinkled, and sometimes, as in the

[1] Determined by Professor J. C. Arthur.

typical form, they are marked by blackish lines. This character is not shown by any of these specimens, but they are apparently old, as only a few of them have any peridiola. Age may also account for the gray color of the peridium in some of the specimens. All are open. The young unopened plant is yet a desideratum.

Family TREMELLACEÆ.

Guepinia lutea Bresadola, sp. nov.‡

Gregaria v. subcæspitosa; tremelloso-tenax, flavo-lutea; conceptaculis cupulari-stipitatis, cupula glabra, complanato-concava margine sinuoso, disco-hymenophora, 2–5 mm. lata; stipes teres, 1–4.5 mm. longus, .5–1 mm. crassus, basi demum fuscidulus; basidia cylindracea, apice subcapitata, 45–50 × 3–4 μ, bifida; sporæ subcylindraceæ, subcurvatæ, 5–9-septatæ, 18–20 × 6–7 μ.

Orca (Trelease, 688). Also in Lowe Inlet, B. C. (Trelease, 592, 594).

Guepiniæ merulinæ, cujus gaudet structura, affinis; differt cupula et stipite lævibus nec non sporibus majoribus majisque septatis.

Dacryomyces deliquescens (Bulliard) Duby.‡

Juneau (Trelease, 589); Sitka (Trelease, 590); Yakutat (Trelease, 598).

One other species of this genus, *D. palmatus* (Schw.) Bresadola, determined by Abbe Bresadola, was collected along Broughton Strait, Vancouver Island (Trelease, 729).

Tremella (?) phyllachoroidea Saccardo, sp. nov. (PL. III, fig. 11.)

Erumpenti-adnata, epiphylla, applanato-pulvinata, ambitu suborbicularis v. oblonga, 2–4 mm. diam., .7–1 mm. crass., uda exquisite gelatinosa, superficie nigra, opaca, minute rugulosa, intus pallidior, tota filamentosa; filamentis seu hyphis angustissime filiformibus, 1.5–2 μ cr., longissimis, varie intricatis, furcatis v. varie ramosis, hyalinis, intus granulosis, apicibus subinde lenissime incrassatis, obtusis; basidiis . . . , sporis. . . .

Sitka (Mertens, on decaying fallen leaves of *Menziesia ferruginea*).

Videtur affinis *Tremella atro-virenti* Fr.; dubia tamen quia sterilis.

Family THELEPHORACEÆ.

Exobasidium vaccinii (Fuckel) Woronin.

CAMPBELL, Amer Naturalist, **33** : 399.

Orca (Trelease, 716, 717, 718, 765; Coville & Kearney, 1639 — all on *Vaccinium ovalifolium?*); Seldovia (Saunders, 714, on *V. oxycoccus*).

Peniophora disciformis borealis Peck, var. nov. †

Yakutat Bay (Trelease, 583).

Differs from the description of the species in having a slight pinkish tint and in its smaller cystidia, which are only half as long and broad as in the species. The disk is covered with a distinct white pruinosity or pulverulence. The specimens are sterile. Fertile specimens may show it to be a distinct species.

Corticium incarnatum (Persoon) Fries.

Farragut Bay (Trelease, 582).

Hymenochæte tabacina (Sowerby) Léveillé †

Sitka (Trelease, 583*a*).

Thelephora laciniata Persoon ‡

Alaska (Evans, 410).

Family POLYPORACEÆ.

Poria crassa Karsten? ‡

Farragut Bay (Trelease, 577).
Sterile and doubtful.

Polystictus radiatus (Sowerby) Fries. †

Kukak Bay (Kincaid, 575).

The specimens are very old, weathered and discolored, but apparently belong here.

Polystictus abietinus Fries. †

Point Gustavus (Coville & Kearney), Orca (Trelease, 579).

Also collected along Lowe Inlet, B. C. (Trelease, 581), where *P. versicolor* L., as determined by Professor Saccardo, was also collected (Trelease, 580).

Fomes fomentarius (Linnæus) Fries.†

White Pass (Trelease, 574, on *Betula*).

Fomes pinicola Fries. †

Orca (Coville & Kearney, a small depressed form; Trelease, 573, the form having a pallid margin), Sitka (Coville & Kearney, the palemargined form).

This species is not limited in its habitat to pine trees or even to coniferous wood.

This species, as determined by Professor Peck, was also collected along Lowe Inlet, B. C. (Trelease, 572), and on Vancouver Island (Trelease, 571).

Though not collected in Alaska, *Fomes lucidus* (Leys) Fr. is very abundant on *Tsuga* in the Vancouver region, where it attains immense proportions. One specimen, by no means the largest observed, which was collected on Broughton Strait (Trelease, 509), measures 16 inches in length and breadth.

F. applanatus (Pers.) Wallr., another species not collected in Alaska, but doubtless occurring there, is represented from Lowe Inlet, B. C. (Trelease, 570), in a singular tabular form, according to Professor Peck's determination.

Fomes igniarius (Linnæus) Fries.†

St. Michael (Nelson, 4266, 43366, in U. S. Nat. Museum); region of Lake Iliamna (Gorman). On *Betula*.

This is the fungus figured by Nelson, without name, in Rept. Bur. Amer. Ethnology, 18^1: 271. *f. 93*, and said by him and Mr. Gorman to be used for making ashes which are mixed with tobacco for chewing.

Polyporus melanopus Schweinitz.†

Orca (Trelease, 578).

Young and not well developed, but scarcely anything else.

Polyporus pubescens (Schumann) Fries.†

Kukak Bay (Kincaid, 576).

The single specimen collected is old and somewhat discolored.

Family AGARICACEÆ.

Psathyrella atomaria Fries.‡

Sitka (Trelease, 555).

Psathyrella disseminata Persoon.‡

Yakutat Bay (Trelease, 559).

Coprinus plicatilis (Curtis) Fries ‡

Hot Springs, Baranof Island (Trelease, 591*g*).

Psilocybe polytrichi Fries.†

St. Paul Island, Bering Sea (Trelease, 521). Among hair-cap moss.

Stropharia magnivelaris Peck, sp. nov.†

Pileus convex, becoming nearly plane, sometimes umbonate, glabrous or obscurely radiately fibrillose or fibrillose-squamose with innate or appressed fibrils, ochraceous buff when dry; lamellæ moderately close, blackish-brown when mature; stems long, slender, glabrous, solid, slightly thickened at the base, whitish, the ring large, membranous, white, persistent; spores elliptic-oblong, 14–16 µ long, 7–8 µ broad.

Pileus 2–3 cm. broad; stem 5–7 cm. long, 2–4 mm. thick.

Yakutat (Trelease, 501, 503).

The species is well marked by the large, firm, persistent white ring, which is sometimes flocculose on the lower surface. The pileus may be somewhat glutinous when moist, and the drying of the gluten may give the fibrillose or squamose appearance exhibited by some of the specimens.

Agaricus campester Linnæus.*

Kadiak (Trelease, 504).

Cortinarius sp. ?

MACOUN, Rept. Fur Seal Investigations, Pt. 3, 584.

St. Paul Island, Bering Sea.

Tubaria brevipes Peck, sp. nov.†

Pileus thin, convex, glabrous, ferruginous; lamellæ broad, arcuate, distant, adnate or slightly decurrent, ferruginous; stem short, slender, glabrous, hollow, brown; spores elliptic, uninucleate, 10–12 µ long, 7–8 µ broad.

Pileus 6–10 mm. broad; stem 6–14 mm. long, scarcely 1 mm. thick.

Port Cluence (Trelease, 562, 567).

The dried specimens resemble in color those of *Omphalia campanella*, but the color of the spores and the ferruginous hue of the lamellæ easily distinguish this species from any species of *Omphalia*.

Galera sphagnorum (Persoon) Fries.†

Kadiak (Trelease, 511); Yakutat (Trelease, 514a, 516).

Naucoria vernalis Peck.†

Orca (Trelease, 506).

Naucoria badipes Fries? ‡

Juneau (Trelease, 568b).

Naucoria camerina Fries.‡

Orca (Trelease, 508).

Flammula fulvella Peck.

MACOUN, Rept. Fur Seal Investigations, Pt. 3, 583.

St. Paul Island, Bering Sea.

Pholiota marginata Batsch.‡

Muir Glacier (Trelease, 525).

Pholiota unicolor Wahlenberg ‡

Yakutat Bay (Trelease, 520).

Pholiota præcox sylvestris Peck.†

Yakutat Bay (Trelease, 502, 514, 517).

In these specimens the whole surface of the pileus has the reddish yellow or rusty brown color that in the typical form is limited to the center.

Eccilia conchina (Fries).‡

Juneau (Trelease, 564).

Nolanea juncea Fries ‡

Sitka (Trelease, 507).

Nolanea ? sp.

Nolaviea ? sp MACOUN, Rept Fur Seal Investigations, Pt 3, 584

St Paul Island, Bering Sea.

Entoloma clypeatum (Linnæus) Fries.†

Glacier Bay (Coville, 505).

The specimens appear to belong to this species, but the reference is doubtful to the extent that it is not possible to affirm that the pileus is hygrophanous when fresh, as there are no notes with the samples that indicate it.

Marasmius androsaceus Fries?‡

Virgin Bay (Trelease, 528).

Marasmius filipes Peck?‡

Orca (Trelease, 529a, on needles of *Tsuga*).

Marasmius perforans Host.‡

Orca (Trelease, 529, on needles of *Tsuga*).

Cantharellus bryophilus Peck, sp. nov.†

Pileus thin, dimidiate, flabellate, or subspatulate, rarely lobed, glabrous, mostly white tomentose or downy at the base, sessile by a more or less broad base; lamellæ very narrow, branched or forked, distant; spores broadly elliptic or subglobose, 6–7 μ long, 5–6 μ broad.

Pileus 1–2 5 cm. broad.

Muir Glacier (Trelease, 552, 563, in moss).

The dried specimens have the pileus partly blackened. They are mostly whitish or pallid at and near the base, blackish toward and on the margin. They are probably white or whitish when fresh and assume the blackish color with age or in drying. Though inhabiting mosses, the species may be distinguished from *C. muscigenus* by the zoneless and differently colored pileus, by the entire absence of a distinct stem, and by the smaller spores. In one specimen the pileus is slightly fibrillose.

Russula nigrodisca Peck.

MACOUN, Rept. Fur Seal Investigations, Pt. 3, 583.

St. Paul Island, Bering Sea.

Hygrophorus limacinus (Scopoli) Fries.†

' Alaska ' (Evans, 263).

The specimens are small and pale.

Omphalia semivestipes Peck.†

Orca (Trelease, 522, 524).

These specimens have the stems longer than they are in the type, but they are evidently the same species.

Omphalia campanella (Batsch) Fries †

Sitka (Trelease, 536‡, 540, 561 ‡); Orca (Trelease, 530, 550, 565).

Omphalia montana Peck †

St. Paul Island, Bering Sea (Trelease, 551).

Omphalia sphagnophila Peck, sp. nov.†

Pileus at first narrowly obconic and centrally depressed, becoming tubiform or subinfundibuliform, thin, glabrous, whitish or pale yellow; lamellæ moderately broad, distant, very decurrent, yellow, the interspaces sometimes venose; stem short, solid or stuffed, pruinose or minutely downy, whitish with a white mycelium at the base; spores broadly elliptic, $6-7\,\mu$ long, $4-5\,\mu$ broad.

Pileus 1-2 cm. broad, stem 1-2 cm. long, 2-4 mm. thick.

Port Clarence (Trelease, 558). Growing among and attached to the stems and branches of *Sphagnum*.

This species is closely related to *O. umbellifera*, of which it may possibly be a variety, but it is easily separated by its peculiar shape, especially when young, and by its more narrow and much more decurrent lamellæ.

Omphalia umbellifera (Linnæus) Fries.†

Cape Fox (Trelease); Juneau (Trelease, 568*a*); Sitka (Trelease, 539, 544-6); Orca (Trelease, 538, 543); Virgin Bay (Trelease, 548);

Port Wells (Trelease, 549); Yakutat (Trelease, 542); Bering Sea: Hall Island (Trelease, 537); St. Lawrence Island (Trelease, 556).

Omphalia gracillima Weinmann.‡

Port Clarence (Trelease, 557).

Omphalia pseudo-androsacea Bulliard.‡

Juneau (Trelease, 564a); Sitka (Trelease, 554).

Omphalia pyxidata hepatica Batsch.‡

Yakutat Bay (Trelease, 566).

Mycena atrocyanea Batsch.‡

Yakutat (Trelease, 532a?); Orca (Trelease, 533?); Virgin Bay (Trelease, 531, forma *minor*).

Mycena debilis Fries.‡

Sitka (Trelease, 553).

Mycena stannea Fries.‡

Hot Springs, Baranof Island (Trelease, 591f?); Orca (Trelease, 534); Yakutat (Trelease, 532).

Collybia dryophila (Bulliard) Fries.†

Wrangell (Trelease, 512); Juneau (Trelease, 564a); Sitka (Trelease, 509, 510, 560); Kadiak (Trelease, 519).

Collybia velutipes spongiosa Peck, var. nov.†

Yakutat (Trelease, 515).

The distinguishing characters of this variety are found in the short, rather fragile stem, which is clothed throughout with a rather dense but soft tawny tomentose stratum .5–1 mm. thick. The stems are scarcely more than 2.5 cm. long. The soft spongy texture of this tomentose coat is suggestive of the name given.

Clitocybe diatreta Fries.

MACOUN, Rept Fur Seal Investigations, Pt 3, 583

St. Paul Island, Bering Sea.

Clitocybe laccata Scopoli.

MACOUN, Rept. Fur Seal Investigations, Pt. 3, 583.

St. Paul Island, Bering Sea.

Clitocybe cyathiformis Fries.

MACOUN, Rept. Fur Seal Investigations, Pt. 3, 583.

St. Paul Island, Bering Sea.

Tricholoma melaleucum Persoon.‡

Orca (Trelease, 523)

STERILE MYCELIA.

Sclerotium varium Persoon

Kadiak (Trelease, 737a, in decaying stems of *Heracleum*).

Sclerotium durum Persoon.

Orca (Trelease, 730a, in decaying stem of *Veratrum*, associated with *Patinella aloysii-sabaudiæ*.)

PSEUDO-FUNGI.

The following mite-galls, formerly placed in the pseudo-genus *Erineum*, occur in Alaska

Erineum alneum Persoon.[1]

Muir Glacier (Trelease, 711); Kadiak (Cole). On leaves of *Alnus*.

Erineum roseum Schult.

HOOKER & ARNOTT, Bot Beechey 134 — ROTHROCK, Smithsonian Rept 1867 463 — TURNER, Cont Nat Hist Alaska 85

Alaska Doubtless on leaves of *Betula*, unless it refers to the preceding

Erineum aucupariæ Kunze.[1]

Wrangell (Evans, 64, on leaves of *Sorbus*).

Erineum pyrinum Persoon *

Cape Fox (Trelease, 666, on leaves of *Pyrus rivularis*).

INDEX TO HOST GENERA.[2]

ACONITUM.
  Æcidium circinans f aconiti delphinifolii
AGROSTIS
  Leptosphæria leersiana.
  Septoria grylli.
  Sphærella californica.
  Sphærella ignobilis
AIRA
  Didymosphæria arenaria
  Stagonospora graminum.

ALNUS
  Didymosphæria nana.
  Erineum alneum
  Gnomoniella tubiformis
  Hypoxylon majusculum
  Lunacinia? alaskensis
  Nectria episphæria.
  Sphærella alni-viridis.
  Sphærella stellarinearum
ANEMONE.
  Æcidium ranunculacearum

[1] Determined by Professor Farlow.

[2] A few indefinite references, such as wood, moss, etc., are to be found at end of the generic index

ANEMONE.
　Physalospora borealis
　Rhabdospora camptospora
　Stagonospora pulsatillæ.
ANGELICA
　Cercospora apii var. angelicæ.
　Septoria dearnesii.
ARABIS.
　Peronospora parasitica.
　Puccinia thlaspeos.
ARENARIA.
　Pseudopeziza cerastiorum var. arenariæ
　Pyrenophora comata.
ARNICA
　Ramularia arnicola.
ARTEMISIA
　Sphærella eriophila.
ASPIDIUM.
　Phyllachora filicina
ASTER
　Æcidium asterum.
　Puccinia asteris
ASTRAGALUS.
　Æcidium astragali-alpini.
　Uromyces lapponicus.
BETULA
　Dothidella betulina.
　Erineum rosaceum.
　Fomes fomentarius.
　Fomes igniarius.
　Sphærella harthensis.
CAMPANULA
　Ramularia macrospora.
CARDAMINE
　Phoma oleracea.
CAREX
　Phacidium diminuens.
　Phyllosticta caricicola
　Puccinia caricis
　Sphærella leptospora.
　Sphærella wichuriana
　Stagonospora heleocharidis subsp. caricina
CHAMÆCYPARIS.
　Uredo nootkatensis.
CIRCÆA
　Puccinia circææ

CLAYTONIA.
　Æcidium claytonianum.
CŒLOPLEURUM.
　Puccinia bullata.
CONIOSELINUM.
　Puccinia bullata.
　Septoria petroselini subsp. treleaseana.
COPTIS.
　Phyllosticta helleboricola var. coptidis.
CORNUS
　Glomerularia corni
　Puccinia porphyrogenita
　Septoria canadensis.
DRABA.
　Pleospora media.
DRYAS
　Massarina dryadis
　Sphærella ootheca.
DUPONTIA
　Pleospora pentamera.
ELYMUS.
　Puccinia procera.
EMPETRUM
　Metasphæria empetri.
　Physalospora crepiniana.
EPILOBIUM
　Æcidium epilobii
　Ramularia cercosporoides.
　Sphærella adusta.
ERIOPHORUM
　Septoria chamissonis.
　Septoria eriophorella
FESTUCA
　Leptosphæria ophiopogonis.
FRASERA.
　Æcidium fraseræ
FRITILLARIA.
　Uromyces erythronii.
GERANIUM.
　Æcidium violascens
　Puccinia geranii-silvatici.
　Venturia circinans.
HABENARIA.
　Æcidium alaskanum
HERACLEUM
　Heterosphæria patella.
　Leptosphæria doliolum.

HERACLEUM
  Phoma complanata.
  Phyllachora? heraclei
  Ramularia heraclei.
  Sclerotium varium
  Sphærographium abditum
HEUCHERA
  Puccinia heucheræ.
  Puccinia tiarellæ
LEDUM
  Uredo ledicola
LONICERA.
  Botrytis vulgaris
LUPINUS.
  Leptosphæria fœniculacea subsp lupina
  Trichopeziza earoleuca
LUZULA
  Stagonospora aquatica subsp luzulicola
MENYANTHES
  Physoderma menyanthis.
MENZIESIA
  Tremella? phyllachoroides.
MONESES
  Chrysomyxa pirolæ.
MYRICA
  Ovularia sommeri.
NEBRIA
  Laboulbenia nebriæ
ORCHIS
  Æcidium alaskanum.
OXYRIA
  Ustilago vinosa.
OXYTROPIS
  Pleospora herbarum.
  Pyrenophora chrysospora.
PARNASSIA
  Æcidium parnassiæ
PARRYA
  Leptothyrium vulgare f. parryæ
PHEGOPTERIS.
  Hyalospora polypodii-dryopteridis
PHYLLODOCE
  Antennaria rectangularis
PICEA
  Hypoxylon ohiense
  Sporonema strobilinum

PINUS
  Peridermium cerebrum
POA.
  Pleospora infectoria
  Sphærella graminum
POLEMONIUM
  Pyrenophora polyphragmoides
POLYGONUM
  Bostrichonema alpestre
  Pseudopeziza bistortæ
  Ustilago bistortarum
  Ustilago bistortarum var. inflorescentiæ
POTENTILLA
  Ramularia punctiformis
PRASIOLA
  Guignardia alaskana
PRENANTHES
  Puccinia prenanthis.
PIROLA
  Chrysomyxa pirolæ
  Leptosphæria marginata
PYRUS
  Erineum pyrinum
RANUNCULUS
  Æcidium ranunculacearum.
  Peronospora ficariæ.
  Pleospora herbarum
  Ramularia æquivoca.
RHODODENDRON
  Rhytisma? rhododendri
RIBES.
  Æcidium grossulariæ.
  Diaporthe pungens
  Diaporthe strumella
  Godronia urceolus
  Pseudovalsa ribesia
  Rhynchophoma raduloides.
ROSA
  Phragmidium subcorticium
RUBUS
  Fabræa cincta
  Leptothyrium vulgare.
  Phragmidium rubi
  Phragmidium rubi-idæi
  Septoria rubi
  Venturia kunzei
  Venturia kunzei var. ramicola.

Rumex.
　Ramularia pratensis.
　Sphærella rumicis.
Salix.
　Lophodermium maculare.
　Melampsora alpina.
　Melampsora farinosa.
　Rhytisma salicinum.
　Sphærella grossulariæ var. salicella.
Sanguisorba.
　Ovularia bulbigera.
Saxifraga.
　Cæoma saxifragarum.
　Læstadia saxifragæ.
　Puccinia heucheræ.
　Puccinia laurentiana.
　Puccinia saxifragæ.
Scirpus.
　Leptosphæria juncicola.
Selinum.
　Cercospora apii var. selini-gmelini.
Silene.
　Leptosphæria silenes-acaulis.
Sorbus.
　Erineum aucupariæ.

Spirogyra.
　Lagenidium entophytum.
　Pythium gracile.
　Vampyrella spirogyræ.
Tellima.
　Puccinia heucheræ.
Trientalis.
　Tuburcinia trientalis.
Tsuga.
　Ciboria sp.
　Microthyrium harrimani.
　Sporonema strobilinum.
Vaccinium.
　Exobasidium vaccinii.
　Lophodermium oxycocci.
　Thecopsora vacciniorum.
Valeriana.
　Puccinia valerianæ.
Veratrum.
　Patinella aloysii-sabaudiæ.
　Sclerotium durum.
Viola.
　Puccinia fergussoni.

UNIDENTIFIED ORGANIC MATERIAL.

Bark.
　Hypoxylon majusculum.
　Hypoxylon ohiense.
　Lachnea scutellata.
　Microcera brachyspora.
　Nectria sanguinea.
　Scleroderris treleasei.
Dung (of ptarmigan?).
　Sporormia ambigua.
Fungi (Sphæriaceæ).
　Nectria episphæria.
Insects.
　Cordyceps militaris.
　Laboulbenia nebriæ.
Leaves.
　Diderma niveum.
　Dothidella betulina subsp. yakutatiana.
　Eurotium herbariorum.
　Phialea carneola.
　Scolecotrichum graminis.
Mosses.
　Cantharellus bryophilus.

Mosses—continued.
　Diderma niveum.
　Omphalia sphagnophila.
　Psilocybe polytrichi.
Snow.
　Diderma niveum.
Stems and Twigs.
　Amphisphæria applanata.
　Botrytis vulgaris.
　Diaporthe anisomera.
　Fusarium illosporioides.
　Helotium fumigatum.
　Leptosphæria agnita subsp. labens.
　Nidularia candida.
　Patinella aloysii-sabaudiæ.
　Pirottæa yakutatiana.
　Speira effusa.
　Speira minor.
　Trichopeziza relicina.
Wood.
　Coniosporium atratum.
　Corticium incarnatum.
　Cudonia circinans.

Wood—continued.
  Dacryomyces deliquescens.
  Fomes applanatus.
  Fomes igniarius.
  Fomes pinicola.
  Guepinia lutea.
  Helotium alaskæ.
  Helotium lenticulare.
  Hymenochæte tabacina.
  Lachnea scutellata.

Wood—continued
  Lycoperdon piriforme
  Peniophora disciformis var. borealis.
  Polyporus melanopus.
  Polyporus pubescens.
  Polystictus abietinus.
  Polystictus radiatus.
  Poria crassa
  Thelephora laciniata.
  Vibrissea truncorum.

PLATE II.

Fig 1 *Microthyrium harrimani* Sacc *a*, fungus, ×5 ; *b*, perithecia duo binata, *c*, contextus perithecii , *d*, ascus , *e*, sporidia
2 *Phialea carneola* Sacc *a*, fungus, ×5 , *b*, cupulæ varia ætate ; *c*, ascus , *d*, sporidia
3 *Helotium alaskæ* Sacc *a*, fungus, ×5 , *b*, ascoma sectum , *c*, ascus ; *d*, sporidia
4 *Pirottæa yakutatiana* Sacc. *a*, fungus, ×4 ; *b*, ascomata magis aucta , *c*, pili fimbriati ; *d*, setula ; *e*, ascus , *f*, sporidia.
5 *Trichopeziza earoleuca* (B. & Br.) Sacc *a*, fungus, ×4 ; *b*, seta , *c*, ascus et sporidia
6 *Patinella aloysii-sabaudiæ* Sacc *a*, fungus, ×1 , *b*, cupulæ, ×5 ; *c*, sectio , *d*, pili seu cellulæ marginales solutæ ; *e*, ascus et paraphyses , *f*, conidia ; *g*, sporidia.

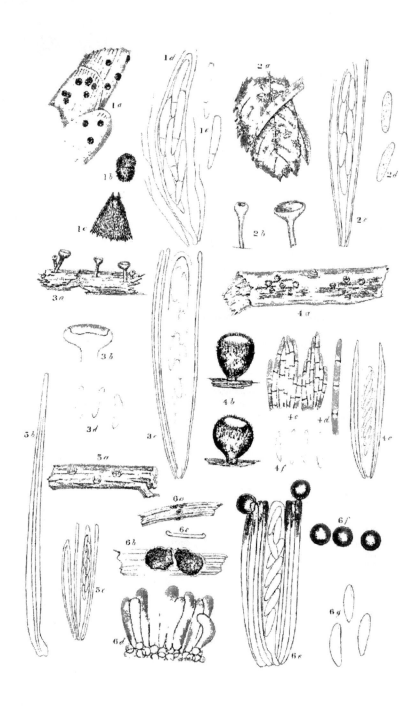

PLATE III.

FIG 7 *Scleroderris treleasei* Sacc   *a*, fungus, ×1 ; *b*, ascomata, ×5 ; *c*, ascoma juvenile sectum, *d*, ascoma adultum sectum; *e*, ascus, *f*, asci apex, *g*, sporidia.
8. *Ramularia punctiformis* Sacc   *a*, fungus, ×5; *b*, cæspituli hyphæ, *c*, conidia
9. *Antennaria rectangularis* Sacc. *a*, hyphæ parum auctæ; *b*, hyphæ fragmentum valde auctum
10 *Fusarium illosporioides* Sacc. *a*, fungus, ×3, *b*, hyphæ sporophoræ variæ ; *c*, conidia varia ætate.
11 *Tremella ? phyllachoroidea* Sacc. *a*, fungus auctus sectus ; *b*, hyphæ.

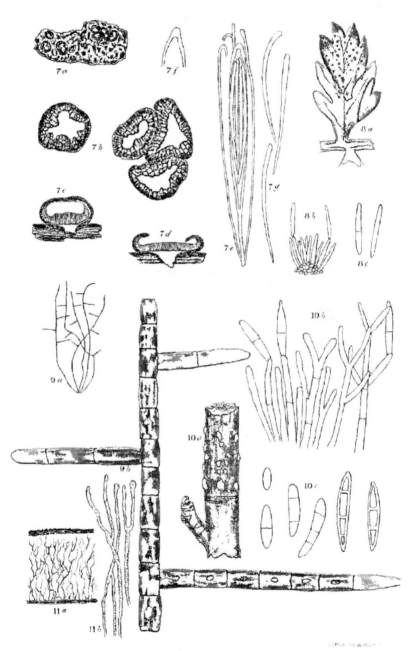

ALASKA FUNGI

PLATE IV.

FIG. 1. *Limacinia? alaskensis* Sacc. & Scal. *a*, fungus, × 1; *b, c,* hyphæ; *d*, conidium; *e*, perithecia aucta; *f*, asci immaturi
2. *Hypoxylon ohiense* Ell. & Everh. *a*, fungus sectus, × 1; *b*, ascus; *c*, sporidia
3. *Læstadia saxifragæ* Sacc. & Scal. *a*, fungus, × 1; *b*, perithecium sectum; *c*, asci; *d*, sporidia
4. *Physalospora borealis* Sacc. & Scal. *a*, fungus, × 1; *b*, perithecia aucta; *c*, ascus; *d*, sporidia
5. *Sphærella graminum* Sacc. & Scal. *a*, fungus, × 1; *b*, perithecium auctum; *c*, asci; *d*, sporidia
6. *Sphærella grossulariæ salicella* Sacc. & Scal. *a*, fungus, × 1; *b*, perithecium auctum; *c*, ascus; *d*, sporidia. (In folio salicino adest quoque *Rhytisma salicinum*.)
7. *Sphærella leptospora* Sacc. & Scal. *a*, fungus, × 1; *b*, perithecium auctum; *c*, asci; *d*, sporidia
8. *Venturia kunzei ramicola* Sacc. & Scal. *a*, fungus, × 1; *b*, perithecia aucta; *c*, setula perithecii; *d*, ascus; *e*, sporidia
9. *Didymosphæria arenariæ macrospora* Sacc. & Scal. *a*, fungus, × 1; *b*, perithecium auctum; *c*, ascus; *d*, sporidia

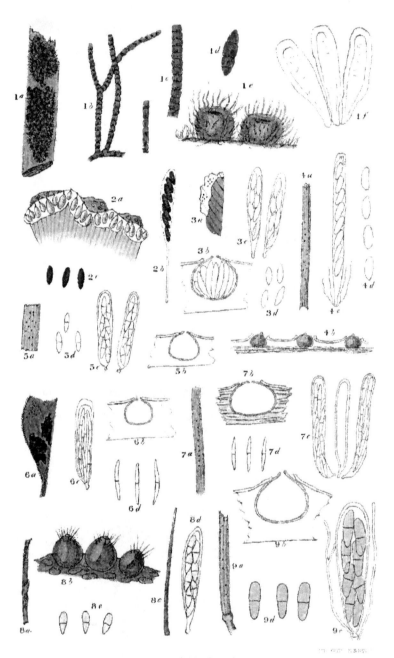

ALASKA FUNGI

PLATE V.

FIG. 10 *Diaporthe (Chorostate) anisomera* Sacc. & Scal. *a*, fungus, ✕ 1, *b*, acervulus sectus horizontaliter; *c*, acervulus sectus verticaliter; *d*, ascus; *e*, sporidia.
11. *Leptosphæria agnita labens* Sacc. & Scal. *a*, fungus, ✕ 1, *b*, perithecium sectum; *c*, ascus; *d*, sporidia.
12. *Leptosphæria fœniculacea lupina* Sacc. & Scal. *a*, fungus, ✕ 1; *b*, perithecia secta; *c*, ascus; *d*, sporidia.
13. *Pyrenophora polyphragmoides* Sacc. & Scal. *a*, fungus, ✕ 1; *b*, perithecium auctum; *c*, setula perithecii; *d*, ascus, *e*, sporidium.
14. *Pseudovalsa ribesia* Sacc. & Scal. *a*, fungus, ✕ 1, *b*, acervulus sectus; *c*, ascus; *d*, sporidia.
15. *Phyllachora filicina* Sacc. & Scal. *a*, fungus, ✕ 1; *b*, stroma sectum; *c*, loculus sectus auctus; *d*, ascus; *e*, sporidia.
15′. *Dothidella betulina yakutatiana* Sacc. & Scal. *a*, stroma sectum, *b*, ascus; *c*, sporidia.
16. *Fabræa cincta* Sacc. & Scal. *a*, fungus, ✕ 1, *b*, ascoma sectum; *c*, asci; *d*, sporidia.
17. *Rhynchophoma raduloides* Sacc. & Scal. *a*, fungus, ✕ 1, *b*, perithecia; *c*, contextus prosenchymaticus perithecii; *d*, basidia, *e*, sporulæ.

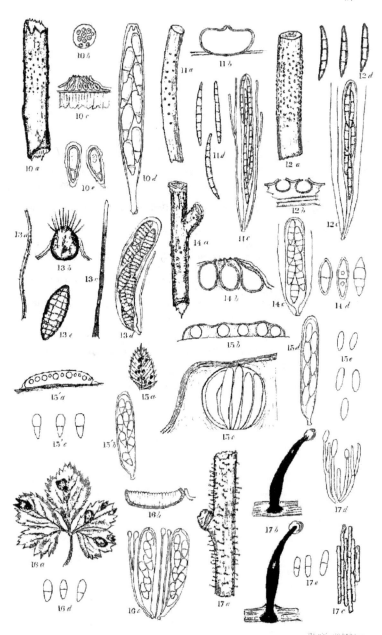

ALASKA FUNGI

PLATE VI

FIG. 18. *Phyllosticta caricicola* Sacc. & Scal. a, fungus, × 1 b, perithecium sectum; c, sporulæ.
19. *Phyllosticta helleboricola coptidis* Sacc. & Scal. a, fungus, × 1 b, perithecium sectum; c, sporulæ
20. *Stagonospora aquatica luzulicola* Sacc. & Scal. a, fungus, × 1; b, perithecium sectum, c, sporulæ.
21. *Stagonospora heleocharidis caricina* Sacc & Scal a, fungus, × 1. b, perithecium sectum; c, sporulæ
22. *Stagonospora graminum* Sacc. & Scal a, fungus, × 1; b, perithecium sectum, c, sporulæ
23. *Septoria petroselini treleaseana* Sacc & Scal a fungus, × 1 b, perithecia secta; c, sporulæ
24. *Septoria eriophorella* Sacc & Scal a, fungus, × 1; b, perithecium sectum; c, sporulæ.
25. *Septoria chamissonis* Sacc & Scal a, fungus, × 1; b, perithecium sectum, c, sporulæ
26. *Rhabdospora camptospora* Sacc & Scal a, fungus, × 1; b, perithecium auctum; c, sporulæ
27. *Sphærographium abditum* Sacc & Scal a, fungus, × 1, b, perithecia aucta, c, sporulæ
28. *Microcera brachyspora* Sacc & Scal a, fungus, × 1, b, sporodochium auctum sectum; c, hyphæ variæ, d, conidia

(62)

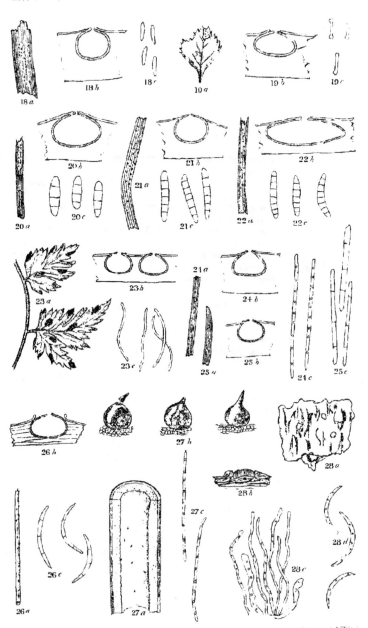

ALASKA FUNGI

PLATE VII.
Guignardia alaskana Reed.

Fig 1 Thallus, × 2
2. Asci and spores, × 435
3 Vertical section, × 192
4 Section through the fruit, × 100
5 Section, × 384

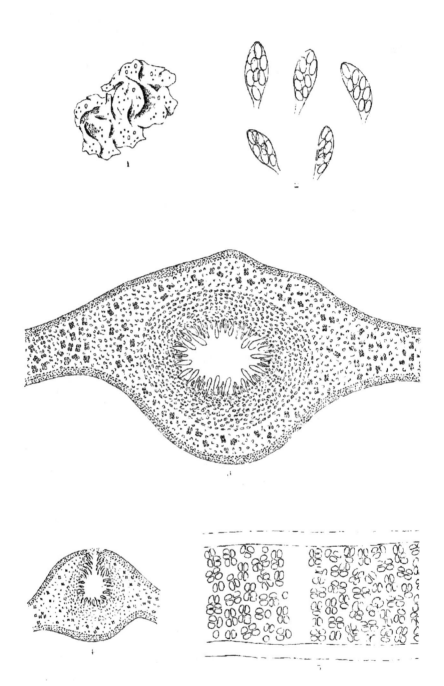

ALASKA FUNGI

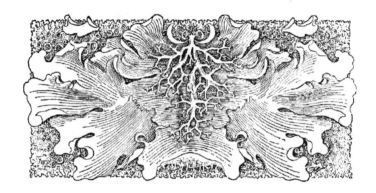

THE LICHENS OF ALASKA

BY CLARA E. CUMMINGS

OUR knowledge of the lichens of Alaska and their distribution has been materially increased by the collections of the Harriman Expedition. Over 800 specimens were collected, representing 217 species, 75 of which were new to Alaska. At the same time that I received the Harriman lichens, various specimens from the United States National Herbarium were placed in my hands. These were collected by C. H. Townsend, in connection with the work of the U. S. Fish Commission Steamer *Albatross* at Attu Island; by Frederick Funston, in the upper Yukon Valley; and by Walter H. Evans and J. Henry Turner. These collections add 5 species new to Alaska which are not represented in the Harriman collection, and 3 species not new to Alaska, but not otherwise represented in this enumeration. Later, the lichen collections made in Alaska in the summer of 1899 by the botanical faculty of the University of California were sent to me for determination. These collections, chiefly the work of Professor Setchell, numbered 135 specimens, representing 82 species, 4 of which were new to Alaska. The collection of Professor Setchell was also valuable for the new localities added, most of the specimens having been collected at Cape Nome or St. Michael, where no collecting had been done by the members of the Harriman Expedition. Summing up, we find 84 species new to Alaska recorded in this list. Of these, 6 are reported in Dr. Nylander's list as occurring on the coast of Siberia, 3 are new to America, and 2 are new to science.

Reviewing briefly the previous collections made in Alaska, we find that Hooker and Arnott[1] enumerate 16 species; Babington,[2] 21 species and varieties; Rothrock,[3] 40 species; Hooper,[4] 4 species, Rothrock,[5] 110 species and varieties. The material on which this last list is based was collected by Dr. T. H. Bean in 1880, in Alaska and the adjacent region. Knowlton[6] adds one species. In 1888 appeared Dr. Nylander's Enumeratio Lichenum Freti Behringii.[7] The collection upon which this was based was made by Dr. E. Almquist, who was connected with the Expedition of the Vega. Dr. Almquist collected at three points on the Asiatic coast, St. Lawrence Bay, Konyam Bay, and Bering Island, while only two Alaskan stations were explored, St. Lawrence Island and Port Clarence. Dr. Nylander lists 197 species, 4 varieties, and 16 forms, a total of 217, the same number as in the present enumeration. In comparing these lists, however, allowance should be made for the well-known fact that Dr. Nylander was inclined to multiply species, while Professor Tuckerman, whose arrangement I have in the main followed, showed a tendency to group somewhat varying forms under one specific name. In 1891, Miss Grace E. Cooley collected in Alaska, the lichens being submitted to me[8] for determination. The list numbers 31 species and

[1] Hooker and Arnott, in Botany of Beechey's Voyage to the Pacific and Behring's Strait, 133-134. 1841.
[2] Babington, Churchill, in Botany of the Voyage of H. M. S. Herald by Seeman, 47, 49. 1852-1857.
[3] Rothrock, in Flora of Alaska, Smithsonian Report. 1867.
[4] Hooper, in Cruise of the Corwin. 1881.
[5] Rothrock, in Proceedings of the United States National Museum, 1-9. 1884.
[6] Knowlton, in Proceedings of the National Museum. 1886.
[7] Nylander, William. Enumeratio Lichenum Freti Behringii. 1-91. 1888.
[8] Cummings, Clara E., in Cooley Miss Grace E., Plants Collected in Alaska and Nanaimo, B. C., July and August 1891. Bull. Torr. Club, vol. XIX, 248, 249. 1892.

varieties. That same year Dr. Charles Willard Hayes, of the U. S Geological Survey, collected a few lichens in Alaska, which were also submitted to me.[1] The list comprises 20 species and varieties. In the Report of the Fur Seal Investigation,[2] J. M. Macoun publishes a list of 70 species; he also publishes a list of 9 species collected by William Palmer and determined by W. J. Calkins.[3] In the summer of 1900 Mr. Arthur J. Collier, in connection with the work of the U. S. Geological Survey, collected 10 species and varieties, which were submitted to me[4] for determination. Kurtz, in his Chilcat Flora,[5] mentions two species, while Professor Farlow[6] records 4 from Point Barrow. Professor Tuckerman[7] gives various Alaska stations for different species, collected principally by Wright and Kellogg. Wainio, in his recently published monograph on *Cladonia*,[8] gives additional localities for species of this genus. Summing up, we find that before the publication of the present list 386 species and varieties had been enumerated. The present list adds 76 species and varieties new to Alaska, making a total of 462 species and varieties.

The lichen flora of Alaska is essentially like that of other northern regions. Constant comparison has been made with the works of Fries,[9] Lindsay,[10] and Arnold,[11] for the distribu-

[1] Cummings, Clara E., in An Expedition through the Yukon District, by Charles Willard Hayes, National Geographic Magazine, vol iv, 160–162. 1892.

[2] Macoun, J. M., in Dr Jordan's Report on the Fur Seals and Fur Seal Islands of the North Pacific, Part 3. 1899.

[3] Calkins, W J, in Jordan's Report on the Fur Seals and Fur Seal Islands of the North Pacific, Part 3. 1899.

[4] Cummings, Clara E, in Reconnaisances in the Cape Nome and Norton Bay Regions, Alaska, in 1900, by Alfred H. Brooks, George B. Richardson, Arthur J. Collier and Walter C. Mendenhall, United States Geological Survey, 167. 1901.

[5] Kurtz, Die Flora des Chilcatgebietes, Engler's Botanische Jahrbucher, vol XIX, 431. 1895.

[6] Farlow, William G., in Ray's Report of the International Polar Expedition to Point Barrow, Alaska, 192. 1885.

[7] Tuckerman, Synopsis North American Lichens, vol I, 1882, vol. II, 1888.

[8] Wainio, Monographia Cladoniarum, vol I, 1887, vol. II, 1894.

[9] Fries, Th. M. Lichenes Arctoi. 1860.

[10] Lindsay, W Lauder. Observations on the Lichens collected by Dr Robert Brown in West Greenland in 1867. Transactions of the Linnæan Society of London, vol. XXVII, 305–368, tab. 48–52. 1871.

[11] Arnold, Dr F, in Labrador. 1896.
Arnold, Dr F. Lichenologische Fragmente, 35, Newfoundland, Separat-Abdruck aus der 'Oester botan. Zeitschrift,' Jahrg 1896, Nr. 4 u. ff

tion of the species, as well as structural characteristics. One element which has added to the difficulty of determination is the frequency with which different genera and species were found growing together, one small fragment of rock, not more than an inch square, showing often four distinct species, sometimes as many genera The commingling of earth forms, which is so common a characteristic of northern lichens, is also noticeable.

I would acknowledge my great indebtedness to Dr. Farlow for the free use of the Tuckerman Herbarium of Lichens, without which I should have found it impossible to do this work, as well as for many other courtesies; to Dr. Trelease of the Missouri Botanical Garden, and Miss Day of the Gray Herbarium, for assistance in finding the literature of the subject; and to Miss Maude Metcalf, graduate student of Wellesley College, for her kindness in making the drawings.

This paper was presented in part before the Society for Plant Morphology and Physiology at its meeting held at Columbia University December 31, 1901, and January 1, 1902.

Family VERRUCARIACEÆ.

PYRENULA.

1. **Pyrenula gemmata** (Ach) Naeg & Hepp.
Verrucaria gemmata ACHARIUS, Meth Lich 120 1803
Pyrenula gemmata NAEGELI & HEPP, Flecht Eur No 104.

Disenchantment Bay (Trelease, 803*b*, 821, 842 in part, 1170 in part). On bark of shrubs, associated with *Buellia*. New to Alaska.

Common in New England, according to Tuckerman, but no other American localities are given in his Synopsis.

VERRUCARIA

KEY TO THE SPECIES.

Thallus obsolete .... *thelodes*.
Thallus evident.
    Thallus yellowish-white, margining the apothecium.. . *fulva*.
    Thallus brownish or blackish
        Thallus breaking up into small areolæ . . .. *fuscella*
            Apothecia entirely immersed, level with the surface of the thallus . . . . *mucosa*
            Apothecia elevated above the surface of the thallus...., *maura*.

2. Verrucaria maura Wahl.

Verrucaria maura WAHLENBERG in Achanus, Meth. Lich. 19. 1803.—SOW-
ERBY, Eng Bot *t 2456*

Sitka (Trelease, 958), Port Wells, Prince William Sound (Trelease, 934) Rothrock reports it from Port Alexander, in Bristol Bay, and from Cook Inlet Nylander, from St. Lawrence Island.

3. Verrucaria mucosa Wahl.

Verrucaria mucosa WAHLENBERG in Acharius, Meth Lich Suppl. 23 1803.

Orca (Trelease and Saunders, no number, and 303). New to Alaska
Though new to Alaska, this has been reported from St. Lawrence Bay, Siberia, by Nylander.

4. Verrucaria fuscella (Turn.) Ach.

Lichen fuscellus TURNER, Trans. Linn. Soc 7. 90 *t 8 fig 2.* 1804.—SOW-
ERBY, Eng Bot *t 1500*
Verrucaria fuscella ACHARIUS, L U. 289. 1810.

Hot Springs, Baranof Island (Trelease, 959, 960). On rock. New to Alaska. Reported by Tuckerman in Genera Lichenum from only Alabama and Vermont.

5. Verrucaria thelodes Smrft.

Verrucaria thelodes SOMMERFELDT, Suppl. 140

Hidden Glacier Inlet, Yakutat Bay (Trelease, 946). On rock The species is credited to Port Clarence by Nylander.

6. Verrucaria fulva sp nov

Thallus a small rounded body from .75-1.5 mm. in diameter, either distinct or aggregated in masses which may equal 5 mm. in diameter The thallus is of a creamy color, chinky-areolate, nearly or entirely concealing the embedded apothecium. Gonidia abundant, scattered throughout the medullary layer Apothecia .20-.35 mm in diameter, dark brown. ampithecium yellowish-brown. Paraphyses distinct in young specimens, gelatinizing in older ones. Spores muriform-multilocular, brown, $\frac{63-84}{24-38}$ μ. Number of spores in ascus unknown.

Collected by Prof. William Trelease at Port Wells, June 26, 1899, on rocks (No. 918) and on moss (No. 1175). Type specimen (No. 918) in the Herbarium of the Missouri Botanical Garden; a duplicate in my own herbarium.

The fact that the walls of the ascus gelatinize so early rendered it impossible to determine the number of spores in an ascus. In no case were mature spores seen within the ascus.

The species would seem to approach nearly *V. verrucosa-areolata* Nyl., but differs markedly in that the perithecium is entire and brown, while in the species cited it is dimidiate and black.

The limits of the genus *Verrucaria* are very differently placed by different authors. Some, as Th. Fries in Lichenes Arctoi, admit only such species as have simple colorless spores, while other authors, as Professor Tuckerman and Dr. Nylander, recognize great diversity in spore types, from simple to muriform-multilocular. Equally diverse characters are given for the perithecium, which varies from colorless to coal black.

While this species hardly has the appearance of the more typical Verrucarias, in view of these admitted variations it seems best to place it here until a thorough revision of these lower forms is made.

The following additional species of *Verrucaria* have been reported from Alaska or adjacent islands: *V. lævata* Ach., *V. acrotella* Ach., *V. aurantii* Mass., *V. sublectissima* Nyl., *V. chlorotica* Ach., *V. leptaleoides* Nyl., on rock, St. Lawrence Island (Nylander), *V. fallax* Nyl., on branches, St. Lawrence and Port Clarence (Nylander); *V. pyrenophora* Ach., *V. muralis* Ach., forma *dolosula* Nyl., *V. integra* Nyl., *V. hymenogonia* Nyl., *V. obnigrescens* Nyl., *V. prominula* Nyl., *V. obtenata* Nyl., *V. exalbida* Nyl., *V. discedens* Nyl., *V. thelodes* Smrft., on rock, Port Clarence (Nylander); *V. intercedens*, on argillaceous schistose rocks, Port Clarence (Nylander) and Cape Lisburne (Rothrock); *V. punctiformis* Ach., on branches, Port Clarence (Nylander); *V. nigrata* Nyl., *V. pernigrata* Nyl., *V. bryospila* Nyl., *V. bryophila* (Loennr.) Nyl., on mossy earth, Port Clarence (Nylander); *V. intermedia*, no definite locality (Rothrock); *V. ceuthocarpa* Wahl., Fort Alexander, in Bristol Bay (Rothrock). James M. Macoun records *Verrucaria* sp. (?) as occurring on rocks, St. George Island, one of the Pribilof Islands. Tuckerman, in his Genera Lichenum, credits Mr. Wright with having collected *V. terrestris* (Th. Fr.) Tuck. on earth, at Bering Strait. Dr. Nylander[1] segregates the following additional species, based upon material collected by Dr. Bean, which formed the basis of Dr. Rothrock's lists:[2] *V. subumbrina* Nyl., on rock, Cape Lisburne; *V. maurioides* (Schaer.) Nyl. and forma *conyzoides* Nyl., no locality given.

[1] Nylander, Dr. William. Enumeratio Lichenum Freti Behringii 1888.
[2] Rothrock, J. T. Lists of and Notes upon the Lichens collected by Dr. T. H. Bean in Alaska and the adjacent region in 1880. Proceedings of the United States National Museum 1884.

Family SPHÆROPHORIACEÆ.

SPHÆROPHORON

KEY TO THE SPECIES.

Thallus densely cæspitose, slightly branched, branches of same size.
fragile.
Thallus more open, freely branched, terminal branches very fine.
coralloides.

7. Sphærophoron coralloides Pers

Sphærophoron coralloides PERSOON in Ust. Ann. 1 23. 1794

Alaska (Brewer and Coe, 30½); Lowe Inlet, British Columbia (Trelease, 1277); Sitka (Trelease, 1278); Broughton Strait (Trelease, 1267); Juneau, 2000 ft. (Trelease, 1273); Yakutat (Trelease, 1289); Wrangell (Brewer and Coe, 405); Orca (Trelease, 1271), Point Gustavus, Glacier Bay (Brewer and Coe, 781, 782); Hall Island (Trelease, 1213, 1282; Brewer and Coe, 2060, 2062); St. Matthew Island (Trelease, 1216); St. Lawrence Island (Trelease, 1210, 1275, 1285); St. Michael (Setchell), Unalaska (Setchell); Cape Nome (Setchell).

Dr. Nylander reports its occurrence on earth and moss on St. Lawrence Island; Dr. Rothrock credits it to Alaska, with no definite station. Under the synonym *S. globiferus* (L.) DC., it is reported by J. M. Macoun as growing on rock on St. Paul and St. George Islands. Dr. Grace Cooley collected it at Loring, and also at Salmon Creek, near Juneau, and Dr. Bean at Port Mulgrave and on Little Koniuji Island, of the Shumagin group. It seems to be one of the most widely distributed of the Alaska lichens, the material collected by the members of the Harriman Expedition being obtained on the mainland and on islands near the coast from British Columbia to Cape Nome.

All the specimens are sterile excepting those from Glacier Bay and St. Michael, which are large and well fruited. Usually the southern forms are more finely divided than those from the northern stations. This species seems to be more abundant and more widely distributed than the following one.

8. Sphærophoron fragile (Crantz) Pers.

Lichen fragilis CRANTZ, Inst 7 h 1 78 1766
Sphærophoron fragile PERSOON, Ust N Ann 1 23 1794.—SOWERBY, Eng Bot *t 2474*

Summit of White Pass, 3000 ft. (Trelease, 1284, 1286); St. Matthew Island (Trelease, 1283), Port Clarence (Trelease, 1280); St. Michael Island (Setchell); Cape Nome (Setchell).

Dr. Nylander records it as growing on earth and moss on St. Lawrence Island; Dr. Rothrock and J. M. Macoun record its occurrence, but give no localities. The specimen from St. Matthew Island is fruited, the others are sterile.

The genus *Siphula* was not found among the Harriman collections, but *Siphula dactyliza* Nyl. and *S. ceratites* (Wahl.) Tr. are reported by Dr. Nylander as growing on quartz rock on St. Lawrence Island, the latter species also on moss associated with *Lecidea suballinita* Nyl. In Tuckerman's Genera Lichenum *S. ceratites* is credited to Bering Strait (Mr. Wright), the only American locality given for it.

Family ARTHONIACEÆ.
ARTHONIA.

9. Arthonia punctiformis Ach.

Arthonia punctiformis ACHARIUS, L. U. 141. 1810.

Sitka (Trelease, 839). New to Alaska.

Growing on *Alnus oregana*. Spores 2-3-4-septate. Thallus not uniform, and thus varying from most of the specimens in the Tuckerman Herbarium. A widely distributed species.

Arthonia mediella alnicola Nyl. is reported by Dr. Nylander as having been collected on branches at Port Clarence.

Family OPEGRAPHIACEÆ.
GRAPHIS.

10. Graphis scripta (L.) Ach.

Lichen scriptus LINNÆUS, Spec. Pl. ed. 2. 2: 1606. 1764.
Graphis scripta ACHARIUS, L. U. 265. 1810.—SOWERBY, Eng. Bot. *t 1813*.

Orca (Trelease, 1801). New to Alaska.

Growing on the bark of dead coniferous trees. Reported from Newfoundland by Arnold, but I find no record of its occurrence in Greenland.

No. 811, collected at Sitka by Trelease, is evidently a *Graphis*. Unfortunately the spores are not developed, and therefore it is impossible to place it. Apparently it belongs in the section *Fissurina*, which is characteristically tropical.

XYLOGRAPHA.

11. Xylographa opegraphella Nyl.

Xylographa opegraphella NYLANDER, Enum. Lich. 128. 1857.

Alaska (Trelease, number lost). On dead wood with *Lecidea enteroleuca* and *Placodium ferrugineum*.

Collected at Cook Inlet by Dr. Bean.

In addition to the species given above, Dr. Bean collected *X. parallela pallens* Nyl. on an island in Cross Sound.

OPEGRAPHA.

12. Opegrapha varia Pers.

Opegrapha varia PERSOON, Ust. Ann. Bot. 7: 30 1794.

Port Wells (Trelease, 835 in part); Orca (Setchell, 1218). New to Alaska.

No. 835 is on the bark of coniferous trees with *Biatora cinnabarina* and *Heterothecium sanguinarium affine*. The spores are broader than usual and often 3-septate. Common throughout the United States.

Family LECIDIACEÆ.

BUELLIA.

KEY TO THE SPECIES.

Thallus yellow.
    Areoles of the thallus scattered.................*geographica atrovirens*.
    Areoles of the thallus massed.
        Hypothallus distinct............................*geographica*.
        Hypothallus not evident............................*geographica contigua*.
Thallus never yellow.
    Spores bilocular.
        Growing on the earth or dead mosses.....................*papillata*.
        Growing on trees or rocks.
            Thallus smooth, whitish ....*parasema*.
            Thallus scurfy, variously colored.
                Thallus ash-colored ....*myriocarpa*.
                Thallus greenish ash-colored........*myriocarpa chloropolia*.
    Spores plurilocular or muriform-multilocular.
        Thallus brownish or blackish ....*petræa*.
        Thallus variously colored.
            Thallus ash-colored, apothecia small..........*petræa grandis*.
            Thallus violet-colored, apothecia large .... *petræa montagnæi*.

13. Buellia geographica (L.) Tuck.

Lichen geographicus LINNÆUS, Spec. Pl ed. 2 2: 1607. 1764.—SOWERBY, Eng Bot. t. 245.

Buellia geographica TUCKERMAN, Gen. Lich. 190. 1872.

Summit of White Pass (Trelease, 951 in part, 951a); Kadiak (Trelease, 899, 900, 902, each in part); Hall Island (Trelease, 891b, 893, each in part); St. Matthew Island (Trelease, 999); Port Wells (Trelease, 936 in part); Port Clarence (Trelease, 890); Cape Nome (Setchell); St. Michael Island (Setchell) Collected on Alaska Peninsula by Dr. Bean, and on St George Island by J. M. Macoun

All the specimens are on rock and are associated with various species of *Parmelia*, *Lecanora*, *Pertusaria*, and *Lecidea*. This is one of the most widely distributed of alpine and arctic lichens. Small bits of the sterile thallus were found with several rock specimens which are not listed above

14. Buellia geographica contigua (Schaer.).
Lecidea geographica a contigua SCHAERER, Spicil 124 1828.

Haenke Island, Disenchantment Bay (Coville and Kearney, 1116), Kadiak (Trelease, 897, 898, each in part, 901); Hall Island (Trelease, 891, 891a in part). New to Alaska.

Associated with species of *Pertusaria*, *Lecanora*, and *Lecidea* No. 1116 has the thallus more distinctly areolate than any specimen in the Tuckerman Herbarium

15. Buellia geographica atrovirens (L.) Tuck.
Lichen atrovirens LINNÆUS, Spec. Pl ed 2 2 1607. 1764

Summit of White Pass, 3000 ft. (Trelease, 888, in part). New to Alaska

On rock, associated with *Lecanora cinerea gibbosa*

16. Buellia petræa Tuck
Lecidea petræa WULF. in Jacq Coll. III, 116 *t 6 f 2 a* 1789
Buellia petræa TUCKERMAN, Gen Lich 190 1872 —SOWERBY, Eng Bot *t 246*

Broughton Strait (Trelease, 850); Plover Bay, Siberia (Trelease, 993); St. Michael (Setchell)

The specimen from Broughton Strait is on wood, those from Plover Bay and St Michael on rock. The species has been recorded by Rothrock from St. Paul Island, from Kadiak and Port Clarence, Alaska, and from Plover Bay, Siberia.

17. Buellia petræa grandis (Flk.) Tuck
Lecidea petræa β *fuscoatra* C *grandis* FLOERKE, Flora 620 1828.
Buellia petræa b *grandis* TUCKERMAN, Syn N A L 2 102. 1888.

Alaska, locality lost (Trelease, 968) New to Alaska. Previously reported from Greenland to California and southward

Compares well with the specimen in the Tuckerman Herbarium which was collected in the White Mountains of New Hampshire.

18. **Buellia petræa montagnæi** (Flot.) Tuck.

Lecidea montagnæi FLOTOW in Koerb Syst 258 1855.
Buellia petræa c *montagnæi* TUCKERMAN, Syn N A L. 2 102 1888

Hot Springs, Baranof Island (Trelease, 964); summit of White Pass, 3000 ft. (Trelease, 952); Kadiak (Trelease, 914a in part, 945 in part, 946), Unalaska (Trelease, 923); St. Paul Island (Trelease, 931). Specimens were collected at Cook Inlet and Port Clarence by Dr. Bean. Nylander records its occurrence at St. Lawrence Island under the synonym *Lecidea geminata* Flot.

All the specimens are on rock, No. 914a being associated with *Lecanora cinerea*.

19. **Buellia myriocarpa** (DC) Mudd

Patellaria myriocarpa DE CANDOLLE, Fl Franc 2 346 1805
Buellia myriocarpa MUDD, Man Brit Lich 217 1861

Port Clarence (Trelease, 939 in part).

Associated with *Lecanora varia* and its variety *intricata*, and with *Parmelia saxatilis omphalodes*. Dr. Rothrock and Dr. Nylander report its occurrence at St. Lawrence Bay and Konyam Bay, Siberia, Dr. Rothrock at Port Clarence, Alaska.

20. **Buellia myriocarpa chloropolia** (Fr.) Th. Fr.

Lecidea chloropolia FRIES, S V Sc 1 115 1846
Buellia myriocarpa chloropolia TH FRIES, Lich Scand 595. 1871.

Kadiak (Trelease, 1170 in part). New to Alaska

On dead wood, associated with *Theloschistes lychneus*. Tuckerman does not recognize this variety, and I find no other American record of it.

21. **Buellia papillata** (Smrft) Tuck.

Lecidea papillata SOMMERFELDT, Suppl 154 1827.
Buellia papillata TUCKERMAN, Gen Lich 186. 1872.

Alaska (Funston, 8). New to Alaska.

The specimen grows on earth. It has been reported from Greenland. Wright collected the variety *albo-cincta* on the islands of Bering Strait.

22. **Buellia parasema** (Ach) Th. Fr.

Lecidea parasema ACHARIUS, Meth Lich 35 1803
Buellia parasema TH. FRIES, Lich Scand 589 1871.

Disenchantment Bay (Trelease, 842 in part); Yakutat (Trelease, 844 in part); Fairagut Bay (Trelease, 837); Kukak Bay, Alaska Peninsula (Trelease, 836 in part, Kincaid, 836a in part); St. Michael (Setchell).

In addition to the stations mentioned above, it was collected by Dr. Hayes at Prince William Sound and by Dr. Bean at Port Clarence, Alaska, and at Plover Bay, Siberia.

On bark and dead wood. Associated with species of *Physcia*, *Lecanora*, *Placodium*, and *Pyrenula*.

23. **Buellia parasema triphragmia** (Nyl) Th. Fr.
Lecidea triphragmia NYLANDER, Prod 141. 1857
Buellia parasema triphragmia TH FRIES, Lich Scand 590 1871.

Oica, 1150 feet (Tielease, 813), St. Michael (Setchell). New to Alaska.

On *Alnus*. The thallus is exceptionally smooth and not limited by the hypothallus. An examination of numerous specimens shows that the thallus is usually smoother when growing on the bark of living trees than it is on decaying trees or on the earth.

Widely distributed; may occur anywhere.

In addition to the species named above, Rothrock records the following species as having been collected by Dr. Bean: *B. albo-atra* (Hoffm Nyl) Th. Fr., at Unalaska; *B. atro-alba* Fr., on St. Paul Island and Unalaska Island and at Plover Bay, Siberia; *B. atro-alba chlorospora* Nyl., on Chamisso Island in the Arctic Ocean. The two latter species are given by Tuckerman as synonyms of *B. colludens* (Nyl.) Tuck. J. M. Macoun collected *B. alpicola* (Nyl.) Anz. at St. George Island, also a *Buellia*, species undetermined. Tuckerman records the occurrence of *B. parmeliarum* (Smrft.) Tuck., parasitic on *Cetraria fahlunensis*, collected by Wright on islands in Bering Strait.

LECIDEA.

KEY TO THE SPECIES.

Thallus interspersed with reddish tubercles................................*panæola*.
Thallus not interspersed with reddish tubercles.
  Apothecia innate ....*tessellata*.
  Apothecia superficial, or if innate, becoming emergent.
    Apothecia innate, becoming emergent.
      Thallus yellowish-white, apothecia medium size ..... *contigua*.
      Thallus grayish, apothecia very small.............*nigrocinerea*.
    Apothecia always superficial.
      Thallus smooth.
        Thallus thick.
          Thallus glaucescent.........................*albocærulescens*.
          Thallus orange-red *albocærulescens flavocærulescens*.

Thallus thin or obsolete.
    Apothecia small, thallus usually evident .   *platycarpa*
    Apothecia large, thallus obsolete . *platycarpa steriza*
Thallus granulate.
    Surface of the apothecium shining as if polished.
                                                melancheima.
    Surface of the apothecium dull
      Thallus ash-colored
        Apothecia small   *enteroleuca*
        Apothecia large ..   *confluens*
      Thallus yellowish .   *enteroleuca flavida.*

24. Lecidea melancheima Tuck.

Lecidea melancheima TUCKERMAN, Syn Lich N E 68. 1848.

St Lawrence Island (Trelease, 832 in part). New to Alaska.

The specimen is on wood associated with *Placodium ferrugineum*. Tuckerman reports its occurrence in New England and Colorado.

25. Lecidea enteroleuca Ach.

Lecidea enteroleuca ACHARIUS, L U 177 1810 —SOWERBY, Eng Bot. *t 1450*

Sitka (Trelease, 825*a* in part); Hot Springs, Baranof Island (Trelease, 963); Port Clarence (Trelease, 942); St Michael (Setchell). Both Nylander and Rothrock report this from Port Clarence Rothrock also lists it for Sitka, Chamisso Island, and Cape Lisburne, collected by Dr. Bean.

26. Lecidea enteroleuca flavida Fr

Lecidea enteroleuca δ flavida FRIES, Vet Akad Handl 261 1824

Sitka (Trelease. 825*a* in part). New to Alaska.

On wood associated with *L. enteroleuca, Placodium*, and *Xylographa*

This differs from the specimens in the Herb. Tuck. in not having limiting hypothallus Professor Tuckerman records its occurrence in New England, and suggests that it probably occurs throughout the United States and Canada.

27 Lecidea platycarpa Ach.

Lecidea platycarpa ACHARIUS, L U 1810.

Alaska (Trelease, 967); Hot Springs, Baranof Island (Trelease, 983 in part), White Pass, 1250 ft. (Trelease, 965), 1925 ft. (Trelease, 955); summit of White Pass, 3000 ft. (Trelease, 954), Kadiak (Trelease, 897 in part, 902 in part, 914*a*), Port Wells (Trelease,

905); Unalaska (Setchell); St. Matthew Island (Trelease, 999 in part). New to Alaska.

On rock associated with various species of *Lecanora* and *Buellia*. A widely distributed species.

28. Lecidea platycarpa forma steriza (Ach.).

Lecidea confluens steriza ACHARIUS, Meth. Lich. 40. 1803.

Orca (Trelease, 912); Kadiak (Trelease, 944). New to Alaska.
Reported from Newfoundland and Labrador by Arnold. The locality given by Tuckerman is the White Mountains of New Hampshire, no western stations being given.

29. Lecidea albocærulescens (Wulf.) Schaer.

Lichen albo-cærulescens WULFEN. in Jacq. Coll. 2: 184. *t. 15. f. 1.* 1788.
Lecidea albocærulescens SCHAERER, Spicil. 142. 1828.

Orca, 1000 ft. (Trelease, 906, 912*a*), 1200 ft. (Trelease, 907); Kadiak (Trelease, 910, 910*a*). Collected in Alaska by Dr. Bean, as recorded by Rothrock; locality not given.

The specimen from Kadiak numbered 910 has apothecia which are almost entirely without the pulverulence which is so characteristic of this species.

30. Lecidea albocærulescens flavocærulescens Schaer.

Lecidea albocærulescens b. *flavocærulescens* SCHAERER, Spicil. 143. 1828.

Summit of White Pass, 3000 ft. (Trelease, 919), Kadiak (Trelease, 909), Unalaska (Setchell); Hall Island (Trelease, 908); Cape Nome (Setchell); St. Michael (Setchell). Collected by Dr. Bean on Alaska Peninsula, as recorded by Rothrock.

31. Lecidea confluens (Web.) Ach.

Lichen confluens WEBER, Spicil. 180 *t. 2* (excl. syn.) 1778.
Lecidea confluens ACHARIUS, Meth. Lich. 40. 1803.—SOWERBY, Eng. Bot. *t. 1964.*

St. Michael (Setchell). New to Alaska.

On rock. Professor Tuckerman gives as known localities on this continent, Arctic America and Greenland.

32. Lecidea contigua Fr.

Lecidea contigua FRIES, L. E. 208. 1831.

Kadiak (Trelease, 896 in part, 898 in part, 913*a*, 914, 915), Hall Island (Trelease, 891*a* in part, 891*b* in part, 903).

Nylander records it for the three Asiatic stations in his Bering Sea list, while Rothrock adds three other Alaskan stations. Unalaska,

Alaska Peninsula and Chamisso Island, Eschscholtz Bay, the material having been collected by Dr. Bean. Tuckerman's records are New York and New England. The specimens are variously associated with *Lecanora atrosulphurea* and *Buellia geographica*.

33. Lecidea nigrocinerea Nyl.
Lecidea nigrocinerea NYLANDER, Lich. Pyreno-Orient. 25 in notula 1891.

Port Wells (Trelease, 936 in part). New to Alaska. Tuckerman makes no record of its occurrence in North America.

Though this species is new to Alaska, Nylander lists it for Lawrence Bay, Konyam Bay, and St. Lawrence Island, Siberia.

34. Lecidea panæola Ach.
Lecidea panæola ACHARIUS, L. U. 201. 1810.

Summit of White Pass, 3000 ft (Trelease, 950); Cape Nome (Setchell); St. Michael (Setchell). Also collected by Dr. Bean at Unalaska.

35. Lecidea tessellata Flk.
Lecidea tessellata FLOERKE, D Lich 64 1821.

St. Michael (Setchell). New to Alaska.

On rock. Previously reported in America from New England, Greenland, Rocky Mts., California, and other localities.

OTHER ALASKA SPECIES

In addition to the species given above, Tuckerman records the occurrence of *Lecidea enteroleuca muscorum* Koerb., *L. arctica* Sommerf., *L. assimilata* Nyl., all collected by Wright at Bering Strait; the last species is credited to St Lawrence Island and Port Clarence by Nylander. Rothrock records the following species as having been collected by Dr. Bean, no definite locality being given *L. contigua speirea* (Ach.) Nyl., *L. enteroleuca latypea* (Ach.) Nyl., *L. fuscoatra* Fr. Nylander records fifty-two additional species divided into thirteen groups. Many of these sections would be variously distributed among different genera by other writers, but in this list I shall retain the arrangement made by Nylander. With the exception of *L subduplex* Nyl., which was collected on rock at Port Clarence, all the members of the first group grow on wood, moss, or on the earth. These species might be placed in the genus *Biatora*. Nine were collected at Port Clarence only, namely *L. albohyalina* Nyl., *L. meiocarpa* Nyl., *L internectens* Nyl., *L. insperabilis* Nyl., *L denotata* Nyl., *L. sabuletorum* Flk., *L. syncomista* Flk., *L. meiobola* Nyl., *L. triplicans* Nyl.; seven were found only on St. Lawrence Island, namely:

L. epiphæa Nyl., *L. ramulosa* Fr., *L. atrorufa* Ach., *L. sanguineoatra* (Fr.) Nyl., *L. pallidella* Nyl., *L. ternaria* Nyl., *L. suballinita* Nyl., while *L. tornoensis* Nyl. was collected at both localities. In the second group are two species collected at Port Clarence on the earth or on moss : *L. muscorum* (Sw.) Nyl. and *L. subfuscula* Nyl. In the third group only two species are represented, one, *L. fecunda* Fr. fil., collected on earth and moss at Port Clarence, the other, *L. pezizoidea* Ach., found in similar habitats both on St. Lawrence Island and at Port Clarence. The fourth group is also represented by two species—*L. limosa* Ach. and *L. dovrensis* Nyl., the former on earth, the latter on rock, at Port Clarence. In the fifth group are the following species. *L. subnegans* Nyl., *L. candida* Ach., *L. parasema*, forma *euphora* Flk., and *L. incongrua* Nyl. The sixth group includes : *L. tenebrosa* forma *subsparsa* Nyl., *L. laurentiana* Nyl. *L. brachyspora* Fr., growing on rock on St. Lawrence Island; *L. contigua* forma *merospora* Nyl. and *L. crustulata* (Ach.) Nyl., on rock, collected at Port Clarence. Of the seventh group there is only one representative—*L. disciformis* forma *insignis* Naeg. There are three representatives of the eighth group : *L. jemtlandica* (Fr. fil.), on earth, St. Lawrence Island; *L. atroalbens* Nyl., on rock, St. Lawrence Island, and *L. chionea* Norm., on rock, Port Clarence. In the ninth group the following species are included : *L. confervoides* (DC.) Nyl., *L. atrocæsia* Nyl., *L. geminata* Flot., *L. excentrica* Ach., the first three on rock on St. Lawrence Island, the last one on rock at Port Clarence. The tenth group is represented by *L. alpicola* Schaer., growing on rock on St. Lawrence Island. The eleventh group contains one species—*L. rhexoblephara* Nyl., which was found on earth on St. Lawrence Island. In the twelfth group are *L. sanguinaria* Ach., growing on the earth on St. Lawrence Island, and *L. affinis* Schaer., growing on the earth on St. Lawrence Island and at Port Clarence. The thirteenth group is represented by *L. paraphanella* Nyl., on rock from St. Lawrence Island. The following species are given in the body of the text, but not arranged in the foregoing groups : *L. associata* Fr. fil., *L. hypopodia* forma *subassimilata* Nyl., growing on the earth on St. Lawrence Island, and *L. scabrosa* Ach., growing on the earth at Port Clarence. In addition to the list based upon the specimens collected by Dr. Almquist, Nylander revises Rothrock's[1] list with the following changes : *L. spilota* Fr. = *L. plana* Lahm., *Buellia petræa* = *Lecidea geminata* Flot.; *L. enteroleucodes* Nyl.

[1] Rothrock Dr. J. T. List of, and Notes upon, the Lichens collected by Dr. T. H. Bean in Alaska in 1880. Proc. U. S. Nat. Museum, 1884.

is classed as *Buellia parasema* by Rothrock. One new species is described—*Lecidea alaskensis* Nyl., based upon material collected by Dr. Bean and forwarded to Nylander by Willey. Macoun indicates that two species of *Lecidea* were collected on rocks on St. George Island, but no specific names are given.

HETEROTHECIUM.

KEY TO THE SPECIES.
Hypothecium red .... *sanguinarium*.
Hypothecium colorless. .. ..*sanguinarium affine*.

36 **Heterothecium sanguinarium** (L.) Flot.
Lichen sanguinarius LINNÆUS, Sp. Pl. ed 2. 2 : 1607. 1764.
Heterothecium sanguinarium FLOTOW in Bot. Zeit. 1850. — SOWERBY, Eng. Bot. t. 155

Vancouver Island, Broughton Strait (Trelease, 807), Yakutat (Trelease, 840, 843); White Pass, 1300 ft. (Trelease, 834); Virgin Bay (Trelease, 847); Port Wells (Trelease, 835*b* in part); Unalaska (Setchell). In addition to the stations mentioned above it was collected by Wright on the islands of Bering Strait; by Dr Cooley at Juneau and at Sheep Cove, near Juneau; and by Dr. Bean at Eschscholtz Bay, Yakutat Bay, and Cook Inlet.

On the bark of various trees. In this species there is usually only a single spore in an ascus. Tuckerman says: "The lichen is now bisporous in Europe." The measurements given for a single spore are $\frac{54-92}{24-48}$ μ. No. 840 from Yakutat and the specimen from Broughton Strait are bisporous, with spore measurements $\frac{45-52}{31}$ μ.

37. **Heterothecium sanguinarium affine** (Schaer.) Flot.
Lecidea affinis SCHAERER, Enum. 132 1850.
Heterothecium sanguinarium affine FLOTOW in Bot. Zeit. 1850

Orca (Trelease, 841, 848); Virgin Bay (Trelease, 1119). New to Alaska.

On the bark of coniferous trees. While the forma *affine* is new to Alaska, the species was collected on the islands of Bering Strait by Wright.

In addition to the species given above, Tuckerman notes that *H. pezizoideum* (Ach.) Flot. was collected by Wright on mosses on the islands of Bering Strait.

BIATORA.

KEY TO THE SPECIES.
Apothecia scarlet......... .. ..*cinnabarina*.
Apothecia variously colored.
    Apothecia lemon-yellow... ....*lucida*.

Apothecia brick-colored, brown or blackening.
   Spores simple.
      Apothecia difform and conglomerate................*granulosa.*
      Apothecia not difform and conglomerate.
         Thallus white................................ *apochrœiza.*
         Thallus grayish-green....................... *viridescens.*
   Spores compound.
      Spores 1-2-locular ....*vernalis.*
      Spores 4-9-locular..............................*hypnophila.*

38. Biatora hypnophila (Turn.) Tuck.

Lecidea hypnophila TURNER in Ach. L. U. 199. 1810.
Biatora hypnophila TUCKERMAN, Syn. N. A. L. 2. 35. 1882. — SOWERBY, Eng. Bot. *t. 2217.*

Yakutat (Trelease, 830); St. Michael (Setchell); Unalaska (Setchell). New to Alaska.

On bark of living trees (Trelease); on earth (Setchell). The thallus of the specimen on bark is not granulate and the apothecia are somewhat larger than most of those in the Tuckerman Herbarium. The spores are usually bilocular. The range of this plant is from Greenland to Florida.

39. Biatora lucida (Ach.) Fr.

Lichen lucidus ACHARIUS, Lich Suec. Pr. 39. 1798.
Biatora lucida FRIES, L. E. 279. 1831.—SOWERBY, Eng. Bot. *t. 1550.*

White Pass (Trelease, 973). New to Alaska.
Growing on earth. Previously reported from Arctic America.

40. Biatora vernalis (L.) Fr.

Lichen vernalis LINNÆUS, Syst Nat 3: 234. 1767.
Biatora vernalis FRIES, L E. 260. 1831.—SOWERBY, Eng. Bot. *t. 845.*

Disenchantment Bay (Trelease, 803c); Orca, 1105 ft. (Trelease, 813). Reported by Nylander from Port Clarence under synonym of *Lecidea vernalis* (L.).

The specimen from Disenchantment Bay is on the bark of dead shrubs. The thallus is almost obsolete and the apothecia are smaller and more regular than in the specimens on moss. The thallus seems entirely obsolete in the specimen from Orca. This species has been reported from Greenland.

41. Biatora cinnabarina (Smrft.) Fr.

Lecidea cinnabarina SOMMERFELDT, Vet Ak Handl. 115. 1821.
Biatora cinnabarina FRIES, Lich Arct 191. 1860.

Summit of White Pass, 3000 ft. (Trelease, 833); Port Wells (Trelease, 835a). New to Alaska.

The specimen from Port Wells is only a fragment on the bark of a coniferous tree associated with *Opegrapha* and *Heterothecium*. The species has been reported from Labrador and Greenland, but not from the western coast.

42. Biatora viridescens (Schrad.) Fr.

Lichen viridescens SCHRADER in Gmel Syst. Nat. 2 : 1361. 1791.
Biatora viridescens FRIES, Act. Acad Sc. Stockh. 268. 1822

Farragut Bay (Trelease, number lost). New to Alaska.

On bark of trees and shrubs. Apothecia smaller and more regular, thallus smoother and not so well developed as in the specimens on dead wood in the Tuckerman Herbarium. A widely distributed species.

43. Biatora granulosa (Ehrnb.) Mass.

Lichen granulosus EHRENBERG, Crypt. N 145. 1785.
Biatora granulosa MASSALONGO, Ric. 124. 1852.—SOWERBY, Eng. Bot. t. 1185.

St. Matthew Island (Trelease, 852). New to Alaska.

On dead wood. The apothecia are rather smaller and more numerous and the thallus less developed than in the specimens in the Tuckerman Herbarium. Previously reported from Arctic America, Canada, New England, Rocky Mts., Oregon, and other localities.

44. Biatora apochrœiza (Nyl.).

Lecidea apochrœiza NYLANDER, Flora 443. 1885.

Hall Island (Trelease, 863a; Coville and Kearney, 206c).

Growing over mosses. Reported from St. Lawrence Island by Nylander.

A specimen numbered 822, collected on dead wood at Sitka, may possibly be referred to *Biatora varians*. The spores are immature and the determination is therefore uncertain.

ADDITIONAL ALASKA SPECIES.

The following species of *Biatora* have been reported from Alaska which do not occur in the Harriman collection: *B. cuprea* (Sommerf.) Fr and *B. artyla* (Ach.) Tuck., collected by Wright on the Islands of Bering Strait; *B. laureri* (Hepp.) Tuck., collected in Alaska by Hall; *B. milliaria* Fr., Shumagin group of islands, and *B. sanguineo-atra* Fr., on logs at old Sitka, collected by Dr. Bean; and *B. sphæroides* (Dicks.) Tuck., collected by Wright on the islands of Bering Sea, and, under the synonym *Lecidea sphæroides*, reported by Nylander from Port Clarence.

BÆOMYCES.

45. Bæomyces æruginosus (Scop.) DC.
Lichen æruginosus SCOPOLI, Fl. Carn. ed. 1. 1760.
Bæomyces æruginosus DE CANDOLLE, Fl. Franç. 2, 353. 1805.

Orca (Trelease, 828, 1006, 1016*a*), Sitka (Trelease, 1015); Hot Springs, Baranof Island (Trelease, 1080); Fraser Reach (Trelease, 1013); Farragut Bay (Trelease, 1014); Port Wells (Trelease, 1079). Collected by Dr. Bean at Sitka and Port Althorp; by Dr. Cooley at Loring and at Salmon Creek, near Juneau, by Dr. Hayes on Prince William Sound; and by Hall at Sitka. Under the synonym *B. icmadophilus* (Ehrh.) Nyl., Nylander reports its occurrence at Port Clarence, and Rothrock at Sitka and Port Althorp.

Family CLADONIACEÆ.

THAMNOLIA.

KEY TO THE SPECIES.

Thallus very slender, prostrate............ *vermicularis subuliformis*.
Thallus swollen, more erect.. .... *vermicularis taurica*.

46. Thamnolia vermicularis subuliformis Schaer.
Thamnolia vermicularis subuliformis SCHAERER, Enum. 243. 1850.

Metlakatla (Trelease, 1218), St. Lawrence Island (Trelease, 1212), Unalaska (Setchell); Cape Nome (Setchell). New to Alaska.

The specimen from St. Lawrence Island is very lax and long. With the other specimen is this note "Floating masses in ponds."

47. Thamnolia vermicularis taurica Schaer.
Thamnolia vermicularis taurica SCHAERER, Enum. 243. 1850.

Agattu Island (Townsend, 77); Hall Island (Trelease, 1228; Brewer and Coe, 673); St. Matthew Island (Trelease, no number), St. Lawrence Island (Trelease, 1232). New to Alaska.

Nylander records the occurrence of the species at St. Lawrence Island and Port Clarence. In his synopsis he does not recognize either variety, both being given as synonyms of the species itself. It is probable that both varieties were represented. As I have followed Tuckerman in separating the varieties, this makes the first Alaskan record of the distinct varieties.

CLADONIA.

KEY TO THE SPECIES.

Apothecia scarlet.
  Cups of the podetia large and evident.
    Cups cupulæform and erect..... . . . .*deformis*.

Cups dilated and cyathiform.
  Podetia smooth or squamulose ....*coccifera.*
  Podetia powdery above ....*coccifera pleurota.*
Cups of the podetia small or obsolete.
  Podetia without squamules.
    Podetia powdery above........................... .*macilenta.*
    Podetia not powdery above... .... *bellidiflora hookeri.*
  Podetia with squamules.
    Podetia scarcely branched ...., *bellidiflora.*
    Podetia freely branched.
      Squamules on the podetia few, thin, appressed.
                bellidiflora coccocephala
      Squamules on the podetia numerous, thick, spreading.
                bellidiflora ramulosa
Apothecia never scarlet.
  Apothecia pale flesh-colored or reddish.
    Podetia unbranched. ....,..........,......................*carneola.*
    Podetia branched.
      Dichotomously branched . .. . *uncialis*
      Irregularly branched ... . *amaurocræa.*
  Apothecia brown.
    Thallus sulphur-colored or straw-colored.
      Thallus densely thyrsoid entangled .. ..*alpestris.*
      Thallus open, not densely thyrsoid entangled
                sylvatica sylvestris
    Thallus grayish-green or brownish.
      Podetia club-shaped.
        Bearing squamules.
          Podetia not subulate.
            Branches not proliferous........ ..,.. ......*squamosa.*
            Branches proliferous from the margin.. ..*crispata*
          Podetia subulate.
            Epidermis granulate ....*squamosa muricella.*
            Epidermis smooth . . *furcata racemosa.*
        Without squamules
          Podetia cancellate-carious .. . ... *cariosa corticata.*
          Podetia not cancellate-carious.
            Thallus irregularly branched. ...... *furcata palamæa.*
            Thallus dichotomously or trichotomously branched
                rangiferina
      Podetia not club-shaped.

Bearing squamules.
 Podetia powdery............................*fimbriata simplex.*
 Podetia not powdery.
  Cups proliferous
   From the center............................., *verticillata.*
   From the margin.
    Podetia smooth..................*gracilis dilatata.*
    Podetia granulate-furfuraceous......*degenerans.*
  Cups not proliferous......................*pyxidata.*
Without squamules
 Podetia short..........................*pyxidata.*
 Podetia elongated
  Podetia powdery.........................*cornuta.*
  Podetia smooth.
   Podetia very slender, subulate....*gracilis chordalis.*
   Podetia not so slender, often ventricose.
           gracilis elongata.

48. Cladonia macilenta Hoffm.

Cladonia macilenta HOFFMANN, Deutschl. Fl. 126. 1795.

Wrangell (Trelease, 1318). Collected at Loring by Dr. Cooley.

Wainio, in his Monographia Cladoniarum, reports its occurrence on Vancouver Island.

49. Cladonia deformis (L.) Hoffm.

Lichen deformis LINNÆUS, Spec. Pl. 2. 1152. 1753.
Cladonia deformis HOFFMANN, Deutschl. Fl. 120. 1795.—SOWERBY, Eng. Bot. t. 1394.

Alaska (Evans, 504); Wrangell (Trelease, 1290; Coville and Kearney, 412); White Pass (Trelease, 1332a); St. Michael (Turner, 852); Keystone Pass (Tibetts). Babington and Rothrock report its occurrence at Kotzebue Sound, while Nylander credits it to Port Clarence.

No. 412 from Wrangell is large and well fruited, the others are sterile or have only immature apothecia.

50. Cladonia bellidiflora (Ach.) Schaer.

Lichen (Scyphophorus) bellidiflorus ACHARIUS, Meth. Lich. 335. 1803.
Cladonia bellidiflora SCHAERER, Lich. Helv. Spic. 21. 1823.—SOWERBY, Eng. Bot. t. 1894.

Alaska (Evans, 39, 193, 399, 502); Fraser Reach, Princess Royal Island, B. C. (Trelease, 1314; Brewer and Coe, 300); Wrangell (Brewer & Coe, 413); New Metlakatla (Trelease, 1317); Yakutat

(Trelease, 1324); Vancouver Island, Broughton Strait (Trelease, 1315); Sitka (Trelease, 1321, 1322, 1355); Hot Springs, Baranof Island (Trelease, 1319, 1319a); White Pass (Trelease, 1325); summit of White Pass, 3000 ft. (Trelease, 626a); Orca (Trelease, 1323; Setchell, 1220); Port Wells (Trelease, 1326); Virgin Bay (Trelease, 1327); Attu Island (Townsend, 72); St. Matthew Island (Trelease, 2117); St. Lawrence Island (Trelease, 1329); Cape Nome (Setchell). In addition to the localities given above, Nylander reports its occurrence on St. Lawrence Island, Macoun states that it is common on St. George and St. Paul Islands, while Wainio credits it to St. Paul Island and to Sitka.

One of the most widely distributed of all the lichens of this collection. It varies greatly in size and in the development of the squamules. Usually the plants are abundantly fruited.

51. **Cladonia bellidiflora coccocephala** (Ach.) Wainio.

Cenomyce coccocephala ACHARIUS, L U. 540 1810
Cladonia bellidiflora coccocephala WAINIO, Monographia Cladoniarum 224. 1887.

Juneau 1800 ft. (Saunders, 1331); White Pass (Trelease, 1325a); Virgin Bay (Trelease, 1312, 1328). Under the synonym *C. bellidiflora* f. *gracilenta*, Nylander reports its occurrence on St. Lawrence Island.

52. **Cladonia bellidiflora hookeri** (Tuck.) Nyl.

Cladonia hookeri TUCKERMAN, Syn Lich N E 55 1848.
Cladonia bellidiflora hookeri NYLANDER, Syn 221 1860.

Broughton Strait (Trelease, 1316); Wrangell (Trelease, 1318 in part); Hot Springs (Trelease, 1320 in part). Wainio reports its occurrence at Sitka and St. Paul Island.

The specimens from Wrangell and Hot Springs are mixed with the species.

53. **Cladonia bellidiflora ramulosa** Wainio.

Cladonia bellidiflora ramulosa WAINIO, Monographia Cladoniarum, 1 : 210. 1887.

Hall Island (Trelease, 1330, 1335); St. Lawrence Island (Trelease, 1333); Cape Nome (Setchell). New to Alaska and to America.

The specimens agree with the descriptions of this variety excepting that the podetia are very scaly, while the variety is described as lacking scales, or somewhat scaly.

54. Cladonia coccifera (L.) Willd.

Lichen cocciferus LINNÆUS, Spec Pl. 2. 1151. 1753.
Cladonia coccifera WILLDENOW, Fl Berol 361. 1787.—SOWERBY, Eng. Bot. *t.* 2051

Alaska (Funston, 3); Broughton Strait (Trelease, 1336); Wrangell (Trelease, 1337); Sitka (Trelease, 1343); White Pass (Trelease, 1332); summit of White Pass, 3000 ft. (Trelease, 626, 1332*a*, 1332*b*); Point Gustavus, Glacier Bay (Coville and Kearney, 769); Popof Island (Kincaid, no number); Hall Island (Coville and Kearney, 2065); St. Paul Island (Trelease, 1342, 1342*a*); St Matthew Island (Coville and Kearney, 2123), Port Clarence (Trelease, 1345), St. Michael (Setchell); Cape Nome (Setchell). Under the synonym *C. cornucopioides* (L.) Fr., Babington records its occurrence at Kotzebue Sound and makes this note: "Very fine, fertile." Under the same name Nylander credits it to St Lawrence Island and Port Clarence, Rothrock to Port Althrop (Dr. Bean, collector), while Macoun states that it is common on St Paul and St George Islands.

Very variable, many of the specimens sterile or with immature fruit. The specimen from Point Gustavus is infected with a small black fungus.

55 Cladonia coccifera pleurota (Floerk.) Schaer.

Capitularia pleurota FLOERKE, Beschr Rothfr Becherfl 218 1808
Cladonia coccifera pleurota SCHAFRER, Lich Helv Spic. 25 1823

Virgin Bay (Trelease, 1346, sterile). Seward Peninsula (Collier). In Nylander's list the species is credited to St. Lawrence Island and Port Clarence.

56. Cladonia uncialis (L.) Web.

Lichen uncialis LINNÆUS, Spec Pl 1153 1753
Cladonia uncialis WEBBER in Wiggers, Prim Fl Hols. 90. 1780, pr. p.—SOWERBY, Eng Bot. *t. 1247*

Sitka (Trelease, 1243); Unalaska (Setchell); St. Lawrence Island (Trelease, 1250); Port Clarence (Trelease, 1255; Cole, no number); Reindeer Station, Port Clarence (James L. White); St. Michael (Setchell); Cape Nome (Setchell), Seward Peninsula (Collier). In addition to these stations, Babington credits it to Kotzebue Sound and Rothrock records its occurrence at Sitka and Kotzebue Sound. Under the synonym *Cenomyce uncialis* Ach., Hooker and Arnott include it in their list of species from Kotzebue Sound, while Nylander credits it to Port Clarence as *Cladonia uncialis* (Hoffm.).

A widely distributed northern lichen. Most of the specimens are the form recognized by Tuckerman as var. *adunca*. Wainio, in his

Monographia Cladoniarum, gives forty-five different varietal names which have been applied to different forms of this protean lichen, and therefore he seems wise in excluding all these varieties.

57. Cladonia amaurocræa (Floerk.) Schaer.

Capitularia amaurocræa FLOERKE, Beschr. Braunfr. Becherfl. 334. 1810.
Cladonia amaurocræa SCHAERER, Spicil 34. 1823.

St. Michael Island (Turner, 843; Setchell); St. Lawrence Island (Trelease, 1230); Fort Cosmos (Huff, no number); Cape Nome (Setchell). Also found at Port Clarence, according to Nylander.

A subalpine and arctic lichen.

58. Cladonia carneola Fr.

Cladonia carneola FRIES, Lich. Eur. 233 (a) 1831.

Sitka (Trelease, 1344). New to Alaska
Other North American stations are Greenland, Oregon, and Washington.

59. Cladonia alpestris (L.) Rabenh.

Lichen rangiferinus alpestris LINNÆUS, Spec. Pl. 1153. 1753.
Cladonia alpestris RABENHORST, Clad Eur 11. 1860 — DILL. Hist. Musc. t. 16. f 29.

Summit of White Pass, 3000 ft. (Trelease, 1244); Orca (Coville and Kearney, 1203; Trelease, 1246); Virgin Bay (Saunders, 1248; Coville and Kearney, 1224); Columbia Fiord, Prince William Sound (Coville and Kearney, 1402); Kadiak (Trelease, 1239); Hall Island (Coville and Kearney, 2061); St. Matthew Island (Trelease, 1256); St. Michael Island (Turner, 844; Setchell); St. Lawrence Island (Trelease, 1249, 1251, 1258; Coville and Kearney, 2009; Cole, no number); Port Clarence (Trelease, 1253); Cape Nome (Setchell); Seward Peninsula (Collier). Under the synonym *Cladonia rangiferina alpestris*, Nylander records its occurrence on St. Lawrence Island, while Macoun states that it is common on St. George Island.

This is a common alpine and arctic form, and shows great variation in the delicacy and fineness of the thallus. This is one of the finest collections of this species that I have ever seen.

60. Cladonia sylvatica sylvestris Oed.

Cladonia sylvatica sylvestris OEDER in Fl Dan. 3: 4. t. 539. 1770.

Alaska (Funston, no number; Townsend, 57a); New Metlakatla (Trelease, 1241); Juneau (Trelease, 1259), Sitka (Trelease, 1242; Coville and Kearney, 881 in part); summit of White Pass, 3000 ft. (Brewer and Coe, 625); Port Wells (Trelease, 1245); Orca (Trelease,

1262); Virgin Bay (Trelease, 1247, 1260); Sturgeon River Bay, Kadiak Island (Trelease, 1240); Akun Island (Townsend, no number), Attu Island (Townsend, 73); Atka Island (Townsend, 90); Hall Island (Trelease, 1252 in part); Pastoliak River (Newhall), Seward Peninsula (Collier). Nylander records *C. sylvatica* (Hoffm.) as occurring at Port Clarence, and *C. rangiferina sylvatica* on St Lawrence Island. Under the synonym *C. rangiferina* var. *sylvatica*, Macoun records its occurrence on St. George Island, Rothrock credits it to 'all Russian America,' while Dr. Cooley collected it at Salmon and Sheep Creeks, near Juneau

All the specimens are sterile. Associated with this species are mosses and various other lichens growing in inextricable confusion.

61. Cladonia rangiferina (L.) Web.
Lichen rangiferinus LINNÆUS, Spec Pl 2 1153 pr. p. 1753
Cladonia rangiferina (L.) WEBBER in Wiggers, Prim. Fl Hols 90 n 994, pr. p 1780.—SOWERBY, Eng. Bot *t. 2249*.

Alaska (Evans, 389); Wrangell (Coville and Kearney, 406), White Pass (Trelease, 1264); Orca (Trelease, 1263); Hall Island (Coville and Kearney, 2063 in part); St. Lawrence Island (Trelease, 1238 in part); Fort Cosmos (Huff, *c*); St. Michael (Setchell); Cape Nome (Setchell). Reported by Nylander from Port Clarence and from St. Lawrence Island; by Macoun as common on St. Paul and St. George Islands; by Dr. Cooley from Salmon Creek and Sheep Creek, near Juneau, by Rothrock from 'all Russian America'; collected also on St. Paul Island by William Palmer and determined by W. W. Calkins. Under the synonym *Cenomyce rangiferina* Hooker and Arnott report its occurrence at Kotzebue Sound.

Some of the specimens are mixed with other species of *Cladonia*, *Thamnolia*, and *Cetraria*. The specimens vary greatly, some being very delicate and finely branched, while others are coarse and not so profusely branched.

62. Cladonia furcata racemosa (Hoffm.) Floerk.
Cladonia racemosa HOFFMANN, Deutschl. Fl 2: 144 1795
Cladonia furcata racemosa FLOERKE, Clad Comm 152 1828.

Alaska (Evans, 195). Also collected by Macoun on St. Paul Island and St. George Island.

63. Cladonia furcata palamæa (Ach.) Nyl.
Bæomyces spinosus b. *palamæus* ACHARIUS, Meth. Lich. 359 1803
Cladonia furcata palamæa NYLANDER, Lich. Scand. 56. 1861.—DILL Hist Musc *t. 16. f. 25, 27*.

Orca (Trelease, 1261); Sturgeon River Bay, Kadiak Island (Trelease, 1225); St. Matthew Island (Trelease, 1223). Macoun collected it on the earth on St. Paul Island and on St. George Island. Hooper figures it in Cruise of the Corwin, plates 1-2.

64. Cladonia crispata (Ach.) Flot.
Cenomyce allotropa C. *crispata* ACHARIUS, Meth. Lich. 341. 1803.
Cladonia crispata FLOTOW, Merkw. Hirschb. 4 1839.

Wrangell (Trelease, 1288); Virgin Bay (Trelease, 1293). Credited to Port Clarence in Nylander's list.

Specimens very finely divided.

65. Cladonia squamosa (Scop.) Hoffm.
Lichen squamosus SCOPOLI, Fl Carn ed 2. 2: 368. 1772.
Cladonia squamosa HOFFMANN, Deutschl. Fl. 2: 125. 1795.—SOWERBY, Eng. Bot. *t. 2362*.

Alaska (Evans, 29). Reported by Nylander as occurring at Port Clarence, by Rothrock at Sitka, and by Dr. Cooley at Sheep Creek, near Juneau.

Plants fertile.

66. Cladonia squamosa muricella (Del.) Wainio.
Cenomyce squamosa muricella DEL. in Dub Bot. Gall. 626. 1830.
Cladonia squamosa B. *muricella* WAINIO, Mono. Clad. 1 431. 1887.

New Metlakatla, Annette Island (Coville and Kearney, 3686), Sitka (Trelease, 1056); Cape Nome (Setchell). New to Alaska. Wainio reports its occurrence on Vancouver Island.

67. Cladonia cornuta (L.) Schaer.
Lichen cornutus LINNÆUS, Spec. Pl. 1152. n. 63. pr. p. 1753.
Cladonia cornuta SCHAERER, Lich. Helv. Spic. 373 1836.—HORNEM. Fl. Dan. 13 *t. 2210*.

Alaska (Funston, 10). Credited to Sitka by Wainio.

Lyell and Macoun had collected this species in British Columbia, and it has been collected from the Asiatic side of Bering Strait.

68. Cladonia verticillata Hoffm.
Cladonia verticillata HOFFMANN, Deutschl. Fl. 2; 122. 1795.

Port Clarence (Trelease, no number). New to Alaska.

A very diminutive specimen likewise collected at Port Clarence may be referred here.

69. Cladonia gracilis elongata (Jacq) Floerk.
Lichen elongatus JACQ. MISC 378 1781.
Cladonia gracilis elongata FLOERKE, Clad. Comm. 38 1828.—JACQ. Misc. 2. *t 11. f. 1*.

Summit of White Pass, 3000 ft. (Trelease, 1234); St. Matthew Island (Trelease, 1229); St. Lawrence Island (Trelease, 1230*a*, 1231,

1233); Port Clarence (Trelease, 1222, 1227, 1235); Cape Nome (Setchell), St Michael (Setchell), Seward Peninsula (Collier). Nylander credits it to St. Lawrence Island and Port Clarence, while Macoun states that it is rare on St. Paul Island Wainio gives as additional stations, Sitka and Kotzebue Sound. Kurtz and Knowlton credit it to Alaska as *Cladonia gracilis elongata macroceras*

70. **Cladonia gracilis chordalis** (Floerk.) Schaer.
Capitularia gracilis B *chordalis* FLOERKE, Beschr. Braunfr Becherfl 324, 1810, in part
Cladonia gracilis chordalis SCHALRER, Lich Helv. Spic 32. 1823. — SOWERBY, Eng. Bot. t. 2260

Juneau (Coville and Kearney, 600; Saunders, 1220); Wrangell (Trelease, 1291, 1292); summit of White Pass, 3000 ft. (Trelease, 1219, 1287); Port Wells (Trelease, 1226), Unalaska (Setchell); Hall Island (Trelease, 1221); St. Lawrence Island (Trelease, 1224); Keystone Pass (Tibbett). Collected also on St. Lawrence Island, according to Nylander

71. **Cladonia gracilis dilatata** (Hoffm.) Wainio.
Cladonia dilatata HOFFMANN, Deutschl Fl 126 1795.
Cladonia gracilis dilatata WAINIO, Monog Clad 2 : 87 1894. — DILL. Hist. Musc. t 14 fig 13A

Glacier Cascade (Canby, 509). Reported from Kotzebue Sound by Babington as *Cladonia gracilis* B *hybrida*

72. **Cladonia degenerans** (Floerk.) Spreng
Baeomyces degenerans FLOERKE in Berl. Magaz. 283 1807
Cladonia degenerans SPRENGEL, Linn Syst Veg. 4 : 273 1827

Alaska (Evans, 503 Funston, 11); New Metlakatla (Coville and Kearney, 368c), Wrangell (Trelease, 1254, Coville and Kearney, 429); Juneau, 1800 ft. (Saunders); Hot Springs (Trelease, 1353); Yakutat (Trelease, 1351), St. Lawrence Island (Trelease, 1359); St. Michael (Setchell); Cape Nome (Setchell). On earth, St. Paul Island, collected by Macoun; and under the synonym *Cladonia degenerans* f. *trachyna* (Ach.) Nylander records its occurrence at Port Clarence.

The specimen from St. Lawrence Island is smaller and less branched than most of the others. It most closely resembles a specimen from Labrador in the Tuckerman Herbarium

73. **Cladonia fimbriata simplex** (Weis) Flot.
Lichen fimbriatus c *simplex* WEIS, Pl. Crypt. 84. 1770 —DILL Hist Musc. t. 14. fig 6A.
Cladonia fimbriata simplex FLOT

Locks of the Columbia River, Oregon (Coville and Kearney, 253); New Metlakatla (Trelease, 1352), Sitka (Trelease, 1309); Point

Gustavus, Glacier Bay (Coville and Kearney, 786, 786a), Hidden Glacier, Russell Fiord (Coville and Kearney, 966); Yakutat (Brewer and Coe, 645b — a fragment); Farragut Bay (Trelease, 1306, Brewer and Coe, 623a). It appears in Dr Cooley's list under the synonym *Cladonia fimbriata* b. *tubæformis*, collected at Sheep Creek, near Juneau.

Cladonia fimbriata is one of the most variable of the *Cladonias*. Wainio, in his Monographia Cladoniarum Universalis, recognizes thirty-one varieties and forms of this species. Though new to Alaska, it has been collected in California by Bolander.

74. Cladonia pyxidata (L.) Fr.

Lichen pyxidatus LINNÆUS, Spec Pl. 2 1151 pr p. 1753
Cladonia pyxidata FRIES, Nov. Sched. Crit. 21 1826

Alaska (Evans, 67; Funston, 61; Trelease, 1313); New Metlakatla (Coville and Kearney, 368); Juneau (Trelease, 1331a, 1338); Egg Island, Disenchantment Bay (Coville and Kearney, 1019); Hidden Glacier Inlet (Trelease, 1347); Point Gustavus, Glacier Bay (Trelease, 787); Yakutat (Trelease, 1348, 1349, 1350; Saunders, 1152), Indian Camp, Yakutat Bay (Brewer and Coe, 645a), Unalaska (Setchell); Hall Island (Trelease, 1341), St. Paul Island (Coville and Kearney, 1822); St. Lawrence Island (Trelease, 1340); Port Clarence (Trelease, 1360); Plover Bay, Siberia (Trelease, 1339); St. Michael (Setchell). Additional localities: Dr. Bean collected this species on Chamisso Island, at Elephant Point, Eschscholtz Bay; and on Alaska Peninsula, according to Rothrock, who reports its occurrence at Kotzebue Sound; Macoun collected it on St. Paul and St. George Islands.

75. Cladonia cariosa corticata Wainio.

Cladonia cariosa γ *corticata* WAINIO, Monog. Clad. Univ. 2 53. 1894.

Alaska (Funston, 55). New to Alaska.

ADDITIONAL SPECIES.

The following species, arranged according to Wainio's Monographia Cladoniarum, have been reported from Alaska: *C. papillaria* (Ehrh.) Hoffm., collected on St. Paul Island by William Palmer, determined by W. W. Calkins; *C. digitata* Schaer, collected at Sitka by Dr. Bean; *C. coccifera stemmatina* Ach., credited to Sitka by Wainio; *C. reticulata* (Russell) Wainio, reported by Nylander under the synonym *Cladina lacunosa* as occurring on St. Lawrence

Island; *C. furcata* (Huds.), collected on St. Paul Island by William Palmer, determined by W. W. Calkins; *C. rangiformis* Hoffm., reported for Kotzebue Sound by Hooker and Arnott, under synonym *Cenomyce pungens* Del., *C. crispata* f. *divulsa* (Del) Arn., recorded by Nylander for Port Clarence under the synonym *C. crispata* f *cetrariæformis* Del.; *C. subsquamosa* Nyl. (Emend), recorded by Nylander as occurring at Port Clarence; *C. cenotea* (Ach) Schaer., reported by Nylander as occurring at Port Clarence, and by Rothrock as having been collected by Dr. Bean on an island in Cross Sound, while forms were brought from Cook Inlet and Sitka which are doubtfully referred here; *C. mitrula* Tuck., collected at Juneau by Dr. Cooley; *C. decorticata* (Floerke) Spreng., collected by Macoun on St Paul Island; *C. acuminata* (Ach.) Norrl., reported by Nylander as having been collected at Port Clarence; *C. gracilis* (L.) Willd., reported by Rothrock[1] for Sitka and Kotzebue Sound, figured by Hooper[2] (pl. 1–2), and recorded for Kotzebue Sound by Hooker and Arnott under the synonym *Cenomyce ecmocyna* Ach.; *C gracilescens* (Floerk.) Wainio, reported by Nylander, under the synonym *Cladina lepidiota* (Ach) Nyl., as having been collected on St Lawrence Island; *C. pyxidata pocillum* (Ach) Flot , collected on the islands of Bering Strait by Wright, reported from Port Clarence by Nylander, who also separates a form as f *cervina* which is included by Wainio under the var *pocillum; C. fimbriata* (L.) Fr., collected by William Palmer on St Paul Island, determined by W. W. Calkins, also collected at Loring by Dr. Cooley, by whom a doubtful form was collected at Sheep Creek, near Juneau; *C fimbriata radiata* (Schieb.) Coem., reported by Hooker and Arnott for Kotzebue Sound under the name *Cenomyce radiata* Ach., *C foliacea alcicornis* (Lightf.) Schaer , collected by Macoun under damp, overhanging rocks on St. Paul Island, and recorded as *C. alcicornis,* and *C cyanipes* (Sommerf.) Wainio, reported by Nylander as collected at Port Clarence.

PILOPHORUS.

KEY TO THE SPECIES.

Podetia short, stout, apothecia elongated............ . .. *cereolus hallii.*
Podetia more elongated, apothecia rounded.. . . *cereolus acicularis.*

76. Pilophorus cereolus hallii Tuck.

Pilophorus cereolus hallii TUCKERMAN, Obs. Lich. 4 · 177. 1877

Orca, 1500 ft. (Trelease, 1305). New to Alaska.

[1] Rothrock, Dr J. T Flora of Alaska, Smithsonian Report, 1867
[2] Hooper, Cruise of the Corwin, 1881.

The only specimen in the Tuckerman Herbarium is from the Cascade Mountains in Oregon. This specimen is much more delicate, being not more than two-thirds as long as the Alaska plants, while the apothecia are about half as thick.

77 **Pilophorus cereolus acicularis** (Ach.) Tuck.
Bæomyces acicularis ACHARIUS, Meth Lich 328 1803
Pilophorus cereolus acicularis TUCKERMAN, Suppl L 427 1858-9

Broughton Strait (Trelease, 1302); Sitka (Trelease, 1303, Setchell, 1265); Mount Verstovia, Sitka (Coville and Kearney, 929); Juneau (Coville and Kearney, 584; Setchell, 1245); Orca (Trelease, 1304; Setchell, 1222). Reported by Rothrock[1] as occurring in Russian America; collected by Dr. Bean at Sawmill Creek, Sitka, by Dr Cooley at Juneau, 3000 ft. alt., and at Salmon Creek and Gold Creek Canyon, near Juneau.

One additional variety of this genus has been reported from Alaska, *P. cereolus robustus* Tuck., which was collected by Wright on the islands of Bering Strait; Macoun collected it "under overhanging rocks" on St. Paul Island. Nylander records its occurrence at Port Clarence, under the synonym *Pilophoron polycarpum* Tuck.

STEREOCAULON.

KEY TO THE SPECIES.

Thallus dwarfed.
    Tomentose, phyllocladia wart-like . . . . *tomentosum alpinum*.
    Not tomentose, phyllocladia confluent . . . . *denudatum*.
Thallus of good size.
    Slightly tomentose, apothecia subterminal, dilated . . . . . . *paschale*.
    Densely white tomentose, apothecia lateral, minute, not dilated.
                                                        tomentosum.

78. **Stereocaulon denudatum** Flk.
Stereocaulon denudatum FLOERKE, Deutsch. Lich Anmerk 4: 13 1821.— TUCKERMAN, Syn. N A L. 1 233

Unalaska (Setchell); St. Michael (Setchell)

Dr. Nylander records this species as occurring at Lawrence Bay, on the Siberian coast According to Professor Tuckerman it has been collected in Alaska by Dr. Kellogg. Common in Greenland and Scandinavia. Reported also from Newfoundland. Pennsylvania is the most southern station given in Tuckerman's North American Lichens.

[1] Rothrock, Dr. J. T Flora of Alaska Smithsonian Report. 1807.

79. Stereocaulon tomentosum Fr.

Stereocaulon tomentosum FRIES, Sched Crit 20 1826.

Juneau, 1200–1800 ft (Saunders, 1274; Coville and Kearney, 609); Muir Glacier, Glacier Bay (Trelease, 1298, 1299, 1300, 1301); Hidden Glacier Inlet, Yakutat (Trelease, 1294), Disenchantment Bay, Yakutat Bay (Trelease, 1296, 1297), Nunatak moraine, Yakutat Bay (Coville and Kearney, 1295); Point Gustavus, Glacier Bay (Coville and Kearney, 761); Hidden Glacier, Russell Fiord (Coville and Kearney, 981), Orca (Trelease, 1269), Kadiak (Trelease, 1311); Hall Island (Trelease, 1267), St. Matthew Island (Coville and Kearney, 2121); Port Clarence (Trelease, 1266); Postoliak River (Newhall).

Other Alaskan localities are: Port Clarence, as listed by Nylander; Kotzebue Sound, recorded by Babington; while Dr Cooley collected it at Sheep Creek, near Juneau, and at Davidson Glacier.

80. Stereocaulon tomentosum alpinum (Laur.) Th. Fr.

Stereocaulon alpinum LAURER in Fries, L E 204 1821.
Stereocaulon tomentosum alpinum TH FRIES, Lich. Scand. 48. 1871–74 — SCHEUCHZ It. Alp 2 *t 19*.

Alaska (Evans, 196, Funston, 16; Turner); locality lost (Trelease, 6112); Muir Glacier, Glacier Bay (Trelease, 1307, 1298*a*); summit of White Pass, 3000 ft (Trelease, 1270), Disenchantment Bay, Yakutat Bay (Trelease, 1310), Kadiak (Trelease, 1279), St. Matthew Island (Trelease, 1268). The species was collected on the islands in Bering Strait by Wright and reported from St Lawrence Island in Nylander, Lich Fr Behr.

Many of the specimens are beautifully fruited. A widely distributed alpine and arctic lichen, and in some of its forms only with difficulty separated from *S. paschale*.

81. Stereocaulon paschale (L.) Ach.

Lichen paschalis LINNÆUS, Sp Pl ed 2 2· 1621 1764
Stereocaulon paschale ACHARIUS, Meth Lich 315 1803.—SOWERBY, Eng. Bot *t 282*

Hidden Glacier, Russell Fiord (Coville and Kearney); Muir Glacier, Glacier Bay (Trelease, 1300), Orca (Trelease, 1272); St. Michael (Setchell); Cape Nome (Setchell). Reported by Hooker and Arnott as having been collected at Kotzebue Sound. Dr. Rothrock, in his report on Dr. Bean's collection, writes. "Common and everywhere met."

Sterile, poorly developed specimens.

Two additional species have been credited to Alaska : *S. coralloides* Fr., collected on St. Paul Island by William Palmer, determined by W. W. Calkins, and *S. wrightii* Tuck., collected by Wright on the islands of Bering Strait.

Family LECANORIACEÆ.

PERTUSARIA.

KEY TO THE SPECIES.

Plants growing on the earth, incrusting mosses, etc.
    Lobes of the thallus finger-shaped, apothecia solitary..... *dactylina*.
    Lobes of the thallus flat, apothecia crowded................ *glomerata*.
Plants growing on bark or on rocks.
    Apothecia underneath the bark, becoming emergent. *carneopallida*.
    Apothecia external.
        Apothecia compound, difform.
            Apothecia and spores medium to large size ....*communis*.
            Apothecia and spores small.. .... *pustulata*.
        Apothecia not compound.
            Thallus thin, not sorediate, apothecia soon powdery.
                                                                               multipuncta.
            Thallus irregularly thickened, often sorediate, apothecia not powdery... . . . . *pocillaria*.

82. Pertusaria glomerata (Ach.) Schaer.

Porina glomerata ACHARIUS, L U 310 *t 7 f 2* 1810.
Pertusaria glomerata SCHAERER, Spicil 66 1823

Hall Island (Trelease, 863) ; Port Clarence (Trelease, 864).

The specimens which grow over mosses are well fruited. A specimen which Rothrock lists was collected at Port Mulgrave. Wright collected it on the islands of Bering Strait, while Nylander records it for Konyam Bay and Bering Island, on the Asiatic side of the Strait, and Dr. Bean collected it at Port Mulgrave. It has been collected on the White Mountains, but I find no record for **Labrador**, **Newfoundland**, or **Greenland**.

83. Pertusaria pustulata (Ach.) Nyl.

Porina pustulata ACHARIUS, L U 309 1810
Pertusaria pustulata NYLANDER, Prodr. Gall. 195. 1857.

Yakutat Bay (Trelease, 819), Farragut Bay (Trelease, 523). New to Alaska.

The most northern station recorded in North America is Oregon, where it was collected by Hall; its most southern record is Florida. It occurs also in tropical America, Japan, and Australia.

84. Pertusaria communis DC.
Lichen pertusa HOFFMANN, Enum. 16. *t. 3 f. 3.*
Pertusaria communis DE CANDOLLE, Fl Fr 2: 320. 1805.

Kadiak (Trelease, 897 and 900 in part, 917, 947, 948, 981); St. Michael (Setchell).

On rocks associated with various species of *Lecanora*, *Lecidea*, and *Buellia*. As listed by Rothrock it occurs also at Port Clarence, Cape Lisburne, and Port Althorp.

85. Pertusaria carneo-pallida (Nyl.) Nyl.
Lecidea carneo-pallida NYLANDER in Bot Notis 183. *t. 853.* 1853.
Pertusaria carneo-pallida NYLANDER, Lich Fr. Behr. 65. 1888.—SOWERBY, Eng. Bot. *t. 2010.*

Disenchantment Bay, Yakutat Bay (Trelease, 802, 803, 820). On bark. Reported from Port Clarence by Nylander.

A lichen which is common in Scandinavia and other European countries, but whose only other American station is Port Clarence, as noted above.

86. Pertusaria dactylina (Ach.) Nyl.
Lichen dactylinus ACHARIUS, Prod. 89. 1798.
Pertusaria dactylina NYLANDER, Lapp Or. 240. 1867.

Alaska (Trelease, 921).

Sterile, on the earth. Reported by Nylander from Port Clarence; by Rothrock from Alaska Peninsula, collected by Dr. Bean; and by Tuckerman from the islands of Bering Strait, where it was also collected by Wright.

A strictly alpine and arctic species.

87. Pertusaria multipuncta (Turn.) Nyl.
Variolaria multipuncta TURNER, Trans Linn. Soc. 9: 137. 1808.
Pertusaria multipuncta NYLANDER, Not Sallsk. F. 1857.

Yakutat (Trelease, 804); Sitka (Trelease, 812). New to Alaska. On bark. No. 812 is sterile, but is without doubt referable here. Common throughout the United States.

In addition to the species of *Pertusaria* given above, several sterile specimens were collected. One of them may probably be referred to—

88. Pertusaria rhodocarpa Koerb.
Pertusaria rhodocarpa KOERBER, Syst Lich. Ger. 384. 1855.

Farragut Bay (Trelease, 806).

Another may well be referred to—

89. **Pertusaria communis isidioidea** Schaer.

Port Wells, Prince William Sound (Trelease, 969). On moss.

No. 80 (Trelease, Sitka) is on the bark of shrubs. The whitish thallus is very smooth. Immature apothecia are present with a lecanorine disk of a yellowish color.

No. 827 (Trelease, Sitka) is on dead wood. The thallus is very smooth and thin, scarcely evident, of a light pink color. The immature apothecia are single, with a lecanorine disk, the disk being flesh-colored, with a lighter margin.

90. **Pertusaria pocillaria** sp. nov.

Thallus rather thin, creamy white, verrucose, sorediate. Apothecia lecanorine, small, .5 mm. in diameter. Spores colorless, simple, 2–8 in an ascus, $\frac{28-45}{17-28}$ μ. Paraphyses slender, branched.

Type specimen in the herbarium of the Missouri Botanical Garden, and a duplicate in my own herbarium; collected by Prof. William Trelease on *Alnus* at Farragut Bay, June 5, 1899, no. 806a.

The species approaches *Pertusaria xanthostoma* (Sommerf.) Fr., but differs in the distinctly smaller spores. The measurement given for the spores of *P. xanthostoma* is $\frac{55-74}{22-38}$ μ.

In many cases the hymenial layer of the apothecium has fallen out, leaving the exciple as an empty cup, a fact which has suggested the specific name chosen. Undoubtedly this fact has an ecological significance in the distribution of the spores, as M. Miyoshi[1] has recorded for *Sagedia macrospora*.

The following additional species of the genus *Pertusaria* are credited to Alaska: *P. bryontha* (Ach.) Nyl., collected by Wright on the islands of Bering Strait, by Dr. Bean on Unalaska Island, and reported by Nylander as collected at Port Clarence, by Dr. Almquist; *P. panyrga* (Ach.) Nyl., collected by Macoun on rocks on St. Paul Island and reported by Nylander as having been collected at Port Clarence; *P. velata* (Turn.) Nyl., collected by Dr. Bean at Warm Springs, Sitka; *P. trochiscea* Norm., *P. subobducens* Nyl., *P. subdactylina* Nyl., *P. sommerfeldtii* (Flk.) Nyl., all collected by Dr. Almquist at Port Clarence; *P. subplicans* Nyl., *P. glomerata corniculata* Nyl., and *P. rhodoleuca* Fr. fil., collected on St. Lawrence Island by Dr. Almquist, determined by Nylander. In his correction

---

[1] Miyoshi, M. Ueber die Sporocarpenevacuation und darauf erfolgendes Sporenausstreuen bei einer Flechte. The Journal of the College of Science Imperial University, Tokyo, Japan. 15² 367–370 *t. 18.* 1901.

of Dr. Rothrock's list of the species collected by Dr. Bean, Nylander states that under the name *P. communis* DC. rock forms of *P. rhodoleuca* Fr. fil. are included.

RINODINA.

KEY TO THE SPECIES.

Thallus incrusting mosses....................................*turfacea.*
Thallus on wood or rock.
    Thallus brown, hypothallus conspicuous......*sophodes atrocinerea.*
    Thallus white, hypothallus inconspicuous .. *.sophodes confragosa.*

91. Rinodina sophodes confragosa (Ach.) Tuck.

Parmelia confragosa ACHARIUS, Meth. Lich. Suppl. 33. 1803.
Rinodina sophodes confragosa TUCKERMAN, Syn N. A L 208. 1882.

Farragut Bay (Trelease, 826). On old boards. According to Rothrock, Dr. Bean collected this species in Alaska, but no definite locality is given. Tuckerman, Syn. N. A. L. 208, indicated the Pacific Coast as the habitat of this species in this country; I can find no other records of it.

92. Rinodina sophodes atrocinerea (Diks.) Nyl.

Lichen atrocinereus DIKSON, Crypt. Brit 14. *t. 9. f. 2.* 1785–1801.
Rinodina sophodes b *atrocinerea* NYLANDER, Lich. Par. N. 43. 1855.—SOWERBY, Eng. Bot *t 2096*

Plover Bay, Siberia (Trelease, 992). On rock. New to the Alaskan region.

93. Rinodina turfacea (Wahl.) Th. Fr.

Lichen turfaceus WAHLENBERG, Fl. Lapp. 408 1812
Rinodina turfacea TH. FRIES, Lich. Arct. 126. 1860

St. Matthew Island (Trelease, 866 in part); St. Michael (Setchell). The specimen from St. Michael grew on moss with *Biatora hypnophila* and *Placodium jungermanniæ.* Collected by Wright on the islands of Bering Strait, and recorded by Rothrock as occurring in Dr. Bean's collection, but with no definite locality. Nylander records it under the synonym *Lecanora turfacea* as collected at Port Clarence. Reported also from British Columbia, Greenland, and Labrador.

Additional Alaskan species of *Rinodina* are as follows: *R. nimbosa* (Fr.) Th. Fr and *R. sophodes* (Ach.) Nyl., collected by Dr. Bean, no definite locality being recorded, *R. sophodes* being listed also by Nylander for Port Clarence; *R. turfacea roscida* Th. Fr. and *R. turfacea miniarea* Nyl., collected by Wright on islands in Bering Strait.

LECANORA.

KEY TO THE SPECIES.

Thallus lobed, subfoliaceous
  Thallus having brown radiately chinked warts ... .*gelida.*
  Thallus not having brown radiately chinked warts.
    Thallus crustaceous-foliaceous ... ... *muralis.*
    Thallus monophyllous, of many round-lobed, branch-like divisions.
      Disk of apothecia olivaceous or black.. .... .*rubina opaca.*
      Disk of apothecia yellowish or red
        Thallus black beneath, margin of apothecia reflexed .*rubina.*
        Thallus white beneath, margin of apothecia not reflexed.
                        straminea.
Thallus nearly uniform.
  Apothecia innate, becoming emergent.
    Spores many, very small.. . . ... *privigna revertens.*
    Spores few, medium size.
      Thallus incrusting mosses ... ...*occulata.*
      Thallus on rocks.
        Thallus subtartareous, areolæ smooth . ... *cinerea.*
        Thallus tartareous, areolæ prominent .... *cinerea gibbosa.*
  Apothecia superficial.
    Spores medium size.
      Disk of apothecium black or greenish-black.
        Disk greenish-black.
          Apothecia small, margin entire, reflexed..*varia intricata*
          Apothecia larger, crenate, not reflexed ... *atrosulphurea.*
        Disk of apothecium shining black.
          Margin of apothecium dark gray . *subfusca coilocarpa.*
          Margin of apothecium shining white.
            Apothecia more or less pruinose, margin crenulate.
                        pacifica.
            Apothecia not pruinose, margin entire .. .. *atra.*
      Disk of apothecia never black.
        Apothecia buff-colored
          Thallus cream-colored, disk of apothecia white pruinose.
                      pallida
          Thallus pale-greenish or yellowish, apothecia not pruinose.
                      varia.
        Apothecia reddish-brown.
          Thallus smooth, thin, whitish.
            Apothecia very small and crowded.... . ...*hageni.*

Apothecia medium size.
  Disk of apothecium shining brown.
    subfusca argentata.
  Disk of apothecium pruinose .... *.pacifica.*
Thallus not smooth, dirty white or yellowish.
  Margin of apothecia reflexed .... *.varia symmicta.*
  Margin of apothecia not reflexed.
    Thallus of rounded, turgid warts.......... *frustulosa.*
    Thallus contiguous, chinky.
      Apothecia rather small, margin entire. ...*subfusca.*
      Apothecia medium size, margin flexuose and crenate ...., *subfusca allophana.*
Spores very large.
  Thallus chinky or plicate........... ....*pallescens.*
  Thallus not chinky, either tartareous, granulate, or nodulose.
    Lobes of the thallus short............................... *tartarea.*
    Lobes of the thallus elongated.
      Thallus finely divided......................*tartarea frigida.*
      Thallus coarsely divided.... .... *tartarea pterulina.*

94. Lecanora privigna revertens Tuck.

Lecanora privigna revertens TUCKERMAN, Syn. N. A. L. 1 : 204. 1882.

Kadiak (Trelease, 900 in part). New to Alaska.

With *Buellia geographica, Lecanora varia intricata,* and *Pertusaria communis.* This variety has been collected in California by Bolander.

95. Lecanora cinerea (L.) Smrft.

Lichen cinereus LINNÆUS, Mant. 132 1767
Lecanora cinerea SOMMERFELDT, Suppl. Lapp. 99. 1826.—SOWERBY, Eng Bot. *t. 1751.*

Summit of White Pass, 3000 ft (Trelease, 951 in part); Kadiak (Trelease, 945); Port Clarence (Trelease, 941). All on rock. Collected by Dr. Bean at Port Clarence, Icy Cape, and Cape Lisburne.

The specimen from White Pass, which is mixed with *Buellia geographica,* differs from the more common form, in that the thallus is not continuous, but broken into areoles. The specimen from Port Clarence has the apothecia urceolate, and sometimes white pruinose. Interspersed in the thallus are reddish-gray, granulose warts. This is a very variable and widely distributed species, which has been classified under several generic names. Common in Greenland and in alpine and arctic regions.

96. **Lecanora cinerea gibbosa** (Ach.) Tuck.

Urceolaria gibbosa ACHARIUS, Meth. Lich. 144. 1803.
Lecanora cinerea gibbosa NYLANDER, Lich Scand 154 1861.—TUCKERMAN, Syn. N. A. L. 1 : 198. 1882.

Summit of White Pass, 3000 ft. (Trelease, 888, 851 in part); Kadiak (Trelease, 894, 895); Muir Glacier, Glacier Bay (Trelease, 887); Cape Nome (Setchell). *Buellia geographica* and its variety *atrovirens* are with the specimens from White Pass. Rothrock lists this variety as collected by Dr. Bean, but gives no locality. Nylander records its occurrence at Konyam Bay, on the Siberian coast of Bering Strait.

97. **Lecanora occulata** (Diks.) Ach.

Lichen occulatus DIXSON, Pl Cr. Br 2 : 17. *t. 5 f 5* 1785-1801
Lecanora occulata ACHARIUS, Syn 148 1814.—SOWERBY, Eng. Bot. *t. 1833*.

Kadiak (Trelease, 1217); Unalaska (Setchell); Cape Nome (Setchell); Hall Island (Trelease, 1204); St. Matthew Island (Trelease, 1020). Growing over mosses and other lichens. Reported by Macoun from St. Paul Island; by Tuckerman as collected by Wright on the islands of Bering Strait; and by Nylander, under the synonym *Pertusaria occulata*, from St. Lawrence Island.

A widely distributed northern lichen.

98. **Lecanora tartarea** (L.) Ach.

Lichen tartareus LINNÆUS, Sp Pl. 2 : 1141 1753.
Lecanora tartarea ACHARIUS, L. U. 371. 1810 —SOWERBY, Eng Bot *t. 156*.

Alaska (Dr. Kellogg, no number); summit of White Pass, 3000 ft. (Trelease, 1137); Unalaska (Trelease, 975; Setchell); Hall Island (Trelease, 862); St. Matthew Island (Trelease, 867, 868, 972); St. Lawrence Island (Trelease, 1019); Cape Nome (Setchell). Most of the specimens are sterile. Macoun reports it as "common and variable" on St. George and St. Paul Islands. Rothrock adds Cape Lisburne, Unalaska, and the Shumagin group of islands as localities where it was collected by Dr. Bean.

The species, with its varieties, is one of the most abundant of the northern lichens, and was formerly of considerable commercial value in the coloration of fabrics and the manufacture of litmus.

99. **Lecanora tartarea frigida** (L. fil.) Sw.

Lichen frigidus LINNÆUS FIL. in SWARTZ, Meth Musc. 1781.
Lecanora tartarea frigida SWARTZ, Meth Musc *t. 1 f. 4* 1781 —SOWERBY, Eng. Bot *t 1879*.

Kadiak (Trelease, 871); Hall Island (Coville and Kearney, 2066); St. Lawrence Island (Trelease, 1018). The specimen from St Lawrence Island is well fruited, the others are sterile. The variety has been reported from St Paul Island by Macoun and from Port Clarence by Nylander; and under the synonym *Parmelia tartarea frigida* it is recorded by Babington as collected at Kotzebue Sound.

100. **Lecanora tartarea pterulina** Nyl

Lecanora tartarea pterulina NYLANDER, Lich. Fr. Behr 44. 1888

Kadiak (Trelease, 870); Hall Island (Trelease, 869. 1017; Coville and Kearney, 2064); St. Matthew Island (Brewer and Coe, 678).

The specimens are very fine. The one from Kadiak was growing on dead herbaceous spermatophytes. The material examined by Nylander was collected on St. Lawrence Island. Dr Lindsay, in his Observations upon West Greenland Lichens, gives an interesting account of the variation of *L. tartarea* as exhibited by the Greenland specimens.

101. **Lecanora pallescens** (L.) Schaer.

Lichen pallescens LINNÆUS, Sp Pl. 2: 1142. 1753.
Lecanora pallescens SCHAERER, Enum. 78. 1850.—HOFFM Plant. Lich. *t. 21. f. 2 a, b*

Broughton Strait, Vancouver Island (Trelease, 851). On dead wood. The other Alaskan records are Sheep Creek (Dr. Cooley); Chugachik Bay, Cook Inlet (Rothrock); and Port Clarence (Nylander).

102. **Lecanora varia** (Ehrh.) Ach.

Lichen varius EHRHART, Plant Crypt. Dec 7: n 68. 1785.
Lecanora varia ACHARIUS, L. U. 377. 1810.—SOWERBY, Eng Bot. *t. 1666.*

Chichagof Bay (Palache, 925); Sitka (Trelease, 810, 822a), Kadiak (Trelease, 899 in part); Port Clarence (Trelease, 890 in part, 939 in part), Whale Island, St. Michael (Setchell). Specimens are on bark of *Alnus oregona*, on dead wood and on rock. Mixed with this species are *Buellia geographica*, *B. myriocarpa*, *Lecanora atrosulphurea*, and *Parmelia saxatilis omphalodes*. New to Alaska.

Though new to Alaska, it has been reported by Rothrock from Plover Bay, Siberia, collected by Dr. Bean.

103. **Lecanora varia intricata** (Ach.) Nyl.

Lecanora intricata ACHARIUS, L. U. 380. 1810
Lecanora varia intricata NYLANDER, Lich. Scand 164. 1861

Kadiak (Trelease, 900 in part), Port Clarence (Trelease, 939 in part, 940). Mixed with *Buellia geographica*, *B. myriocarpa*, *Lecanora varia* and *L. privigna revertens*, *Pertusaria communis*, and *Parmelia saxatilis omphalodes*. New to Alaska. Reported from Konyam Bay by Nylander.

An alpine and arctic species.

104. Lecanora varia symmicta Ach.

Lecanora varia symmicta ACHARIUS, L U 379 1810.

St. Lawrence Island (Trelease, 1156 in part). On dead wood, with *Parmelia saxatilis omphalodes*. New to Alaska.

Lecanora varia, with its varieties, is a widely distributed species, and it is therefore rather surprising that three new Alaskan records should be made for this species and its varieties in this collection.

105. Lecanora atrosulphurea (Wahl.) Ach.

Lichen atrosulphureus WAHLENBERG, Fl Lapp 471 1812
Lecanora atrosulphurea ACHARIUS, Syn 149 1814

Kadiak (Trelease, 891a, 896, 897, 898, 899 in part); Plover Bay, Siberia (Trelease, 994). The specimens are all on rock. Those from Kadiak are mixed with various species of *Lecanora*, *Pertusaria*, *Buellia*, and *Lecidea*. Nylander records it as occurring on St. Lawrence Island. It has been collected in Arctic America and Greenland.

106. Lecanora pacifica Tuck.

Lecanora pacifica TUCKERMAN, Syn N A L 1 191 1882

Port Wells (Trelease, 828). On bark. New to Alaska.
It has been reported from Oregon and California.

107. Lecanora atra (Huds) Ach.

Lichen ater HUDSON, Fl Angl. ed. 2 530 1798
Lecanora atra ACHARIUS, Syn 146 a 1814 —SOWERBY, Eng Bot *t 949*

Alaska (Funston, 25a); Port Wells (Trelease, 935a). The specimen from Port Wells is too old for satisfactory determination, but seems better placed here than elsewhere. Rothrock's locality is Cape Lisburne In Nylander's list it is given as occurring at Konyam Bay and Bering Island on the Siberian side of Bering Strait.

108. Lecanora hageni Ach.

Lecanora hageni ACHARIUS, L U. 367 1810 —HAG Hist Lich. 1. *f 5*.

Muir Glacier (Trelease, 933). On rock. The species has been reported from Port Clarence in Nylander's list, and from Cape Lisburne by Rothrock. It is found also in Greenland, the Rocky Mts., and California

109. Lecanora subfusca (L) Ach.

Lichen subfuscus LINNÆUS, Spec Pl ed 2 2 1609 1764
Lecanora subfusca ACHARIUS, L U 393 1810.—SOWERBY, Eng Bot *t. 930, 2109*

Yakutat (Trelease, 817, 844 in part, 928), Kukak Bay (Kincaid, 836a in part). On bark and rock. No. 844 is with *Buellia para-*

sema, and 836*a* with *Buellia parasema*, *Placodium cerinum*, etc. The localities that Rothrock gives are Cook Inlet, Unalaska, and Port Clarence. Nylander reports its occurrence on Bering Island, on the Asiatic side of Bering Strait.

110. **Lecanora subfusca allophana Ach.**
Lecanora subfusca allophana ACHARIUS, L U 395 1810

Mouth of Sturgeon River, Kadiak Island (Trelease, 857 in part); St. Lawrence Island (Trelease, 854); Cape Fox (Trelease, 855); St. Michael (Setchell). New to Alaska

All except the specimen from St Michael growing on dead wood, and all well fruited. *Theloschistes lychneus pygmaeus* is with No. 857. Reported from Greenland, and common throughout the United States

111. **Lecanora subfusca argentata Ach.**
Lecanora subfusca argentata ACHARIUS, L U 393 1810

Cape Fox (Trelease, 856). On dead wood. New to Alaska. The most northern record for this variety.

112. **Lecanora subfusca coilocarpa Ach**
Lecanora subfusca coilocarpa ACHARIUS, L U 393 1810

Muir Glacier, Glacier Bay (Trelease, 814, on *Salix*); Virgin Bay, Prince William Sound (Trelease, 978, on rock with *Placodium murorum*). New to Alaska

I find no record for Greenland, but reference is made to it in Dr. Arnold's list of Newfoundland lichens.

113. **Lecanora frustulosa (Diks) Ach.**
Lichen frustulosus DIKSON, Crypt. Brit 3 13 *t.* 8 *f.* 1 1785–1801
Lecanora frustulosa ACHARIUS, L U 405. 1810 —SOWERBY, Eng. Bot *t.* 2273

Kadiak (Trelease, 911, 943); St. Michael (Setchell). No spores are developed, and therefore the determination is not absolutely certain. It compares well with authentic specimens in the Tuckerman Herbarium. It has been found in Greenland. A specimen collected by Dr. Hayes at Taku seems to belong here.

114. **Lecanora pallida (Schreb.) Schaer.**
Lichen pallidus SCHREBER, Spicil 155 1771
Lecanora pallida SCHAERER, Enum 78 1850 —SOWERBY, Eng. Bot. *t. 2154*

Orca (Trelease, 808) On bark. New to Alaska, though reported from Arctic America by Richardson.

115. **Lecanora straminea** (Wahl.) Ach.
Parmelia straminea WAHLENBERG in Ach Meth Suppl 47 1803
Lecanora straminea ACHARIUS, L U. 432. 1810 —WAHL Fl Lapp. *t. 28. f. 1* 1812.

Kadiak (Trelease, 902 in part), Unalaska (Setchell), St. Paul Island (Trelease, 883, 888, 1136); St. Matthew Island (Trelease, 881) The specimen from Kadiak is mixed with *Buellia geographica, Lecidea platycarpa*, and *Parmelia stygia.* Nylander reports it from St. Lawrence Island.

116. **Lecanora muralis** (Schreb) Tuck.
Lichen muralis SCHREBER, Spicil 130. 1771.
Lecanora muralis TUCKERMAN, Syn N A. L. 1: 184. 1882 —HOFFM. Enum. 64 *t 9 f 1*

Alaska (Funston, 20). Rothrock reports that it is " apparently very common in Alaska," and gives the following definite localities where Dr. Bean collected specimens: cliffs on St. Matthew Island, St. Paul Island; Sitka; and Unalaska.

117. **Lecanora rubina** (Vill.) Ach.
Lichen rubinus VILLARS, Dauph 3: 977. 1789
Lecanora rubina ACHARIUS, L U. 412. 1810 —HOFFM Pl Lich. *t 32. f. 1.*

Alaska (Trelease, 1140 in part; Funston, 25); Hot Springs, Baranof Island (Trelease, 961); St. Paul Island (Trelease, 882, 884); Cape Fox (Trelease, 1142) No. 1140 is mixed with fragments of *Physcia cæsia* and *Theloschistes lychneus.* New to Alaska.

Reported from Arctic America by Richardson, and from Greenland.

118. **Lecanora rubina opaca** (Ach) Tuck.
Lecanora chrysoleuca β *opaca* ACHARIUS, L U 411 1810
Lecanora rubina opaca TUCKERMAN, Syn. N. A. L 1: 183. 1882.

St Matthew Island (Trelease, 926); Bering Island; Plover Bay, Siberia (Trelease, 994 in part). New to Alaska.

Both specimens are on rock. The one from Bering Island is mixed with *Theloschistes lychneus pygmæus.* This variety has been collected in the Rocky Mts and in California.

119. **Lecanora gelida** (L.) Ach.
Lichen gelidus LINNÆUS, Succ. Prod. 74
Lecanora gelida ACHARIUS, L U 428 1810.

Muir Glacier (Trelease, 986, 987, 987a, 987b, 987c, 987d, 987e, 989); Hidden Glacier Inlet, Yakutat Bay (Trelease, 924); Port Wells (Trelease, 979), Port Clarence (Trelease, no number), Cape

Fox (Trelease, 997, 998). This species has been reported from Greenland and British Columbia. In Alaska it has been discovered on Chernofski Island, Unalaska, and Belkofski, Alaska Peninsula, by Dr Bean.

ADDITIONAL SPECIES.

The following species were collected by Dr Almquist and determined by Nylander : *Lecanora fuscolutea* (Diks.) Nyl., *L. cæsiorufa* (Ach) Nyl., on earth and moss only; *L. contractula* Nyl., *L. subradiosa* Nyl., *L. atrynea* Ach., *L. atrynea* forma *cenisia* Ach., *L. epiglypta* Norl., *L. subradians* Nyl., *L. lacustris* (With.) Nyl., *L. fuscata* (Schrad.) Nyl., on rock only; *L. lobulata* (Sommerf.) Nyl. and *L. crenata* Nyl., on earth and on rock, all collected on St. Lawrence Island. The following species were collected by Dr. Almquist at Port Clarence *L. tetraspora* Nyl., *L. stillicidiorum* forma *chloroleuca* (Sommerf.) Nyl., *L. cæsiorufella* Nyl., *L. pyracea ramulicola* Nyl., *L. mniarœa* Ach., *L. mniarœa pachnea* Ach., *L. hypnorum deaurata* (Ach.) Nyl., *L. epibrya* Ach., *L. chlarona* Ach., *L. subintricata* Nyl., *L. upsaliensis* (L.) Nyl., *L. inæquatula* Nyl., *L. gyalectina* Nyl., all growing on the earth or upon moss (*L. tartarea upsaliensis* is reported from Kotzebue Sound by Hooker and Arnott) ; *L. pyracea* (Ach.) Nyl., *L. irrubata* (Ach.) Nyl., *L. disceptans* Nyl., *L. umbrina* (Ehrnb.) Nyl., *L. ochromicra* Nyl., *L. quadruplans* Nyl., *L. suaveolens* (Ach.) Nyl., *L. lævata* var. *candida* Anzi, *L. belonioides* Nyl., all rock forms. *L. stillicidiorum* (Oed.) Nyl. was found growing upon earth and moss, both at St. Lawrence Island and at Port Clarence *L. smaragdula* (Whlnb.) Nyl. was found growing upon rock on St. Lawrence Island. Nylander, in his correction of Rothrock's list, states that *L. cervina* should be called *L. smaragdula*. *L. ventosa* (L.) Ach. was collected by Wright on the islands of Bering Strait, by Macoun on rocks on St. George Island, and reported by Hooker and Arnott for Kotzebue Sound. In Rothrock's list, based upon Dr. Bean's collection, the following additional species are found : *L. glaucomela* Tuck., no definite locality given, *L. subfusca hypnorum* Schaer., Port Clarence and Cape Lisburne—also collected by Wright on the islands of Bering Strait; *L. cervina* (Pers.) Nyl., Eschscholtz Bay, Arctic Ocean ; *L. cervina discreta* Sommerf., Port Clarence; and *L. verrucosa* (Ach.) Laur., Eschscholtz Bay, Arctic Ocean. Dr Cooley has collected two additional species : *L. elatina ochrophœa* Tuck., at Sheep Creek, near Juneau, and *L. pallescens rosella* Tuck., in the same locality. Mr. William Palmer collected *L. thamnitis* Tuck. on St. Paul Island. Mr. J. M. Macoun has made the following addition. *L. occulata gonatodes* Ach., on rock on St. Paul Island. Of another plant he notes: "*Lecanora saxicola* Schaer. —Specimens which may prove to represent a new species have been provisionally referred here by Mr. Branth."

PLACODIUM.

KEY TO THE SPECIES

Thallus well developed, typically lobed at the circumference.
    Thallus orange-colored.. .... *elegans*.
    Thallus bright yellow................................... ....*murorum*.
Thallus poorly, or not at all, developed, not lobed at the circumference.
    Spores simply bilocular.
        Thallus orbicular, crenate-granulose....... . ...*crenulatum*.
        Thallus effuse, granules usually crowded into heaps, sometimes scattered. . ... *vitellinum*.
    Spores polar-bilocular.
        Growing over mosses.. .... *jungermanniæ*.
        Growing on wood or stone.
            Thallus very uneven, warted...................... *aurantiacum*.
            Thallus comparatively smooth.
                Hypothallus bluish-black.. . ...*cerinum*.
                Hypothallus obsolete.
                      Apothecia orange-colored beneath and on the margin.
                                                        cerinum.
                      Apothecia greenish beneath and on the margin.
                                                      fuscoatra.

120. **Placodium vitellinum (Ehrh.) Naeg. & Hepp.**
Lichen vitellinus EHRHART, Crypt. n. 155. 1785.
Placodium vitellinum NAEGELI & HEPP, Sporen der Flecht. Eur. n. 70. 1853.
— SOWERBY, Eng. Bot. t. *1792*.

Hot Springs, Baranof Island (Trelease, 963 in part). On rocks with *Lecidea enteroleuca* and *Parmelia saxatilis*. Wright collected this species at Bering Strait, while Rothrock reports it from Port Clarence. Under the synonym *Lecanora vitellina* Ach., Nylander reports its occurrence on St. Lawrence Island.

It is a widely distributed species and closely related to the following, which may, perhaps, be considered as developed from it.

121. **Placodium crenulatum (Wahl.) Tuck.**
Lichen murorum γ *crenulatus* WAHLENBERG, Lapp. 416. 1812.
Placodium crenulatum TUCKERMAN, Syn. N. A. L. 1: 180. 1882.

Hot Springs, Baranof Island (Trelease, 984); Plover Bay, Siberia (Trelease, 995, 996). On stones. In Rothrock's list this is reported from Plover Bay, Siberia, and Sitka, which is on Baranof Island. Thus the localities are practically identical. Nylander, in Lich. Fr. Behr., records it from Konyam Bay and Bering Island, Siberia

Several specimens show new thalli forming on the decaying remnants of old thalli.

122. Placodium fuscoatrum (Bayrh.).
Lecanora fuscoatra BAYRHOFFER, Zw. Exs. 96.

Kadiak (Trelease, 949). On rock. New to Alaska and to America.

123. Placodium ferrugineum (Huds.) Hepp.
Lichen ferrugineus HUDSON, Fl. Ang. ed 2 526 1778
Placodium ferrugineum HEPP, Sporen der Flechten Europas 1853 —
  SOWLRBY, Eng Bot *t. 1650*

Alaska (Dr. Kellogg, no number); Sitka (Trelease, 825c); Yakutat (Trelease, 831); Farragut Bay (Trelease, 829); St Lawrence Island (Trelease, 832 in part). A lichen of wide distribution; reported by Tuckerman as having been collected in Alaska by Dr. Kellogg. Rothrock reports its occurrence at Port Clarence, as determined from the collection of Dr. Bean, Nylander states in his correction of Rothrock's list that this specimen should be named *Lecanora caesiorufa* (Ach.).

On bark and dead wood. The specimen from St. Lawrence Island is on bark, with *Lecidea melancheima*. The specimen from Sitka is very small and is associated with *Lecidea enteroleuca*.

124. Placodium jungermanniæ (Vahl) Tuck.
Lichen jungermanniæ VAHL, Nat Selsk Sk 2. 29
Placodium jungermanniæ TUCKERMAN, Syn N. A. L. 1: 176 1882

Unalaska (Setchell); St. Matthew Island (Trelease, 866 in part); St. Michael (Setchell). Collected on the islands of Bering Strait by Wright, Nylander reports it from St. Lawrence Bay, Konyam Bay, and Bering Island, all on the Asiatic side of Bering Strait.

The St. Matthew specimen was growing on moss, with *Rinodina turfacea* and the sterile thallus of a *Pertusaria*, the St. Michael specimen was on moss, with *Rinodina turfacea* and *Biatora hypnophila*.

125. Placodium cerinum (Ehrh.) Naeg. & Hepp.
Lichen cerinus EHRHART, Plant Crypt. n 216 1785
Placodium cerinum NAEGELI & HEPP, Sporen der Flechten Europas 1853 —
  SOWERBY, Eng. Bot *t. 627*.—HEDW Stirp. Crypt. 2 62 *t. 21. f B*

Kukak Bay (Kincaid, 836a in part); Kadiak (Trelease, 1134). The locality given for this in Dr. Rothrock's list is Icy Cape, Arctic

Ocean. Tuckerman records it as having been collected in Arctic America (on mosses) by Wright. Th. Fries, in Lichenes Arctoi, states that it is common in Scandinavia, Spitzbergen, and Greenland.

The specimen from Kukak Bay is on bark, with *Buellia parasema* and a *Physcia*. The specimen from Kadiak has immature spores and is doubtfully referred here. On the same piece of wood are three different species of *Cetraria* and three of *Parmelia*.

126. **Placodium aurantiacum** (Lightf.) Naeg. & Hepp.

Lichen aurantiacus LIGHTFOOT, Fl. Scot. 2. 810. 1777.
Placodium aurantiacum NAEGELI & HEPP, Sporen der Flechten Europas 1853.

St. Lawrence Island (Trelease, 853). On dead wood. New to Alaska.

This species was collected in Arctic America by Richardson.

127. **Placodium murorum** (Hoffm.) DC.

Lichen murorum HOFFMANN, Enum. 63 *t 9 f 2*. 1784.
Placodium murorum DE CANDOLLE, Fl. Fr. 2. 378. 1805.

Virgin Bay, Prince William Sound (Trelease, 978 in part); Kadiak (Trelease, 982, on slate rock). New to Alaska. Collected by Richardson in Arctic America.

With no. 978 is a specimen of *Lecanora subfusca coilocarpa*.

128. **Placodium elegans** (Link) DC.

Lichen elegans LINK, Ann. 1. 37. 1791.
Placodium elegans DE CANDOLLE, Fl. Fr. 2. 379 n. 1026. 1805.—SOWERBY, Eng. Bot. *t 2181*.

Alaska (Funston, 24); White Pass, 900 ft. (Trelease, 980); Vancouver Island, Broughton Strait (Trelease, 985 in part), Unalaska (Setchell); St. Michael (Setchell). Collected by Wright on the islands of Bering Strait, by Dr. Bean on Chamisso Island, at Elephant Point, in Eschscholtz Bay, and on Chernofski Island, and by Macoun on St. Paul Island. This lichen has been reported from various points in Arctic America, and it seems to be common through all the mountainous and northern regions of America, from the Atlantic to the Pacific.

No. 985 has with it a lichen which is apparently a sterile *Lecidea*.

129. **Placodium coralloides?** Tuck.

Placodium coralloides TUCKERMAN, Syn. N. A. L. 1: 169. 1882.

St. Paul Island (Trelease, 1000). On the earth.

A very interesting specimen which may possibly be referred here. Unfortunately it is not fruited, and therefore its classification is uncertain. It differs from *P. coralloides* in its stouter branches and lighter color. The thallus is sorediate, with a dull surface, while *P. coralloides* is not sorediate and has a shining surface.

Additional Alaskan species of the genus are: *Placodium variabile* (Pers.) Nyl., collected at Port Clarence by Dr. Bean, and *P. nivale* (Koerb.) Tuck., collected by Dr. Bean, but no definite locality given. According to Tuckerman, *P. sinapispermum* (Auct.) Hepp was collected by Wright on the islands of Bering Strait. Nylander, in his revision of Rothrock's list, records *P. granulosum* Muell., named by Rothrock, as growing on rock on St. Matthew Island, and also states that *P. murorum miniatum* Tuck., of Rothrock's list, should be named *P. elegans tenue* (Wahlb.).

Family COLLEMACEÆ.
LEPTOGIUM.

KEY TO THE SPECIES.

Thallus fringed with white cilia .... *albociliatum*.
Thallus not fringed with white cilia
    Thallus granulate above .... *myochroum*.
    Thallus not granulate above . .   *myochroum saturninum*.

130. Leptogium myochroum (Ehrh.) Tuck.

Lichen myochrous EHRHART, Plant Crypt. n. 286. 1785 — SCHAERER, Spicil. 534. 1771. — SOWERBY, Eng. Bot. *t. 1980.*
Leptogium myochroum TUCKERMAN, Genera 99. 1872.

Disenchantment Bay (Trelease, 1098*b*). A small, sterile fragment, perhaps best placed here.

131. Leptogium myochroum saturninum (Schaer.) Tuck.

Leptogium saturninum SCHAERER, Spicil. 534. 1840.
Leptogium myochroum saturninum TUCKERMAN, Syn. N. A. L. 1 · 166. 1882.

Muir Glacier (Trelease, 1131); Disenchantment Bay (Trelease, 1095, 1097*a*). New to Alaska.
Rhizoids on the under surface poorly developed.

132. Leptogium albociliatum Desmaz.

Leptogium albociliatum DESMAZIÈRES, Ann. Sci. Nat. IV. 4. 132. 1855.

Port Wells, Prince William Sound (Trelease, 1161). It is recorded by Tuckerman for California and Oregon. New to Alaska. On rocks near tide.

This is represented only by a very small specimen on which the cilia are not abundant.

The following additional species of the genus *Leptogium* have been reported from Alaska: *L. muscicolum* (Sw.) Fr., *L. tenuissimum* (Diks.) Koerb, *L. myochroum tomentosum* Tuck., collected by Wright on the islands in Bering Strait; *L. tremelloides* (L. fil.) Fr., collected by Dr. Cooley at Salmon Creek, near Juneau; *L. scotinum* Ach. and *L. parculum* Nyl., reported from Port Clarence by Nylander.

COLLEMA.

This genus is represented by two specimens, both of which are sterile. One was collected by Frederick Funston under NO. 21, locality not given. The other was collected by Trelease. The latter specimen is numbered 1160, but bears no other data. It may possibly be referred to *C. pulposum*. No. 21 is so fragmentary and incomplete that no determination can be made.

Species of *Collema* recorded for Alaska: *C. melænum polycarpum* Schaer., collected by Wright on the islands of Bering Strait, *C. melænum* Ach., *C. triptodes* Nyl., *C. tenax* Ach., *C. furvum subhirsutulum* Nyl., reported from Port Clarence by Nylander; and *C. pulposum* (Bernh.) Ach., collected by Dr. Bean at Cape Lisburne. Nylander records *Collemopsis flotoviana* (Hepp) as having been collected at Port Clarence.

EPHEBE.

133. Ephebe pubescens Fr.

Ephebe pubescens FRIES, S. O. V. 356. 1825. —NYL. Syn. I : *t 2 1* and 17-20 1860

Mountain west of Muir Glacier (Trelease, 974). Sterile. New to Alaska. It has been reported from Greenland, but I find no record of it for Newfoundland or Labrador.

Family PANNARIACEÆ.

PANNARIA.

KEY TO THE SPECIES.

Thallus white, powdery..*lanuginosa*.
Thallus brown or blackening.
    Thallus of rounded branchlets.................*lepidiota coralliphora*.
    Thallus squamulose.
        Thallus yellowish and reddish-brown, apothecia sessile, with a broad, thin, light-colored margin..................*hypnorum*.
        Thallus darker, apothecia appressed or immersed, margin not so conspicuous and of nearly the same color as the disk *brunnea*.

134. **Pannaria lepidiota coralliphora** Tuck.
Pannaria lepidiota coralliphora TUCKERMAN, Syn. N. A. L. 1 : 122. 1882.

Hot Springs (Trelease, 962). New to Alaska.

A small specimen on rock. This variety was described from material collected at Vancouver Island by Professor John Macoun. I have carefully compared this with the type specimen in the Tuckerman Herbarium. The apothecia are not quite so convex as in the type where the margin is excluded. The thallus of the type specimen is nearly black, while this is a dark gray. No other localities are recorded for the variety.

135. **Pannaria brunnea** (Sw.) Mass.
Lichen brunneus SWARTZ in Act. Upsal. 4 : 247. 1784.
Pannaria brunnea MASSALONGO, Ric. 115. 1852.—SOWERBY, Eng. Bot. *t. 1246*

Alaska (Evans, 272); Hot Springs, Baranof Island (Trelease, 858, 874); Hidden Glacier Inlet, Yakutat Bay (Trelease, 861); Unalaska (Setchell), Hall Island (Trelease, 878a). Collected by Wright on the island in Cross Sound and on Chernofski Island, and by Macoun on earth and rock on St. George Island.

A common alpine and arctic lichen.

136. **Pannaria hypnorum** (Vahl) Koerb.
Lichen hypnorum VAHL, Fl. Dan. 6 : *t. 956.* 1787.
Pannaria hypnorum KOERBER, Syst. Lich. Germ. 108. 1855.—SOWERBY, Eng. Bot. *t. 740.*

Hidden Glacier, Russell Fiord (Coville and Kearney, 965); Disenchantment Bay (Trelease, 860, 879, 879a, 970); Egg Island, Disenchantment Bay (Coville and Kearney, 1018), Muir Glacier (Trelease, 876, 877, 877a); Hidden Glacier Inlet, Yakutat Bay (Trelease, 859); Orca (Trelease, 873); Port Wells (Trelease, 872); Unalaska (Setchell); Hall Island (Trelease, 878a), Plover Bay, Siberia (Trelease, 875); St. Michael (Setchell). This is a very common and widely distributed alpine and arctic lichen, although the only other Alaskan record is Unalaska, where it was collected by Dr. Bean.

The specimens are usually well fruited, the apothecia varying greatly in size and in the indentation of the margin, which is sometimes nearly entire.

137. **Pannaria lanuginosa** (Ach.) Koerb.
Parmelia lanuginosa ACHARIUS, Meth. Lich. 207. 1803.
Pannaria lanuginosa KOERBER, Syst. Lich. Germ. 106. 1855.—HOFFM. Enum Lich *t. 10 f. 9.* 1784.

White Pass, 1925 ft. (Trelease, 971). Sterile. New to Alaska.

I find no record of this for Newfoundland, Labrador, or Greenland. Th. Fries, in his Lichenes Arctoi, 79, records its occurrence in Finland, and expresses his conviction that it is found in many other northern localities.

Nylander credits *Pannaria nigra* (Huds.) Nyl. to Port Clarence under the synonym *Pannularia nigra* (Huds.).

Family PELTIGERIACEÆ.
SOLORINA.

KEY TO THE SPECIES.

Thallus orange-saffron-colored beneath.................................*crocea*.
Thallus white beneath..*saccata spongiosa*.

138. Solorina saccata spongiosa (Sm.) Nyl.

Solorina spongiosa SMITH in Sowerby, Eng Bot *t 1374*.
Solorina saccata spongiosa NYLANDER, Syn 331 1860

Disenchantment Bay (Trelease, 880). One fragmentary specimen. This is a common alpine and arctic lichen. Collected at Bering Strait by Wright and reported from Port Clarence by Nylander, both much more northern localities than the present record.

139. Solorina crocea (L.) Ach.

Lichen croceus LINNÆUS, Fl. Suec. ed. 2 1101 1755
Solorina crocea ACHARIUS, L. U. 149. 1810.—SOWERBY, Eng Bot *t 498*.—
HOFFM Pl Lich *t. 41. f. 2–4.*

Disenchantment Bay (Burroughs, 1106); Point Gustavus (Coville and Kearney); Orca (Trelease, 1104); Pinnacle Rock, Chichagof Bay, 2700 feet (Palache, 1082); St Matthew Island (Trelease, 1078, 1083).

A common alpine and arctic lichen. Collected on St. Paul Island by Macoun and on the shores of Bering Strait by Wright.

According to Tuckerman, *Solorina saccata* (L.) Ach. was collected by Wright on the islands of Bering Strait.

PELTIGERA.

KEY TO THE SPECIES.

Thallus small, veins underneath black...........................*venosa*.
Thallus medium-sized to large.
  Upper surface of thallus besprinkled with brown warts......*apthosa*.
  Upper surface of thallus without warts.
    Surface of the thallus smooth.
      Thallus small, cream-colored underneath.........*canina spuria*.
      Thallus of medium size or large.

Thallus very thin, covered beneath with a network of cream-colored veins... . . . *canina membranacea.*
Thallus thicker, veins dark-colored.
    Apothecia transversely oblong, veins blackening
                                                        horizontalis.
    Apothecia elongated, revolute, veins brown *polydactyla.*
Surface of the thallus downy or granulate.
    Thallus granulate............ . . . . . *pulverulenta.*
Thallus downy.
    Thallus reddish-brown, crisped on the edges...... *rufescens.*
    Thallus greenish-gray or ash-brown, not crisped on the margins.
        Thallus with distinct veins underneath...................*canina.*
        Thallus covered with a spongy nap underneath.
                                                canina spongiosa

140. **Peltigera canina** (L) Hoffm.

Lichen caninus LINNÆUS, Fl. Suec. 1100. 1755.
Peltigera canina HOFFMANN, Fl. Germ 2: 106 1795.—SOWERBY, Eng Bot. t *1119.*

    Locality not given (Coville and Kearney, 576); Lowe Inlet, B. C. (Trelease, 1089), Vancouver Island, Broughton Strait (Trelease, 1084); Yakutat (Trelease, 1065, 1065*a*); Aguadulce River, Yakutat Bay (Trelease, 1064); Hidden Glacier Inlet, Yakutat Bay (Trelease, 1063, 1093*b*); Disenchantment Bay, Yakutat Bay (Trelease, 1091, 1096, 1097, 1098); Juneau (Setchell, 1243, 1249); Muir Glacier (Trelease, 1054, 1100*z*); Farragut Bay (Trelease, no number); Orca (Trelease, 1061), Port Wells (Trelease, 1056*c*), Kadiak (Trelease, 1055, 1075), Agattu Island (Townsend, 76), Cape Fox (Trelease, 1070, 1085). Other Alaskan records are: Sitka, Port Mulgrave, Unalaska, Port Chatham in Cook Inlet, Dr Bean, collector; St. Paul Island and St George Island, collected by Macoun. Dr. Cooley collected specimens at Salmon Creek, near Juneau, which are doubtfully referred to this species. Under the synonym *Peltidea canina* Ach., Babington reports its occurrence at Kotzebue Sound.

    With these specimens were fragments of *Leptogium, Nephroma,* and other species of *Peltigera.* A number of the specimens are sterile.

141. **Peltigera canina spongiosa** Tuck.

Peltigera canina spongiosa TUCKERMAN, Genera Lichenum 38. 1872.

    Alaska (Funston, 12); St Paul Island (Trelease, 1086). Collected by Macoun on St. Paul and St. George Islands.

142. **Peltigera canina membranacea** (Ach.) Nyl.

Peltidea canina membranacea ACHARIUS, L U 518. 1810
Peltigera canina membranacea NYLANDER, Syn. 324 1860

Alaska (Evans, 184); head of Russell Fiord (Trelease, 959); Sitka (Trelease, 1042; Setchell, 1272); Hot Springs, Baranof Island (Trelease, 1039a), Vancouver Island, Broughton Strait (Trelease, 1033, 1058, 1084); Point Gustavus, Glacier Bay (Coville and Kearney, 778); Farragut Bay (Coville and Kearney, 474a); Unalaska (Trelease, 1043); St. Paul Island (Trelease, 1044); St. Michael (Setchell); Pastoliak River (Newhall)

The specimens from Sitka are especially large and well developed. Most of the specimens are fertile. This is a common form on the northwest coast of America.

143 **Peltigera canina spuria** (Ach.) Nyl.

Peltidea canina spuria ACHARIUS, L. U. 518. 1810.—SOWERBY, Eng. Bot t 1542
Peltigera spuria NYLANDER, Syn. 325 1860.

Lowe Inlet, B. C. (Trelease, 1059a); Yakutat (Trelease, 1065b). Collected on St. Paul Island by Macoun

Both specimens well developed and fertile.

144. **Peltigera rufescens** (Neck.) Hoffm.

Lichen rufescens NECKER, Meth Musc. 79 1771
Peltigera rufescens HOFFMANN, Fl Germ. 2 107 1795 —SOWERBY, Eng Bot t 2300.

Wrangell (Trelease, 1101b, 1127); Juneau (Setchell, 1246); Muir Glacier (Trelease, 1102a, 1102b); Cape Fox (Trelease, 1070a); St. Michael (Setchell). New to Alaska Nylander reports it from Konyam Bay on the Asiatic side of Bering Strait.

145. **Peltigera pulverulenta** (Tayl.) Nyl.

Peltidea pulverulenta TAYLOR in Hook Lond Journ Bot 6 184 1847.
Peltigera pulverulenta NYLANDER, Syn 325 1860

Alaska (Evans, no number); Disenchantment Bay (Trelease, 1096b); Port Wells (Trelease, 1056, 1056b); Hall Island (Trelease, 1067); Cape Nome (Setchell). New record for Alaska

Tuckerman, in his Syn. N A. L., 108, records it as being in Herb. Babington, from Kotzebue Sound. In Babington's list of the Flora of Western Eskimaux Land no mention is made of this species, although four other species of *Peltigera* are recorded from Kotzebue Sound. The specimens vary greatly in the amount of granulation of the thallus, no. 1056 being the most typical in that respect.

146. **Peltigera polydactyla** (Neck.) Hoffm.

Lichen polydactylus NECKER, Meth Musc 132. 1771.
Peltigera polydactyla HOFFMANN, Fl Germ 2 106 1795 —DILL Hist Musc.
  t. 28, f. 107–108.

Lowe Inlet, B. C. (Coville and Kearney, 343); Sitka (Trelease, 1041; Setchell, 1271); Hot Springs (Trelease, 1039); Farragut Bay (Trelease, 1034; Coville and Kearney, 472), Orca (Trelease, 1036a, 1037, 1060); Unalaska (Setchell). Collected by Dr. Cooley at Gold Creek Cañon, near Juneau. Rothrock records its occurrence at 'Kotzebue Sound, Sitka, etc.,' but does not give the names of the collectors.

Most of the specimens are sterile, and the determination is therefore not without question. After careful comparison with the large series of specimens in the Tuckerman Herbarium it seems best to refer these specimens here.

147. **Peltigera horizontalis** (L.) Hoffm.

Lichen horizontalis LINNÆUS, Mant 132 1771
Peltigera horizontalis HOFFMANN, Fl Germ 2: 107 1795 —SOWERBY, Eng.
  Bot *t 888.*

Aguadulce River, Yakutat Bay (Trelease, 1099); Yakutat (Trelease, 1094); Egg Island, Disenchantment Bay (Coville and Kearney, 1010).

All the specimens are sterile, and therefore there must remain some question about their determination.

148. **Peltigera apthosa** (L.) Hoffm.

Lichen apthosus LINNÆUS, Fl Suec 1098 1755.
Peltigera apthosa HOFFMANN, Fl Germ 2: 107 1795 —SOWERBY, Eng. Bot.
  t. 1119.

Multnomah Falls, Oregon (Trelease, 1053); locality lost (Trelease, 1032); Alaska (Evans, 409); Fort Cosmos (Huff, 6); Lowe Inlet, B. C. (Trelease, 1059, 1103); Wrangell (Trelease, 1101), Hot Springs, Baranof Island (Trelease, no number, also 1040); Juneau (Trelease, 1090); Hidden Glacier Inlet, Yakutat Bay (Trelease, 1062, 1093); Kadiak (Trelease, 1076); Orca (Trelease, 1036, 1036a); Port Wells (Trelease, 1056a); Virgin Bay (Trelease, 1035), Farragut Bay (Brewer and Coe, 705); Egg Island, Disenchantment Bay (Coville and Kearney, 1009), Shumagin Islands, Popof Island (Saunders, 1081); Attu Island (Townsend, 74), Unalaska (Setchell), Pastoliak River (Newhall) Rothrock reports the species as having been collected at Port Mulgrave, Yakutat Bay, by Dr Bean, and also as having been collected at 'Kotzebue Sound, Sitka, etc.,' the collectors' names not being given. Dr. Cooley collected it at Loring and at Sheep Creek, near Juneau; Macoun adds St. George Island and St. Paul Island to the list of localities. Under the synonym *Peltidea apthosa* Ach., Nylander credits it to Port Clarence, in the lists of Hooker and Arnott, and Babington, it is reported from Kotzebue Sound.

There is great difference in the size of the fronds in the different specimens. No. 1040, from Hot Springs, is characterized by very long and narrow lobes, the specimen being sterile. The three fertile specimens, 1053, 1062, and 1076, are all small.

149. Peltigera venosa (L.) Hoffm.

Lichen venosus LINNÆUS, Fl Suec. ed. 2. 1097 1755.
Peltigera venosa HOFFMANN, Pl. Lich *t. 6 f. 2* 1790-1801 —SOWERBY, Eng. Bot *t. 887.*

Juneau (Setchell, 1242); Hidden Glacier Inlet, Yakutat Bay (Trelease, 1077, 1105); Unalaska (Setchell). Fertile. Collected by Wright on the islands of Bering Strait. In Rothrock's Flora of Alaska it is credited to Kotzebue Sound, under the synonym *Peltidea venosa* (L.) Nyl. Babington records its occurrence at Kotzebue Sound, Nylander lists it as collected at Port Clarence.

Other Alaska species of the genus are: *P. scabrosa* Fr., reported by Nylander from St. Lawrence Island and Port Clarence; *P. canina sorediata* Schaer., collected by Wright on banks of islands in Bering Strait; and *Peltidea polydactyla scutata* Fries, reported by Babington as having been collected at Kotzebue Sound.

NEPHROMA.

KEY TO THE SPECIES.

Thallus greenish straw-colored .. .. *arcticum.*
Thallus brown.
    Thallus tomentose beneath .... *tomentosum.*
    Thallus naked.
        Thallus not sorediate. .... *lævigatum.*
        Thallus sorediate ... . *lævigatum parile.*

150. Nephroma lævigatum Ach.

Nephroma lævigatum ACHARIUS, Syn. 242. 1813.—SOWERBY, Eng Bot *t. 305.*

Juneau (Setchell, 1244); Sitka (Trelease, 1072); Yakutat Bay (Trelease, 1065a, 1092, 1100 in part); Virgin Bay (Trelease, 1073), Port Clarence (Trelease, 1071, 1087c); Cape Nome (Setchell). New to Alaska.

No. 1100 is with *Physcia tribacea* and *Sticta crocata*. Most of the specimens are sterile. A common northen lichen.

151. Nephroma lævigatum parile Nyl.
Nephroma lævigatum parile NYLANDER, Syn 320. 1860—SOWERBY, Eng. Bot. *t. 2360.*

Disenchantment Bay (Trelease, 1091*b*, 1097, 1098*c*). New to Alaska.

No. 1098*c* was found with *Peltigera* and *Leptogium*. No. 1097 is very large, measuring 150 cent in diameter. All the specimens are sterile. Nylander, in Lich. Fr. Berh., reports its occurrence on Bering Island, under the name of *Nephromium parile*.

152. Nephroma tomentosum (Hoffm.) Koerb.
Peltigera tomentosa HOFFMANN, Fl. Germ 2: 108 1795
Nephroma tomentosum KOERBER, Systema Lich. Ger. 56 1855.
Lichen resupinatus DILLEN , Hist. Musc. *t. 28 f. 105.* 1741

Point Gustavus (Coville and Kearney, 775*b*). A small fragment of a thallus with large thin apothecia. Found with *Sticta anthraspis*. Reported by Dr. Cooley from Salmon Creek, near Juneau.

153. Nephroma arcticum (L.) Fr.
Lichen arcticus LINNÆUS, Sp. Pl. 2 1148 1753.
Nephroma arcticum FRIES, Lich. Arct. 41. 1860.
Lichen grœnlandicus Fl. Dan. *t. 466.*

Virgin Bay (Trelease, 1047) , Orca (Trelease, 1046 in part) ; summit of White Pass, 3000 ft. (Trelease, 1048); St. Lawrence Island (L. J. Cole, no number); Hall Island (Trelease, 1049) ; St. Matthew Island (Trelease, 1050; Coville and Kearney, 2122); St. Michael Island (Turner, 835; Setchell), Port Clarence (Trelease, 1052, Coville and Kearney, 1923, 1923*a*); Cape Nome (Setchell); Seward Peninsula (Collier). Collected by Dr. Bean on Chamisso Island, in Eschscholtz Bay, and by Dr. Hayes at Taku. Under the synonym *Nephroma polaris* Ach. Babington reports its occurrence at Kotzebue Sound.

With these specimens are usually found various species of *Cladonia*, *Sphagnum*, and *Dicranum*. With the specimen from Orca are fragments of *Thamnolia*. The specimen from Virgin Bay is fertile. This is a very common arctic and alpine lichen.

Additional Alaska species are: *Nephroma expallidum* Nyl., reported by Nylander as having been collected by Dr. Almquist at Port Clarence, and *Nephroma lætevirens*, reported by Macoun under the synonym *Normandina lætevirens* Turn. and Borr., as growing among tufts of moss on St. George Island.

STICTA.

KEY TO THE SPECIES

Thallus sorediate.
    Soredia lemon-colored ....*crocata*.
    Soredia grayish....... .. ..*anthraspis*.
Thallus not sorediate.
    Thallus greenish-yellow, edges very finely cut . . .*oregana*.
    Thallus brownish, edges not very finely cut.
        Thallus with urceolate cyphels.. . . . .*quercizans*.
        Thallus without cyphels.
            Thallus large, with elongated lobes. . . . *pulmonaria*.
            Thallus small, with round, crenate lobes.. *pulmonaria linita*.

154. **Sticta anthraspis** Ach.

Sticta anthraspis ACHARIUS, Meth. Lich. 280. 1803.

Point Gustavus, Glacier Bay (Coville and Kearney, 775) New to Alaska.

Plant well developed, but sterile. Acharius founded the species on material collected on the coast of California by Menzies. Tuckerman records it as found in Oregon by Hall. Macoun's Canadian Lich. No. 153 was collected at Victoria.

155. **Sticta crocata** (L.) Ach.

Lichen crocatus LINNEUS, Mant. 310. 1771.
Sticta crocata ACHARIUS, Meth. Lich. 277. 1803.—DEL. Stict. 56. *t. 4. f. 10.*

Yakutat (Trelease, 1100 in part). Sterile specimen on dead coniferous twigs with *Nephroma lævigatum* and *Physcia tribacea*. New to Alaska.

This is a widely distributed lichen. Arnold records it from Newfoundland, J. M. Macoun from Canada. It is not mentioned in Fries' Lich. Arct., and the Yakutat station would seem to be the most northern one established on this continent.

156. **Sticta quercizans** (Michx.) Ach.

Lichen quercizans MICHAUX, Fl. Bor. Amer. 2 : 524. 1803.
Sticta quercizans ACHARIUS, Syn. 234. 1814.

Unalaska (Setchell). New to Alaska.

A small sterile specimen, growing on the earth.

Described from material collected by Michaux on Grandfather Mountain, North Carolina. It is common throughout the Southern States, ranging northward to Canada and Oregon.

157. **Sticta oregana** Tuck.

Sticta oregana TUCKERMAN, Bull. Torr. Club 5 : 4, 20. 1873

Lowe Inlet, B. C. (Trelease, 1023 ; Coville and Kearney, 339, 350) ; Fraser Reach, Princess Royal Island, B. C. (Coville and Kearney, 305, 311) ; Sitka (Setchell, 1218) ; Broughton Strait (Trelease, 1021), Juneau (Setchell, 1248) ; Yakutat (Trelease, 1028) ; Point Gustavus, Glacier Bay (Coville and Kearney, 779). Collected by Dr. Cooley at Loring and at Sheep Creek, near Juneau. Tuckerman, in his Syn. N. A. L., gives Oregon as the only station for this species. In my own herbarium I have specimens from Vancouver Island and Washington.

All the specimens are sterile with the exception of NO. 339.

158. **Sticta pulmonaria** (L.) Ach.

Lichen pulmonarius LINNÆUS, Fl. Suec. 1087. 1755
Sticta pulmonaria ACHARIUS, L. U. 449. 1810 —SOWERBY, Eng. Bot. *t 572*.—
DELIS Stict *t 14 f. 60–65.*

Alaska (Evans, 6) ; Fraser Reach (Coville and Kearney, 311 in part) ; Lowe Inlet, B. C. (Trelease, 1024) ; Juneau, 1800 ft. alt. (Trelease, 1026, 1057) ; Juneau (Coville and Kearney, 608), Broughton Strait (Trelease, 1022) ; Farragut Bay (Trelease, 1025, Coville and Kearney, 474) ; Point Gustavus, Glacier Bay (Coville and Kearney, 780), Orca (Trelease, 1030, 1031, 1031*a*, 1038, 1045), Port Wells (Trelease, 1029, 1029*a*) ; Aguadulce River, Yakutat Bay (Trelease, 1027) ; Attu Island (Townsend, 71). Dr. Cooley collected it at Salmon Creek, near Juneau, Dr. Bean at Port Althorp and Sitka. The specimens collected by Dr. Bean are placed by Nylander under the following number as *Lobaria linita* (Ach.). Under the synonym *Sticta pulmonacea* Ach., Babington[1] reports its occurrence at Kotzebue Sound. He writes: "The specimens are rather small, neatly crisped, and pale ferrugineous below, approaching the form called *S. linita.*"

This Alaska form differs from the type in various particulars. The lobes of the thallus are broader and much more irregularly divided. The lobes are usually round and crenate at the apex, while the type is described as 'retuse-truncate.' The upper surface of the thallus is lighter brown in color and not so deeply lacunose, while the under surface shows fewer white spots. These specimens fruit much more freely than the type. The apothecia are large, chestnut brown, granulate on the under side, and are scattered over the thallus and not confined to the edges, as is usually the case in *Sticta pulmonaria.*

[1] Botany of the voyage of H. M. S. Herald, by Seeman. Lichens determined by Churchill Babington, 1852–1857.

The spores are similar to those of the type. The specimen from Fraser Reach shows also fragments of *Sticta oregana*. Judging from the specimens submitted, this must be one of the most abundant and characteristic lichens of the Alaskan coast. It is noticeable that in the collection here listed the species does not appear north of the Aleutian Islands. In the northern region its place is taken by the variety *linita*, which is represented by nine specimens, only three of which were collected south of the Aleutian Islands, and those all at one place. Arnold reports it from Newfoundland but not from Alaska. Dr. Lindsay[1] says of it: "Not in the present collection and not given at all by Th. Fries as a Greenland lichen. But in the Kew Herbarium I saw specimens of the ordinary form labeled 'Davis Straits.' The labels, however, unfortunately did not inform us on which coast the plant was collected, east or west." Fries reports it from Lapland, Norland, and the Samoyede country. Nylander records its occurrence in Scandinavia, but not its frequency. Tuckerman has recorded it for California.

159. Sticta pulmonaria linita (Ach.) Nyl.

Sticta linita ACHARIUS, Syn. 234. 1814.—DELIS. Stict. 145. *t. 18. f. 65* 1825. *Sticta pulmonaria linita* NYLANDER, Syn. 96. 1860.

Lowe Inlet, B. C. (Coville and Kearney, 339*b*, 342, 344); Unalaska (Setchell); Hall Island (Trelease, 1088); St. Matthew Island (Trelease, 1069); Port Clarence (Trelease, 1068, 1087, 1087*a*, 1087*b*); Cape Nome (Setchell). All sterile. Collected by Macoun on St. Paul Island. It is reported from Port Clarence by Nylander.

Nylander, in his revision of Rothrock's list, states that Dr. Bean's specimen, which is listed as *Sticta pulmonaria* by Rothrock, should be placed under this variety. This rock form is the more widely distributed alpine and arctic form.

Additional Alaska species of the genus are: *Sticta limbata* (Sm.) Ach., collected by Dr. Cooley at Sheep Creek and at Salmon Creek, near Juneau; and *Sticta scrobiculata* (Scop.) Mass., credited by Rothrock to Kotzebue Sound, no collector being given.

Family UMBILICARIACEÆ.

UMBILICARIA.

KEY TO THE SPECIES.

Thallus with fibrils on the under side.
  Thallus blackish-brown.
    Thallus one-leaved, not lacerate underneath............*proboscidea*.

[1] Lindsay, Dr. W. Lauder. Observations on the Lichens collected by D. Robert Brown, M.A., F.R.G.S., in West Greenland in 1867. Transactions of the Linnæan Society, vol. xxvii, 327. 1871.

Thallus often many-leaved, lacerate and shaggy underneath.
muhlenbergii alpina.
Thallus of a grayish color.
Fibrils pale . . .. *hirsuta.*
Fibrils black ....*cylindrica*
Thallus without fibrils on the under side.
Thallus of a grayish color................... . . . . *vellea tylorrhiza*
Thallus blackish-brown.
Upper surface of thallus smooth, not perforate on the edge.
anthracina.
Upper surface of the thallus not smooth, more or less perforate on the edge.
Thallus smooth underneath .... *hyperborea.*
Thallus ridged underneath. . ...*erosa.*

160. **Umbilicaria vellea tylorrhiza** Nyl.

Umbilicaria vellea tylorrhiza NYLANDER, Lich Lapp Orient 122 1867

Alaska, locality lost (Trelease, 1101); summit of White Pass (Trelease, 1002) Both sterile. New to Alaska.

The only record we have for this continent is southern Colorado, Brandegee. Nylander records it for eastern Asia and Europe

161. **Umbilicaria hirsuta** (Ach.) Stenh.

Umbilicaria hirsuta ACHARIUS in Vet. Ac. Handl. 1794. *t. 3, f 1* 1821.
Umbilicaria hirsuta STENHAMMER, Sched Crit 4 . 1825. DILL. Hist. Musc *t 30. f. 117.*—SOWERBY, Eng Bot *t. 2486.*

Muir Glacier (Trelease, 1006). Sterile New to Alaska.

Professor Tuckerman does not give definite notes of its distribution in North America in his Syn. N. A. L. I find no mention of it in Arnold's lists of the lichens of Newfoundland and Labrador. Lindsay does not mention it in his West Greenland Lichens Branth and Grönlund, in Grönland's Lichen-Flora, recognize the var. *papyria*, giving three stations for it. In the alpine and arctic regions of Europe it seems to be quite widely distributed.

162. **Umbilicaria muhlenbergii alpina** Tuck.

Umbilicaria muhlenbergii alpina TUCKERMAN, Syn New Eng Lich 74 1848.

Locality lost (Trelease, 1004). New to Alaska.

The variety was described from specimens from "Alpine rocks in the White and Green Mountains, Tuckerman; and in Hastings county, Canada, Macoun."

163. **Umbilicaria erosa** (Web.) Hoffm.

Lichen erosus WEBER, Spicil. Fl Götting. 259. 1778.
Umbilicaria erosa HOFFMANN, Pl Lichen. 3^1: 7. *t.* 70. 1801.—SOWERBY, Eng. Bot. 29. *t.* 2066. 1809.

Muir Glacier (Trelease, 1007), Kadiak (Trelease, 1009); St. Michael (Setchell). Reported from St Paul and St. George Islands by Macoun.

Fertile One of the specimens which was collected at Muir Glacier (1007*b*) might perhaps be separated out as forma *subradicans* Nyl.

164. **Umbilicaria hyperborea** Hoffmann.

Umbilicaria hyperborea HOFFMANN, Fl. Germ. 110. 1795.

Muir Glacier (Trelease, 1007*b*); summit of White Pass, 3000 ft. (Trelease, 1003); Sturgeon River, Kadiak Island (Trelease, 1008); Hall Island (Trelease, 1010, 1010*b*), Cape Nome (Setchell); Seward Peninsula (Collier). In Rothrock's List it is given as collected at Plover Bay, Siberia, and at Unalaska by Dr. Bean. It has also been collected on St Paul Island by William Palmer.

Fertile. A widely diffused northern form.

165. **Umbilicaria anthracina** (Wulf.) Schaer.

Lichen anthracinus WULFEN in Jacq Misc **2** 84 *t 9 f 4* 1781
Umbilicaria anthracina SCHAERER, Helv no 154 1823–1852

Kadiak (Trelease, 1005). Sterile. New to Alaska.

This is an alpine and arctic form which has been reported from Arctic America, Greenland, Newfoundland, and from northern Europe.

166. **Umbilicaria proboscidea** (L.) DC.

Lichen proboscideus LINNÆUS, Sp. Pl. **2**: 1150. 1753.—Fl. Dan *t.* 471 *f. 3.*
Umbilicaria proboscidea DE CANDOLLE, Fl. Franç. **2**: 410. 1805.

Muir Glacier (Trelease, 1007*c*); Unalaska (Setchell), St. Matthew Island (Trelease, 1011); Cape Nome (Setchell). Rothrock reports it from St. Matthew Island, and Macoun from St. Paul and St. George Islands. Under the synonym *Gyrophora proboscidea* Dr. Nylander records its occurrence on St. Lawrence Island.

The specimen from Muir Glacier is doubtfully referred here. It is small, with branching fibrils beneath. The development of fibrils on this specimen is much more evident than on the more mature specimens.

167. Umbilicaria cylindrica (L.) Dub.

Lichen cylindricus LINNÆUS, Afz. Act. Sc. Sv. 1788.
Umbilicaria cylindrica DUBY, Bot. Gall. 595. 1829.—DILL. Hist. Musc. *t. 29. f. 116*

Unalaska (Setchell). Collected by Macoun on St. Paul and St. George Islands, Bering Sea.

A common and widely distributed northern lichen.

Additional species of *Umbilicaria*: Wright collected *U. flocculosa* Hoffm. at Bering Strait, Macoun collected *U. rugifera* Nyl. on rocks on St. Paul and St. George Islands.

Family PARMELIACEÆ.

PHYSCIA.

KEY TO THE SPECIES.

Thallus brown.
    Thallus closely adnate to the substrate, lobes very thin and flat.
        adglutinata.
    Thallus not closely adnate to the substrate, the tips rounded and erect.. *pulverulenta*.
Thallus gray.
    Thallus granulate or sorediate
        Lobes of thallus very narrow, granulate at tips.......... *tribacea*.
        Lobes of thallus rather wide, sorediate .... *cæsia*.
    Thallus neither granulate nor sorediate.
        Lobes of thallus rather broad, with white fibrils underneath.
            stellaris.
        Lobes of thallus narrow, with black fibrils beneath.
            stellaris apiola.

168. Physcia adglutinata (Floerk.) Nyl.

Lecanora adglutinata FLOERKE in Deutsch Lich Lief 4: 7. 1815
Physcia adglutinata NYLANDER, Syn. 428. 1860
Lichen elænius SOWERBY, Eng. Bot. *t. 2158.*

Muir Glacier (Trelease, 1154*b*). New to Alaska. On *Salix* with *Parmelia olivacea*. Specimen fertile.

Not recorded as occurring in Greenland, Newfoundland, or Labrador, but widely distributed to the west and south.

169. Physcia cæsia (Hoffm.) Nyl.

Lichen cæsius HOFFMANN, Enum *t. 12. f. 1.* 1784
Physcia cæsia NYLANDER, Syn. 426. 1860.—SOWERBY, Eng. Bot. *t. 1052.*

Yakutat (Trelease, 1139*b*); Farragut Bay (Trelease, 1141); Kukak Bay, Alaska Peninsula (Coville and Kearney, 1515*c* in part);

St. Paul Island (Trelease, 1147). Credited to St. Lawrence Island by Nylander.

The specimens from Muir Glacier and St. Paul Island are fertile. With the specimen from Kukak Bay are small fragments of *Theloschistes polycarpus*.

170. **Physcia tribacea** (Ach.) Tuck.
Lecanora tribacea ACHARIUS, Syn. 191, in part, 1814.
Physcia tribacea TUCKERMAN, Syn N. A L. 75. 1884.

Yakutat (Trelease, 1100, 1144). No. 1144 is on dead twigs of Coniferæ No. 1100 is associated with *Nephroma lævigatum* and *Sticta crocata*. Reported from Port Clarence by Nylander.

171. **Physcia stellaris** (L.) Nyl.
Lichen stellaris LINNÆUS, Fl Suec ed. 2. 1082 1755.
Physcia stellaris NYLANDER, Syn. 424. 1860.—SOWERBY, Eng. Bot. *t. 1697*.

Muir Glacier (Trelease, 1133, 1135); Unalaska (Setchell). On bark of trees. Collected by Dr. Bean on Chamisso Island, in Eschscholtz Bay, on Little Koniuji Island, of the Shumagin group, and on Glacier Spit, in Cook Inlet. Nylander, in his enumeration of Rothrock's list based upon Dr. Bean's collection, states that *Physcia melops* (Duf.) Nyl. appears under the name *Physcia stellaris*. Arnold reports this from Newfoundland, Lindsay from West Greenland, and Fries[1] writes of it as being widely distributed in Scandinavia as well as in West Greenland.

No. 1133 is especially well fruited.

172. **Physcia stellaris apiola** (Ach.) Nyl.
Parmelia apiola ACHARIUS, Meth Lich 209 1803.
Physcia stellaris apiola NYLANDER, Lich. Scand III 1861.—DILL. Hist. Musc. *t. 24. f. 70*.

Alaska (Funston, 23); Yakutat (Trelease, 1139), Muir Glacier (Trelease, 1012); Virgin Bay (Trelease, 977); St. Michael (Setchell) New to Alaska.

All the specimens are sterile.

173. **Physcia pulverulenta** (Schreb.) Nyl.
Lichen pulverulentus SCHREBER, Spicil 128 1771.
Physcia pulverulenta NYLANDER, Syn. 419. 1860.—HOFFM. Pl. Lich. *t. 8. f 2*

St. Paul Island (Trelease, 1116, 1116*a*). New to Alaska. Dr. Lindsay mentions it in his West Greenland Lichens,[2] and mentions

[1] Fries, Th M. Lichenes Arctoi, 64 1860.
[2] Lindsay, W Lauder Observations on the Lichens collected by Dr. Robert Brown in West Greenland in 1867. Transactions of the Linnæan Society, vol. XXVII, 332 1871.

having seen a specimen in the Kew Herbarium which was collected by Parry and labeled as from the 'North Pole.' Dr. Arnold makes no mention of its occurrence in Newfoundland or Labrador in his lists of the lichens of those regions. Neither of the St Paul specimens shows apothecia, and both are only slightly pulverulent. They may possibly be referred to *P. muscigena* of Fries' Lichenes Arctoi

Additional Alaska species: *P. obscura* (Ehrnb.) Nyl., listed by Rothrock as having been collected at Kotzebue Sound, *P. obscura sciastra* (Ach.) Nyl., and *P. muscigena* (Wahl.) Nyl., both recorded by Nylander as occurring at Port Clarence; and *P. melops ossicola* Nyl., collected on St. Lawrence Island, as recorded by Nylander.

PARMELIA.
KEY TO THE SPECIES.

Thallus straw-colored.
    Thallus large, often isidiophorous, lobes variously divided..*conspersa*.
    Thallus small, sorediate, dichotomously divided.. . ...*ambigua*.
Thallus variously colored
    Thallus olivaceous brown.
        Lobes of thallus flat, rounded crenate . . . . . . *olivacea*.
        Lobes of thallus linear or terete.
            Palmately divided. . . . . *stygia*.
            Dichotomously divided. . . . . *lanata*.
    Thallus glaucescent or blackening.
        Thallus small, dichotomously divided, sorediate
                                ambigua albescens.
        Thallus large, not dichotomously divided.
            Thallus gray, sometimes with blackening borders.
                Thallus more or less reticulate, not inflated.
                      Thallus whitish, sorediate .. ..*saxatilis*.
                      Thallus grayish, not sorediate . . . *saxatilis sulcata*.
                Thallus not reticulate, inflated.
                      Lobes of thallus wide and much inflated, not black-margined .. .. *physodes enteromorpha*.
                      Lobes of thallus narrow, somewhat inflated.
                          Lobes of thallus not black-margined . ... *physodes*
                          Lobes of thallus black-margined ... *physodes vittata*.
    Thallus blackening all over.
        Lobes of thallus flat, broad, not inflated.
                                saxatilis omphalodes.
        Lobes of thallus rounded, narrow, inflated
                                physodes obscurata.

174. **Parmelia ambigua** (Wulf.) Ach.
Lichen ambiguus WULFEN in Ap Jacq Coll 4 239 *t 4 f. 2* 1790
Parmelia ambigua ACHARIUS, Meth 207 1803

Alaska (Funston, 36); Juneau (Setchell, 1247); Virgin Bay (Trelease, 1143). Sterile, on dead wood Reported by Nylander as occurring at Port Clarence, under the synonym *Parmeliopsis ambigua* (Wulf.).

175. **Parmelia ambigua albescens** Wahl.
Parmelia ambigua albescens WAHLENBERG, Fl Suec 852 1826
Parmelia ambigua albescens SCHAERER, Spicil. 468 1840.—Fl Dan. *t. 2512 f 1 b & d.*

Virgin Bay (Trelease, 846). Sterile, on dead wood. New to Alaska.

Neither *Parmelia ambigua* nor the variety *albescens* is mentioned in Fries' Lichenes Arctoi, or by Branth and Gronlund in Gronlands Lichen Flora, or in Dr. Lindsay's West Greenland Lichens. *Parmelia ambigua* has been reported from Arctic America (Richardson) and from British Columbia (Macoun).

176. **Parmelia conspersa** (Ehrh.) Ach.
Lichen conspersus EHRHART in Ach Prod 118 1798
Parmelia conspersa ACHARIUS, Meth. Lich 205 1803.—SOWERBY, Eng. Bot. *t. 2097*

Sitka (Trelease, 1146); summit of White Pass, 3000 ft. (Trelease, 1138); St Michael (Setchell). New to Alaska.

No. 1138, which bears apothecia, has finely divided lobes approaching the variety *stenophylla* of Acharius. The other specimen is sterile.

177. **Parmelia lanata** (L.) Wallr.
Lichen lanatus LINNÆUS, Fl Suec 1125. 1755
Parmelia lanata WALLROTH, Fl Germ 529 1831.—SOWERBY, Eng Bot *t 846*.

Hot Springs, Baranof Island (Trelease, 1176); Unalaska (Setchell); Muir Glacier (Trelease, 1159, 1177). New to Alaska.

All the specimens are sterile No. 1176 is much more finely divided than any specimen in the Tuckerman Herbarium. The species has been reported from Arctic America

178. **Parmelia stygia** (L.) Ach.
Lichen stygius LINNÆUS, Sp Pl 2 · 1143 1753
Parmelia stygia ACHARIUS, Meth. Lich 203. 1803—SOWERBY, Eng. Bot. *t 2048*

Summit of White Pass, 3000 ft (Trelease, 1162*b*); Kadiak (Trelease, 902). On rocks. New to Alaska.

No. 902 is mixed with *Buellia geographica, Lecanora straminea,* and *Lecidea platycarpa* Common in Arctic regions.

179. **Parmelia olivacea** (L.) Ach.

Lichen olivaceus LINNÆUS, Sp. Pl. 2 1143 1753.
Parmelia olivacea ACHARIUS, L. U 462 1810.—SOWERBY, Eng. Bot. *t. 2180.*—NYL. Syn *t. 1. f. 1.*

Wrangell (Trelease, 1153); Hidden Glacier Inlet (Trelease, 991); Sitka (Trelease, 1107*b*, 1117); Muir Glacier (Trelease, 988, 990, 1154); Whale Island, St Michael (Setchell). On bark of *Alnus oregona* and on rock. Reported by Nylander as having been collected at Port Clarence.

The specimens are well developed, but all but two are sterile. Dr. Lindsay states in West Greenland Lichens, 331, that all the forms which he examined were sterile. All the specimens which I have collected in Massachusetts are sterile, but more northern forms from Maine, New Hampshire, Idaho, and Oregon show apothecia well developed.

The species has been reported from Alaska but once before. It was found at Port Clarence, a much more northern locality than any reported in this list. It appears to be a common arctic form, and therefore its comparative scarcity in Alaska is the more noticeable.

180. **Parmelia physodes** (L.) Ach.

Lichen physodes LINNÆUS, Fl Suec. ed 2 1755.
Parmelia physodes ACHARIUS, Meth Lich 250. 1803.—SOWERBY, Eng Bot *t 126.*

Alaska (Evans, 255), with *Usnea longissima*, etc.; Sitka (Trelease, 1149, 1149*a*, 1151); Kadiak (Trelease, 1134, on dead wood); Fraser Reach (Coville and Kearney, 296). Recorded by Rothrock as occurring at Elephant Point, Eschscholtz Bay, Arctic Ocean, Port Mulgrave, Yakutat Bay, and Fort Alexander, in Cook Inlet.

Specimens small and sterile. No. 299 may be considered a transitional form approaching the variety *vittata*.

181. **Parmelia physodes obscurata** Ach.

Parmelia physodes obscurata ACHARIUS, Syn 218 1814

Unalaska (Setchell); St. Matthew Island (Trelease, 1163*b*, also a specimen with no number); Hall Island (Trelease, 1164*b*); Port Clarence (Trelease, 1112), mixed with *Cetraria cucullata*, *Parmelia saxatilis*, and *Alectoria divergens*.

The unnumbered specimen from St. Matthew Island is well fruited, the others are sterile. Mixed with this specimen is a sterile fragment, apparently a *Cladonia*, and also *Alectoria divergens*. This variety has been reported from Alaska but once before. Tuckerman records that it was collected by Wright on the islands of Bering Strait.

Acharius, in establishing the variety, records it as occurring in Helvetia, on the limbs of pines. No reference is made to it in Lichenes Arctoi by Fries, or in the Lichen Flora Grönland's, by Branth and Grönlund.

182. Parmelia physodes enteromorpha (Ach.) Tuck.

Parmelia enteromorpha ACHARIUS, Meth. Lich. 252. 1803
Parmelia physodes enteromorpha TUCKERMAN, Syn. N. A. L. 1. 60. 1882.

Broughton Strait (Trelease, 1108, 1114); Sitka (Trelease, 1126; Setchell, 1273); Wrangell (Coville and Kearney, 403); Farragut Bay (Coville and Kearney, 466); Glacier Bay (Coville and Kearney, 769); Orca (Trelease, 1110); Kadiak (Trelease, 1134a). Collected by Dr. Cooley at Sitka, Loring, and Juneau, and at Sheep Creek, near Juneau. Tuckerman states that it was collected in Alaska by Dr. Kellogg.

On several of the specimens were minute, black, cup-shaped fungi, either scattered or so crowded that the cups formed a continuous stroma-like mass. These fungi were most abundant in Nos. 1108, 1114, and 769.

Two-thirds of the specimens were fruited, the apothecia often large, one measuring 25 μ.

This variety was described from specimens from California, and seems to be very abundant on our northern coast. It has also been reported from northern Asia, Australia, and New Zealand.

183. Parmelia physodes vittata Ach.

Parmelia physodes vittata ACHARIUS, Syn. 218. 1814.

Wrangell (Trelease, 1109); Point Gustavus, Glacier Bay (Coville and Kearney, 784); Virgin Bay (Trelease, 1111), with *Polytrichum*. Collected at Loring by Dr. Cooley and on St. Paul Island by Macoun.

Parmelia physodes seems to be more widely distributed than any of its varieties. It is found in Europe, North and South America, Asia, Africa, New Zealand, etc. The variety *vittata* has been reported from Europe, North America, and South America.

184. Parmelia saxatilis Ach.

Parmelia saxatilis ACHARIUS, Meth. Lich. 204. 1803 —SOWERBY, Eng. Bot. *t. 603.*

Alaska (Evans, 368); Sitka (Trelease, 1148, 1150); Hot Springs (Trelease, 1123, 1123a, 1113, and 963 in part); Yakutat (Trelease, 1066, 1121a, 1121b); Virgin Bay (Trelease, 1074); Sturgeon River Bay (Trelease, 1134b, also a specimen with no number); Kukak (Coville and Kearney, 1515); Unalaska (Setchell); St. Michael (Setchell); Port Clarence (Trelease, 1113, 1112, fragments with *Cetraria*, etc.). Reported by Babington from Kotzebue Sound, by Nylander for St. Lawrence Island; collected by Dr. Bean at Cape Lisburne, Unalaska, and on logs in Cross Sound, and by Macoun on St. Paul and St. George Islands.

This species is represented entirely or in part by sixteen different numbers, and exhibits great variation as to color of thallus and presence or absence of isidioid growths. The most normal forms are represented by numbers 1113 and 1150. It will be noted that 1113 was collected at Port Clarence, the most northern station for this species, and 1150 at Sitka, the most southern station.

Numbers 1123a, 1066, and 1074 are characterized by a change of color of a portion, or in 1074 of nearly all, of the thallus, to a reddish-brown. Macoun notes the same fact in the following words: "Frequently found abnormally colored from a red brown to a beautiful violet" This is a change which often occurs in specimens of a normal color which have been kept in a damp condition in a collecting box for two or three days. Certain specimens, as No. 368, show a tendency toward the blackening which is characteristic of the variety *omphalodes*.

The most interesting variation, however, is that caused by the development of the isidioid growths. This is only slightly evident in 1121a and 1123, but very strongly developed in Nos. 368, Evans; 1515, Coville and Kearney; 1130 and 1134b, Trelease. In these cases the greater portion of the thallus, the periphery being excepted, is densely covered with a growth which resembles minute specimens of *Sphærophoron coralloides* or *Cladonia papillaria*. This is the form which Dr. Lindsay refers to as *sphærophoroidea*, in his Observations on West Greenland Lichens, 328 None of the reddish-brown forms show any isidioid growths. Macoun collected an isidiferous form on earth on St. George Island.

No. 1066 is interesting as showing the development of minute secondary laciniæ upon the surface or at the edge of the lobes of the thallus.

Only two of the sixteen specimens bear fruit, or one-eighth of the whole number, and the apothecia are poorly developed in these cases. An examination of eleven specimens in my herbarium, including material from Canada and Newfoundland, shows that six of the eleven specimens (more than half) are fruited. The sterility of these Arctic forms has been noted by Dr. Lindsay in his Observations upon the Lichens of West Greenland.

185. **Parmelia saxatilis sulcata** (Tayl.) Nyl.
Parmelia sulcata TAYLOR in Mack. Fl Hib. 145. 1836.
Parmelia saxatilis sulcata NYLANDER, Syn. 1: 389. 1860.—MICH. Ord. 22. *t. 49.* C. D.

Alaska (Funston, 7); Sitka (Trelease, 1149); Yakutat (Trelease, 2299); Virgin Bay (Trelease, 1118). Collected by Macoun on St. George Island and reported by Nylander under the synonym *Parmelia sulcata* Tayl. as occurring on St. Lawrence Island and at Port Clarence.

In NO. 1121 the lobes are short and somewhat overlapping, tending toward the variety *panniformis*, while in NO. 1118 they are narrow, more elongated and spreading. All the specimens are sterile.

186. **Parmelia saxatilis omphalodes** (L.) Fr.
Lichen omphalodes LINNÆUS, Fl Suec. 1755.
Parmelia saxatilis omphalodes FRIES, L. E. 62. 1831.—DILL. Hist. Musc. *t. 24 f 80.*—SOWERBY, Eng. Bot. *t. 604.*

Kadiak (Trelease, 1132); summit of White Pass, 3000 ft. (Trelease, 1120); St. Paul Island (Trelease, 1115); St. Matthew Island (Trelease, 1165); St. Lawrence Island (Trelease, 1156), associated with *Lecanora varia symmicta;* Port Clarence (Trelease, 1129); St. Michael (Setchell); Cape Nome (Setchell). Collected by Dr. Bean near Cape Lisburne and reported by Nylander under the synonym *P. omphalodes* (L.) as occurring on St. Lawrence Island.

No. 1129 shows the development of minute laciniæ and NO. 1105 of isidia which have been mentioned as characteristic of some forms of *Parmelia saxatilis.* No apothecia are developed on any of these specimens.

Additional Alaska species: *P. austerodes* Nyl., recorded by Nylander as having been collected on St. Lawrence Island and at Port Clarence; and *Parmeliopsis aleurites* (Ach. Sommerf) Nyl., recorded by Nylander as occurring at Port Clarence. Rothrock reports *P. perlata* (L.) Ach., *P. perforata* (Jacq.) Ach., and *P. tiliacea* (Hoffm.) Floerk., as having been collected at Kotzebue Sound. Hooker and Arnott, in their list of Kotzebue lichens, include *P. diatrypa* Ach., which may be referred to *P. pertusa* (Schrank.) Schaer

THELOSCHISTES.

KEY TO THE SPECIES.

Thallus not powdery on the margin . . . .*polycarpus.*
Thallus powdery on the margin.
    Lobes flat, linear, profusely granulate. . . . .*lychneus.*
    Lobes erect, terete, branched . . . . *lychneus pygmæus.*

187. Theloschistes lychneus (Nyl.) Tuck.

Physcia parietina lychnea NYLANDER, Syn 411. 1860.
Theloschistes lychneus TUCKERMAN, Syn. N A L. 1: 50. 1882.—HEPP, Sporen. *t. 99 f 871*

Sitka (Trelease, 1169); Kadiak (Trelease, 1170 in part); Unalaska (Trelease, 1154); St. Paul Island (Trelease, 930). Collected on St. Paul Island by William Palmer, and reported by Nylander, under the synonym *Physcia lychnea* (Ach.) Nyl., as occurring on St. Lawrence Island

All sterile, on rocks or old rails. The specimen from Kadiak was on rails with *Buellia myriocarpa chloropolia.*

188. Theloschistes lychneus pygmæus (Fr.) Tuck.

Parmelia parietina 1 *pygmæa* FRIES, L. E. 73.
Theloschistes lychneus pygmæus TUCKERMAN, Syn. N A L 1: 51 1882.

Muir Glacier (Trelease, 1167), Sturgeon River Bay, Kadiak Island (Trelease, 1171); Unalaska (Setchell); St Paul Island (Trelease, 886, 1173); St. Matthew Island (Trelease, 1172); St. Michael (Setchell). This species has been collected on St Paul Island by J. M. Macoun, who states that it is 'rare.' Also collected on St. Paul Island by William Palmer, and in Alaska, no locality given, by Dr. Kellogg, and on the islands in Bering Strait by Wright

Nos. 1172 and 1173 are sparingly fruited. No 1173 was found growing with fragments of *Physcia* on tufts of moss.

189. Theloschistes polycarpus (Ehrh.) Tuck.

Lichen polycarpus EHRHART, Plant Crypt. 136 1785
Theloschistes polycarpus TUCKERMAN, Syn N A L 1 50 1882.—SOWERBY, Eng Bot *t. 1795*

Muir Glacier (Trelease, 1168) on *Salix*, Kukak Bay, Alaska Peninsula (Coville and Kearney, 1515*b*); St Paul Island (Trelease, 1174). Mixed with the specimen from Kukak is a fragment of *Physcia* sp All are fertile. A specimen collected by Professor Setchell at St. Michael may possibly be placed here. Rothrock, in his list based upon Dr Bean's collection, places this as a variety under *T. parietinus*, and writes: "Widely diffused over the Arctic regions and apparently very common, being obtained at a number of points." In his correction of Rothrock's list, Nylander refers the specimen to *Physcia lychnea*, a synonym for *T. lychneus.*

One additional species of this genus has been collected in Alaska— *T. parietinus* (L) Norm, collected by Dr Bean at Port Clarence, and reported by Babington under the synonym *Parmelia parietina* Ach., as occurring at Kotzebue Sound.

Family USNEACEÆ.
ALECTORIA.

KEY TO THE SPECIES.

Thallus straw-colored.
  Not blackening at the tips
    Divaricately branched. . . . . *ochroleuca.*
    Densely intertangled .. . . *ochroleuca sarmentosa.*
  Blackening at the tips.
    Branches rounded. . . . . *ochroleuca rigida.*
    Branches flattened.. . . . . *ochroleuca circinata.*
Thallus variously colored.
  Thallus light brown . . . . *nigricans.*
  Thallus chestnut-colored or blackish-brown
    Thallus robust, tips forked. . . . . *divergens.*
    Thallus slender, tips not forked.
      Thallus paler at the ends . . . . *jubata bicolor.*
      Thallus all the same color.
        Thallus pendulous . . . . *jubata.*
        Thallus prostrate or subpendulous... *jubata chalybeiformis.*

190. Alectoria ochroleuca (Ehrh.) Nyl.

Lichen ochroleucus EHRHART, Beytr. 3 82 1788.
Alectoria ochroleuca NYLANDER, Prod. 47 1857.
Usnea ochroleuca HOFFMANN, Pl Lich 2 *t 26 f 2.*

    Unalaska (Setchell). Nylander reports its occurrence on St. Lawrence Island and at Port Clarence, Hooker and Arnott credit it to Kotzebue Sound, under the synonym *Cornicularia ochroleuca* Ach., and Babington to the same locality, under the synonym *Evernia ochroleuca* Fries.

191. Alectoria ochroleuca rigida (Vill.) Fr.

Lichen rigidus VILLARS, Dauph 3 938 1789
Alectoria ochroleuca rigida FRIES, Lich Arct 27 1860 —SOWERBY, Eng. Bot. *t. 2374.*

    Alaska (Evans, 428), Orca (Trelease, 1202), Kadiak (Trelease, 1189). All sterile.
    Intermixed with these specimens are fragments of *Alectoria jubata, Sphærophorus,* and various mosses. This is an alpine and arctic species. Collected at Taku by Dr. Hayes, and at Seward Peninsula by Arthur J. Collier.

192. **Alectoria ochroleuca sarmentosa** (Ach.) Nyl.

Lichen sarmentosus ACHARIUS, Prod. 180 1798.
Alectoria ochroleuca sarmentosa NYLANDER, Syn. 282. 1860.—HOFFM. Pl. Lich. *t.* 72.

New Metlakatla (Trelease, 1186); Broughton Strait (Trelease, 1184); Wrangell (Coville and Kearney, 398); Yakutat (Trelease, 1028*b*, 1188). Collected at Sitka by Dr. Bean, and in the same locality by Dr. Cooley, who also found it at Salmon Creek and Sheep Creek, near Juneau.

All the specimens sterile except NO. 1188 from Yakutat. That is fertile and especially well developed.

193. **Alectoria ochroleuca circinata** (Fr.) Tuck.

Evernia ochroleuca circinata FRIES, Lich Eur. 22 1831.
Alectoria ochroleuca circinata TUCKERMAN, Syn. N. A. L. 1: 45. 1882.
Lichen sarmentosus SOWERBY, Eng. Bot. *t.* 2040.

Unalaska (Setchell). New to Alaska.

The range of this lichen as given in Tuckerman's Synopsis N. A. L. is limited, only two stations being noted, Newfoundland and the White Mountains. Various stations are given for it in Fries' Lichenes Arctoi.

194. **Alectoria nigricans** (Ach.) Nyl.

Cornicularia ochroleuca β nigricans ACHARIUS, L. U. 615
Alectoria nigricans NYLANDER, Lich. Scand 71 1861 —NYL Syn. *t. 8 f. 17.*

Agattu Island (Townsend, 78), Unalaska (Setchell); St. Michael (Turner, 840 and an unnumbered specimen; Setchell); St. Lawrence Island (Trelease, 1265); Cape Nome (Setchell). All sterile. Reported by Nylander as occurring on St. Lawrence Island and at Port Clarence, and collected by Dr. Bean at Chernofski, Unalaska. Macoun records it, under the synonym *Alectoria thulensis* Th. Fr., as occurring on St. Paul and St. George Islands.

This is essentially an alpine and arctic form. It has been reported from Labrador and Newfoundland, though not reported from Greenland. Mixed with some of the specimens are fragments of mosses and other lichens.

195. **Alectoria jubata** (L.) Ach.

Lichen jubatus LINNÆUS, Fl. Suec. 1124. 1755.
Alectoria jubata ACHARIUS, L. U. 592. *t. 13 f. 1.* 1810.

Alaska (Evans, 255 in part); between Cook Inlet and Tanana River (Capt. Glenn, no number); Broughton Strait (Trelease, 1179, 1185); Hot Springs (Trelease, 1183), Sitka (Trelease, 1178); Wrangell (Coville and Kearney, 402*b*). Collected by Dr. Bean, no locality being given.

All sterile. The specimen collected by Mr. Evans is on the bark of spruce and is intermixed with *Usnea longissima, Parmelia physodes,* and *Cetraria glauca.*

196. Alectoria jubata bicolor (Ehrh.) Tuck.

Lichen bicolor EHRHART, Beytr 3 82 1788
Alectoria jubata bicolor TUCKERMAN, Syn. N. A. L. 1 44. 1882.—SOWERBY, Eng. Bot. *t. 1853.*

Broughton Strait (Trelease, 1184*b* in part), Sitka (Trelease, 1132); Yakutat (Trelease, 1181). New to Alaska

The specimen from Yakutat is dwarfed and poorly developed, and shows fragments of *Mnium* and *Dicranum.* The specimen from Broughton Strait is mixed with fragments of *Usnea longissima.*

197. Alectoria jubata chalybeiformis (L.) Ach.

Lichen chalybeiformis LINNÆUS, Sp. Pl. 2: 1155. 1753.
Alectoria jubata chalybeiformis ACHARIUS, L. U. 593. 1810 —Fl Dan *t. 262.*

Alaska (Funston, 13), Sitka (Trelease, 1180). The only other recorded Alaska locality is St. Paul Island, J. M. Macoun, collector.

This variety occurs in a dwarfed form on the earth in alpine regions, elongated and pendulous on trees farther south.

198. Alectoria divergens (Ach.) Nyl.

Cornicularia divergens ACHARIUS, Meth. Lich. 305. *t. 6 f. 1.* 1803.
Alectoria divergens NYLANDER, Syn. 1: 278. 1860.

Kadiak (Trelease, 1194*b* in part, 1208 in part); St. Michael (Turner, 838; Setchell); Agattu Island (Townsend, 78); Hall Island (Trelease, 1209 in part); St. Matthew Island (Trelease, no number); Port Clarence (Trelease, 1112 in part), Cape Nome (Setchell); Seward Peninsula (Collier). Reported by Nylander from Port Clarence and St. Lawrence Island, by Rothrock as occurring in various localities, by Farlow as having been collected at Point Barrow, by Tuckerman as having been collected by Wright on the islands of Bering Strait. Macoun collected it on St. Paul Island, under synonym *Cornicularia divergens* Ach.; Hooker and Arnott report its occurrence at Kotzebue Sound; Babington credits it to Norton Sound and Kotzebue Sound as *Evernia divergens* Fries. It has also been collected on Seward Peninsula by Arthur J. Collier

Mixed with these specimens are fragments of *Cetraria islandica* and *C cucullata, Parmelia saxatilis, Cladonia rangiferina,* and various mosses. The specimen from Agattu Island is the best developed and shows no intermixture of other lichens. All the specimens are sterile. A common arctic form.

The only additional Alaskan species of which I find record is *A. fremontii* Tuck., collected by Dr. Cooley at Sitka and at Salmon Creek, near Juneau.

USNEA.

KEY TO THE SPECIES.

Thallus short, tufted.
    Thallus fine, nearly smooth...*barbata*.
    Thallus coarse, papillate...*barbata florida*.
Thallus elongated, pendulous
    Thallus profusely subdichotomously branched, without spreading fibrils...*barbata plicata*
    Thallus scarcely branched, covered with spreading fibrils, very much elongated ....*longissima*.

199. **Usnea longissima** Ach.

Usnea longissima ACHARIUS, L U 626 1810

Alaska (Dr. Kellogg, 6; Evans, 255 in part), Fort Cosmos (Huff, *a*), Sitka (Setchell, 1259 in part, 1262, 1264); Broughton Strait (Trelease, 1184). Tuckerman records it as having been collected in Russian America by Dr. Kellogg.

The specimen collected by Mr. Evans has with it *Cetraria glauca*, *Alectoria jubata*, *Parmelia physodes* and *U. barbata plicata*. No. 1259, collected by Professor Setchell at Sitka, is mixed with *Alectoria jubata*. With the specimen from Broughton Strait is the following note: "Strangling evergreens close to the seaside." Mixed with the specimen are fragments of *Alectoria* and of species of *Dicranum* and *Polytrichum*.

200. **Usnea barbata** Fr.

Usnea barbata FRIES, Sched Crit 9 34 1824-1833.

Fraser Reach (Coville and Kearney, 301); Broughton Strait, Vancouver Island (Trelease, 1184*e*), with *Usnea longissima*. Both specimens sterile. Collected by Dr. Bean, but no definite locality given.

201. **Usnea barbata florida** (L) Fr

Lichen floridus LINNÆUS, Fl Suec 1130 1755
Usnea barbata florida FRIES, L U 18 1831 —SOWERBY, Eng Bot *t 872*.

Sitka (Trelease, 1180*b*). A very much dwarfed, sterile specimen, which would seem best placed here. New to Alaska.

202. Usnea barbata plicata (L.) Fr.

Lichen plicatus LINNÆUS, Fl. Suec. 1122 1755.
Usnea barbata plicata FRIES, L. E. 18 1831.—SOWERBY, Eng. Bot. *t. 257*.

Alaska (Evans, 255 in part); Hot Springs, Baranof Island (Trelease, 1187). New to Alaska.

The specimen from Hot Springs is finely developed, though sterile. It measures nine centimeters in length and is freely branched.

I have found record of only one additional form, *U. barbata dasypoga* Fr., collected by Dr. Bean at old Sitka.

CETRARIA

KEY TO THE SPECIES.

Thallus straw-colored or yellow.
   Thallus depressed, sorediate . . . . *juniperina pinastri.*
   Thallus erect, more or less branched, not sorediate.
     Thallus finger-shaped, hollow . . . . *arctica.*
     Thallus flat, lobed.
       Margins of thallus connivent . . . . *cucullata.*
       Margins of thallus not connivent . . . . *nivalis.*
Thallus chestnut brown . . . . *ciliaris.*
Thallus variously colored.
   Thallus erect, branching.
     Lobes of thallus connivent . . . . *islandica.*
     Lobes of thallus not connivent.
       Lobes of thallus narrow, freely branched . . *islandica delisæi.*
       Lobes of thallus broad, moderately branched.
                              islandica platyna.
   Thallus flat, lobed.
     Lobes of thallus narrow, elongated, channeled . . . *fahlunensis.*
     Lobes of thallus not channeled.
       Thallus ciliate on the margin, sorediate.
                              sæpincola chlorophylla.
       Thallus not ciliate on the margin.
         Thallus deeply lacunose . . . . *lacunosa.*
         Thallus not lacunose . . . . *glauca.*

203. Cetraria juniperina pinastri Ach.

Cetraria juniperina pinastri ACHARIUS, Meth. Lich. 298. 1803.—HOFFM. Plant. Lich. *t. 7. f. 1.*

Alaska (Funston, 4); St. Michael (Setchell), Cape Nome (Setchell). New to Alaska, though it has been reported from Arctic America by Richardson.

204. **Cetraria glauca** (L.) Ach.

Lichen glaucus LINNÆUS, Fl. Suec ed. 2 1094. 1755.
Cetraria glauca ACHARIUS, Meth. Lich. 296. 1803.—SOWERBY, Eng. Bot. *t. 1606*

Broughton Strait, Vancouver Island (Trelease, 1108 in part), Sitka (Trelease, 1124); Wrangell (Coville and Kearney, 402); Point Gustavus, Glacier Bay (Coville and Kearney, 786*b*); Orca (Trelease, 1122). Collected by Dr. Cooley at Sheep and Salmon Creeks, near Juneau, and at Sitka; by Dr. Hayes at Prince William Sound, and by Dr. Bean at Cook Inlet. Rothrock reports that it has been collected at Kotzebue Sound.

The specimens from Sitka and Point Gustavus show a fine development of the coralloid branchlets on the margin of the lobes.

205. **Cetraria lacunosa** Ach.

Cetraria lacunosa ACHARIUS, Meth. Lich. 295. *t. 5 f. 3*. 1803.

Sitka (Trelease, 1125); Virgin Bay (Trelease, 1089); Kadiak (Trelease, 1134*e*); Unalaska (Trelease, 1128; Setchell). Collected by Dr. Hayes at Prince William Sound; by Macoun on St. George and St. Paul Islands; and by Dr. Bean, "sterile specimen from logs on an island in Cross Sound, Baranof Island, Sitka."

The specimen from Unalaska, collected by Professor Trelease, in its general aspect and coloration suggests *Parmelia saxatilis omphalodes*, but it is undoubtedly a *Cetraria*. The specimen from Virgin Bay shows a change in coloration to reddish-brown, but it is especially interesting as showing the development of isidia, which are very characteristic of *Cetraria glauca*, but of which no mention is made in any description of *Cetraria lacunosa* to which I have access.

206. **Cetraria sæpincola chlorophylla** (Humb.) Th. Fr.

Lichen chlorophyllus HUMBOLDT, Fl. Fri. Sp 1793
Cetraria sæpincola chlorophylla TH. FRIES, Lich Arct. 40. 1860.

Sitka (Trelease, 1107); Yakutat (Trelease, 1155). Sterile. New to Alaska.

The only stations which Tuckerman gives in Syn. N. A. L. 1: 35, are Oregon and the coast of California. Th. Fries, Lichenes Arctoi, 40, records its occurrence in Finland.

207. **Cetraria ciliaris** Ach.

Cetraria ciliaris ACHARIUS, L. U. 50. 1810.

Kadiak (Trelease, 1134*d*). New to Alaska.

Fibrils on the margins of the thallus poorly developed. Apparently not common so far north.

208. Cetraria fahlunensis (L.) Schaer.

Lichen fahlunensis LINNÆUS, Fl. Suec. no. 107. 1755.
Cetraria fahlunensis SCHAERER, Spicil. 255. 1833.—SOWERBY, Eng Bot. t. 653.

Muir Glacier (Trelease, 1158), summit of White Pass (Trelease, 1162); Kadiak (Trelease, 1134c); Unalaska (Setchell); Hall Island (Trelease, 1164); St. Matthew Island (Trelease, 1163, 1166); Cape Nome (Setchell). Collected on St. Paul Island by Macoun. Rothrock includes it in his list of species collected by Dr. Bean, but with no indication of special locality.

Schaerer recognizes two forms, one indicated as *a. major*, having lobes of the thallus broad and granulate on the margin, the other *b. minor*, having the lobes of the thallus narrow and scarcely at all granulate on the margins. No. 1166 is a good example of the first form, and 1164 of the second, while 1158 and 1162 are transition forms. An examination of material in my herbarium from the mountains of New Hampshire and from Labrador shows that both forms are found on the same specimen, and therefore it hardly seems worth while to attempt to discriminate.

209. Cetraria nivalis (L.) Ach.

Lichen nivalis LINNÆUS, Fl. Suec. 413. 1755.
Cetraria nivalis ACHARIUS, Meth. Lich. 294. 1803.—SOWERBY, Eng Bot. t. 1994.

Alaska (Funston, 32); Agattu Island (Townsend, 75); St. Michael (Turner, 836); St. Matthew Island (Trelease, 1190). Collected by Dr. Hayes at Taku; by J. M. Macoun on St. George and St. Paul Islands. Under the synonym *Platysma nivale* (L.) Nylander records its occurrence at Port Clarence.

The specimen from Agattu Island by C. H. Townsend is a specimen from the U. S. Fish Commission Steamer *Albatross*. The segments of the thallus are dwarfed and, at the same time, broader than the common forms. No. 836, from St. Michael, has fragments of *Cladonia rangiferina* mixed with it.

210. Cetraria cucullata (Bell.) Ach.

Lichen cucullatus BELLARDI, App. Fl. Pedem. 1792.
Cetraria cucullata ACHARIUS, Meth. Lich. 293. 1803.—HOFFM. Plant. Lich. t. 66 f. 2.

Agattu Island (Townsend, 756); Unalaska (Setchell); St. Michael (Turner, 842; Setchell); St. Lawrence Island (Trelease, 1238, a fragment with *Cladonia rangiferina*); St. Lawrence Island, North-east Cape (Coville and Kearney, 2008); Port Clarence (Trelease, 1254, 1112, the latter a fragment mixed with *Parmelia saxatilis*, *Parmelia physodes* and *Alectoria divergens*), Cape Nome (Setchell). All specimens sterile. Collected at Taku by Dr. Hayes, and on St. Paul Island by J. M. Macoun; Hooker and Arnott report its occurrence at Kotzebue Sound, and Babington credits it to the same locality. Nylander lists *Platysma cucullata* Hoffm. as occurring at Port Clarence.

This species is distributed from about latitude 40° N to the Arctic regions, both in the Old and New Worlds.

211. **Cetraria islandica** (L.) Ach.

Lichen islandicus LINNÆUS, Fl. Suec. 1085. 1755.
Cetraria islandica ACHARIUS, Meth. Lich. 293. 1803 —SOWERBY, Eng Bot. *t. 1330.*—NYL. Syn. *t. 8. f. 32.*

Summit of White Pass (Trelease, 1193), Kadiak (Trelease, 1194, 1194*a*, 1194*b*), mixed with *Alectoria* and *Cladonia;* Unalaska (Setchell); Hall Island (Trelease, no number), St. Matthew Island (Coville and Kearney, 2113); St. Lawrence Island (Trelease, 1206); Port Clarence (Trelease, 1198, 1207); St. Michael (Setchell); Cape Nome (Setchell). Babington reports its occurrence at Norton Sound and Kotzebue Sound; Hooker and Arnott credit it to the latter locality. J. M. Macoun collected it on St. Paul and St. George Islands, the forms *gracilis* and *robustus* growing with the type. Also collected on Seward Peninsula by Arthur J. Collier.

This is a very variable species, and the transition forms between the species and its varieties are very puzzling. No. 1207 may be considered one of the most typical forms, though these specimens are somewhat lighter than is normal. The thallus grows nearly upright, branching freely. The fibrils on the edge of the lobes of the thallus are short and unbranched. The specimen from Port Clarence (NO. 1198) is much abbreviated, and in the broadening of its shining lobes tends toward the variety *platyna*. The most interesting variation, however, is in the specimens from the summit of White Pass (NO. 1193) and from Kadiak Island (NO. 1194*a*). In these specimens the lobes are long, narrow, and flexuous, thickly beset on the edge with long fibrils, which in the specimen from White Pass are variously branched. Dr. Lindsay, in West Greenland Lichens, 321, suggests that this state "might appropriately bear the name (if name is required) of form or variety *leucomeloides*" because of its resemblance to *Physcia leucomela*. All these specimens are sterile.

212. Cetraria islandica delisei (Bory.) Schaer.

Cetraria delisei BORY in Schaerer, Enum 16 1850
Cetraria islandica delisei SCHAERER, Enum 16 1850 —WESTR. Faergh *t. 16 c.*

Hall Island (Trelease, 1197); St. Matthew Island (Trelease, 1195, 1205); St Lawrence Island (Trelease, 1196); Plover Bay, Siberia (Trelease, 1199); Cape Nome (Setchell). Recorded by Farlow as having been collected on the expedition to Point Barrow; J. M. Macoun collected it on St. Paul Island; Nylander credits it to St. Lawrence Island.

It is noticeable that the development of the marginal fibrils is very slight in the variety *delisei*. No 1205 from St Matthew Island shows a few fibrils on the finer branches, near the apex of the fronds. All these forms are somewhat coarser than those of the variety *delisei* in the Tuckerman Herbarium, and all are sterile. With the specimen from Hall Island is a species of *Dicranum*.

213. Cetraria islandica platyna (Ach.) Th. Fr.

Cetraria platyna ACHARIUS, Syn. 229 1814.
Cetraria islandica platyna TH. FRIES, Lich Arct. 35. 1860

Hall Island (Trelease, 1201, 1202); St Lawrence Island (Trelease, 1200); Plover Bay, Siberia (Trelease, 1203). New to the Alaska region.

The specimens of this variety have a much richer chestnut color than the type, while the surface of the thallus is very highly polished and the marginal fibrils are very slightly developed. Not mentioned in Tuckerman's Synopsis of N A Lichens, but given by Fries as occurring in Greenland.

214. Cetraria arctica (Hook.) Tuck.

Dufourea arctica HOOKER in Richards., Frankl. Narr. 762, append. 47 *t. 31.* 1823.
Cetraria arctica TUCKERMAN, Syn. N. A. L. 1: 30. 1882.

Locality lost (Trelease, 1236); St. Matthew Island (Coville and Kearney, 2117a). Plover Bay, Siberia (Trelease, 1237, Coville and Kearney, 1850). Sterile. Reported by Farlow as occurring at Point Barrow; collected by Macoun on St. Paul Island, and by Dr Hayes at Taku. Hooker and Arnott report it from Kotzebue Sound under the synonym *Dufourea arctica* Br., and Nylander records its occurrence at Port Clarence and on St. Lawrence Island under the synonym *Dactylina arctica* (Hook.).

Mixed with it are *Cetraria islandica* and various mosses.

Additional Alaska species: *Cetraria delisei submedia* Nyl., Port Clarence; *C. crispa* (Ach.), Port Clarence; *C. nigricans* Nyl., Port Clarence and St. Lawrence Island; *Platysma tilesii* Ach., Port Clarence; and *P. sæpincola* forma *minuta* Nyl., Port Clarence — all recorded by Nylander only; *Platysma septentrionale* Nyl., listed by Nylander from Port Clarence and by Rothrock from Kotzebue Sound; *C. glauca substraminea* Babington, reported by Babington from Kotzebue Sound. Dr. Bean collected two species, *C. juniperina* (L.) Ach., sterile specimens, on Chamisso Island in Eschscholtz Bay, and *C. aleurites* (Ach.) Th. Fr. at Cook Inlet and, on the bark of coniferæ, at Eschscholtz Bay. Concerning the latter species Rothrock[1] writes: "Stein has said of this species that it is an evident transition, resembling *Cetraria* in its fruit and spermagonia, and *Parmelia* in habit, and hence often placed by later lichenologists in the latter genus." J. M. Macoun collected *C. aculeata* (Schreb.) Fr. on St. Paul Island and Nylander reports its occurrence at Port Clarence. Dr. Hayes added one species to the list, *C. glauca stenophylla* Tuck., collected at Prince William Sound. Tuckerman reports two additional species, *C. ramulosa* (Hook.) Tuck., a common alpine and arctic form, and *C. chrysantha* Tuck. The range of the latter species is very interesting. It was collected by Wright on the islands in Bering Strait, and is represented by a specimen in the Babington Herbarium collected on rocks at Kotzebue Sound; the only other locality given is Japan, where fertile specimens were collected by Wright.

RAMALINA.

KEY TO THE SPECIES.

Thallus rather elongated, finely divided . . . . . *pusilla geniculata*.
Thallus short, compressed, coarsely divided . . . . *polymorpha*.

215. Ramalina polymorpha Ach.

Ramalina polymorpha ACHARIUS, L. U. 600. 1810.

Unalaska (Setchell); St. Paul Island (Trelease, 1192). Sterile. An alpine and arctic species. Previously reported from the islands in Bering Strait, collected by Wright, and from St. Paul Island by Macoun and Dr. Bean. Rothrock's determination of Dr. Bean's specimen is revised by Nylander, who makes it *R. polymorpha emplecta*.

[1] Rothrock, Dr. J. T. List of and Notes upon the Lichens collected by Dr. T. H. Bean in Alaska and the Adjacent Regions in 1880. Proceedings of the United States National Museum, 7: 1884.

216. **Ramalina pusilla geniculata** (Hook. & Taylor) Tuck.

Ramalina geniculata HOOKER & TAYLOR, Lond. Jour. Bot. 3 - 655. 1844.
Ramalina pusilla geniculata TUCKERMAN, Syn. N. A. L. 1 26 1882

Fraser Reach, Princess Royal Island, British Columbia (Coville and Kearney, 304); St. Michael (Setchell); St. Matthew Island (Trelease, 1191, 1257). All the specimens are sterile. A specimen collected by Dr. Bean and determined by Rothrock was referred here. Nylander, in his revision of Rothrock's list, places the specimen under the species *R. minuscula* Nyl., which Nylander records as also occurring at Port Clarence and on St. Lawrence Island.

No. 304 is very finely divided, many of the branches ending in capitate soredia. It resembles specimens in the Tuckerman collection from Anticosti and the Gaspé coast. The species as represented in the Tuckerman Herbarium shows great variation in the fineness of the division of the terminal segments and in the regularity of branching as well as in the presence of soredia.

Additional Alaska species are: *R. cuspidata*, collected by J. M. Macoun on St. Paul Island, and *R. calicaris farinacea* Fr. collected by Dr. Bean on Little Koniuji Island, Shumagin group.

ADDITIONAL GENERA.

Five genera of which there are no specimens in the Harriman collection have been recorded as occurring in Alaska. A list of these, with the recorded species, is appended.

Varicellaria microsticta Nyl., reported by Nylander from Port Clarence; *Sphinctrina turbinata* (Pers.) Nyl., from the same locality as the preceding; *Pycnothalia cladinoides*, collected by William Palmer on St. Paul Island, determined by W. W. Calkins; *Urceolaria scruposa* (L.) Ach., collected by Dr. Bean, no special locality being recorded; *Gyalecta convarians* Nyl., reported for Port Clarence by Nylander; *Gyalecta rhexoblephara* (Nyl.) Tuck., collected by Wright on the islands of Bering Sea; and *Evernia thamnodes* (Flot.) Nyl., reported from Port Clarence by Nylander.

BIBLIOGRAPHY

Hooker, Sir William Jackson, and Arnott, G. A. Walker.
    1841 Botany of Beechey's Voyage to the Pacific and Behring's Strait, 133-134.
Babington, Churchill.
    1852-7 Botany of the Voyage of H. M. S. Herald by Seeman, 47-49.

Fries, Th. M.
 1860 Lichenes Arctoi.

Rothrock, J. T.
 1867 Flora of Alaska Smithsonian Report.

Lindsay, W Lauder
 1871 Observations on the Lichens collected by Dr Robert Brown in West Greenland in 1867. Transactions of the Linnæan Society of London, vol xxvii, 305-368, tab 48-52

Hooper, Capt. C. L
 1881 Cruise of the Corwin

Tuckerman, Edward.
 1882 Synopsis North American Lichens, Part I; Part II, 1888

Rothrock, J. T.
 1884 Proceedings of the United States National Museum, vol. VII, 1-9

Farlow, Dr William G.
 1885 Ray, Report of the International Polar Expedition to Point Barrow, Alaska, 192

Knowlton
 1886 Proceedings of the National Museum, vol IX.

Wainio, Edv
 1887 Monographia Cladoniarum, vol I; vol II, 1894

Turner, Lucien M
 1888 Contributions to the Natural History of Alaska.

Nylander, Dr William
 1888 Enumeratio Lichenum Freti Behringii, 1-91 Bull Soc Linn de Normandie, vol 1, 1888

Cummings, Clara E.
 1892 Cooley, Miss Grace E., Plants collected in Alaska aud Nanaimo, B C., July and August, 1891 Bull Torr Club, vol XIX, 248, 249
 1892 An Expedition through the Yukon District, by Charles Willard Hayes. National Geographic Magazine, vol IV, 160-162.

Arnold, Dr F.
 1896 Labrador.
 1896 Lichenologische Fragmente, 35, Newfoundland Separat-Abdruck aus der "Oester botan. Zeitschrift," Jahrg XLVI

Kurtz, F.
 1895 Die Flora des Chilcatgebietes in Sudostlichen Alaska nach der Sammlungen der Gebruder Krause Engler's botanische Jahrbucher, vol. XIX, 327-431

Macoun, J. M
 1899 Jordan's Report on the Fur Seals and Fur Seal Islands of the North Pacific, pt 3.

Calkins, W. J.
 1899 Jordan's Report on the Fur Seals and Fur Seal Islands of the North Pacific, pt 3

Cummings, Clara E.
  1901 Reconnaissances in the Cape Nome and Norton Bay Regions, Alaska, in 1900, by Alfred H. Brooks, George B. Richardson, Arthur J. Collier and Walter C. Mendenhall, United States Geological Survey, 167

Miyoshi, M.
  1901 Ueber die Sporocarpenevacuation und darauf erfolgendes Sporenausstreuen bei einer Flechte The Journal of the College of Science, Imperial University, Tokyo, Japan, vol. xv, pt 3, pp 367-370 tab 18.

PLATE VIII.

Verrucaria fulva sp nov.

FIG. 1. Thalli showing grouping ($\times 5$).
2. Spores ($\times 250$).
3. Section of apothecium ($\times 48$). *a*, ampithecium; *p*, perithecium, *m*, medullary layer; *g*, gonidia, *c*, cortical layer.

The figures are drawn from specimens collected by Dr. Trelease at Port Wells. (No. 918)

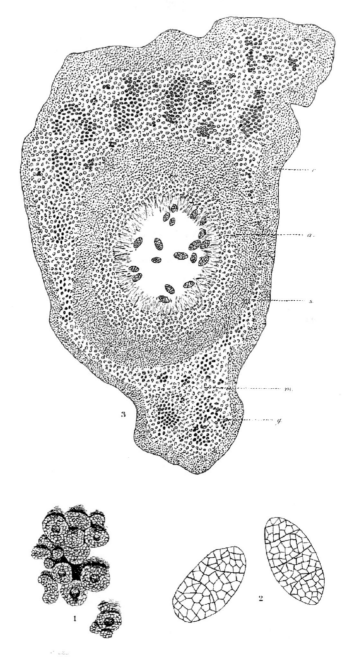

ALASKA LICHENS

PLATE IX.

Pertusaria pocillaria sp. nov.

Fig 1. Portion of fruited thallus ($\times 8$). *c*, cup formed by the evacuation of the asci.
2. Vertical section of thallus and apothecia ($\times 24$).
3. Vertical section of apothecium ($\times 96$).
4. Asci and paraphyses ($\times 187$).
5. Spores ($\times 375$).

The figures are drawn from specimens collected by Dr. Trelease at Farragut Bay. (NO. 806*a*)

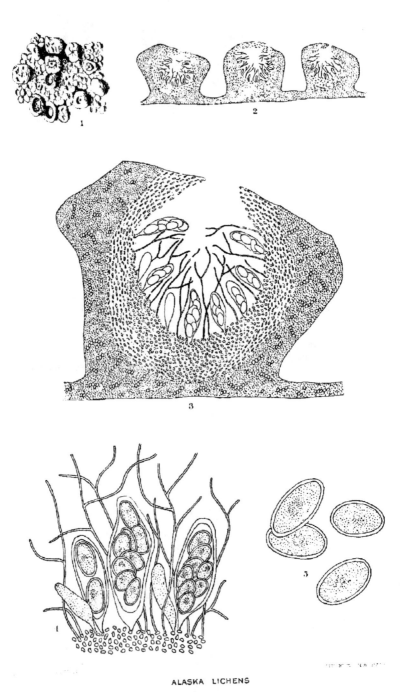

ALASKA LICHENS

The following paper on the Algæ of the Expedition, by Prof. De Alton Saunders, was originally published in the Proceedings of the Washington Academy of Sciences, vol. III, pp. 391–486, Nov 15, 1901. It is here reprinted from the same electrotype plates, so that it may be quoted exactly as if it were the original. The original pagination has been preserved and transferred to the inner or hinge side of the page, where it is enclosed in brackets, thus [392], while the consecutive pagination of the present volume has been added in the usual place. In the plates the original numbers and running headline, slightly abbreviated, have been preserved [in brackets], while the volume designation and serial plate numbers have been added in the usual place. The original text references to the plates are unchanged. The present headpiece and title have been substituted for the running heading of the Academy's Proceedings and the original title, which was: *Papers from the Harriman Alaska Expedition. XXV. The Algæ.* No other alterations have been made.

The author desires to record the following corrections

Page 156 [392], seventh line from bottom, for 'vagnum' read *vagum*.
Page 160 [396]
    Seventh line from top in table, for 'Gloiosiphonia' read *Gloiopeltis*.
    Sixth line from bottom of table, for 'yendori' read *yendoi*.
Page 159 [395] and 203 [439], for 'Calithamnion' read *Callithamnion*.
Page 161 [397], fifth line from top, for 'mirabilis' read *mirabile*.
Page 163 [399], fourth line from bottom for 'biasolletiana' read *biasolettiana*
Page 178 [414], seventeenth line from top and seventh line from bottom, for 'arctica' read *arcta*
Page 181 [417], tenth line from bottom, for 'stilophorea' read *stilophoræ*
Page 183 [419]
    Seventeenth line from bottom, for 'cirrosa' read *cirrhosa*.
    Seventh line from bottom, for 'Zoostera' read *Zostera*.
Page 185 [421], thirteenth line from bottom, for 'lepidum' read *lepidium*.
Page 186 [422]
    Seventh line from top, for 'Systophyllum lepidum' read *Cystophyllum lepidium*
    Sixteenth line from bottom, for 'Rhodamea' read *Rhodomela*.
Page 190 [426], fifth line from top, for 'cryptostomata' read *hairs*.
Page 202 [438], eighteenth and eleventh lines from bottom, for 'perithecia' read *cystocarps*.
Page 203 [439], eleventh line from top, for 'pekeanum' read *pikeanum*
Page 204 [440], thirteenth line from bottom, for 'Gratloupiaceæ' read *Grateloupiaceæ*.
Page 205 [441], fourth line from bottom, for 'patens' read *patena*
Page 206 [442], eighteenth line from top for 'yendori' read *yendoi*
Page 236 [472], for 'lacticosta' read *laticosta*.

EDITOR.

(154)

THE ALGÆ OF THE EXPEDITION

BY DE ALTON SAUNDERS

CONTENTS

Introduction 155
Geographic distribution 156
Catalogue of species 160

INTRODUCTION

COLLECTIONS of algæ were made by the writer and other members of the Harriman Alaska Expedition at Victoria, in British Columbia, and at the following localities in Alaska: Wrangell, Annette Island, Juneau, Glacier Bay, Sitka, Yakutat Bay, Prince William Sound (near Orca and in Virgin Bay), Cook Inlet, Kukak Bay, Kadiak Island, and Popof Island and Unga Island of the Shumagin group. This paper contains an enumeration of the species collected at these localities. Except where otherwise stated, the numbers representing localities are those of the collections made by the writer.

The list of Chlorophyceæ, except the Oedogoniaceæ which were determined by Dr. K. E. Hirn, was prepared by Mr. F.

S. Collins. Most of the Oscillatoriaceæ were determined by Dr. Maurice Gomont, and the list of Bacillariaceæ is entirely the work of Professor A. M. Edwards. Acknowledgment is also due Dr. F. R. Kjellman, who examined many of the Alarias and the species of *Fucus* and named the entire collection of Corallinaceæ; to Dr. W. A. Setchell for examining several species of *Laminaria* and Cyanophyceæ; and to Dr. W. G. Farlow for determining several species of the Rhodophyceæ. My thanks are also due to Dr. C. E. Bessey for the loan of valuable books, to Professor Conway MacMillan for library and herbarium privileges and for the loan of books, and to Miss Josephine E. Tilden for the privilege of examining material, preserved in fluid, of her entire Puget Sound collection.

In this paper are catalogued 380 species of algæ, of which nine are new to science and 240 new to Alaska.

The number of species, both fresh water and marine, in each of the six classes of algæ is:

	FRESH WATER	MARINE	TOTAL
Schizophyceæ	26	2	28
Conjugatæ	96	0	96
Chlorophyceæ	18	26	44
Phæophyceae	0	70	70
Rhodophyceæ	1	68	69
Bacillariaceæ	32	41	73

GEOGRAPHIC DISTRIBUTION.

Though the algal flora of the Pacific coast in not well enough known to enable a map showing the exact distribution of species to be made, yet, enough collecting has been done to indicate the general distribution.

The Cyanophyceæ, Chlorophyceæ, Bacillariaceæ and the single freshwater species of the Rhodophyceæ (*Batrachospermum vagnum*) are so largely cosmopolitan that they have been disregarded in the table which follows. Of the remaining 126 species, comprising the Phæophyceæ and Rhodophyceæ, only seven are found on the southern California coast, 37 occur on the central California coast, 68 range from Puget Sound northward into Alaska waters, 49 are peculiar to the Pacific coast of North America, and 55 are either circumpolar or inhabitants of the north Atlantic. Furthermore, of the 126 species, 39 are reported from Bering Sea, and of these, 18 are circumpolar or north Atlantic forms and 21 are peculiar to the Pacific coast of North America.

At least three distinct regions may be distinguished in the algal flora of the Pacific coast of North America; a southern, a Californian, and a northern.

The southern region extends from Point Conception southward, perhaps to the equator. It is characterized by *Nereocystis giganteus, Sargassum agardianum, Taonia lennebackeræ, Zonaria tournefortii* and many other tropical species.

The Californian region extends from Point Conception on the south, to Puget sound on the north, and is characterized by forms like *Dictyoneuron, Postelsia, Laminaria sinclairii, Laminaria andersonii,* and *Fucus harveyanus*. It may more properly be limited on the north by the mouth of the Columbia River and the shore line between that point and Puget Sound may be regarded as a transitional area.

The northern region begins at Puget Sound and extends northward to and including Bering Sea. It is characterized by such species as *Odonthalia aleutica, Polysiphonia bipinnata, Euthora cristata, Rhodymenia pertusa, Constantinea rosamarina, Fucus evanescens megacephalus, Agarum turneri, Cymathere triplicata, Laminaria bongardiana, Laminaria bullata, Dictyosiphon fœniculaceus,* and *Myelophycus intestinalis.*

GEOGRAPHIC DISTRIBUTION OF ALASKAN ALGÆ ON THE PACIFIC COAST

Names.[1]	Southern California to Alaska	Central California to Alaska	Puget Sound to Alaska	From Dixon Entrance northward	Circumpolar or North Atlantic	Peculiar to the Pacific Coast of North America	British Columbia	Bering Sea
Streblonema minutissima			*			*		
Streblonema pacifica						*		
Streblonema irregularis	*					*		
Phycocelis baltica				*	*			
Ectocarpus tomentosus		*			*			
Ectocarpus confervoides	*				*			*
Pylaiella littoralis			*		*			
Sphacelaria cirrosa				*	*			*
Sphacelaria racemosa arctica				*	*		*	
Homeostroma undulata	*				*			
Homeostroma latifolia	*						*	
Homeostroma lobata				*	*			
Punctaria plantaginea			*		*			*
Phyllitis fascia		*		*	*			
Scytosiphon lomentarius	*				*			*
Scytosiphon bullosus		*				*		*
Coilodesme californica		*	*					
Coilodesme bulligera			*					
Coilodesme linearis				*		*		
Myelophycus intestinalis			*					
Colpomenia sinuosa	*				*			*
Soranthera ulvoides		*						
Elachista lubrica				*	*			*
Dictyosiphon foeniculaceus			*		*			*
Desmarestia aculeata		*	*		*			
Desmarestia viridis		*			*			
Liebmannia sp				*				*
Endesme virescens				*	*	*		
Myrionema strangulans		*	*		*			
Mesogloia simplex			*			*		
Chordaria flagelliformis					*			
Chordaria abietina		*				*		*
Ralfsia deusta				*	*			
Ralfsia clavata	*				*		*	*
Chorda filum				*	*		*	
Alaria cordata			*			*		
Alaria fragilis				*		*		
Alaria laticosta				*		*		*
Alaria lanceolata						*		*
Alaria fistulosa				*		*		*
Laminaria bullata			*			*		*
Laminaria bongardiana			*			*		*
Laminaria cuneata				*	*			
Laminaria solidungula			*	*	*			
Laminaria saccharina			*			*		
Hedophyllum sessile			*			*		
Hedophyllum subsessile		*	*	*		*		
Cymathere triplicata			*			*		*

[1] Black face type indicates new species

THE ALGÆ

Names	Southern California to Alaska	Central California to Alaska	Puget Sound to Alaska	From Dixon Entrance northward	Circumpolar or North Atlantic	Peculiar to the Pacific Coast of North America	British Columbia	Bering Sea
Pleurophycus gardneri			*			*		
Thalassiophyllum clathrus				*		*		*
Eisenia arborea		*				*		
Macrocystis pyrifera		*				*		
Nereocystis priapus		*				*		*
Agarum turneri			*		*	*		*
Agarum gmelini				*		*		
Costaria mertensii		*				*		
Fucus evanescens			*					
Cystophyllum lepidum			*			*		
Bangia atropurpurea pacifica						*	*	
Porphyra laciniata				*	*			*
Porphyra perforata	*							
Porphyra amplissima					*			
Porphyra miniata cuneiformis		*			*			
Porphyra tenuissima				*	*			
Choreocolax polysiphoniæ				*		*		
Endocladia muricata		*				*		
Iridæa membranacea			*					
Iridæa laminarioides							*	
Gigartina papillata		*				*		
Gigartina pacifica				*		*		
Kalymenia californica		*				*		
Ahnfeldtia plicata		*			*			
Turnerella mertensiana		*				*		
Euthora cristata			*		*			
Rhodymenia pertusa					*			
Rhodymenia palmata					*			
Plocamium coccineum uncinatum					*			
Halosaccion fucicola			*			*		*
Halosaccion ramentaceum					*			*
Halosaccion firmum				*		*		*
Halosaccion tilesii				*		*?		*
Halosaccion microsporum			*		*			*
Nitophyllum ruthenicum				*		*		*
Delesseria bærii			*		*			
Delesseria alata					*		*	
Delesseria sinuosa				*	*			*
Delesseria crassifolia								*
Delesseria serrata								*
Rhodomela floccosa		*				*		*
Rhodomela larix		*			*?			*
Odonthalia aleutica			*			*		*
Odonthalia kamtschatica				*		*		*
Polysiphonia bipinnata			*			*		*
Polysiphonia arctica					*			
Calithamnion floccosum pacificum		*				*		
Calithamnion plumula							*	
Calithamnion pikeanum		*				*		*
Ptilota asplenoides				*				
Ptilota plumosa				*	*			

Names	Southern California to Alaska	Central California to Alaska	Puget Sound to Alaska	From Dixon Entrance northward	Circumpolar or North Atlantic	Peculiar to the Pacific Coast of North America	British Columbia	Bering Sea
Ptilota serrata				*	*			
Antithamnion boreale		..		*	*		..	*
Ceramium rubrum		*			*			*
Ceramium codicola		*		..	....		*	....
Microcladia borealis		*				*	*	..
Rhodochorton rothii						*		*
Gloiosiphonia furcata			*		..		*	
Gloiosiphonia californica		..						
Cryptonemia obovata		....	*	...			*	
Dumontia filiforme		....		*	*			..
Cryptosiphonia grayana			*	..			*	..
Dilsea californica	*			..	..		*	
Dilsea arctica		..		*	*			*
Constantinea rosa-marina			*		...		*	*
Hildenbrandtia rosea		*			*		....	*
Melobesia patens		*	..		*		*	....
Lithophyllum farlowii		*	..					
Lithophyllum compactum		....		*	*		....	
Lithophyllum glaciale				*				
Lithothamnion læve				*	....			
Clathromorphum circumscriptum				*			*	
Lepidomorphum yendoi				*			*	*
Amphiroa tuberculosa				*			*	
Amphiroa epiphlegmoides			....	*				
Amphiroa planiuscula								....
Corallina arbuscula		*?					*	
Corallina pilulifera filiformis				*			*	

CATALOGUE OF SPECIES.

SCHIZOPHYCEÆ.

Family CHROOCOCCACEÆ.

Chroococcus turgidus (Kuetz.) Naegeli.

Distributed through a mass of *Microcystis marginata* which formed a slimy coating on a perpendicular cliff over which water was trickling. Juneau (75).

Chroococcus rufescens (Bréb.) Naegeli.

Forming with *Stigonema* a reddish coating on a rock five hundred feet above sea level. Prince William Sound (Trelease 501).

Schizothrix lardacea (Cesati) Gomont.

Forming bright rose-red tufts on rocks exposed to fresh water spray, near Orca, Prince William Sound (304). Identified by Gomont.

Schizothrix lacustris A. Braun.

In a freshwater pool with *Stigonema* near Prince William Sound (300). Identified by Setchell.

Microcoleus vaginatus (Vaucher) Gomont.

Forming, with *Scytonema mirabilis*, a thin coating on damp ground recently covered by snow. Glacier Bay (104).

Family *NOSTOCACEÆ*.

Nostoc commune Vaucher.

Forming thin leathery thalli of indefinite size and shape on damp ground near Glacier Bay (106); Hidden Glacier, Yakutat Bay (502).

Cells spherical or oblong, 12–18 μ in diameter; often two to four cells coalesced. Tegument colorless; cytoplasm finely granulated.

Aphanothece microspora Naegeli.

Forming with *Chroococcus turgidus* a slimy coating on a perpendicular cliff over which water was trickling. Juneau (75).

Microcystis marginata Naegeli.

Forming a slimy coating on a perpendicular cliff near Juneau (75).

Dermocarpa prasina Born. & Thur.

Abundant on *Sphacelaria racemosa arctica* and *Sphacelaria cirrosa*. From Puget Sound to the Shumagin Islands.

Dermocarpa fucicola sp. nov. (Plate XLVI, figs. 4 and 5.)

Phycotheca Boreali-Americana, No. 801

Plant forming dark violet brown patches 2–12 mm. in extent, cells 40–60 μ high, 18–25 μ broad, ovate, clavate or spatulate, much narrowed below; schizospores abundant. On *Fucus evanescens megacephala*, Puget Sound (440). Forming orbicular or irregular patches which become confluent into irregular masses of indefinite extent.

This plant is closely related to Savageau's *D. biscayensis*, but differs from it in the larger size of the patches and the shape and size of the individual cells. In *D. biscayensis* the plant forms orbicular patches 1 mm. broad and the cells are 25–30 μ broad.

Family *OSCILLATORIACEÆ*.

Oscillatoria amœna (Kuetz.) Gomont.

The plant formed a soft, felt like, dark bluish-green mass 3–10 mm. thick, of indefinite extent, lining the bottom of the outlet of a hot spring. The water in the outlet where the plant was abundant ranged from 80° F. some distance from the spring to 120° F. near the spring. Near Sitka (158). Identified by Gomont.

Phormidium autumnale (Ag.) Gomont.

Forming a thin dark blue coating on small rocks in a rapid stream emptying into Kukak Bay (332). Identified by Gomont.

Phormidium laminosum (Ag.) Gomont.

Forming a thin membranaceous stratum on perpendicular rocks moistened by spray from a waterfall, Orca (301) Identified by Gomont.

Lyngbya ærugineo-cœrulea (Kuetz.) Gomont.

In a felt-like mass of filaments of *Vaucheria* Juneau (74); with *Zygnema* sp. in a small pond on an island in the Muir Glacier (107).

Nostoc sphæroides Kuetz.?

Forming a soft bluish green coating on rocks near Juneau (75). This species was submitted to Dr. Setchell, who says of it "The *Nostoc* is a minute spherical one very often found but I am uncertain as to whether it is *N. sphæroides* or not."

Desmonema wrangelii (Ag.) Bor. & Fla.

Mixed with *Tolypothrix tenuis* from a clear brook emptying into Glacier Bay (103). In a similar locality and associated with the same species on Popof Island (404).

Family *SCYTONEMACEÆ*.

Scytonema varium Kuetz.

On rocks moistened by spray from a waterfall near Juneau (76). Identified by Setchell.

Scytonema myochrous (Dillw.) Ag.

With *Tolypothrix tenuis*, forming small tufts on rocks in a brook emptying into Glacier Bay. Identified by Setchell.

Scytonema mirabile Bornet.

On moist ground near Glacier Bay, with *Microcoleus vaginatus* (104) On the perpendicular surface of a rock, with *Vaucheria*, moistened by dripping water, Kukak Bay (347).

Scytonema figuratum Ag.

In a freshwater stream emptying into Glacier Bay (103 *b*).

Tolypothrix tenuis Kuetz.

Forming brownish or blue-green tufts attached to rocks in fresh water. Glacier Bay (300); Popof Island (404). Identified by Setchell.

Family *STIGONEMATACEÆ*.

Hapalosiphon pumilus (Kuetz.) Kirchner.
In a freshwater pond near Seldovia, Cook Inlet (424).

Stigonema minutum (Ag) Hassall.
Forming a thin brown coating with *Chroococcus rufescens* on damp rocks several hundred feet above sea level, Prince William Sound (Trelease 501).

The threads are about 1 mm. high, 13-25 μ broad, irregularly branched and flexuously curved; sheath yellowish brown, internal tegument much darker; main filament usually of one layer of cells; the branches usually of two or more, heterocysts abundant, yellowish, lateral or intercalary.

Stigonema ocellatum (Dillw.) Thur.
On rocks in a rapid stream emptying into Glacier Bay, floating in a quiet freshwater pool, Prince William Sound (300, 302).

The plant forms dark brown, loosely cæspitose tufts 2-7 or 8 mm. high which are attached at first but finally are floating, irregularly branched, branches elongated, patent, primary filaments one or two cells thick (35-50 μ) all bearing hormogones, trichomes 21-40 μ broad; sheath broad, indistinctly lamellose, yellowish brown except near the ends on young branches, cells 25-35 μ, shorter than broad, surrounded by a dark brown tegument; heterocysts lateral, scarce; hormogones 13 μ broad, 50-65 μ long.

Family *RIVULARIACEÆ*

Calothrix fusca (Kuetz.) Bornet.
Imbedded in the gelatinous coating of *Batrachospermum vagum* from a freshwater pond, Cook Inlet (423); Kadiak Island (504).

The plants, which were apparently immature, resemble the form of *C. æruginosa* of Kuetz [1] The threads are loosely gregarious, broad, curved and somewhat enlarged at the base; sheath broad, ochraceous with age, produced into long thread-like articulations; heterocysts 10 μ broad.

Calothrix scopulorum (Weber & Mohr) Ag.
In salt water, Puget Sound.

Rivularia biasolletiana Menegh.
On rocks in freshwater streams, Juneau (76); Glacier Bay (102). Identified by Setchell.

[1] Kuetz Tab Phyc 2: Pl 45, Figs 5 and 6

The plant forms minute, hard, dark bluish green thalli 1-3 mm. in diameter, which finally become agglutinated into hollow indefinite masses.

Family *HYDRURACEÆ*.

Hydrurus penicillatus Ag.

Plant forming dark olive-green filaments attached to smooth round pebbles in a rapid brook emptying into Kukak Bay (351).

The filaments are 7-20 mm. in length, having long primary branches bearing many short penicillate ones.

CONJUGATÆ.

Family *DESMIDIACEÆ*.

Mesotænium braunii De Bary. (Plate XLIII, fig. 29.)

In a freshwater pond near Cook Inlet.

The cells are cylindrical, $2\frac{1}{4}$ times as long as broad; 16 to 18 μ broad, 38-45 μ long.

Penium interruptum Bréb.

In a freshwater pond near Seldovia, Cook Inlet.

Plant 24-40 μ wide, 130-145 μ long. Slightly smaller in all its dimensions but agrees otherwise with the description.

Penium closterioides Ralfs.

In a freshwater pond on Popof Island.

Diameter 140 μ, length 150 μ.

Penium margaritaceum (Ehrenb.) Bréb.

Occasional in freshwater, Kukak Bay.

Cells 25 μ wide, 100 μ long.

Penium polymorphum Perty.

In quiet water near Kukak Bay.

Cells 22 μ wide, 35 μ long. Very delicately punctate-striate.

Penium oblongum De Bary.

In a freshwater pond near Virgin Bay, Prince William Sound (302).

Diameter 21 μ, length 64 μ.

Penium digitus (Ehrenb.) Breb. (Plate XLIV, fig. 3.)

In quiet water, Virgin Bay. Rare.

Diameter 54 μ, length 183 μ. The plant averages almost a third smaller in all its parts than the measurements given by various authorities

Closterium juncidum Ralfs.

In quiet water near Seldovia, Cook Inlet (422).

Diameter 10 μ, length 240 μ. The plant is slightly bent, but little contracted toward the ends, which are obtusely rounded; membranes smooth, light brown; vacuoles not apparent.

Closterium angustatum reticulatum Wolle.

Occasional in a freshwater pond near Cook Inlet.

Diameter 16–19 μ, length 340 μ. The plant is dark brown, marked with delicate longitudinally and spirally arranged striæ.

Closterium acerosum (Schrank) Ehrenb. (Plate XLIII, fig. 27.)

In a freshwater pond near Seldovia, Cook Inlet.

Diameter 18–29 μ, length 200–300 μ.

Virgin Bay, Prince William Sound.

Diameter 29 μ, length 265–300 μ.

Closterium striolatum Ehrenb.

In quiet water in Kukak Bay (283).

Diameter 25–30 μ, length 275–300 μ.

Closterium brebissonii Delp.

In a freshwater pond near Cook Inlet (224).

Diameter 18 μ, length 650 μ.

Closterium lunula (Muell.) Nitzsch.

Occasional in quiet water near Kukak Bay.

Diameter 70 μ, length 450 μ.

Closterium acutum (Lyngb.) Bréb.

In a freshwater pool near Prince William Sound (300).

Diameter 8–9 μ, length 85–100 μ. The plant is small and slightly bent, ten times as long as broad, tapering from the middle to the rounded ends; cytoderm smooth and colorless.

Closterium dianæ Ehrenb.

Freshwater pool, Prince William Sound (302). Only one specimen seen.

Diameter 16 μ, length 180 μ.

Closterium venus Kuetz. (Plate XLIII, fig. 15.)

In a pond near Seldovia, Cook Inlet (422).

Diameter 9 μ, length 85 μ.

Closterium parvulum Naeg. (Plate XLIII, fig. 14.)

Very abundant in freshwater pond near Seldovia, Cook Inlet (424). Diameter 8–12 μ, length 100 μ.

Tetmemorus brebissonii (Menegh.) Ralfs.
In freshwater near Prince William Sound: frequent.
Diameter 23 μ, length 78 μ.

Tetmemorus lævis (Kuetz.) Ralfs.
In a freshwater stream, Virgin Bay (300); Yakutat Bay.
Diameter 21–24 μ, length 91–100 μ. The plant is slightly constricted and not at all punctate.

Pleurotænium nodosum (Bail.) Lund.
Common in a freshwater pond, Popof Island.
Diameter 40–45 μ, length 290–325 μ.

Pleurotænium truncatum (Bréb.) Naeg.
In a freshwater pond near Seldovia, Cook Inlet.
Diameter 45 μ, length 216 μ.

Disphinctium cucurbita (Bréb.) Reinsch.
In a freshwater pond near Prince William Sound (302).
Diameter 27 μ, length 67 μ.

Disphinctium connatum (Bréb.) DeBary. (Plate XLIII, fig. 30.)
In a freshwater pond near Seldovia, Cook Inlet. Only one specimen was seen.
Diameter 24 μ, length 38 μ.

Docidium baculum Bréb.
In a freshwater pond, Popof Island.
Diameter 27 μ, length 228 μ. The plant is slightly wider than the description given, but is not at all narrowed as are the other species.

Docidium coronulatum Grun.
In a freshwater pool near Kukak Bay.
Diameter 40 μ, length 432 μ.

Docidium dilatatum (Cleve.) Lund.
In a freshwater pond, Popof Island.
Diameter 13 μ, length 165 μ. The plant has five pearly granules at each end.

Docidium gracile Wittr.
Triploceras gracile BAIL. Micr.
Common in fresh water near Prince William Sound.
Diameter 27 μ. The plant has two rows of rather long spines.

Docidium minutum Ralfs.
Pleurotænium ? minutum (Ralfs) Delponte
In freshwater near Prince William Sound.
Diameter 11 μ, length 135 μ.

Arthrodesmus convergens Ehrenb. (Plate XLIV, fig. 14.)
In a freshwater pond near Seldovia, Cook Inlet (422). Rare.
Diameter 32 μ, length 32 μ without the spines.

Xanthidium antilopæum (Breb.) Kuetz. (Plate XLIII, fig. 38.)
In a freshwater pond near Cook Inlet.
Diameter 55 μ, length 55 μ including the spines. The spines near the apex of the semi-cells are more nearly straight than in the figures given of this species.

Xanthidium armatum (Bréb.) Ralfs. (Plate XLIV, fig. 18.)
In a freshwater pond near Virgin Bay, Prince William Sound.
Diameter 81 μ, length 128 μ. Most of the spines are bifurcated, with the points divergent.

Cosmarium granatum Bréb. (Plate XLIII, fig. 8.)
In a freshwater pond near Seldovia, Cook Inlet.
Diameter 18 μ, length 32 μ.

Cosmarium constrictum Delp. (Plate XLIII, figs 33, 34.)
In a freshwater pool near Virgin Bay, Prince William Sound (300).
Diameter 40 μ, length 65 μ.

Cosmarium bioculatum Bréb. (Plate XLIII, fig. 28.)
Common in a freshwater pond, Seldovia, Cook Inlet (422).
Diameter 16–18 μ, length 17–18 μ.

Cosmarium hammeri Reinsch. (Plate XLIII, fig 7.)
In a freshwater pond near Seldovia, Cook Inlet (422).
Diameter 10–14 μ, length 18–22 μ. Very close to the variety *subangustatum* of Boldt. The angles are a little more acute than in the type; the apex of the semicells is very emarginate.

Cosmarium depressum (Naeg.) Lund. (Plate XLIII, fig. 17.)
In a freshwater pond near Seldovia, Cook Inlet.
Diameter 16–20 μ, length 18 μ.

Cosmarium holmiense Lund. (Plate XLIV, fig. 28.)
In freshwater near Kukak Bay.
Diameter 32 μ, length 54 μ.

Cosmarium venustum (Bréb.) Arch.
In a freshwater pond near Seldovia, Cook Inlet.

Diameter 18 µ, length 27 µ. In its measurements the Alaskan plant agrees with Nordstedt's variety *induratum* but has the form of the type.

Cosmarium latum Bréb. (Plate XLIV, fig. 4.)
In a freshwater pool near Kukak Bay.
Diameter 68 µ, length 100 µ.

Cosmarium contractum Kirch. (Plate XLIV, fig. 16.)
In freshwater near Kukak Bay.
Diameter 22 µ, length 22 µ.

Cosmarium sexangulare Lund. (Plate XLIII, fig. 39.)
In a freshwater pond near Seldovia, Cook Inlet.
Diameter 27 µ, length 32 µ.

Cosmarium tumidum Lund. (Plate XLIV, fig. 21.)
In a freshwater pond near Seldovia, Cook Inlet.
Diameter 27–30 µ, length 35–38 µ. Several specimens were found, all of which belong to Kirchner's variety *subtile*, the cytoderm being delicately punctate over the whole surface.

Cosmarium parvulum Bréb. (Plate XLIII, fig. 6.)
In freshwater, Virgin Bay, Prince William Sound.
Diameter 17–19 µ, length 35–38 µ. Some of the specimens have a smooth cytoderm and on some it is delicately punctate.

Cosmarium kitchelii Wolle. (Plate XLIV, fig. 17.)
In a freshwater pond Seldovia, Cook Inlet.
Diameter 43 µ, length 51 µ. The plant agrees in all three views with Wolle's description except that the three central rows of granules are neither longer nor more conspicuous than the marginal ones.

Cosmarium pyramidatum Bréb. ? (Plate XLIII, fig. 40.)
In a freshwater pool near Juneau; Kukak Bay.
Diameter 35 µ, length 54 µ, isthmus 11 µ wide; cell membranes very delicately punctate.

Cosmarium pachydermum Lund. (Plate XLIV, fig. 12.)
In a freshwater pond near Seldovia, Cook Inlet.
Diameter 73 µ, length 103 µ.

Cosmarium undulatum Corda. (Plate XLIV, fig. 9.)
In a freshwater pond near Seldovia, Cook Inlet (422).
Diameter 38 µ, length 59 µ, cytoderm smooth, edge crenate, ten crenæ to a semicell; sinus enlarged outward.

Cosmarium pseudogranatum Nordst. (Plate XLIII, fig. 21.)
In a freshwater pond, Popof Island.
Diameter 35 μ, length 51 μ.

Cosmarium botrytis Menegh. (Plate XLIII, fig. 11.)
In freshwater, Popof Island.
Diameter 35–43 μ, length 40–52 μ.

Cosmarium conspersum Ralfs. (Plate XLIII, fig. 1.)
In a freshwater pond, Cook Inlet (424).

Cosmarium cælatum Ralfs. (Plate XLIII, fig 2.)
In a freshwater pond, Glacier Bay; only one specimen seen.
Diameter 40–45 μ.

Cosmarium portianum nephroideum Wittr. (Plate XLIII, figs. 12, 13.)
Freshwater pond, Seldovia, Cook Inlet.
Diameter 21 μ, length 32 μ; isthmus 9 μ broad, sinus 5 μ wide. The verrucæ are short, absent from the sinus.

Cosmarium ochtodes Nordst. (Plate XLIII, fig 10.)
In a freshwater pond near Seldovia, Cook Inlet.
Diameter 64 μ, length 97 μ.

Cosmarium intermedium Delp. (Plate XLIV, fig. 1.)
In a freshwater pond near Seldovia, Cook Inlet.
Diameter 74 μ, length 66 μ, isthmus 12 μ wide. The plant is covered all over with large pearly granules.

Cosmarium subcrenatum Hantzsch. (Plate XLIII, fig. 20.)
In freshwater ponds, Glacier Bay; Kukak Bay.
Diameter 26–30 μ, length 35–40 μ.

Cosmarium phaseolus Bréb. (Plate XLIV, fig. 8.)
In freshwater near Seldovia, Cook Inlet.
Diameter 24 μ, length 27 μ; sinus 3 μ broad; isthmus 4 μ broad.

Cosmarium costatum Nordst.
In freshwater near Virgin Bay, Prince William Sound.
Diameter 40 μ.

Cosmarium pulcherrimum Nordst. (Plate XLIII, figs. 18, 19.)
In freshwater near Kukak Bay.
Diameter 38 μ, length 52 μ.

Cosmarium quadrifarium Lund. (Plate XLIII, fig. 22.)
In freshwater near Virgin Bay, Prince William Sound.
Diameter 33 μ, length 40 μ.

Cosmarium broomei Thwaites. (Plate XLIII, figs. 26, 35, 36.)
In freshwater, Popof Island.
Diameter 40 μ, length 40 μ.

Cosmarium ornatum Ralf. (Plate XLIII, fig. 3.)
Very abundant in a freshwater pond, Kukak Bay; Cook Inlet.
Diameter 32-45 μ, length 38-75 μ.

Cosmarium sphalerostichum Nordst. (Plate XLIV, fig. 6.)
In a freshwater pond near Seldovia, Cook Inlet.
Diameter 16 μ, length 16 μ.

Cosmarium pseudotaxichondrum Nordst. (Plate XLIII, fig. 5.)
In freshwater ponds near Prince William Sound.
Diameter 33 μ, length 22 μ.

Pleurotæniopsis pseudoconnata (Nordst.) Lagerh.
In a freshwater pond near Seldovia, Cook Inlet.
Diameter 27 μ, length 38 μ. The sinus is broad and very shallow and the margins distinctly striate; cytoderm finely punctate; the end view a perfect circle and the chlorophyll body divided into eight equal arms.

Pleurotæniopsis debaryi (Archer) Lund. (Plate XLIV, fig. 20.)
In a freshwater pond near Seldovia, Cook Inlet.
Diameter 65 μ, length 100 μ, isthmus 40 μ broad. Only one specimen was found and this agrees with Nordstedt's variety *spitsbergensis*.

Pleurotæniopsis ralfsii (Bréb.) Lund.
In a freshwater pond near Seldovia, Cook Inlet.
Diameter 54 μ, length 70 μ.

Staurastrum dejectum Bréb. (Plate XLIV, fig. 5.)
In a freshwater pond near Seldovia, Cook Inlet (422).
Diameter 21 μ, length 21 μ.

Staurastrum dejectum mucronatum (Ralfs) Kirchn.
Occurs with the type.
Diameter 27 μ, length 27 μ.

Staurastrum ravenelii Wood. (Plate XLIV, fig. 29.).
In a freshwater pond, Seldovia, Cook Inlet.

Staurastrum pygmæum Bréb.
In a freshwater pond near Seldovia, Cook Inlet.
Diameter 27 μ, length 30 μ.

Staurastrum calyxoides Wolle. (Plate XLIII, fig. 31.)
In freshwater near Prince William Sound (300).
Diameter 10 μ, length 20 μ.

Staurastrum furcigerum Bréb.

In a freshwater pond near Seldovia, Cook Inlet (422).

Diameter 45 μ, length 50 μ.

Staurastrum arctiscon (Ehrenb.) Lund.

In a freshwater pool, Virgin Bay, Prince William Sound (302). Common.

Diameter 116 μ.

Staurastrum polymorphum Bréb. (Plate XLIII, figs. 23, 24.)

In a freshwater pond near Seldovia, Cook Inlet (402).

Diameter 40 μ, length 45 μ. The end view shows four arms rounded at the ends.

Staurastrum echinatum (Perty) Rab. (Plate XLIII, fig. 16.)

In a freshwater pond near Seldovia, Cook Inlet.

Euastrum verrucosum Ehrenb. (Plate XLIII, fig. 9.)

In freshwater, Popof Island.

Diameter 81 μ, length 88 μ.

Euastrum gemmatum Bréb.

In a freshwater pond near Seldovia, Cook Inlet.

Diameter 40 μ, length 67 μ. The plant agrees exactly with Brébisson's description except that the terminal lobe is not emarginate.

Euastrum pokornyanum Grun.

In a freshwater pond near Kukak Bay.

Diameter 21 μ, length 43 μ. The basal lobe of the trilobe semicell is crenate, the terminal lobe subcuneate, truncate and excised; membrane smooth.

Euastrum oblongum (Grev.) Ralfs. (Plate XLIII, fig. 37.)

In a freshwater pond near Prince William Sound.

Diameter 67 μ, length 130 μ. The semicells are five lobed, all of the lobes having the broad shallow marginal cavity.

Euastrum crassum (Bréb.) Kuetz. (Plate XLIII, fig. 4.)

In a freshwater pond near Seldovia, Cook Inlet.

Diameter 68 μ, length 148 μ.

Euastrum didelta (Turp.) Ralfs. (Plate XLIV, Fig. 24.)

In freshwater near Kukak Bay.

Diameter 46–60 μ, length 86–120 μ, sinus 16 μ deep, bridge 11 μ wide.

Euastrum ansatum Ralfs.

In a freshwater pond near Yakutat Bay.

Diameter 27 μ, length 54 μ

Euastrum elegans (Bréb.) Kuetz. (Plate XLIV, figs. 2, 25, 26, 30.)
Common in freshwater near Yakutat Bay; Prince William Sound; Popof Island
Diameter 13–15 μ, length 20–30 μ.

Euastrum affine Ralfs. (Plate XLIII, fig. 32.)
In freshwater material from Glacier Bay
Diameter 60 μ wide, length 121 μ.

Micrasterias truncata (Corda) Ralfs. (Plate XLIV, fig. 7.)
In a freshwater pond near Glacier Bay.
Diameter 92 μ, length 97 μ.

Micrasterias oscitans pinnatifida (Kuetz.) Rabenh. (Plate XLIV, fig. 27.)
In a freshwater pond near Seldovia, Cook Inlet.
Diameter 60 μ, length 60 μ. Plant is considerably smaller than the measurements given by various authors but agrees perfectly as to shape and markings.

Micrasterias rotata (Grev.) Ralfs. (Plate XLIII, fig. 25.)
In a freshwater pond, Prince William Sound.
Diameter 190–220 μ. The plant varies considerably in the length of the processes on the ultimate division of the semicells.

Micrasterias denticulata (Bréb.) Ralfs. (Plate XLIV, fig. 11.)
In a freshwater pond near Kukak Bay.
Diameter 90 μ, length 110 μ.

Micrasterias fimbriata elephanta Wolle. (Plate XLIV, fig. 31.)
In freshwater pond near Seldovia, Cook Inlet
Diameter 350 μ, length 350 μ.

Micrasterias kitchelii Wolle. (Plate XLIV, fig. 23.)
In a freshwater pond near Seldovia, Cook Inlet.
Diameter 135 μ, length 135 μ.

Sphærozosma excavatum spinulosum (Del Ponte) Hansg
In a freshwater pond near Seldovia, Cook Inlet
Diameter 8–10 μ, length 11 μ.

Desmidium swartzii Ag.
In a freshwater pond near Seldovia, Cook Inlet.
Diameter 35 μ.

Gymnozyga (?) longata (Wolle) Nordst.
In a freshwater pond near Seldovia, Cook Inlet.
Diameter 35 μ.

Family *ZYGNEMACEÆ*.[1]

Spirogyra varians (Hass) Kuetz.
In a freshwater pond near Seldovia, Cook Inlet.
Diameter 38-40 μ.

Spirogyra porticalis (Muell.) Cleve.
In running water, Popof Island.
Diameter of the zygospores 32-42 μ.

CHLOROPHYCEÆ.

Family *PLEUROCOCCACEÆ*.

Oocystis solitaria crassa (Wittr.) Hansgirg.
Forming a mucous coating on damp rocks near waterfalls. Juneau (75). Identified by Setchell.

Family *PROTOCOCCACEÆ*.

Sphærella lacustris (Girod.) Wittr.
On snow near Yakutat Bay, June 23.
This is the so-called "red snow" found in standing rain water and on snow throughout Europe and North America. It was also observed by members of the party on Muir Glacier and on snow above Orca, Prince William Sound.

Family *HYDRODYCTIACEÆ*

Pediastrum boryanum (Turp.) Menegh.
In freshwater, Popof Island.

Pediastrum angulosum (Ehrenb.) Menegh.
Abundant in a freshwater pond, Popof Island.
The plant is discoidal, 32-celled, the cells all angled.

Family *ULVACEÆ*.

Monostroma fuscum (Post & Rupr.) Wittr.
On rocks, Muir Inlet, Glacier Bay (105); Sitka (144); Virgin Bay, Prince William Sound (277); Kukak Bay (315); Lowe Inlet (16).

---

[1] Several sterile specimens of *Zygnema* were collected, but no fruiting material was obtained.

Frond 40–60 µ thick, dark green, becoming brownish or blackish when dried, not adhering to the paper; cells in cross-section usually longest at right angles to the surface of the frond.

In the Kukak Bay specimens the frond is about 40 µ thick, and the cells are nearly square in cross section, agreeing with the typical *M. fuscum* In the Lowe Inlet specimen the frond is 30 µ thick, the cells in cross section somewhat rounded, agreeing with the form known as *M. splendens*. The color however is duller than usual in that form

Monostroma vahlii J Ag.
Kukak Bay (316).

Frond persistently tubular, torn at the top so as to form a flat membrane only at a quite late stage; thickness of membrane 15–25 µ; cells about 12 µ in cross section, somewhat arranged in series when seen from the surface.

This species has much resemblance in habit to the genus *Enteromorpha*, at least when young

Monostroma grœnlandicum J Ag.
Kukak Bay (346)

Frond filiform, opening only at the extreme top, when in fruit; thickness of membrane 25–30 µ, cells roundish-angular seen from surface, radiately elongate in cross-section.

Externally the frond of this species is that of a slender, unbranched *Enteromorpha*, but the structure is that of *Monostroma* It has heretofore been found only in the Arctic region and along the Atlantic coast, from Greenland to Nahant, Massachusetts. The specimens from Kukak Bay have cells little more than half the size of those in Greenland and New England specimens, otherwise there is no difference.

Ulva lactuca rigida (J. Ag.) Le Jolis.
Frond usually ovate when young, later becoming of indefinite shape, rather firm.

Common in quiet pools, Virgin Bay, Prince William Sound (278); Shumagin Islands (396).

A very common species, varying in form, texture and dimensions, distributed all over the world.

Ulva lactuca myriotrema Le Jolis.
On rocks and algæ, Sitka (133).

Frond pierced with numerous irregular holes. Rather a form than a definite variety.

Enteromorpha linza (L.) J. Ag.
Yakutat Bay (232)

Frond flattened, the membranes united except for a small space at the margin.

Enteromorpha linza *forma* lanceolata J. Ag.
Yakutat Bay (232).
Margins smooth and even.

Enteromorpha linza *forma* crispata J. Ag
Sitka (156).
Margins and often the whole frond crisped and wavy.

This species connects the genera *Enteromorpha* and *Ulva* and has perhaps been oftenest placed in the latter, but its affinities seem to be more with the present genus.

Enteromorpha intestinalis (L.) Link.
Metlakatla, Annette Island (37).

Frond simple or with a few proliferations at the base, usually enlarged upward; cells arranged in no definite order, 6–12 μ wide, in cross section radiate, 16–30 μ long, the membrane about twice as thick as the cell length in cross section.

Enteromorpha intestinalis *forma* cylindracea J. Ag.
In a protected sandy pool, Kukak Bay with *forma maxima* (316); Sand Point, Popof Island (382).

The frond is long, slender, and of nearly uniform diameter throughout its length.

Enteromorpha intestinalis *forma* maxima J. Ag.
Orca (311), Kukak Bay, with *forma cylindracea* (316); Victoria, British Columbia, a form with small cells and thin membrane, approaching *E. minima* (12).

Frond much inflated, usually contorted.

Enteromorpha micrococca Kuetz.
On cliff, Orca (305), Shumagin Islands (398).

Frond simple, tubular, of small size, much contorted, cells 4–5 μ in diameter, in membrane 18–20 μ thick.

This species usually grows in dense masses on rocks between tide marks.

Enteromorpha prolifera (Muell.) J. Ag.
Annette Island (35).

Frond more or less abundantly branched; branches like main frond, not much smaller; cells arranged in longitudinal series in all but the oldest parts of the frond.

These specimens have few branches.

Enteromorpha crinita (Roth) J. Ag.

Wrangell (65); Sitka (155), Prince William Sound (309).

Frond abundantly branched, usually with a main stem and virgate branches, with cells in longitudinal series, beset with short, tapering ramuli, the smallest of a single series of very short cells.

In specimens from this last locality the habit is that of *E. intestinalis* forma *cylindracea*, but the structure and the branching are those of *E. crinita*.

Family ULOTHRICHACEÆ.

Ulothrix flacca (Dillw.) Thuret.

Glacier Bay (82). Very abundant, forming a dark green coating on rocks and pebbles on the shore, extending up to within a quarter of a mile of the glacier.

Cells one-sixth to two-thirds as long as broad; filaments 20–40 μ in diameter.

Hormidium parietinum (Vauch.) Kuetz.

Yakutat Bay; St. Paul, Kadiak.

Cells one-fourth to one diameter in length, often dividing into two or more lateral series, which may develop into a flat membrane.

As now understood, *H. parietinum* includes two forms that were long considered distinct species, and that in their fully developed condition are of quite different habit,—the filiform *Ulothrix parietina* and the membranaceous *Prasiola crispa*. In the specimens collected at Yakutat both forms are to be found, each apparently usually occurring by itself, but both sometimes together. The frond of the *Prasiola* may reach several millimeters in width. The species occurs on damp ground, not like most other algæ, submerged.

Family ŒDOGONIACEÆ.[1]

Oedogonium concatenatum (Hass.) Wittr.

Popof Island.

This species was reported by Wolle from Pennsylvania and New Jersey; I have also observed it in material from Malden, Mass.

Bulbochæte brebissonii Kuetz.

In a freshwater pond near Seldovia, Cook Inlet.

This species has not been hitherto known to occur in America. The form reported by Wolle does not belong to this species.

---

[1] This family was determined by Dr. K. E. Hirn, of The Royal University of Finland, whose notes are here given in translation.

Bulbochæte intermedia De Bar.

In a freshwater pond near Seldovia, Cook Inlet.

This species according to Wolle is generally distributed throughout the United States. Wittrock records it from north Greenland.

Bulbochæte nordstedtii Wittr.

In a freshwater pond near Seldovia, Cook Inlet.

This species has also been reported by Wittrock from Greenland. I have also found it from Norwich, Conn.

Bulbochæte nana Wittr.

In a freshwater pond, Shumagin Islands.

Reported from north Greenland.

The form which Wolle refers to this species belongs, it seems to me, according to his figures, to *B. monile.*

Bulbochæte insignis Pringsh.

Wolle reports this species as occurring in many lakes in New Jersey.

Family *CLADOPHORACEÆ.*

Trentepohlia iolithus (L.) Wallr.

Orca, on rocks at 1,000 feet elevation (Trelease).

Forming an orange or brick-red coating on rocks; filaments dichotomously or irregularly branched; cells 14–20 μ thick in the middle, much constricted at the ends, 1½ to 2 times as long as broad, thick-walled. This is the Veilchenstein of the Germans. It grows on rocks, requires little moisture and can withstand prolonged drouth. When moistened it has a distinct violet odor.

Urospora penicilliformis (Roth) Aresch.

Phycotheca Boreali-Americana, No. 18.

Forming a light green coating on cliffs, Kukak Bay (349).

Frond 20–60 μ in diameter; cells from one-third to three diameters in length, usually constricted at the nodes.

Chætomorpha cannabina (Aresch.) Kjellm.

Annette Island (46), filaments light green, more curled than usual, generally 80–110 μ in diameter; Cook Inlet, near Seldovia (417), less curled, and filaments coarser than in the previous specimens.

Filaments light green, 80–150 μ in diameter; cells 1 to 4 times as long as broad.

Chætomorpha melagonium *forma* **rupincola** (Aresch.) Kjellm.

Yakutat Bay (243).

Filaments dark green, attached at base, 300–500 μ in diameter; cells 1½ to 3 times as long as broad.

A large and rather coarse species, abundant throughout the whole Arctic region, and as far south as the cold currents extend in the Atlantic and the Pacific.

Rhizoclonium riparium implexum (Dillw.) Rosenvinge.

Yakutat Bay (192), floating in large flocculent masses.

Rather light green in color; filaments 20–30 μ in diameter, cells 1 to 5 times as long as broad.

In these specimens the filaments reach a diameter of 30 μ; the cells are sometimes five times as long as broad. No rhizoidal branches were noted, thus placing the form as variety *implexum*. It is difficult to distinguish this variety technically from species of *Chætomorpha*, but all forms of *Rhizoclonium* have a certain irregularity in form of the cells, which is readily recognized when one becomes familiar with these plants.

Cladophora arctica (Dillw.) Kuetz.

Glacier Bay (91), Ocean Cape, entrance to Yakutat Bay, on rocks (233), near Sand Point, Popof Island (381).

Filaments 40–90 μ in diameter, straight and rather stiff; branches erect; basal parts, especially in older plants, emitting numerous slender rhizoidal descending filaments, by which the whole tuft is matted together.

Cladophora scopæformis (Rupr.) Harv.

Yakutat Bay (225); Sitka, on exposed rocky points (185); Kukak Bay (320, 327), on rocks exposed to direct washing of the waves.

Filaments 100–200 μ in diameter, straight and stiff; branches erect, all but the youngest parts attached to each other by short hooked branches, forming long, simple or branching, slender tufts, from 2 to 10 mm. in diameter.

This is a characteristic species of the coast from California northward, resembling a larger and coarser *C. arctica* in its later stages.

Cladophora flexuosa (Griff.) Harv.

Filaments pale green, flexuous, sparingly branched, 20–60 μ in diameter, cells 2 to 3 times as long as broad; ultimate ramuli short, curved, usually secund.

The determination of these specimens is based on their resemblance to No. 206. Alg. Am.-Bor. Exsicc. The species is found on both sides of the Atlantic, but appears not to have been previously reported from the Pacific.

The following specimens of *Cladophora* can be noted by numbers only, specific determination being impracticable at present.

Annette Island (17, 45, 48); Wrangell (56); on rocks, Glacier Bay (86); forming masses on rocks, Sitka (157), on protected side of exposed rocks, Virgin Bay, Prince William Sound (295).

Family *GOMONTIACEÆ*.

Gomontia polyrhiza (Lagerh.) Born. & Flah.

Popof Island.

Basal layer growing in the substance of marine shells, erect filaments extending to the surface, zoospores formed in sporangia.

Family *DERBESIACEÆ*.

Derbesia vaucheriæformis (Harv.) J. Ag.

On a sponge in Yakutat Bay (234).

Filaments 30–40 μ in diameter, simple below, dichotomous above, branches patent, 20–30 μ wide, often with a cuboidal cell near the base; zoosporangia ovoid or pyriform, 140–200 by 50–80 μ, short-pedicelled.

As there are no mature spores on this specimen, there is a possible doubt as to the identification, but the characters agree well with the species named.

Derbesia marina (Lyng.) Kjellm.

Sitka, in quiet water (149).

Filaments 50–60 μ in diameter at the thickest, tapering slightly, sparingly branched laterally, usually two partitions found at the base of each branch, enclosing a short cell; zoosporangia 150–180 by 90–120 μ, short pediclled.

Family *VAUCHERIACEÆ*.

Vaucheria sessilis (Vauch.) DC.

On an overhanging dripping cliff, Juneau (74).

Filaments up to 70 μ in diameter, oogonia usually two or three together, sessile, ovate or ovate-oblong, about 60–150 μ, beaked; antheridia in the vicinity of the oogonia, formed at the end of a short, hooked or curved ramulus.

With antheridia and oogonia.

Family *CODIACEÆ*.

Codium adhærens (Cabr.) Ag.

Dredged at Kadiak, at 15 meters depth (350). This species usually grows between tide marks and its occurrence at this depth is exceptional.

Forming flat expansions, adherent by the lower surface.

Codium mucronatum californicum J. Ag.

Sitka (170).

Forming a terete, dichotomously branching, fleshy, erect thallus; filaments tipped with a short mucron.

Family *CHARACEÆ*.[1]

Chara contraria A. Braun.

In ponds and streams near Glacier Bay, very abundant (300).

Chara fragilis Desv.

In a freshwater pond, Shumagin Islands (400).

Nitella acuminata subglomerata A. Braun.

In a fresh water pond near Prince William Sound (300).

Nitella opaca Ag.?

In a freshwater pond near Kadiak (419).

PHÆOPHYCEÆ.

Family *ECTOCARPACEÆ*.

Phycocelis baltica (Reinke) Foslie.

Forming minute tufts one mm or less in diameter on *Ralfsia deusta*. Sitka (169a).

The erect filaments are unbranched, 200–300 μ long by 5–7 μ wide; cells 8–10 μ long, plurilocular sporangia 60–80 μ long, 6–9 μ wide, borne on a 3–5-celled stalk, containing 20–30 uniseriate zoospores.

Streblonema minutissima sp. nov. (Plate XLV, fig. 3.)

Plant composed of penetrating filaments ramifying through the cortical filaments of the host, from which arise short erect filaments intermingled with the peripheral filaments of the host, which are once or twice dichotomously branched bearing above a few short branches that become transformed into uniseriate plurilocular sporangia 20–30 μ long by 3–5 μ wide.

---

[1] Determined by Dr. T. F. Allen.

In the branches of *Liebmannia* sp. from Sitka (142*b*).

A very minute plant the erect branches of which might easily be taken for a part of the host plant. The penetrating filaments are 1–2 μ wide, short, sparingly branched; cross partitions few and inconspicuous, at intervals closely applied to the host cells; no hairs or unilocular sporangia were observed.

Streblonema pacifica sp. nov. (Plate XLV, fig. 1*a* and 1*b*.)

Plant composed of irregular branching horizontal threads, from which arise mostly unicellular, haustoria-like filaments which penetrate into the host plant, and erect filaments arising at right angles to the horizontal ones; cells of the horizontal filaments 4–8 μ wide, twice as long as the diameter; erect filaments short, unbranched or once dichotomous, 30–70 μ long, most of them bearing a narrow elliptical plurilocular sporangium 5 μ and 13 μ, which contains about five uniseriate zoospores. The plant forms circular dark brown patches 2–4 mm. in diameter on the sporophylls of *Alaria*. Related to *Streblonema minutulum* of Heydrich, but larger in all its measurements.

Yakutat Bay (438).

Streblonema irregularis sp. nov. (Plate XLV, fig. 2.)

Plant consisting of irregularly branching surface filaments applied closely to the host plant, from which arise numerous simple or sparingly branched erect filaments 1–2 mm. high, 9–14 μ wide, cells as long to twice as long as broad; from the surface filaments, filaments 10–14 μ wide, with cells a little shorter or longer than broad, penetrate the substratum irregularly; plurilocular sporangia linear, lanceolate or ovate, terminal or lateral on the erect filament, 14–18 μ wide, 55–70 μ long; no unilocular sporangia observed.

Forming small brown patches on the bulbs of *Nereocystis priapus*, Sitka (164).

This plant is closely related to *Streblonema stilophorea* in its general appearance and method of branching, but differs from it in the shape of the sporangia and the chromatophores of the vegetative filaments which are small, round and numerous in this species.

Ectocarpus tomentosus (Huds.) Lyngb.

Abundant on *Fucus evanescens*, Sitka harbor (166), and Victoria, British Columbia (49).

The rope-like tufts of the Alaskan specimens are fully as long as those from the Atlantic ocean, while the specimens from the California coast are rarely over three mm. in length.

Ectocarpus confervoides (Roth) Le Jol.

On rocks in Yakutat Bay (226½).

This plant comes very close to the typical form of the species, it is 10 or more centimeters long, closely intertwined, the branches few, ateral, and secund, 20–40 µ broad at the base, the ultimate ones short and pointed; plurilocular sporangia ovate, sessile or short stalked, borne laterally on the main branches, especially abundant on the short ultimate ones, 20–30 µ, by 40–80 µ long.

Ectocarpus confervoides corticulatus Saunders.

Ectocarpus corticulatus SAUNDERS, Phyc Mem 152. *pl. 20.*

On *Desmarestia aculeata*, Popof Island (368).

This species is the same as that described from the California coast though the tufts are longer, and only the main filaments and the lower part of the long primary filaments are uniformly corticated. After examining a large amount of material of this and several other varieties of *E confervoides* the writer is convinced that *E. corticulatus* should be considered as a variety of *E confervoides*.

The plant is of a light olive green, forming flocculent tufts a few mm. to 5 cm. or more in length, the main filament and lower part of the primary branches densely corticated, 60–100 µ broad, ultimate branches short, bearing numerous ovate plurilocular sporangia 16–25 µ broad, and 40–70 µ long.

Ectocarpus confervoides pygmæus (Aresch.) Kjellm.

Forming a velvety covering or minute tufts on various algæ, from Puget Sound to the Shumagin Islands. Yakutat Bay (439); Shumagin Islands (386).

The plant is 2–15 mm high, sparingly branched; filaments 10–20 µ broad, 2 to 3 times as long.

Pylaiella littoralis (L.) Kjellm **acuta,** form nov

Plant 3–10 cm or more long, loosely disposed; main filaments 25–40 µ wide, branches few, alternate or opposite, ultimate filaments short, pointed, but not pilate; unilocular sporangia in the ultimate branches 18–24 µ broad, 5–15 or more in a chain.

This plant agrees with the variety *opposita* Kjellm in its general appearance but is smaller in all its parts and is not pilate.

Very abundant from Wrangell westward to the Aleutian Islands. Kukak Bay (322)

The plants form large loose tufts on *Fucus evanescens macrocephala* and occasionally on rocks in all quiet coves In several instances it was found extending up brooks much beyond the mean tide level. In fact it seemed to be most abundant and to reach its best development in quiet waters at the mouths of brooks where the percent of salt must be perceptibly reduced.

Pylaiella littoralis varia (Kjellm.) Kuck.

Common on rocks, and on *Fucus* and other algæ in quiet water from Puget Sound to Bering Sea. Victoria, Juneau, Yakutat and Shumagin Islands.

This form is 1–10 cm. in length, a light faded brown in color, very intricate, the ultimate branches short and standing at right angles to the axis.

Pylaiella littoralis densa Saunders.

The plant forms rope-like masses 2–4 cm. or more long on *Fucus* and other algæ. Victoria, Sitka, Prince William Sound (294), Shumagin Islands (386).

Pylaiella littoralis macrocarpa (Foslie) Kjellm.

On fruiting tips of *Fucus evanescens macrocephalus*, Victoria.

The plant is 1–3 mm. or more long, the branches and the upper part of the main filament, except for a few-celled stalk at the base and one of the cells at the tip, form plurilocular sporangia. No unilocular sporangia were observed.

Family SPHACELARIACEÆ.

Sphacelaria cirrosa (Roth) Ag.

Forming small light olive tufts on *Fucus evanescens*, Annette Island

Sphacelaria racemosa arctica (Harv.) Reinke.

Wrangell (70); Yakutat Bay (195); Prince William Sound (283).

Forming dark olive-brown, densely tufted mats sometimes several cm. wide and 1 cm high; unilocular sporangia abundant on all material collected at the various stations.

Family ENCOELIACEÆ.

Homeostroma undulatum J. Ag. (Plate XLVI, fig 3.)

On *Zoostera marina* in a quiet cove near Seldovia, Cook Inlet (412).

Fruiting plants 3 cm. long, 1–3 mm. wide.

The plurilocular sporangia project little if at all above the surface of the plant and are massed together more than is indicated in Reinke's figures. The single hairs are very scarce on all the Pacific coast material.

Homeostroma lobatum sp nov. (Plate XLVI, figs. 6a, 6b, 6c.)

Plant broadly linear, lanceolate or ovate, 10 or more cm long, 1–5 cm. wide, narrowed below to a short stipe, dark olive-brown, the edges deeply and irregularly lobed, the lobes irregularly cut and divided; unilocular sporangia scattered over the whole surface of the plant.

Attached to *Zostera marina*. Sitka (114); Prince William Sound (296).

Cross sections of the young plants were two cells thick, those of the older plants 4 cells thick, the central cells slightly larger than the outer but not at all elongated. No plurilocular sporangia were observed.

Homeostroma latifolium (Grev.) J. Ag.

Occasional in quiet sandy coves. Annette Island (39); Sitka (143); Popof Island (367).

Punctaria plantaginea Grev.

On exposed rocks near entrance to Yakutat Bay (229).

The plant is 4–10 mm. wide, and 5–10 cm. long. Both unilocular and plurilocular sporangia are abundant. Some of the specimens approach Foslie's variety *linearis*.[1]

Myelophycus intestinalis sp nov. (Plate XLVII.)

Plant dark reddish brown, loosely cæspitose, cylindrical, hollow with age, much twisted and intestiniform, narrowed below to a distinct solid stipe, 5–12 mm. long; the inner layer of tissue composed of long colorless cells, the intermediate layer composed of 2–4 irregularly arranged rows of thick-walled cuboidal cells giving rise to broad coarse paraphyses composed of 4–8 thick-walled cells; sporangia very abundant, elliptical or obovate, scattered irregularly throughout the frond, 45–60 μ long, 20–30 μ wide, arising like the paraphyses from the intermediate layer of tissue.

Attached to rocks in the sublittoral zone from Puget Sound to the Shumagin Islands. More abundant in quiet coves. Glacier Bay (113); Sitka (192); Yakutat (252); Popof Island (359); Puget Sound (Gardner 215).

This plant was at first referred tentatively by the writer to Foslie's *Chordaria attenuata*. Foslie states[2] however that this plant is a form of *Scytosiphon*; Mr. F. S. Collins has kindly examined specimens of Foslie's plant and agrees that it is a *Scytosiphon* and quite distinct from the Pacific plant. *M. intestinalis* is less firm in texture and is lighter colored than Kjellman's *M. cæspitosa*, in cross section the

[1] Foslie, Om Nogle Arctiske Havalger.
[2] Nya Havalger, Vol. 13 · 97.

paraphyses are much broader and shorter, and the sporangia broader than in *M. cæspitosa* and the central layer of tissue composed of only 2-4 rows of cells while in *M. cæspitosa* there are 10 or more rows.

The plant so closely resembles *Scytosiphon lomentarius* in color and general appearance that it has probably been passed over by collectors. It is however somewhat firmer in texture and not at all constricted. Specimens collected from Puget Sound averaged much smaller than those collected farther north. From Sitka northward the plant is more abundant than *Scytosiphon lomentarius*.

Scytosiphon lomentarius (Lyngb.) J. Ag.

Abundant, Puget Sound, Annette Island (40); Glacier Bay; Sitka (892); Yakutat Bay (2290), Kukak Bay; Shumagin Islands (360).

Scytosiphon lomentarius complanatus Rosenv.

Juneau; Glacier Bay (98).

Scytosiphon bullosus Saunders.

On rocks in the sublittoral zone, Sitka (145); Cook Inlet (408).

Heretofore this species was known only from the type locality, Monterey Bay. (Am. Alg. 251.)

Phyllitis fascia (Muell.) Kuetz.

Abundant in protected places in the littoral zone from Puget Sound to the Shumagin Islands. Annette Island (41); Glacier Bay (94) Yakutat Bay (220), Kukak Bay (319), Cook Inlet (409, 410).

The specimens from the northern localities are much larger than the average plant from the California coast and the Atlantic coast of North America. Those from Cook Inlet are 20-35 cm. long and 2-4 cm. wide.

Colpomenia sinuosa (Roth) Derb. & Sol.

On *Cystophyllum lepidum*, Prince William Sound (268); Yakutat Bay (420).

This widely distributed and usually common species was seen but twice during the trip. It is common in quiet coves from Puget Sound to southern California.

Coilodesme linearis sp. nov. (Plate XLVIII.)

Phycotheca Boreali-Americana No 824.

Plant linear, tubular, olive brown, 8-20 cm. long, narrowed below to a short stalk (1-2 mm. long); tissues thin and delicate, composed of three to four layers of cells; unilocular sporangia scattered singly throughout the plant, 11-14 μ wide, 15-20 μ long.

On *Cystophyllum lepidum*, Popof Island (399); Kukak Bay (320½).

The plant is attached to the host in great numbers. It differs from *C. californica* in its shape, size and the size of the unilocular sporangia. The tissue is more delicate, being composed of from two to three layers of colorless cells, a single row of endodermal cells and one of poorly differentiated epidermal cells.

Coilodesme californica (Rupr.) Kjellm.

Occasional on *Systophyllum lepidum* from Puget Sound to Yakutat Bay. Victoria; Annette Island (38); Wrangell (58); Yakutat Bay (224).

No fruiting plants were seen, but the shape and structure of the specimens obtained are the same as in those of the California coast. It is much less abundant in southern Alaska than on the shores of California and apparently is wholly replaced further north by *C. linearis*.

Coilodesme bulligera Stroemf.

Abundant on rocks in the littoral zone in quiet coves, from Puget Sound to the Aleutian Islands. Wrangell (58); Yakutat Bay (222), Prince William Sound (282, 312); Kukak Bay (345½); Shumagin Islands (390a).

Soranthera ulvoides Post & Rupr.

Saunders, Phyc. Mem. 165 Pl 29, fig 4 and 5

Abundant in the littoral and sublittoral zone, in rather quiet protected places, on rocks, *Rhodomela larix*, and *Rhodamea floccosa*. Victoria (2); Wrangell (69, 120, 162); Yakutat Bay.

Family *DESMARESTIACEÆ*.

Desmarestia viridis (Muel.) Lamour.

In the ellittoral and sublittoral zones, Glacier Bay (110); Prince William Sound (274); not uncommon but less abundant than the next species.

Desmarestia aculeata (L.) Lamour.

One of the most abundant of plants in the ellittoral and sublittoral zones from Puget Sound to the Aleutian Islands. Victoria (8); Sitka (180½); Wrangell, Yakutat Bay (226½); Kukak Bay (322½); Shumagin Islands (369).

Family *DICTYOSIPHONACEÆ*.

Dictyosiphon fœniculaceus (Huds.) Grev.

A common plant on rocks, *Scytosiphon* and other plants from Puget Sound to Bering Strait. Annette Island (42); Wrangell (59);

Juneau (72); Prince William Sound (285); Shumagin Islands (341); Glacier Bay (96).

Family *ELACHISTACEÆ*.

Elachista lubrica Rupr.

Phycotheca Boreali-Americana No 828

On *Rhodymenia palmata* in the littoral zone. Wrangell (66); Glacier Bay (83) (101); Prince William Sound (306); Yakutat Bay (242).

Family *CHORDARIACEÆ*.

Myrionema strangulans Grev. (Plate XLVI, figs. 1, 2.)

On *Ulva lactuca*. Sitka (146). Abundant also on the California coast.

Eudesme virescens (Carm.) J. Ag.

Not uncommon on rocks and *Zostera marina* in the sublittoral and littoral zones. Sitka (115–177); Glacier Bay (194), Shumagin Islands (406½); Prince William Sound (284).

The specimens from Prince William Sound are somewhat doubtfully referred to this species. The plant is much smaller than the other specimens, much more branched throughout and of a light yellow color, resembling in these respects Zanardini's *E. flavescens*. The microscopic structure however is identical with that of *E. virescens*.

Leathesia difformis (L.) Aresch.

On rocks and algæ in the littoral zone from Puget Sound to the Shumagin Islands. Victoria (2½); Annette Island (32); Wrangell (70½); Sitka (142); Yakutat Bay (254).

Mesogloia simplex sp. nov. (Plate L, figs. 3, 4.)

Plant soft mucous, olive-brown, unbranched, tubular or intestiniform, hollow, rounded above, narrowed below to a short indistinct stipe; central filaments few, distinct, irregularly branched; peripheral filament short, simple, 2–3–4-celled; unilocular sporangia ovate or elliptical, pyriform, 15–25 μ by 25–35 μ, arising from the subcortical area.

In structure this plant very closely resembles *Gobia*, agreeing closely with Gobi's figure and description, but lacks the parenchymatous structure of that genus. It is no doubt one of the *Chordariaceæ*, which is given this somewhat provisional name until the plurilocular sporangia are found.

Attached to old worn plants of *Chordaria abietina* Sitka (128).

Small immature specimens of this plant are also found on the specimens of *Chordaria abietina*, from Puget Sound, distributed by Miss J. E. Tilden (Am. Alg., No. 348).

Chordaria flagelliformis (Muell.) Ag.

Abundant in protected places in the sublittoral zone, attached to rocks and to other algæ. Sitka (122); Glacier Bay (96); Yakutat Bay (193, 231).

The plant has frequently been reported from the Atlantic shores of Europe and America, the Baltic Sea, the Arctic Ocean, and the shores of Kamchatka.

Chordaria abietina Rupr.

Attached to rocks in exposed places in the littoral zone. Sitka (126)? Prince William Sound (291); Shumagin Islands (380).

This species is much less abundant than on the California coast and all specimens collected are smaller than the average plant of the species from that region.

? Liebmannia sp. (Plate XLIX.)

A single specimen of a *Mesogloia*-like plant was collected at Sitka (142a). It bears an abundance of unilocular but no plurilocular sporangia, hence its exact position is in doubt. The arrangement and structure of the axial tissue and the peripheral filaments closely resemble those of *Liebmannia*.

Family *RALFSIACEÆ*.

Ralfsia deusta (Ag.) J. Ag.

Sitka (169); Kukak Bay (324) Orca, Prince William Sound (267a).

The plants were loosely attached to rocks in the sublittoral zone. All specimens collected were sterile.

Ralfsia clavata (Carm.) Farl.

Yakutat Bay and Cook Inlet (413½).

Forming light olive-green patches 5–10 mm. in diameter, which finally produce an indefinite coating on rocks; in the sublittoral region.

Family *LAMINARIACEÆ*.

Chorda filum (L.) Lamour.

Found in the sublittoral region. Prince William Sound (273); Popof Island (383).

At both stations the plant was found in quiet sandy coves in great abundance.

Alaria fragilis sp. nov. (Plate LIV.)

Plant of small size (4-8 dm. long); blade lanceolate or linear, undulate on the margin, 1-2 dm. broad, substance thin membranaceous, brittle, drying dark, midrib quadrangular in cross section, protruding equally on each margin; stipe short, rounded at base, slightly flattened above, 7-12 cm. long; rachis 6-15 cm. long, slightly flattened but no broader than the stipe; sporophylls few (8-18), distant, oblong elliptical, often oblique at the base, very obtuse above, narrowed below to a stalk (5-15 mm. long); sporangia confined to the basal third of the sporophyll.

Dr. Kjellman compares this plant to Harvey's specimen labeled *Alaria pylaii* Grev.[1] from Vancouver Island, but he agrees that Harvey's specimen is distinct from *Alaria pylaii* of the Atlantic and Polar Seas and is an undescribed species. This plant differs essentially from the description of *A. pylaii* in having a longer stipe and the sporophylls few and distinct.

In the sublittoral zone. Glacier Bay (80½); Prince William Sound (257); Kukak Bay (333½).

Alaria fragilis forma **bullata** form. nov.

With the last, Glacier Bay (79).

With this species were collected several specimens that agree with it except that the blade is densely covered with small bullations, occasionally a plant being found that had only a very few or almost no bullations. It may be a distinct species but it seems preferable to regard it as a bullate form of the last until it can be further studied.

Alaria laticosta Kjellm. (Plate LV.)

In the sublittoral zone, in protected coves, Kukak Bay (333).

Plant of medium size, 1-2 mm.; stipe short, round, 2-5 mm. long; rachis long muriculate, slightly broader than the stipe; lamina broadly linear, dark brown, drying blackish, undulate on the margin, plicated and fluted, 10-20 cm. broad, tapering below to the transition point, midrib 7-12 mm. broad; sporophylls numerous, long and narrow, rounded at end, gradually narrowed to a short indistinct stalk, fruit usually confined to the lower two-thirds of the sporophyll, varying in size, 10-30 cm. long, 1-2 cm. wide, and borne on a stalk 4 mm. long.

Dr. Kjellman referred the plants sent him to this species with some doubt. He says: " The form, color and consistency of the blade, and the form, width and rigidity of the sporophyll differ somewhat from this species."

[1] Harvey's Notes Col. Alg. N. W. Coast, 165.

Alaria lanceolata Kjellm. (Plate LIII.)

In the sublittoral zone. Glacier Bay (111); Sitka Harbor (178).

The specimens obtained agree well with Kjellman's description, and specimens submitted to him were pronounced to be this species, which is easily recognized by the tufts of long cryptostomata which in no other species are so large and abundant.

Alaria cordata Tilden. (Plate LVI.)

In the sublittoral zone on exposed point of an island opposite the entrance to Yakutat Bay (230). The plant was growing in great abundance at this station but was not seen again on the trip.

The writer's specimens are certainly identical with Miss Tilden's plant, of which, by her kindness, he has seen both herbarium and formalin specimens. There is also in the writer's herbarium a young plant of this species, from Puget Sound, collected by Mr. N. L. Gardner and labelled by Dr. Setchell *Alaria esculenta ?*.

The stipe is of medium length (15 cm.), round, dark and firm; rachis short and broad. The blade is oblong, lanceolate (250–450 cm. long), somewhat undulate, plicate, light olive-green, firm; midrib protruding equally on both sides; medulla slightly swollen near the margins; sporophylls few (7–10 on a side), arising seriately on a short stalk, broadly linear, ovate, cuneate or somewhat cordate at the base; obtuse or occasionally acute above, sporangia covering most of the surface, 25–40 cm. long, 3–6 cm. wide

Alaria fistulosa Post & Rupr. (Plate LVII.)

The first specimen of this large and interesting plant was a fragment of the midrib washed ashore near Wrangell. At Juneau several much worn specimens were obtained but no plants were found *in situ*. In Glacier Bay it was abundant from the lower part of the sublittoral zone to a quarter of a mile from the shore. Although some immature plants measured 12 feet in length the plant does not reach the size nor is it as abundant as farther north. In Yakutat Bay, Prince William Sound, and Cook Inlet a few fragments were found washed ashore but no mature specimens were seen growing. This may be due to the fact that all landings were made in protected places in the bays while this plant loves considerable exposure. Near the mouth of Kukak Bay there are numerous reefs 5–10 fathoms or more below the surface. These reefs are marked by patches of this species, sometimes an acre or more in extent. The plant not only reaches the surface but floats for several meters on the surface.

The plant is of a very dark olive-brown color, the blade being broadly linear, thin, papery, and smooth, 2–8 or 10 dm. broad; the midrib is 15–40 or more mm. broad, the central part inflated, and divided by narrow septa into air vesicles of various lengths; near the base of the blade the septa become indistinct and then disappear, the inflations also disappear some distance above the transition point, the stipe is short (5–10 cm. long), black, solid, and rounded at the base, flattened above and gradually passing into the rachis, which is broad and short; sporophylls very numerous, crowded, spatulate, elliptical or obovate, rounded at the ends and narrowed below to a stipe of considerable length (2–4 cm); fruiting area covering nearly the entire surface of the sporophyll.

No complete specimens of mature plants were measured but many fragments were cast ashore having a blade which measured 3–7 meters in length and 4–10 dm. in width.

De Toni[1] credits this species, on the authority of Dr. Anderson, to California. Dr. Anderson informed the writer that he had seen no specimens from the California coast and had no record of its occurrence there. He admitted that several of the *Laminariaceæ* credited in his list to the northern coast of California had been included in the belief that they might occur there.

Pleurophycus gen. nov. Setchell & Saunders. (Plate LII.) Plant attached to the substratum by hapteres, consisting of a single undivided blade with one central distinct midrib; no perforations or auricles at the base of the blade; stipe simple; muciferous canals wanting, fruiting area confined to the midrib, sporangia and paraphyses as in *Laminaria*.

Pleurophycus gardneri sp. nov. Setchell & Saunders. (Plate LII.)
Tilden's Am. Alg., No 346.

Blade broadly linear in outline, tapering below to the transition point, 7–12 dm and more long, 12–25 cm. wide, thin and soft, striate and "lung like," wrinkled or somewhat regularly pleated near the midrib giving it a bullate appearance which disappears near the base of the blade; midrib broad (3–7 cm.) and flat, 2 mm. thick, narrow above and below; stipe dark brown, drying black (3–7 dm.), firm and solid, round below, much flattened above and gradually passing into the midrib; sorus single, covering the upper part of the midrib.

Yakutat Bay (236); Puget Sound (450).

On June 26, 1899, on an island opposite the entrance to Yakutat Bay the writer collected a few fragments of a plant washed up with several

[1] Syll. Alg. 3 322.

species of kelp that he at once took to represent a new genus. The locality was visited for three successive mornings during the lowest tides and although an abundance of material was washed ashore the plant was not found *in situ*. Several other points in the bay were visited but no sign of the plant was found. If it grows off the shore on which it was collected, and the condition of the material collected would indicate that it does, it must grow well down in the elittoral zone, for twice a careful search was made along the whole shore line at the lowest tide, where one could get out beyond the "kelp line." The location in which the plant was collected and the frayed and torn condition of the ends of the blade would indicate that it grows in exposed localities. In all specimens collected the stipe was broken off apparently just above the holdfast. The only holdfast seen was on an almost perfect specimen (from which Plate LII was drawn) collected by Miss J. E. Tilden in Puget Sound.

Pleurophycus has no midrib in a proper sense, but has a broad shallow furrow indented on one surface and prominent on the other, the surface of which is little thicker than that of the adjacent portion of blade, except in the region of the sorus.

This plant was first collected by Mr. N. L. Gardner in Puget Sound in the summer of 1898 and sent to Dr. Setchell for identification. Dr. Setchell recognized it at once as a new genus and gave it the above manuscript name. The writer not knowing of Dr. Setchell's name gave his specimen a provisional name, but on learning from Mr. Gardner of a previous name offered his specimens for comparison to Dr. Setchell, who at once suggested the joint authorship of the name.

Referring to the distribution of the plant Dr. Setchell writes " while *Pleurophycus* may grow in the elittoral zone, all the evidence in Gardner's and my possession shows that it extends even to the upper sublittoral, as is the case with so many species credited to the elittoral, Gardner found them just below low water mark, but in places much exposed to the fury of the waves Several of Gardner's specimens have holdfasts which show several whorls of hapteres branched in a somewhat irregularly dichotomous fashion and several times, the distal branches being slender.

Pleurophycus stands as the simplest of the subtribe *Agareæ*, forming something of a transition between that subtribe and the *Laminarieæ*.

Laminaria bullata Kjellman.

In the sublittoral zone. Puget Sound; Sitka (188); Prince William Sound.

All specimens collected were quite young and sterile but agree with Kjellman's figures and descriptions.

Laminaria bongardiana P. & R.

Abundant in the sublittoral zone, from Sitka to Shumagin Islands. Sitka (186); Prince William Sound; Kukak Bay (337).

Laminaria solidungula J. Ag.

Occasional in the sublittoral zone from Yakutat Bay northward and westward. Yakutat Bay (260); Kukak Bay (337); Popof Island (387½)

All specimens collected were sterile and of small size; the blade averages 6 dm. long, 3 dm. broad; the stipe is about 17 cm. broad, firm, thick and abundantly supplied with mucous canals as are the broad flattened rhizoids which are fused almost to the tips to form a disklike attachment.

Laminaria cuneifolia J. Ag.

Two specimens of this species were collected from a small rock on Popof Island (387). The rock had apparently been washed up from the sublittoral zone. The blade is very distinctly wedge-shaped, thin, papyraceous, light olive-green, and very brittle in drying, quite regularly wavy on the margin; the stipe is black, very firm, rounded below and slightly flattened above, 6–10 cm., the rhizoids are long and slender, resembling those of *L. saccharina*.

Laminaria saccharina (L.) Lam.

Abundant in the sublittoral zone from Puget Sound to the Shumagin Islands. Two forms were collected.

Forma (a). Blade 300–800 cm. long, cuneate at base, 20–40 cm. wide; stipe 3–5 cm. long, texture thin, papyraceous or membranaceous, drying light-green; sori usually small, 1–3 dm., irregular, confined to the upper part of the frond; muciferous canals small, abundant in blade and stipe.

Glacier Bay (77); Sitka; Wrangell (63); Yakutat Bay; Cook Inlet; Shumagin Islands.

Forma (b). Blade 50–150 cm. long, 5–10 cm. wide; stipe 1–3 cm. long, submembranaceous to coriaceous; sorus occurring as a band in the central part of the blade, extending from a few centimeters to two-thirds the length of the blade; muciferous canals abundant in blade.

Prince William Sound (259½); Kukak Bay (337).

Hedophyllum sessile (Ag.) Setchell.—(Plate LI.)

Laminaria sessilis AG., Syst. Alg., p. 270. TILDEN, Am. Alg., 344.

This species was collected in the sublittoral zone in Yakutat Bay the latter part of July.

The young plants have a short distinct flat stipe 1–2 cm. long and 5 or more mm. broad, the stipe soon disappears or becomes attached to the substratum by its whole length, the old blades are a foot or two in length, irregularly longitudinally torn above, bullate and folded in the lower part.

Hedophyllum subsessile (Aresch.) Setchell (Mss.).

Laminaria bongardiana subsessilis ARESCH , Obs. Phyc. 4 : 5.

Abundant in exposed places, from Puget Sound northward. Yakutat Bay (218), Prince William Sound (259); Kukak Bay (337½).

This plant, heretofore considered a form of *L. bongardiana*, is made the type of a new genus by Dr. Setchell, on account of the prostrate rhizome. The creeping rhizome-like affair is apparent only in old, well developed plants. The stalk is always short, 1–4 or 5 cm., and in mature plants much flattened above, in old specimens being as much as 2 cm. or more wide. The blade is dark brown, thick and leathery, reaching a length of 3 or more meters. It is usually split nearly to the base into 3 somewhat equal parts each one of which is more or less irregularly cut and torn.

Cymathere triplicata (Post & Rupr.) J. Ag.

Abundant from Puget Sound to Shumagin Islands. This species is gregarious and usually found pretty well down in the sublittoral zone or in the upper part of the elittoral zone. While not of extreme size this plant forms a large part of the kelp flora in many places.

Agarum gmelini Mert. (Plate LXI.)

In the sublittoral and elittoral zones in exposed localities. This species and *Desmarestia aculeata* form the majority of the elittoral flora in many places. Prince William Sound; Yakutat Bay; Kukak Bay, Popof Island.

In mature specimens the outline is rotund or reniform and the midrib broad and flat.

Three specimens from different localities gave the following measurements.

Blade.		Stipe.		Midrib
Length	Width	Length	Width.	Width.
cm.	cm.	cm.	mm	mm
60	80	17	10	12
60	60	15	10	14
60	60	wanting		12

Agarum turneri (Post & Rupr.).

Abundant in the sublittoral zone. Yakutat Bay (200a); Prince William Sound (261); Popof Island.

This species differs from the last chiefly in its smaller size, more ovate outline, and the much narrower midrib. Its relationship would probably be better expressed by placing it as a variety rather than a distinct species.

Costaria turneri Grev.

Abundant in the sublittoral zone from Puget Sound to the Shumagin Islands. Victoria; Sitka (187); Yakutat Bay; Prince William Sound; Kukak Bay; Shumagin Islands.

The plant reaches a much larger size on the Alaska coast than on the California and Washington coast. Specimens were seen measuring from 180 to 220 cm. in length and 50 cm. wide at the base.

Eisenia arborea Aresch.

A broken fragment of this plant was obtained at Wrangell and several specimens were obtained in Puget Sound.

Macrocystis pyrifera (Turn.) Ag. (Plate LX.)

In the elittoral zone off rocky points and in unprotected places. Wrangell; Sitka (171, 189); Juneau.

Although a constant watch was kept for this plant it was not seen north of Sitka.

Nereocystis priapus (Gmelin) Saunders. (Plates LVIII, LIX.)

Ulva priapus GMELIN, Hist. Fucorum, 231, 1768.
Nereocystis lutkeanus MERT. FIL. in Linnæa, p. 48, 1829.

Abundant from Puget Sound to the Shumagin Islands. The plant is seldom found growing in protected places, being confined to the elittoral zone at the mouth of bays and in the open ocean from a few yards to a mile or more from shore. The plant, unlike *Macrocystis pyrifera* and *Alaria fistulosa*, does not form floating masses.

Mature plants measure from 50–70 feet long, about two-thirds of which is the long tube-like stipe with its terminal air bulb, which floats the dichotomously torn lamina on the surface of the ocean.

Mertens' statement, copied by Harvey, in which in speaking of the stipes, he says: "They are said to be 45 fathoms long," is probably not true. The writer has measured many fully-developed plants on the California, Oregon, and Washington coasts as well as on the Alaska coast and has never yet found one exceeding the above figures.

Gmelin's figures and description of *Ulva priapus* leave no doubt as to the identity of his plant although he had only an imperfect stipe.

As his description antedates Mertens' by some sixty years it seems best to the writer to reinstate the name given by him.

Family *FUCACEÆ*.

Fucus evanescens *forma* macrocephala Kjellm (Plate LXII, fig. 1.)

Puget Sound; Annette Island; Wrangell; Juneau; Sitka, Glacier Bay; Prince William Sound; Cook Inlet; Kukak Bay; Shumagin Islands

This is by far the most abundant seaweed on the northwest coast. It is found in all quiet bays and protected places from Puget Sound to Bering Sea, forming the characteristic light brown covering extending some distance above the average tide level. In many places the plant is not covered by salt water more than twice a month. It is able to thrive from the moisture in the atmosphere. This species and *Pylaiella littoralis* extend the farthest up the mouths of streams and fresh water bays.

This form is more commonly evesiculose, but there are often found indefinite vesicles just below the fruiting tip, either singly or in pairs. It is a variation of this form from Puget Sound that Dr. Setchell has referred to *F. platycarpus*, which is quite a distinct species.

Identified by Kjellman.

Fucus evanescens *forma* cornuta Kjellm. (Plate LXII, fig. 2.)

Juneau; Yakutat Bay (256); Prince William Sound (264a); Kukak Bay (376); Popof Island.

This form was collected in more exposed places than the last and is not nearly as common. The plant is darker colored and firmer in texture than the last, with narrower branches and fruiting tip. The fruiting tip is usually not at all inflated but in one extreme variation it is inflated 5–7 cm. long.

Cystophyllum lepidum (Rupr.) Harvy.

Victoria, Wrangell, Sitka (121, 190); Yakutat Bay; Kukak Bay; Shumagin Islands.

In slightly protected places in the clittoral zone from Puget Sound to Bering Sea. Mature plants measured from 1 to 3 meters in length.

RHODOPHYCEÆ.

Family *BANGIACEÆ*.

Bangia atropurpurea pacifica J. Ag.

Specimens of this species were collected near Victoria in Puget Sound but it was not obtained in Alaskan waters.

Porphyra laciniata (Lightf.) Ag.[1]

On the stems of *Fucus* and on rocks in the littoral and sublittoral zone, Yakutat Bay.

All specimens obtained were sterile.

Porphyra perforata J. Ag.

On rocks in the littoral and sublittoral zones, Glacier Bay (100); Sitka (130); Shumagin Islands (394).

The most abundant species.

Porphyra amplissima (Kjellm.) Setchell & Hus.

On rocks in the sublittoral zone, Prince William Sound. This large and beautiful species was found growing in great abundance at this station but was not collected again.

Porphyra miniata forma cuneiformis Setchell & Hus.

Usually found floating, occasionally attached to stems of *Nereocystis* and other algæ; Lowe Inlet (20).

Porphyra tenuissima (Stroemf.) Setchell & Hus.

Abundant on rocks and also epiphytic on algæ. Sitka (148a, 137); Yakutat Bay (214).

Not previously reported from the west coast of North America.

Family *HELMINTHOCLADIACEÆ*.

Batrachospermum vagum flagelliforme Siridot.

In ponds, pools and streams near Virgin Bay, Prince William Sound (299), Cook Inlet (423); Kadiak Island.

Plants collected in June and July at or near sea level bore an abundance of mature carpospores.

Family *GELIDIACEÆ*.

Choreocolax polysiphoniæ Reinsch.

On the stems of *Polysiphonia* sp., Sitka (123a).

Plants collected in June bore only tetraspores. The plants are closely attached to the lower part of the main stem of the *Polysiphonia*, spherical, dark brown or black, about ½ mm. in diameter. The tubes of the *Polysiphonia* are much deformed wherever the "parasite" is attached. The central tube is much enlarged, the surrounding ones somewhat so, the walls considerably contorted and thickened. This species has been found in the Atlantic on the European and American shores but has not been previously reported from the Pacific ocean.

---

[1] All specimens of the genus *Porphyra* were identified by Dr. Setchell and Mr. Hus.

Family *GIGARTINACEÆ*

Endocladia muricata (P. & R.) J Ag.

On perpendicular rocks in exposed places at or above the high tide line. Wrangell (62); Prince William Sound (293); Popof Island (370). This species, so common on the California coast, is comparatively rare or local on the Alaskan coast.

Iridæa membranacea J Ag ?

On rocks in the sublittoral zone Sitka (125), Yakutat Bay (207); Shumagin Islands (377) This is the plant distributed from Puget Sound by J. E Tilden as *Iridæa heterocarpa* (Am. Algæ, No. 329). The plant is abundant and evidently ranges from Puget Sound to Bering Sea

To this species Dr Farlow has very questionably referred a plant with small, once to twice dichotomously divided plant body. It is broadly obovate or reniform in outline, tapering below to a short stalk, entire or crenate on the margin or in the sterile plants with few or many tooth-like proliferations. Dr. Farlow says "This plant has made the tour of European algologists * * * Bornet is sure that it is a form of *Iridæa laminarioides* It also agrees with some of Bory's specimens of that species I must admit that having seen a series of the two species in foreign herbaria, I found that I could not tell where one began and the other ended."

The plant is smaller than any of the specimens of *Iridæa laminarioides* seen by the writer, ranging from 5 to 10 cm. in length and the primary division of the plant being 2-10 cm. broad. It is also somewhat thinner in texture, dark red in color, and lighter on the margins. The cystocarps are small and evenly distributed over the entire surface of the blade except the basal part

Iridæa laminarioides Bory.

This plant is abundant in the sublittoral zone in Puget Sound but was not seen in Alaskan waters.

Gigartina papillata Ag. forma **typica.**

Washed ashore, Shumagin Islands (357).

A few small plants 5-8 cm in length, were collected that are identical with the forma *subsimplex* of Setchell (Phycotheca Boreali-Americana, No. 425). Dr. Farlow states that they are identical with typical *G papillata* given him by Agardh. Dr Setchell in a note on the distributed form says "Under this name is included the form figured by C. Agardh as the type."

Gigartina papillata forma **cristata** Setchell.

A single plant of this variety was collected in Kukak Bay (331*a*) which is apparently identical with Dr. Setchell's *cristata*. It is also very closely related to some forms of *G. mamillosa*.

Gigartina pacifica Kjellm.

On rocks in the sublittoral zone. Yakutat Bay (200); Prince William Sound (308), Shumagin Islands (358, 377).

No. 377 agrees exactly with Kjellman's figures and descriptions, the others are somewhat intermediate between *G. pacifica* and *G. papillata*.

Kalymenia californica Farlow.

In tide washings, Kukak Bay (342).

The plant collected in Kukak Bay is much smaller in all of its parts than specimens from the California coast. The proliferations are very numerous, obovate, and only 2–5 cm. long by 1–2 cm. wide.

Ahnfeldtia plicata (Hudson) Fries.

On rocks in the sublittoral zone, Yakutat Bay (250); Prince William Sound (270).

The specimens collected at both stations were sterile and had fewer and shorter branches than the typical forms but agree in structure.

Family *RHODOPHYLLIDACEÆ*.

Turnerella mertensiana (P. & Rupr.) Schmitz.

Washed ashore in exposed places. Kukak Bay (352); Shumagin Islands (453).

The plant is oblong or ovate, fastened to rocks by a basal disk, entire or lobed on the margin, coriaceous, and of a deep dark blood-red color; several specimens were obtained 6 dec. long by 3 dec. wide.

This species was seen at only three stations in Alaska, a large specimen was seen in the herbarium of Mr. N. L. Gardner, collected in Puget Sound. There is also a small sterile specimen in the writer's herbarium, from the central Californian coast, Monterey Bay.

Euthora cristata (L.) J. Ag.

Abundant in the sublittoral zone. Seldovia, near the entrance to Cook Inlet (415); Shumagin Islands (356).

One of the most abundant of the red algæ. It is also reported from

Family *RHODYMENIACEÆ*.

Rhodymenia pertusa (P. & Rupr) J. Ag.

On rocks in the lower part of the sublittoral zone, Yakutat Bay (205); Prince William Sound (267 and 271).

No. 271 is a smaller form and not at all pertuse.

Rhodymenia palmata (L.) J. Ag.

On rocks in the upper part of the sublittoral zone. Glacier Bay (88); Yakutat Bay (206); Prince William Sound, near Orca (310), Kukak Bay (345); Popof Island (378).

The entire form of this species seems to be the more common on the Pacific Coast, though the palmately divided form and the form with numerous proliferations are also abundant.

The plant is gathered in large quantities, dried and eaten by the Indians of the northwest coast, as is *Porphyra pertusa* by the Chinamen on the California coast.

Plocamium coccineum uncinatum J. Ag.

In the sublittoral zone, Sitka (148).

Halosaccion firmum (P. & R.) J. Ag.

In the sublittoral zone in a quiet muddy cove, Cook Inlet (414).

This species was collected at only the one station, but it was abundant there.

Halosaccion fucicola (Post & Rupr.) J. Ag.

On rocks, *Rhodomela larix*, and other algæ in the littoral zone from Puget Sound to Bering Sea. Victoria (5); Annette Island (33); Sitka (115a); Prince William Sound; Popof Island.

Halosaccion ramentaceum (L.) J. Ag.

In the sublittoral and littoral zones. Kukak Bay (331, 317); Cook Inlet (414).

Nos. 317 and 414 agree with the typical form of this variable species. No 331 is very close to the forma *densa* of Kjellm. It was found well up in the littoral zone while the other forms are sublittoral. At each station this species was collected only once.

Halosaccion tilesii (Ag.) Kjellm.

In the littoral zone from Wrangell to Bering Sea. Wrangell (54); Yakutat Bay (235, 248, 249); Prince William Sound (306a); Kukak Bay (453).

Halosaccion microsporum Rupr.

In the littoral zone. Glacier Bay (85, 109); Yakutat Bay (452).

The three numbers, referred to this species somewhat tentatively, represent three very variable and diverse forms which however agree in structure.

Family *DELESSERIACEÆ*.

Nitophyllum ruthenicum (Post & Rupr.) Kjellm.[1]

A single sterile specimen of this plant was collected in the sublittoral zone at Sitka (119).

The plant is 15 cm. high bearing many cuneate branches which are delicately longitudinally striate, especially near the base. It is quite distinct from any of the Californian species of *Nitophyllum*, but is related to *N. latissimum*. The nerves are much more delicate and not branched and disappearing above the middle of the lobes, in this respect it is intermediate between *N. latissimum* and *N. fryeanum*.

Delesseria bærii (Post & Rupr.) J. Ag.

Two small sterile plants of this species were collected in the sublittoral zone near Sitka (183).

Delesseria alata (Huds.) J. Ag.

A few sterile plants of this species were collected in Puget Sound at Victoria (3). It was not seen in Alaskan waters.

Delesseria sinuosa (Good & Wood.) Lamon.

Abundant in the sublittoral zone. Sitka (151); Prince William Sound (265); Kukak Bay (344, 323); Shumagin Islands (371, 389).

A very variable species, some of the forms resembling *D quercifolia* but with a more distinct midrib and opposite nerves. Specimens from Kukak Bay bore an abundance of cystocarps. The species occurs in the Arctic and North Atlantic oceans and has recently been reported by Kjellman from Bering Sea. From Sitka to the Shumagin Islands it is the most common *Delesseria*.

Delesseria crassifolia Rupr.

A specimen of this plant was collected by Prof. Trevor Kincaid in 1898 on the shores of St. Paul Island. It was not collected by the Harriman Expedition in Bering Sea.

Delesseria decipiens J. Ag.

In the sublittoral zone, Prince William Sound (290).

An abundance of cystocarpic material was collected. The plants are much smaller (only 8–15 cm. in length) than those from the California coast, but agree in other respects.

[1] Kjellman, Om Behringshaf Algfl , 25

Delesseria serrata Post & Rupr.

To this species is referred a plant with the general appearance of a broad form of *D. alata*, but the branches are more distant and fewer and the margins of the upper and younger branches are regularly or irregularly serrate. It may be an extreme form of *D. alata* but it seems best to keep it under a separate name until this is proven.

Family *RHODOMELACEÆ*

Rhodomela floccosa Ag.

In the littoral and sublittoral zones from Puget Sound to Bering Sea. Annette Island (30, 56); Wrangell (68), Sitka (139); Yakutat Bay (191, 203), Kukak Bay (321); Popof Island (374).

One of the most abundant plants. It occurs also on the Washington, Oregon, and California coasts.

Rhodomela larix Ag.

Attached to rocks in the upper sublittoral and littoral zones; abundant from Puget Sound to the Shumagin Islands. Sitka (131); Kukak Bay (318).

Odonthalia aleutica (Mertens) J. Ag.

Attached to rocks in the sublittoral zone, Shumagin Islands (385).

The same species has been collected in Puget Sound by the writer. The branches are narrower than in *O. dentata*, the perithecia are racemed and very slightly oblong-urceolate, and the plant turns black in drying.

Odonthalia kamtschatica (Rupr.) J. Ag.

On rocks in the sublittoral zone. Kukak Bay (341); Yakutat Bay (219).

In this species the plant is smaller than the last species and remains a dark blood-red color in drying the perithecia are short, racemed and very strongly urceolate.

Polysiphonia arctica J. Ag.

In the sublittoral zone, Shumagin Islands (364, 366).

Polysiphonia bipinnata Post & Rupr.

Abundant on rocks and on other algæ in the sublittoral zone, from Puget Sound northward. Annette Island (19); Glacier Bay (84); Sitka (117); Yakutat Bay (244).

Several specimens of *Polysiphonia* are undeterminable and for the present can be noted only by numbers as follows; 25, 64, 123, 150, 154, 212, 363.

Family *CERAMIACEÆ.*

Calithamnion floccosum pacificum Harv.

On *Nereocystis priapus* and other algæ, and on rocks. Puget Sound, Lowe Inlet (15), Yakutat Bay (210, 244, 199).

The most abundant species of *Calithamnion* on the Northwest coast.

Calithamnion plumula Lyngb.

This species was collected several times in Puget Sound but was not seen in Alaska waters. It is a comparatively common plant in Puget Sound, while on the central California coast it is very rarely found.

Ceratothamnion pekeanum (Harv.) J. Ag.

On rocks in exposed localities in the littoral and upper sublittoral zones. Sitka (152); Yakutat Bay (211); Shumagin Islands (373).

The northern plant is smaller and with shorter branches than the same species from the California coast.

Ptilota asplenoides Ag.

Abundant on rocks in the sublittoral zone. Yakutat Bay (198, 219); Prince William Sound (269).

Ptilota plumosa Ag.

Attached to rocks and large algæ in the sublittoral zone. Sitka (140); Shumagin Islands (397).

A much finer and more delicately branched plant than the last, with opposite similar branches.

Ptilota serrata Kuetz.

In the sublittoral zone. Shumagin Islands (355).

Antithamnion boreale (Gobi) Kjellm.

Occasional in the sublittoral region. Wrangell (55); Sitka (135).

In its general appearance the plant agrees with *A. boreale corallina* but the branches near the apex are not elongated as in that form.

Ceramium rubrum Ag.

In the sublittoral zone. Sitka (127); Prince William Sound (275).

The Prince William Sound material, collected in June, bears an abundance of mature carpospores.

Ceramium codicola J. Ag.

Attached to *Codium mucronatum californicum*, Sitka (170).

The plants are small and sterile, but agree with specimens of *C. codicola* collected by the writer on the California coast, and with specimens distributed in the Phycotheca Boreali-Americana.

Microcladia borealis Rupr

In the littoral zone, attached to rocks in exposed places, Puget Sound (4).

The plant was not collected in Alaskan waters.

Rhodochorton rothii (Turton) Naegeli.

Forming a dense coating on rocks, especially in caverns in the upper sublittoral or littoral zones, Prince William Sound (292).

The writer has collected this plant also on the central California coast and in Puget Sound

Family *GLOIOSIPHONIACEÆ*.

Gloiopeltis furcata (P. & R.) J Ag.

Attached to rocks in the sublittoral zone from Puget Sound to the Shumagin Islands. Annette Island (26); Sitka (124), Yakutat Bay (201); Shumagin Islands (372).

Not common at any of the stations.

Gloiosiphonia californica (Farl.) J. Ag.

In the sublittoral region in a protected cove, Prince William Sound (277).

This species was originally described by Dr. Farlow from the central California coast. He placed it somewhat questionably in the genus *Nemastoma* on account of having only dry material for examination. J Agardh, in Till Algernes Systematik, transferred the species to *Gloiosiphonia*. Dr Farlow recently stated that since the publication of the species he had examined both living and alcoholic material and believed that Agardh was right in placing it in *Gloiosiphonia*.

Family *GRATLOUPIACEÆ*.

Cryptonemia obovata? J. Ag.

Washed ashore, Prince William Sound (276).

Two sterile specimens of a *Cryptonemia* are referred somewhat questionably to this species. They agree in shape and structure with fruiting specimens collected in Puget Sound which undoubtedly belong to this species.

Family *DUMONTIACEÆ*.

Dumontia filiformis (Lyngb.) Ag

Abundant in the sublittoral zone in protected places from Prince William Sound northward and westward. Prince William Sound (307, 280); Cook Inlet (411); Kukak Bay (340); Shumagin Islands (365).

The specimens from Cook Inlet bear an abundance of cystocarps; the others have tetraspores.

Cryptosiphonia grayana J. Ag.

In the sublittoral zone. Wrangell (162); Sitka (132); Yakutat Bay (208); Kukak Bay (330).

The Yakutat and Kukak Bay specimens bear cystocarps, the Sitka and Wrangell material tetraspores.

Dilsea californica (J. Ag.) Schmitz.

In the sublittoral zone, Orca, Prince William Sound (313).

The large sterile plants (3-5 dm. long by 1-2 dm. broad) were submitted to Dr. Setchell and were referred by him to this species.

Dilsea arctica (Kjellm.)

Attached to rocks in the sublittoral zone, Shumagin Islands (353).

Young plants are broadly ovate or reniform, and of a light rose-red color, older specimens are once to twice longitudinally divided nearly to the base and of a light faded red color.

Constantinea rosa-marina (Gmel.) J. Ag.

In the upper part of the elittoral zone, Prince William Sound (298).

It was observed at several other stations, including the Shumagin Islands, but no collections were made. It occurs in both protected and exposed situations, but seems to be more abundant in exposed localities. Its occurrence in Puget Sound would indicate a general distribution from that locality to Bering Sea.

Family *SQUAMARIACEÆ*.

Hildenbrandtia rosea Kuetz.

Forming a very delicate rose-red crust on rocks in the littoral and sublittoral zones, from Puget Sound to the Shumagin Islands.

The same species is reported by Kjellman from Bering Sea. The writer has also found it common on the central California coast. All specimens were sterile.

Family *CORALLINACEÆ*.[1]

Melobesia patens.

On *Amphiroa epiphlegmoides*, Prince William Sound (423a).

Dr. Foslie is somewhat in doubt as to the species, labeling specimens submitted to him, "*M. patens* or n. sp."

---

[1] Specimens of all Corallinaceæ enumerated were sent to Dr. Kjellman who requested Dr. Foslie to work them over. The determinations are entirely those of Dr. Foslie.

Lithophyllum farlowii Foslie.

On rocks in the littoral zone, Sitka (138).

The young plants were somewhat doubtfully referred to the species by Dr. Foslie.

Lithothamnion compactum Kjellm.

Forming an indefinite coating on rocks in the sublittoral zone, Prince William Sound (431).

Lithothamnion glaciale Kjellm.

In the upper elittoral and lower sublittoral zones. Prince William Sound (430); Kukak Bay (427); Shumagin Islands (426). Abundant in exposed localities.

Lithothamnion læve (Stroemf.) Foslie.

Abundant on rocks in exposed localities in the sublittoral zone, Kukak Bay (425a), with *Clathromorphum circumscriptum*.

Clathromorphum circumscriptum (Stroemf.) Foslie.

On rocks in the sublittoral and elittoral zones. Kukak Bay (425); Sitka (441).

Lepidomorphum yendoi Foslie.

On rocks in the sublittoral zone, Sitka (438).

Amphiroa tuberculosa Rupr.

On rocks in the lower sublittoral zone, Sitka (432).

Amphiroa epiphlegmoides J. Ag.

On rocks and other algæ. Sitka (433); Prince William Sound (423).

Amphiroa planiuscula (Kuetz.) Foslie.

On mussel shells, rocks, etc., in the lower sublittoral zone. Yakutat Bay (255); Prince William Sound (429).

Corallina arbuscula Rupr.

On rocks in the sublittoral zone. Shumagin Islands (438).

Corallina pilulifera filiformis Rupr.

On rocks in the sublittoral zone. Prince William Sound (435).

BACILLARIACEÆ.[1]

Melosira granulata C. G. E.

In a freshwater pond, Popof Island, near Kukak Bay; Kadiak Island; Cook Inlet.

[1] Determined by Prof. A. M. Edwards.

Melosira nummuloides B. de st. V.
  In salt water near Juneau; Glacier Bay.

Melosira sol C. G. E.
  Attached to seaweeds from Annette Island.

Melosira sulcata C. G. E.
  Attached to seaweeds from Annette Island.

Trochiscia moniliformis F. C. M.
  Attached to seaweeds from Annette Island; Glacier Bay.

Coscinodiscus argus C. G. E.
  In salt water material from Annette Island; Yakutat Bay.

Coscinodiscus lineatus C. G. E.
  In salt water from Glacier Bay.

Thalassosira cleve H. H. G.
  In salt water from Glacier Bay.

Triceratium wilkesii J. W. B.
  In salt water near Wrangell.

Chætoceros hispidum C. G. E.
  One specimen was found in material from Annette Island.

Biddulphia aurita L. W. D.
  Attached to seaweeds from Annette Island; Popof Island.

Isthmia obliquata J. E. S.
  In salt water from Yakutat Bay; Victoria, British Columbia.

Rhabdonema biquadratum J. B.
  Material from Annette Island.

Rhabdonema fauriæ P. P.
  Material from Annette Island.

Rhabdonema japonica T. & B.
  Material from Annette Island.

Rhabdonema elegans J. B.
  Material from Annette Island.

Rhabdonema striatulum J. E. S.
  In salt water material from Annette Island; Glacier Bay; Popof Island; Yakutat Bay.

Rhabdonema arcuata F. T. K.
  In salt water, Yakutat Bay.

Tabellaria flocculosa F. T. K.
In a freshwater pond, Popof Island; Kadiak Island; Kukak Bay.

Grammatophora marina (Lyngb.) Kuetz.
In salt water from Yakutat Bay.

Licmophora granulata V.
In salt water from Glacier Bay.

Licmophora cuneata F. C. L.
Attached to seaweeds, Glacier Bay.

Licmophora pennatula V.
In salt water near Juneau; Annette Island; Yakutat Bay; Wrangell; Popof Island.

Meridion circulare C. A. A.
In a freshwater pond, Popof Island.

Diatoma hyemale II. C. L.
In a freshwater pond, Popof Island.

Diatoma pectinale O. F. M.
In a freshwater pond, Popof Island.

Fragilaria construens C. G. E.
In a freshwater pond, Popof Island.

Fragilaria virescens J. R.
In a freshwater pond, Popof Island.

Fragilaria striatula H. C. L.
In material from salt water. Sitka; near Juneau; Popof Island.

Fragilaria exilis A. G.
In salt water, Yakutat Bay.

Synedra crotonensis A. M. E.
In a freshwater pond, Popof Island; Cook Inlet.

Synedra ulna C. L. N.
In a freshwater pond, Popof Island; Kadiak Island.

Synedra prolongata A. S.
In a fresh water pond, Cook Inlet.

Synedra fasciculata C. A. A.
Attached to seaweeds from Annette Island; Glacier Bay; Yakutat Bay.

Eunotia robusta J. R.
In a freshwater pond, Kadiak Island; Cook Inlet; Kukak Bay.

Eunotia gracilis C. G. E.
In a freshwater pond, Popof Island.

Eunotia lunaris C. G. E.
In a freshwater pond, Popof Island; Kadiak Island.

Cocconeis placentula C. G. E.
In a freshwater pond, Kadiak Island.

Cocconeis scutellum C. G. E.
In salt water from Victoria, British Columbia; attached to seaweeds from Annette Island; freshwater pond, Kadiak; salt water, Yakutat Bay; Juneau; Popof Island.

Achnanthes subsessilis C. G. E.
In salt water from Glacier Bay.

Achnanthes lanceolata A. B.
In a freshwater pond, Popof Island; near Kukak Bay.

Achnanthes glabrata A. G.
In salt water, Yakutat Bay.

Cocconema lanceolatum C. G. E.
Material from salt water, Annette Island; in a freshwater pond, Popof Island; Kadiak Island; Cook Inlet.
A freshwater species, the dead shells of which had been carried into the ocean by streams or glaciers.

Navicula silicula C. G. E.
In a freshwater pond, Popof Island.

Navicula cyprinus C. G. E.
In a freshwater pond, Popof Island.

Navicula elliptica F. T. K.
In a freshwater pond, Popof Island; attached to seaweeds from Popof Island.

Navicula major F. T. K.
In a freshwater pond, Popof Island; Annette Island; Kukak Bay.

Navicula radiosa F. T. K.
In a freshwater pond, Popof Island.

Navicula legumen C. G. E.
In salt water material from Annette Island.
A freshwater species, the dead shells of which had been carried into the ocean by streams or glaciers.

Navicula pupula C. A. A.
In salt water material from Annette Island.
A freshwater species, the dead shells of which had been carried into the ocean by streams or glaciers.

Navicula apis C. G. E.
Material from Annette Island; Popof Island.

Vanheurckia rhomboides A. B.
In a freshwater pond near Kukak Bay.

Pleurosigma angulata W. S.
In salt water, Yakutat Bay.

Pleurosigma attenuata F. T. K.
In a freshwater pond, Kadiak Island.

Pleurosigma fasciola C. G. E.
In salt water near Wrangell.

Nitzschia diadema F. T. K.
In salt water, Yakutat Bay.

Nitzschia angularis W. S.
In salt water, Yakutat Bay.

Nitzschia closterium C. G. E.
In salt water material, Annette Island.

Nitzschia sigmoidea C. L. N.
In salt water material from Annette Island.
A freshwater species, the dead shells of which had been carried into the ocean by streams or glaciers.

Nitzschia vermicularis F. T. K.
In a freshwater pond, Popof Island.

Surirella elegans C. G. E.
In a freshwater pond, Popof Island.

Staureoneis phœnicenteron C. L. N.
Material from Annette Island; freshwater pond, Kadiak Island; Kukak Bay.
A freshwater species, the dead shells of which had been carried into the ocean by streams or glaciers.

Amphora ovalis C. G. E.
　In salt water from Glacier Bay.

Amphora elliptica C. A. A.
　In salt water, Yakutat Bay.

Gomphonema geminatum C. G. E.
　In a freshwater pond, Kadiak Island.

Gomphonema affine F. T. K.
　In a freshwater pond, Kadiak Island.

Gomphonema subtile C. G. E.
　In a freshwater pond, Popof Island

Rhoicosphenia curvata F. T. K.
　In salt water material from Annette Island; Yakutat Bay; Popof Island

Cymbella inæqualis C. G. E.
　From salt water material from Annette Island.
　A freshwater species, the dead shells of which had been carried into the ocean by streams or glaciers.

Cymbella ehrenbergii F. T. K.
　In a freshwater pond, Popof Island, Kadiak Island.

Epithemia gibba C. G. E.
　In a freshwater pond, Popof Island, Kadiak Island

Epithemia jurgensii C. A. A.
　In a freshwater pond, Popof Island, Cook Inlet; Annette Island.

Epithemia westermannii C. G. E.
　In a freshwater pond, Popof Island.

PLATE X

[Proc. Wash. Acad. Sci., Vol. III, Pl. XLIII.[1]]

FIG 1. *Cosmarium conspersum* Ralfs
    2.   "   *cælatum* Ralfs
    3.   "   *ornatum* Ralfs
    4. *Euastrum crassum* (Bréb.) Kuetz.
    5. *Cosmarium pseudotaxichondrum* Nordst.
    6.   "   *parvulum* Bréb
    7.   "   *hammeri* Reinsch
    8.   "   *granatum* Bréb
    9. *Euastrum verrucosum* Ehrenb
   10. *Cosmarium ochtodes* Nordst
   11.   "   *botrytis* Menegh.
   12.   "   *portianum nephroideum* Wittr   Front view
   13.   "   "   "   "   End view
   14. *Closterium parvulum* Naeg.
   15.   "   *venus* Kuetz.
   16. *Staurastrum echinatum Pecten* (Perty) Rab.
   17. *Cosmarium depressum* (Naeg.) Lund.
   18.   "   *pulcherrimum* Nordst.
   19.   "   "   "   From Kukak Bay.
   20.   "   *subcrenatum* Hantzsch.
   21.   "   *pseudogranatum* Nordst.
   22.   "   *quadrifarium* Lund.
   23. *Staurastrum polymorphum* Bréb   End view.
   24.   "   "   "   Front view
   25. *Micrasterias rotata* (Grev.) Ralfs.
   26. *Cosmarium broomei* Var. Thwaites.
   27. *Closterium acerosum* (Schrank), Ehrenb.
   28. *Cosmarium bioculatum* Bréb.
   29. *Mesotænium braunii* De Bary
   30. *Disphinctium connatum* (Bréb.) De Bary
   31. *Staurastrum calyxoides* Wolle
   32. *Euastrum affine* Ralfs.
   33. *Cosmarium constrictum* Delp   Side view
   34.   "   "   "   Front view.
   35.   "   *broomei* Thwaites.   End view
   36.   "   "   "   Front view
   37. *Euastrum oblongum* (Grev.) Ralfs
   38. *Xanthidium antilopæum* (Bréb.) Kuetz.
   39. *Cosmarium sexangulare* Lund
   40.   "   *pyramidatum* Bréb.

[1] Plates xliii-lxii are from drawings by Eva M. Saunders, except for plate xlvi, figs. 1 and 2, which were drawn by Edna L. Hyatt.

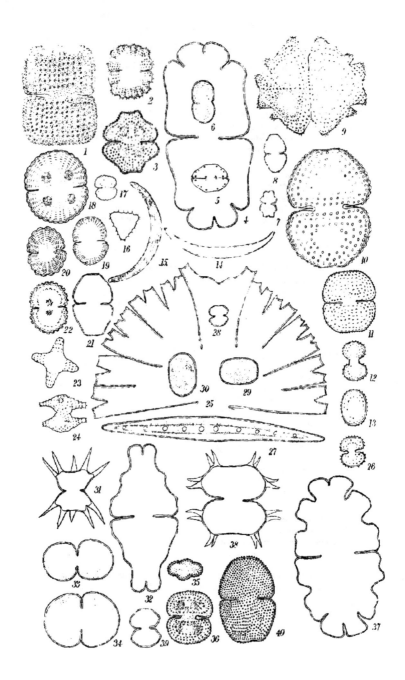

PLATE XI.

[Proc Wash Acad Sci, Vol III, Pl XLIV]

FIG. 1. *Cosmarium intermedium* Delp.
2. *Euastrum elegans* (Bréb.) Kuetz.
3. *Penium digitus* (Ehrenb.) Bréb.
4. *Cosmarium latum* Bréb.
5. *Staurastrum dejectum* Bréb. *a*, *b* and *c*
6. *Cosmarium sphalerostichum* Nordst.
7. *Micrasterias truncata* (Corda) Ralfs.
8. *Cosmarium phaseolus* Breb.
9. *Cosmarium undulatum* Corda.
11. *Micrasterias denticulata* (Bréb.) Ralfs.
12. *Cosmarium pachydermum* Lund.
13. *Tetmemorus brebissonii* (Menegh.) Ralfs.
14. *Arthrodesmus convergens* Ehrenb.
15. *Cosmarium blyttii* Wille.
16. *Cosmarium contractum* Kirch.
17. " *kitchelii* Wolle.
18. *Xanthidium armatum* (Bréb.) Ralfs.
19. *Cosmarium meneghinii braunii* (Reinsch.) Hansg.
20. *Pleurotæniopsis debaryi* (Archer) Lund.
21. *Cosmarium tumidum* Lund.
22. " *ralfsii* Bréb.
23. *Micrasterias kitchelii* Wolle.
24. *Euastrum didelta* (Turp.) Ralfs
25. " *elegans* (Bréb.) Kuetz.
26. " " " Two forms.
27. *Micrasterias oscitans pinnatifida* (Kuetz.) Rabenh.
28. *Cosmarium holmiense* Lund.
29. *Staurastrum ravenelii* Wood *a*, front view; *b*, end view
30. *Euastrum elegans*, large form.
31. *Micrasterias fimbriata elephanta* Wolle.

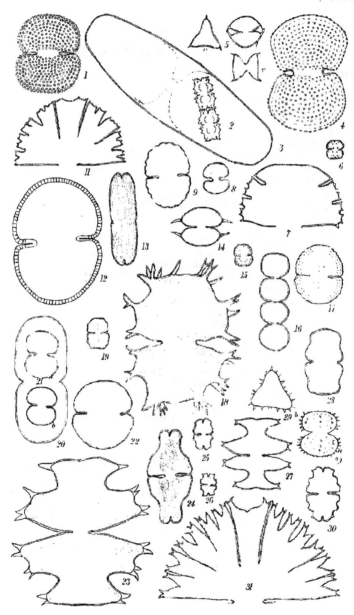

ALASKA ALGAE.

PLATE XII.

[Proc. Wash. Acad. Sci., Vol. III, Pl. XLV.]

FIG. 1. *a* and *b* *Streblonema pacifica* sp. nov.
2. *Streblonema irregularis* sp. nov.
3. " *minutissima* sp. nov.

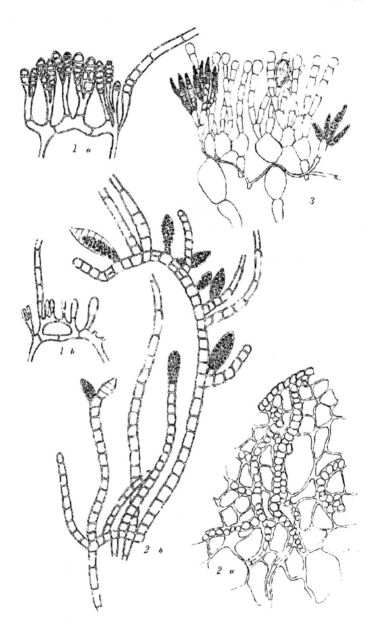

PLATE XIII.

FIG 1. *Myrionema strangulans* Grev , tufts natural size.
2.   "   "   "   section ($\times 400$)
3. *Homeostroma undulatum* J Ag
4. *Dermocarpa fucicola* sp nov.; section ($\times 400$).
5.   "   "   "   natural size.
6a *Homeostroma lobatum* sp nov , natural size.
6b.   "   "   "   portion of edge ($\times 30$)
6c.   "   "   "   section ($\times 400$)

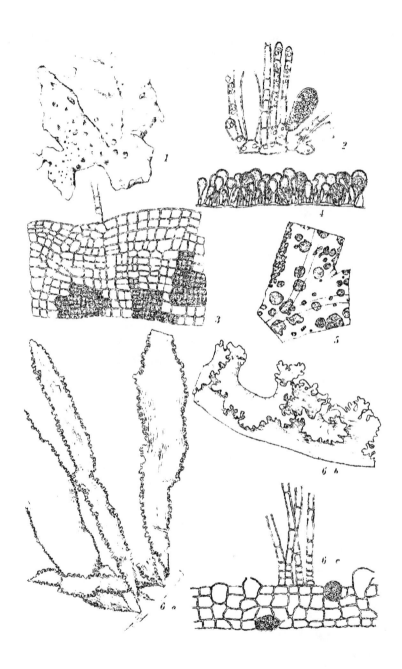

PLATE XIV.

[Proc. Wash. Acad. Sci., Vol III, Pl. XLVII.]

FIG 1 *Myelophycus intestinalis* sp nov ; natural size
    2   "   "   "   cross section ($\times 400$)
    3   "   "   "   longitudinal section ($\times 400$)

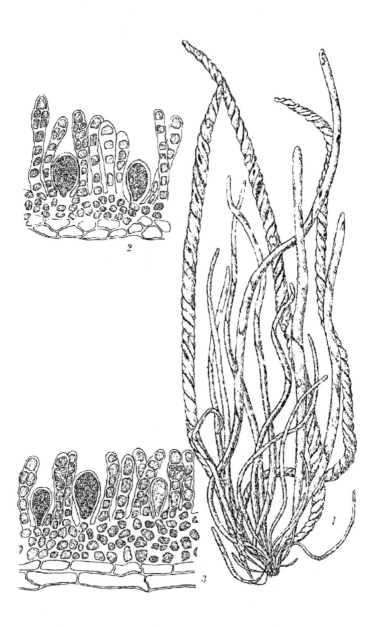

EVA M. SAUNDERS, DEL.   HELIOTYPE PRINTING CO.

ALASKA ALGAE.

PLATE XV.

[Proc. Wash Acad Sci, Vol III, Pl XLVIII]

FIG 1. *Coilodesme linearis* sp. nov.; natural size
    2.   "   "   "   cross section ($\times 400$).

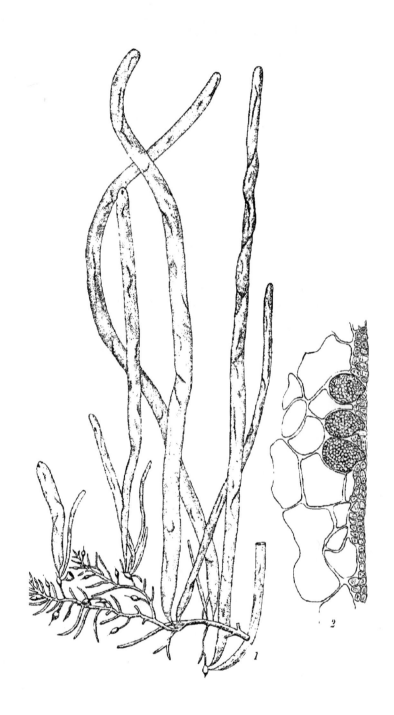

PLATE XVI

[Proc. Wash. Acad. Sci., Vol III, Pl. XLIX]

FIG 1 *Liebmannia* ?, natural size
2 " peripheral filaments (×400).

PLATE XVII.

[Proc. Wash. Acad. Sci., Vol. III, Pl. L.]

FIG 1. *Laminaria cuneifolia* J. Ag.
2. *Mesogloia simplex* sp. nov.
3. " " section ($\times 100$).
4. " " ($\times 400$).

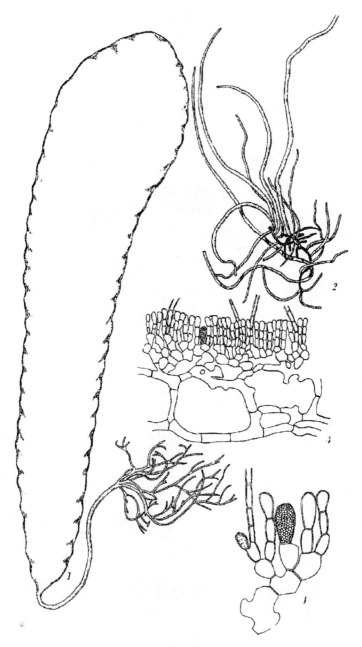

EVA M. SAUNDERS DEL.

HELIOTYPE PRINTING CO.

PLATE XVIII

[Proc. Wash. Acad. Sci., Vol III, Pl LI]

Hedophyllum sessile (Ag.) Setchell

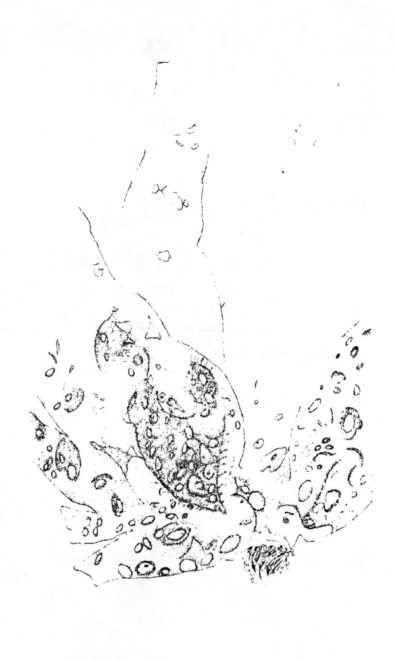

PLATE XIX.

[Proc Wash Acad Sci, Vol III, Pl LII.]

FIG. 1 *Pleurophycus gardneri* gen et sp nov Setchell and Saunders, ¼ natural size
2. " " young plant.
3. " " cross section of blade ($\times 400$).
4 " " longitudinal section of blade, showing fruit
5 " " *a*, section of stipe near the transition point, natural size, *b*, section of stipe near base, natural size, *c*, porton of same ($\times 80$)

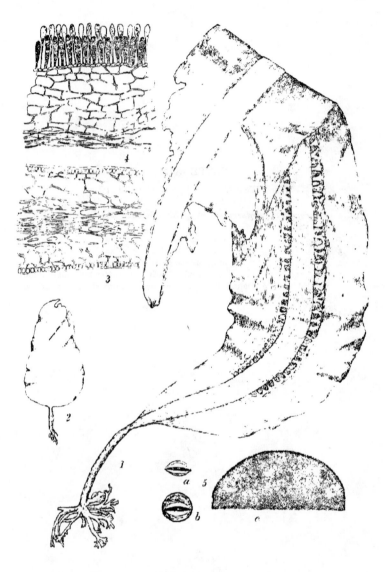

ALASKA ALGAE

PLATE XX.

FIG. 1. *Alaria lanceolata*, Kjellm ; ½ natural size.
    2.   "   "   "   section of blade, natural size.
    3, 4. "   "   "   young plants.

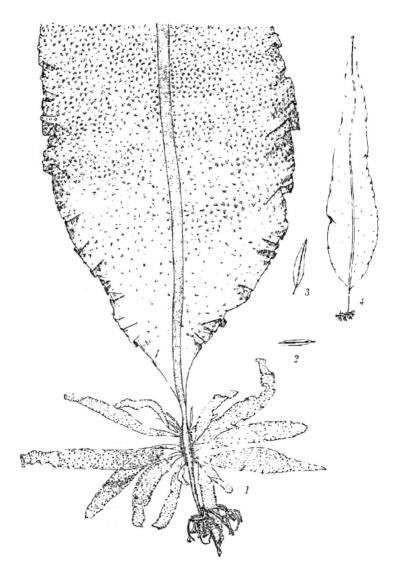

ALASKA ALGAE

PLATE XXI.

[Proc Wash Acad. Sci , Vol III, Pl LIV.]

Alaria fragilis sp nov.

ALASKA ALGAE

PLATE XXII

[Proc Wash Acad Sci , Vol. III, Pl LV.]

Alaria lacticosta Kjellman

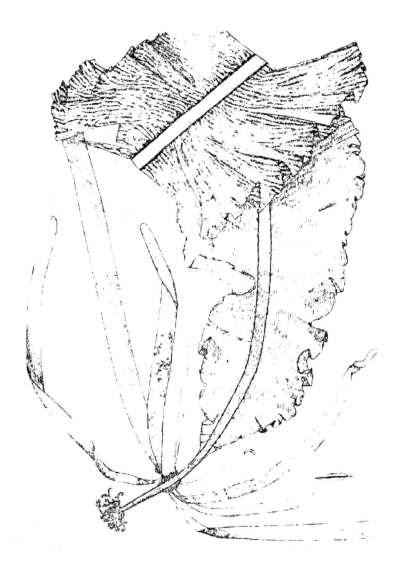

ALASKA ALGAE

PLATE XXIII

Alaria cordata Tilden.

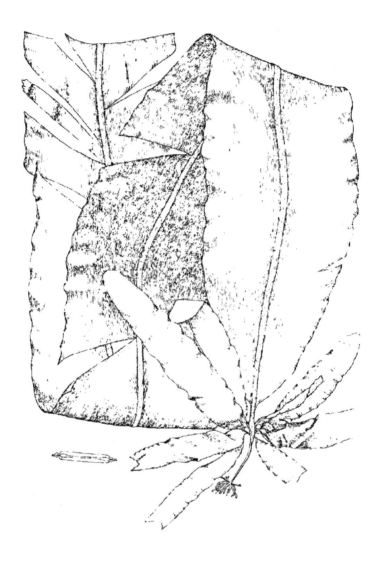

ALASKA ALGAE

PLATE XXIV.

[Proc. W.sh. Acad Sci., Vol. III, Pl. LVII.]

FIG. 1. *Alaria fistulosa* Post & Rupr.; ¼ natural size.
    2.   "   "   "   "   section of midrib; natural size.
    3, 4.   "   "   "   "   portions of the midrib ($\times$ 80).

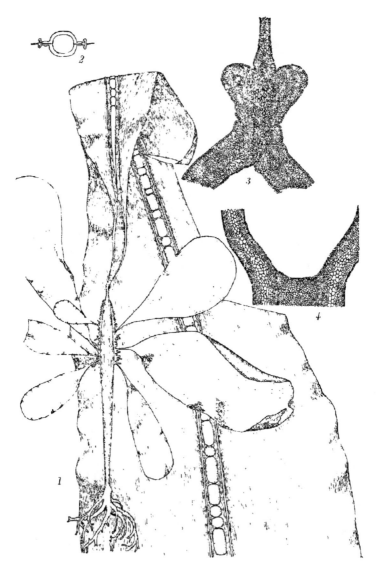

ALASKA ALGAE

PLATE XXV.

FIG. 1. *Nereocystis priapus* (Gmel.) Saunders; much reduced.
　2.　"　"　"　section of blade showing fruit
　3.　"　"　"　longitudinal section showing mucous canals ($\times 40$).
　4. *Nereocystis priapus* (Gmel.) Saunders ($\times 40$).
　5.　"　"　"　cross section of stipe showing mucous canals and secreting cells.

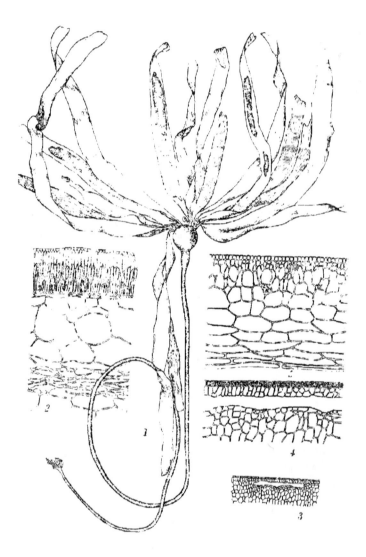

ALASKA ALGAE

PLATE XXVI.

[Proc. Wash. Acad. Sci., Vol. III, Pl. LIX]

FIGS. 1-8. *Nereocystis priapus*, young plants in various stages of development.
    9. " " An abnormal plant.

ALASKA ALGAE

PLATE XXVII.

[Proc. Wash. Acad. Sci., Vol. III, Pl. LX.]

FIG. 1. *Macrocystis pyrifera* (Turner) Ag.
2.   "   "   "
3.   "   "   "
4.   "   "   "
5.   "   "   "

ALASKA ALGAE

PLATE XXVIII

[Proc Wash Acad Sci , Vol III, Pl LXI.]

Agarum gmelini Mert.

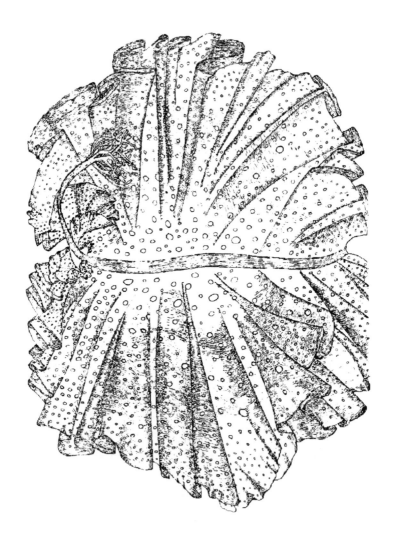

ALASKA ALGAE

PLATE XXIX.

[Proc. Wash. Acad. Sci , Vol III, Pl LXII.]

FIG. 1. *Fucus evanescens* Ag.; forma *macrocephala* Kjellm.
    2. "   "   forma *cornuta* Kjellm.

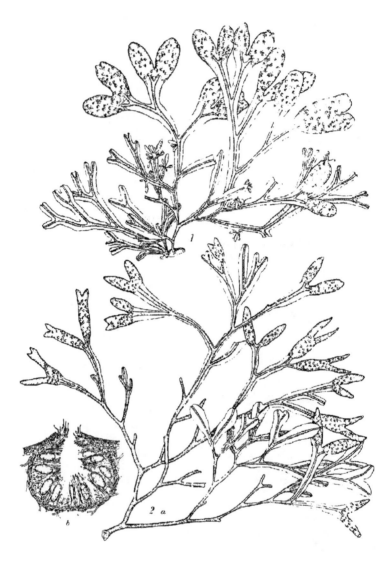

ALASKA ALGAE

The following paper on the Mosses of Alaska, by J. Cardot and I. Thériot, was originally published in the Proceedings of the Washington Academy of Sciences, vol. IV, pp. 293-372, July 31, 1902. It is here reprinted from the same electrotype plates, so that it may be quoted exactly as if it were the original. The original pagination has been preserved and transferred to the inner or hinge side of the page, where it is enclosed in brackets, thus [294]; while the consecutive pagination of the present volume has been added in the usual place. In the plates the original numbers and running headline, slightly abbreviated, have been preserved [in brackets], while the volume designation and serial plate numbers have been added in the usual place. The original text references to the plates are unchanged. The present headpiece and title have been substituted for the running heading of the Academy's Proceedings and the original title, which was: *Papers from the Harriman Alaska Expedition.* XXIX. *The Mosses of Alaska.* No other alterations have been made.

The authors desire to record the following corrections:

Page 255 [295]
Second line from bottom, for *polycarpam* read *polycarpum*.
Page 278 [318]:
Eleventh line from bottom, omit 'pl. VIII, fig. 1.'
Eighth line from bottom, omit 'pl. VIII, fig. 2.'
Fourth line from bottom, omit 'pl. V, fig. 3.'
Page 288 [328], seventh line from bottom, for 'Barclay' read *Boulay*.
Page 303 [343]
Omit line of synonymy under 'Hypnum sarmentosum beringianum'
Seventh line from bottom, omit 'in litt'
Omit line of synonymy under section 'Calliergidium'
The following species should be added to those contained in the paper:
Œdipodium griffithsianum Schwgr, a species not heretofore recorded as American, is added by Mrs. E. G. Britton, from Kadiak (Trelease, 1416).

EDITOR.

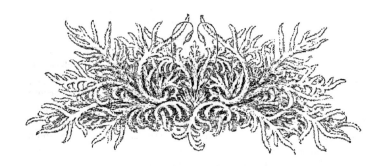

THE MOSSES OF ALASKA

BY J. CARDOT AND I. THÉRIOT

INTRODUCTION

The following catalogue of the mosses of Alaska and some adjacent islands is based primarily upon the collection made by the Harriman Expedition in 1899. For completeness, however, species previously reported from the region are also included.

The whole number here enumerated is 280, of which 124 are new to Alaska and 46 are new to science. The 29 new species and 17 new varieties, except for three species of *Bryum*, are here first described.

The mosses brought back by the Harriman Expedition were collected by Wm. H. Brewer, W. R. Coe, L. J. Cole, F. V. Coville, T. H. Kearney, De Alton Saunders and Wm. Trelease.

Previous collections were made by W. H. Dall, 1867; Krause brothers, 1882; W. G. Wright, 1891; Jas. M. Macoun, 1891–92; B. W. Evermann, 1892; C. H. Townsend, 1893–95 (Exp. of U. S. S. *Albatross*); W. M. Canby, 1897; W. H. Evans, 1897; W. A. Setchell, 1899; F. C. Schrader, 1899.

Subclass ANDREÆALES.
Family ANDREÆACEÆ.

Andreæa petrophila Ehrh. in Hann. Mag., 1784, p. 140, and in Beitr. I, p. 192.

From Orca (Trelease, 2245), Hall Island (Trelease, 2127), St. Matthew Island (Trelease, 2168, 2530). New to Alaska.

Andreæa petrophila sylvicola Bryol. eur., VI, p. 13, pl. 2, e.

From Hall Island (Trelease, 2527). New to Alaska.

Andreæa parvifolia C. Müll. in Flora, 1887, p. 219.

From upper part of Dyea valley (Krause brothers).

Andreæa papillosa Lindb. in Oefv. af Vet. Ak. Forh., XXIII, p. 557.

From St. Lawrence Bay, and Plover Bay, Siberia (W. H. Dall).

Subclass BRYALES.
Family WEISIACEÆ.

Gymnostomum curvirostre scabrum Lindb. Musc. scand., p. 22

From Port Wells (Trelease, 1834). New to Alaska.

Anœctangium compactum Schw. Suppl. I, 1, p. 36, pl. XI.

From White Pass, 1,900 feet (Trelease, 2309); Orca (Trelease, 2259, 2260 in part).

Anœctangium compactum alaskanum var. nov.

Habitu robustiore, foliis madore magis patulis, longioribus latioribusque, cellulis majoribus (mediis 6–9 μ latis, loco 4–6) reteque magis opaco distinctum.

From Port Wells (Trelease, 1832).

Dicranoweisia crispula Lindb. in Oefv. af Vet. Ak. Forh., 1864, p. 230.

From White Pass, 3,000 feet (Trelease, 2492); Port Clarence (Trelease, 2119); Hall Island (Trelease, 2129, 2131, 2134); St. Matthew Island (Trelease, 2153, 2154); Attu Island (J. M. Macoun).

Most of these specimens have the inner perichætial bracts shortly acuminate, which relates them to *D. contermina* Ren. & Card. (*D. roellii* Kindb.), but the alar cells are usually more distinct than on the moss from Oregon and Idaho. Moreover, the comparison with numerous specimens from different regions of Europe and North America proves that the characters on which *D. contermina* has been established are too variable and insufficient to establish a specific distinction. *D. contermina* must therefore be considered as only a variety of *D. crispula*, and the specimens from Alaska and the islands of Bering Sea are nearly all intermediate between the type and this variety.

D. obliqua Kindb., which has been recorded from Alaska, is unknown to us; but, from the description, it is probable that it, likewise, is only a form of *D. crispula*. (Cfr. Kindberg, Notes on Canadian Bryology, 1893, and Eur. and N. Amer. Bryineæ, p. 210.)

Rhabdoweisia fugax Br. eur., fasc. 33–36, p. 4, pl. 41.

From Kodiak (Trelease, 2217, 2218). New to Alaska.

Rhabdoweisia fugax subdenticulata Boul. Musc. de la France, p. 543.

From Juneau (Brewer and Coe, 699a). New to Alaska.

Another species of Weislaceæ, *Oreoweisia serrulata* Sch., has been recorded from Nulato by J. T. Rothrock and by Lesquereux and James (Manual, p. 58).

Family DICRANACEÆ.

Cynodontium torquescens Limpr. Laubm., 1, p. 288.

From Port Clarence (Trelease, 2101, 2102, 2525).

Number 2101 has the peristome smooth or nearly so; it is *C. subalpestre* Kindb. in Mac. Cat. Can. pl., VI, Musci, pp. 17 and 257.

Cynodontium treleasei sp. nov.

(Pl. XIII, figs. 1^{a-i}.)

Monoicum, densiuscule cespitosum. Caulis erectus, brevis, 3–4 millim. altus. Folia siccitate crispata, madore patentia, 2–3 millim. longa, e basi oblonga sat subito constricta, longe et anguste acuminato-subulata, apice sinuato denticulata, marginibus planis et integris, costa percurrente, cellulis inferioribus rectangulis, 2–3 long. quam lat., superioribus irregularibus, plerisque subquadratis, opacis et papillosis, 9–15 μ longis, 8–9 latis, cellulis alaribus majoribus, subinflatis, lutescentibus. Flos masculus in ramo brevi. Folia perichætialia intima vaginantia, longe acuminata. Capsula in pedicello brevi, 7–8 millim. longo, nutans vel inclinata, breviter ovato-convexa, interdum strumulosa, levis vel vix striatula, operculo longe oblique rostrato, basi crenulato. Annulus distinctus. Peristomium elatum, intense purpureum, 0.5 millim. altum, valde papillosum, dentibus irregulariter bi-trifurcatis. Sporæ leves, 16–18 μ crassæ.

From Port Wells (Trelease, 2268, 2271).

This species is only comparable with *C. polycarpam* Sch., from which it is easily distinguished by its smaller size, its shorter, smooth or hardly striate capsule, its more papillose, longer and brighter purple peristome. its shorter leaves with a thinner subula, and its upper cells smaller and less distinct.

Cynodontium polycarpum alaskanum var. nov.

A forma typica differt foliis apice tantum denticulatis, marginibus minus late et minus longe revolutis, reteque levi vel sublevi, cellulis superioribus paulo majoribus et distinctioribus (20 × 13 μ, loco 14 × 11), a var. *laxirete* Dix foliis angustioribus et rete basilari densiore distinctum, ab *Oncophoro suecico* Arn. et Jens. differt foliis inferne revolutis cellulisque alaribus indistinctis vel parum distinctis.

From Juneau (Trelease, 2176); Cape Fox (Trelease, 2374); Indian Camp, Yakutat Bay (Brewer and Coe, 645).

The type has been indicated for Alaska by Kellogg and by Lesquereux and James (Manual. p. 58).

Cynodontium virens Sch. Br. eur Coroll., p. 12.

From Haenke Island (Coville and Kearney, 1110). A doubtful specimen from St. Matthew Island (Trelease, 2155).

Cynodontium virens serratum Sch., loc. cit.

From Haenke Island (Coville and Kearney, 1111); Egg Island (Coville and Kearney, 1016, 1017); Port Wells (Trelease, 2290; Brewer and Coe, 654), St. Matthew Island (Trelease, 1891).

Cynodontium wahlenbergii Hartm. Flor. scand., ed. 10, p. 113.

From Cape Vancouver (J. M. Macoun); Port Wells (Trelease, 1830, 2288 in part, 2289); Port Clarence (Brewer and Coe. 669); Hall Island (Trelease, 1882, 1898, 1899, 2130, 2132), St. Lawrence Island (Trelease 1895, 1896, 1897, 2124); St. Matthew Island (Trelease, 1892, 1906, 2156, 2157, 2162)

Number 2130 is a small form with short leaves, forma *brevifolia*.

Dichodontium pellucidum Sch. Br. eur Coroll., p 12.

From Hidden Glacier Inlet in Yakutat Bay (Trelease, 1816, 2154 in part); Disenchantment Bay (Brewer and Coe, 639 in part); Muir Glacier (Trelease, 1752 in part), Port Wells (Trelease, 1831), Unalaska Island (J. M. Macoun).

Dichodontium pellucidum fagimontanum Sch., loc. cit.

From Juneau (Trelease, 2171); Muir Glacier (Trelease, 1909 in part).

Numbers 1816, 2154 in part and 1831 are forms passing to var. *fagimontanum*.

Dichodontium pellucidum kodiakanum var. nov.

(Pl. XIII, fig. 2*a–b*.)

Magnitudine *D. flavescenti* Lindb. simile, 5–8 centim. altum; folia subintegra, apice late obtuso tantum sinuolata, rete vix papilloso.

From Kodiak (Trelease, 1848).

D. pellucidum serratum Sch. (*D. flavescens* Lindb.) has been recorded from Alaska by Kindberg.

Aongstroemia longipes Br. eur., fasc. 33–36, p. 3, pl. 1.

From Muir Glacier (Trelease, 2422, 2466, 2468); Hidden Glacier Inlet, in Yakutat Bay (Trelease, 2519). New to Alaska.

Dicranella crispa Sch. Br. eur. Coroll., p. 13.

From Yakutat Bay (Trelease, 2334); St. Lawrence Island (J. M. Macoun).

Dicranella grevilleana Sch., loc. cit.

From Port Clarence (Trelease, 2103). New to Alaska.

Dicranella rufescens Sch., loc. cit.

From Prince of Wales Island (J. M. Macoun).

Dicranella heteromalla Sch., loc. cit.

From Juneau (Trelease, 2180, Setchell, 1235); Farragut Bay (Coville and Kearney, 470); Kodiak (Trelease, 2206, 2213, 2214); Douglas Island (Trelease, 2405, 2407, 2411); Prince of Wales Island (J. M. Macoun), Yes Bay (Gorman, 182 in part, 183).

Dicranella heteromalla orthophylla Lesq. & Jam. Manual, p. 67.

From Sitka (Trelease, 2367); Kodiak (Trelease, 2197); Douglas Island (Trelease, 2411).

Dicranella heteromalla latinervis var. nov.

A forma typica differt foliis brevius subulatis costaque latiore, circa ⅓ basis occupante.

From Douglas Island (Trelease, 2389).

D. squarrosa Sch. was recorded from Alaska, teste M. W. Harrington, by Lesquereux and James, and *D. subulata* Sch. and *D. polaris* Kindb. from the islands of Bering Sea, teste Macoun, by Kindberg. The specimen received by us as *D. subulata*, from St. Lawrence Island is *D. crispa*. We have not seen any specimens of the other two species.

Dicranum anderssonii Sch. Syn., ed. 1, p. 689.

From Port Wells (Trelease, 2277). New to Alaska.

This moss undoubtedly belongs to *D. anderssonii* Sch. (*Arctoa anderssonii* Wich. in Flora, 1859, no. 27). In his second edition of the Synopsis, Schimper reunites it to *D. hyperboreum*, from which, however, it seems sufficiently distinct by its smaller, subglobose capsule, turbinate after the fall of the lid, very shortly pedicellate and almost always surrounded and surpassed by the perichætial leaves, and by the cells of the exothecium being smaller, with more solid and more colored walls. According to C. Jensen (Bryophyta of the Faeroes, in his Botany of the Faeroes, p. 159), the capsule of *Dicranum anderssonii* should be destitute of stomates, but in the Port Wells specimen all the capsules bear several stomates at the base of the very short neck.

Dicranum starkei Web. & Mohr, Bot. Taschb., pp. 189, 471.

From Yakutat Bay (Trelease, 2059); Disenchantment Bay (Brewer and Coe, 635). New to Alaska.

Dicranum albicans Br. eur., fasc. 43, Suppl., pl 1.

From Yakutat Bay (Trelease, 2059 in part). New to Alaska.

A form of greener tint than usual and with homomallous leaves.

Dicranum strictum Schl. Pl. crypt. helv., cent. III, no. 26.

From Yakutat Bay (Trelease, 2331, 2336).

Dicranum subflagellare sp. nov.

(Pl xiii, fig 3^{a-e}.)

A *D. flagellari* proximo differt defectu flagellarum, foliis erectis subfalcatis angustioribus parum flexuosis, brevioribus (2–2.5 millim.), acumine canaliculato non subtubuloso, marginibus dorsoque subintegro cellulisque inferioribus angustioribus, superioribus multo minoribus. Specimina pauca, sterilia.

From Kodiak (Trelease, 1899).

Dicranum elongatum Schl. Pl. crypt. helv., cent. III, no. 27.

From Port Clarence (Trelease, 1867 in part, 2117, 2118); Kodiak (Trelease, 2503); St. Lawrence Island (Trelease, 1892, 1894, 1897 in part); St. Matthew Island (Trelease, 2170).

Number 2503 is a short, stunted form, with nearly the facies of *D. miquelonense* Ren. & Card.

Dicranum groenlandicum Brid. Mant. musc., p. 68. Bryol. univ., 1, p. 460.

From the Yukon River (W. H. Dall); Port Clarence (Trelease, 1867 in part). New to Alaska.

Dicranum fuscescens Turn. Musc. hib., p. 60, pl. 5, f. 1.

From Yes Bay (Gorman, 184); Juneau (Brewer and Coe, 699b, 700); Skagway (Canby, 478); Wrangell (Trelease, 2317); White Pass, 3,000 ft. (Trelease, 2313); Farragut Bay (Trelease, 2416, Brewer and Coe, 617), Yakutat Bay (Trelease, 1763, 2340); Point Gustavus (Coville and Kearney, 777); La Perouse Glacier (Trelease, 2498), Sitka (U. S. S. *Albatross*, 53, 55, Canby, 458, 463, Trelease, 2359); Hot Springs (Trelease, 1914); Kodiak (Trelease, 1853); Douglas Island (Trelease, 1908, 2392); Port Wells (Trelease, 2282, 2288); Orca (Trelease, 1918, 1925, 2262; Setchell, 1213), New Metlakatla (Coville and Kearney, 364); Plover Bay, Siberia (Trelease, 1865).

The Yes Bay specimen was associated with *Mnium glabrescens* Kindb. and *Scapania* sp.

The Kodiak specimen (1853) is a paludal form, with entire, shorter, erect leaves. We must point out too a sterile form, collected on Unalaska Island by Mr. C. H. Townsend (U. S. S. *Albatross* exped., 43), which is very near *D. muehlenbeckii* Br. eur. var. *brevifolium* Lindb. The same form was found by Trelease on Hall Island (1907). It differs from the European plant chiefly in having its leaves less flexuous when dry.

Many authors separate *D. congestum* Brid. from *D. fuscescens* Turn. but as it is almost impossible to find two descriptions of *D. congestum* which agree, we can infer that it is one of those species which every author understands in his own way, that is to say a very bad species; and we deem it preferable to merely unite it with *D. fuscescens*.

Dicranum dipteroneuron C. Müll. in Flora, 1887, p. 221.

From valley of the Takhin River (Krause brothers).

Dicranum scoparium Hedw. Fund. musc., II, p. 92, pl. 8, f. 41, 42.

From Point Gustavus (Coville and Kearney, 772 in part.)
A paludal form.

Dicranum neglectum Jur. Laubm. fl., p. 47. Limpr. Laubm., 1, p. 353
D. spadiceum Zett. Musc. pyren., p. 30.

From Port Clarence (Trelease, 1868); Sturgeon River Bay, Kodiak (Trelease, 1929); Unalaska (U. S. S. *Albatross* exped., 7a); St. George Island (U. S. S. *Albatross* exped., 57), St. Lawrence Island (Trelease, 1873, 1874 in part, 1902); St. Matthew Island (Trelease, 1886, 1888 in part, 1980); Hall Island (Trelease, 1988, 1990, 1991). New to Alaska.

Dicranum howellii Ren. & Card. in Bot. Gaz., 1889, p. 93, pl. XII, B.

From Skagway (Canby, 483); New Metlakatla (Trelease, 1906); Point Gustavus (Coville and Kearney, 755), Virgin Bay (Trelease, 2308), Sitka (Setchell, 1255, Trelease, 2360); Kodiak (Trelease, 2202, 2223, 2504), Unga (Saunders, 2294, 2295). New to Alaska.

Dicranum bonjeani De Not. apud Lisa Elencho, p. 29. Epil., p. 616.

From Sturgeon River Bay, Kodiak (Trelease, 1854).

A form nearly allied to var. *schlotthaueri* Barnes by its short and entire leaves. The type was recorded from Sitka and Nulato, teste Rothrock, by Kindberg, Mac. Cat. Can. pl., VI, Musci, p. 32.

Dicranum majus Sm. Fl. brit., III, p. 1202.

From Point Gustavus (Coville and Kearney, 754); Orca (Setchell, 1215); Sitka (Trelease, 1953; U. S. S. *Albatross* exped., 61), Hot Springs (Trelease, 1952).

Number 1215 Setchell, is a slender form.

Dicranum bergeri Bland. Musc. frond. exs., III, no. 114.

From Kodiak (Trelease, 1675a in part).

Dicranum molle Wils. is recorded from St Paul Island and *D. angustifolium* Kindb. from Unalaska by Kindberg, in Mac. Cat. Can. pl., VI, Musci. *D. muehlenbeckii* has also been recorded from Alaska

Dicranodontium longirostre Br. eur., fasc. 41, p. 2, pl. 1

From Orca (Trelease, 1839). New to Alaska.

Dicranodontium aristatum Sch. Syn., ed. 1, p. 695.

From Hot Springs (Trelease, 1809) New to Alaska.

Slightly different from the European plant, the costa being rather less broad, but one fifth or one fourth the width of the leaf base, and having a less rough subula. *Dicranum virginicum* Aust. (*Campylopus virginicus* Lesq. & Jam.) is intermediate between the European and Alaskan forms.

Mr. Kindberg has, teste Macoun, reported from Alaska, *Campylopus schimperi* Milde.

Family SELIGERIACEÆ.

Blindia acuta Br. eur., fasc. 33-36, p. 3, pl. 1

From Juneau (Coville and Kearney, 582), Port Wells (Trelease, 2274, 2275, 2276, 2280, 2291 in part); Hall Island (Trelease, 1881). New to Alaska.

Number 2280 is a form with long innovations, surpassing the capsule.

Blindia acuta flexipes Ren. & Card., in Rev. bryol., 1892, p. 79

Port Wells (Trelease, 2286). New to Alaska.

Family DITRICHACEÆ.

Ceratodon purpureus Brid. Br. univ., 1, p. 480

Very common and variable From Juneau (Setchell, 1233; Coville and Kearney, 589; Trelease, 2175, 2177); New Metlakatla (Trelease, 2240); Wrangell (Trelease, 2316); Port Clarence (Trelease, 2106, 2107, 2108, 2109, 2110, 2111, 2112; Brewer and Coe, 671); Cape Fox (Trelease, 1934), Yakutat Bay (Trelease, 2326, 2332), Disenchantment Bay (Coville and Kearney, 1065, Brewer and Coe, 637); Muir Glacier (Trelease, 1801, 1804, 2443, 2446, 2447, 2450, 2465), Orca (Trelease, 2255, 2256), Bogoslof volcano (Coville and Kearney, 2614 in part); Sitka (Coville and Kearney, 868; Trelease, 2361, Canby, 460), Kodiak (Trelease, 2189, 2198, 2212, 2224, 2226), Douglas Island (Trelease, 2393, 2404); Prince of Wales Island (J. M. Macoun); Bering Island (J. M. Macoun); Hall Island (Trelease, 2139), St Paul Island (Trelease, 1860, 2086); Plover Bay, Siberia (Trelease, 2097, 2531, 2532, 2536, 2537, 2546, Coville and Kearney, 1862)

Ceratodon heterophyllus Kindb. in Ott. nat., v, p. 179. Macoun, Cat. Can. pl., VI, Musci, p 261.

From St Paul Island (J. M. Macoun; B W Evermann, Trelease, 2062, 2070, 2071, 2072, 2075).

Distichium capillaceum Br. eur., fasc. 29–30, p. 4, pl. 1.

From White Pass (Trelease, 2310); Port Wells (Brewer and Coe, 653; Coville and Kearney, 1291 in part; Trelease, 2278, 2291); Orca (Trelease, 1837, 1838, 2260 in part); Yakutat Bay (Brewer and Coe, 644), Port Clarence (Trelease, 2104).

Ditrichum homallum Hpe. in Flora, 1867, p. 182.

From Kodiak (Brewer and Coe, 658 in part) New to Alaska

A slender etiolated form, of which we find only some stems among other mosses, leaves erect, costa narrower, basilar cells broader

Ditrichum flexicaule densum Sch has, teste Rothrock, been recorded from Alaska by Lesquereux and James, and *D glaucescens* Hpe, teste Macoun, from Unalaska, by Kindberg. Kindberg has also, teste Macoun, described a *Leptotrichum tomentosum* from St. Paul Island.

Family POTTIACEÆ.

Pottia heimii beringiana var. nov.

(Pl XIV, fig 2ᵃ⁻ᵉ.)

A forma typica differt foliis brevioribus, limbo lutescente circumductis, costa breviter excurrente mucronatis reteque magis opaco valde

From St. Matthew Island (Trelease, 2151 in part).

We found only a few stems of this moss, mixed with *Barbula brachypoda* Card. & Thér. and a *Bryum*. By the pellucid margin of the leaves, it is nearly related to *P. obtusifolia* C. Müll. (*P. heimii arctica* Lindb.), but it is easily distinguished from it by its pointed leaves. It also closely resembles *Desmatodon systylioides* Ren. & Card., from Labrador, which is probably also a *Pottia* of the same group, but it differs from this species by its ovate, shorter and proportionately wider capsule, its longer and more finely beaked lid, its shorter and more briefly acuminate leaves, and finally by its areolation formed of larger and less obscure cells.

According to J M Macoun *P. heimii* typica has been recorded by Kindberg from St Matthew Island and from Bering Island.

Didymodon rubellus Br. eur., fasc. 29-30, p. 3, pl. 1.

From Juneau (Trelease, 2178); Port Wells (Trelease, 2272, 2283); Agattu Island (U. S. S. *Albatross* exped., 36); St. Matthew Island (Trelease, 2143, specimen in bad condition, and determination doubtful); Bering Island (J. M. Macoun).

Didymodon baden-powelli Kindb. Ott. Nat., v, p. 179. Macoun, Cat Can. pl., VI, Musci, p. 262.

From St. Paul Island (J. M. Macoun).

Contrary to Kindberg's description, the leaves are entire or nearly so on the specimen we have seen. It is probable that this moss is but a form of *D. rubellus*.

Trichostomum cuspidatissimum sp. nov.

(Pl. XIII, fig. 4ᵃ⁻ᵉ.)

Dioicum, elatum, compacte cespitosum, fusco-lutescens. Caulis erectus, circa 5 centim. altus, dense foliosus, rufo-tomentosus, ramis erectis numerosis. Folia siccitate crispata, madore erecto-arcuata, ad apicem caulis et ramorum congesta, fragilia (acumine sæpe effracto), e basi ovata sensim et longissime acuminata, 3-3.5 millim, longa, 0.45-0.7 lata, marginibus planis, superne inflexis, papillis prominentibus crenulatis, costa angusta, 80-90 μ basi lata, in cuspidem acutissimam longe excurrente, cellulis inferioribus rectangulis, 5-6 long. quam lat., lutescentibus, superioribus plerumque quadratis, 10-12 μ latis, opacis, grosse papillosis. Cætera desunt.

From Hall Island (Brewer and Coe, 674).

A fine species, easily distinguished from the large forms of *T. mutabile* Bruch, and its var. *cuspidatum* Limpr. (*T. cuspidatum* Sch.), by the form of the leaves, and more particularly by its narrower costa and its upper cells which are much larger and more distinct (10–12 μ instead of 6–8).

Trichostomum sitkanum sp. nov.
(Pl. XIV, fig 1^{a-e}.)

Dioicum? Cespites densiusculi, superne virides, intus nigrescentes, inferne terra obruti. Caulis 2–3 centim. altus, parum divisus, laxe foliosus. Folia mollia, sicca cirrato-crispata, madore patula, inferiora 2.5–3 millim longa, superiora majora, 4–4 5 millim. longa, e basi longe subvaginante lineari-lanceolata, marginibus planis integris, costa sat valida, basi circa 110 μ lata, in mucronem lutescentem breviter excurrente, cellulis basis subvaginantis rectangulis, hyalinis, 4–6 long. quam lat., cæteris quadrato-hexagonis, 12–14 μ latis, valde papillosis. Cætera desunt

From Sitka (Trelease, 2370).

The aspect, the form of leaves, the looser basal areolation and the upper cells more papillose, easily distinguish this plant from *T. cuspidatissimum* Card. & Thér. It is more closely connected with *T. bambergeri* Sch., but the latter has the costa shining on the back in a dry state, and the hyaline cells of the base going up along the borders of the leaf, as in *Barbula tortuosa* Web. & Mohr.

Desmatodon latifolius Br. eur., fasc. 18–20, p. 5, pl. 1.

From Unalaska (J. M. Macoun).

Barbula brachypoda sp. nov.
(Pl XIV, figs 3^{a-d}.)

Monoica, laxiuscule cespitosa, viridis. Caulis 5–10 millim. altus, erectus, simplex furcatusve. Folia mollia, sicca erecta, madida erecto-patentia, elliptica vel subspathulata, 2.5–3 millim longa, o 6–1 millim. lata, late et breviter acuminata obtusa, subobtusa acutave, marginibus e basi ad medium usque revolutis, deinde planis et pro more limbo lutescente e 3–4 seriebus cellularum composito limbatis, costa angusta (Lat. 50 μ), paulo sub apice evanida, rete levi, in dimidio inferiore laxissimo hyalino, cellulis rectangularibus, 66–88 μ longis, circa 22 latis, superne valde chlorophylloso, cellulis inæqualibus quadrato-rotundatis vel brevissime rectangulis, e costa ad margines sensim minoribus (majoribus 25 μ longis, 16 latis, minoribus quadratis, 14 μ latis). Flos masculus infra femineum situs Folia perichætialia caulinis majora, acuminata, intima angustissima. Capsula in pedicello brevi, crassiusculo, pallido,

5–7 millim. longo, 0.2 millim. crasso, erecta, cylindrica, circa 2 millim. longa, operculo conico tertiam partem capsulae aequante. Annulus latus, distinctus. Peristomium papillosum, membrana basilari brevi, dentibus semel vel bis convolutis. Sporae leves, 12–16 µ crassae.

From St. Matthew Island (Trelease, 2151 in part, 2166).

This species, which belongs to the section *Cuneifoliæ* Sch., is easily distinguished from *B. cuneifolia* Brid. by its leaves revolute below, its longer lower cells, the upper more chlorophyllose with thicker walls, its shorter seta, its broad annulus, etc.

Kindberg has established (in Revue bryologique. 1896, p. 22) a *B. subcuneifolia* from Alaska, which, by some characters, seems to be near to our *B. brachypoda*, but his description is so incomplete that we can neither ascertain whether this *B. subcuneifolia* is identical with the plant here described, nor, with still more reason, mention the characters which might distinguish it from the former.

Barbula saundersii sp. nov.

(Pl. xvi, fig. 1ᵃ⁻ᵈ.)

Dioica? laxiuscule cespitosa, olivaceo-viridis. Caulis brevis, 5–8 millim altus, simplex vel parce divisus. Folia sicca incurvata, madida erecta vel erecto-patentia, 1.5–2 millim longa, 0.8 lata, e basi ovata breviter acuminata, obtusa vel brevissime mucronata, marginibus e basi usque ad ⅔ valde revoluta, superne concava, costa valida, tota fere longitudine aequaliter crassa (0.1 millim.), dorso valde prominente, percurrente, rarius paulisper excedente; rete levi, cellulis inferioribus laxis, rectangulis, lutescentibus, 40 µ longis, 12 latis, sequentibus quadratis, 12–13 µ latis, parietibus incrassatis, mediis et superioribus minutis, 7–8 µ latis, parum distinctis. Folia perichaetialia caulinis majora, sicca erecto-incurvata, madida erecta, appressa. Capsula in pedicello purpureo, circa 10 millim. longo, siccitate sinistrorsum torto, erecta, oblonga vel subcylindrica, 1–1.25 millim. longa, operculo conico longissimo, capsulam aequante. Peristomium purpureum, papillosum, membrana basilari brevi, 30 µ alta, dentibus semel vel bis contortis. Sporae leves, 14–16 µ crassae.

From Hidden Glacier Inlet, Yakutat Bay (Trelease, 2514).

In habit recalls the smallest forms of *B. unguiculata* Hedw., from which it differs by the shorter and proportionately broader leaves, which are shortly ovate-lanceolate, not or hardly mucronate, etc. By the form of the leaves, it is also connected with *B. brachyphylla* Sulliv., but the latter has the stems much longer and the basal areolation of the leaves quite different.

Barbula treleasei sp. nov.
(Pl. xv, fig. 2^{a—g})

Dioica? dense cespitosa, lutescenti-viridis. Caulis 1–2 centim. altus, erectus, divisus. Folia siccitate crispatula, madore erecto-patentia, circa 1.5 millim. longa, 0.6 lata, ovato-lanceolata, breviter acuminata, integra, marginibus e basi longe revolutis, costa valida, rubella, percurrente, basi 80 μ crassa, cellulis inferioribus rectangulis subhyalinis, levibus, mediis superioribusque minutis (diam 8 μ), quadratis, valde papillosis, parum distinctis. Folia perichætialia multo longiora et latiora, sat subito constricta, longe acuminata, madore arcuato-patula, intima subvaginantia, in dimidio inferiore hyalina. Capsula in pedicello 10–11 millim. longo, erecta, oblongo-cylindrica. Cætera desunt.

From Juneau (Trelease, 2179, 2181)

This moss has the aspect of a slender *B. fallax* Hedw.; but the texture of the leaf base, formed of rectangular subhyaline cells, clearly separates it. On the other hand, it differs from *B. vinealis* Brid. and allied forms by the much shorter leaves.

Barbula rigens sp. nov.
(Pl. xv, fig. 1^{a—g})

Rubella, laxe cespitosa vel aliis muscis gregarie intermixta. Caulis gracilis, erectus, rigidulus, divisus, 1–2 centim. altus. Folia sicca crispatula, madida erecto-patentia, stricta, breviter lanceolato-linearia, 1.25–1.5 millim. longa, 0.3 lata, marginibus integris medium versus paululum revolutis, costa valida, tota fere longitudine æqualiter crassa, diam. 56 μ, biconvexa, percurrente vel in mucronem brevem excurrente, cellulis inferioribus rectangulis, hyalinis, plerumque levibus, superioribus opacis, indistinctis, quadrato-rotundatis, utraque pagina dense papillosis, mediis circa 11 μ latis. Cætera ignota.

From Orca (Trelease, 2260; mixed with *Distichium capillaceum* and *Anœctangium compactum*).

This species belongs to the group of *B. rigidula* Mitt., from which it is easily distinguished by its stiff stem and leaves, the latter being shorter and very briefly acuminate and by its much more papillose areolation.

Barbula cylindrica Sch. in Hedwigia, 1873, p. 47. Syn., ed 2, p. 208.

From Prince of Wales Island (J. M. Macoun).

Barbula fragilis Br. eur., fasc. 62–64, Suppl., pl. 4.

From Port Wells (Coville and Kearney, 1291 in part).

Barbula aciphylla Br. eur., fasc. 13-15, p. 42, pl. 26.

Yakutat Bay (Trelease, 1746 in part); Muir Glacier (Trelease, 1802). New to Alaska.

Number 1802 is a rather badly characterized form, which can be ascribed to *B. aciphylla*, but which has also some relationship with *B. ruralis* Hedw.

Barbula ruralis Hedw. Fund., II, p. 92.

From Agattu Island (U. S. S. *Albatross* Exped., 42).

A form having the facies of *B muelleri* Bruch.

'Mr. Kindberg has described from Alaska a *B subcuneifolia* and a *B. ruralis* subsp *alaskana*, of which we have seen no specimens

Family GRIMMIACEÆ.

Grimmia apocarpa Hedw. Descr., 1, p. 104, pl. 39.

From Juneau (Trelease, 2183); Muir Glacier (Trelease, 2432); Kodiak (Trelease, 2215); Hall Island (Trelease, 2128); St. Paul Island (Trelease, 2079).

Grimmia apocarpa gracilis Web. & Mohr, Taschenb., p. 131.

From White Pass (Trelease, 2493); Muir Glacier (Trelease, 1789, 2454); Hidden Glacier Inlet, Yakutat Bay (Trelease, 1790, 2058); Kodiak (Trelease, 1788); Hall Island (Trelease, 1880).

Grimmia apocarpa alpicola Hook. & Tayl. Muscol. brit., p. 87.

From Portage Bay (U. S. S. *Albatross* Exped.); Cape Fox (Trelease, 2386); St. Paul Island (Trelease, 2080).

A form allied to this variety by the dimension of its spores, but differing from it by its sharp pointed leaves, the upper ones ending in a hyaline point, was collected at Wrangell (Canby, 471); Cape Fox (Trelease, 2385) and at Hot Springs, near Sitka (Trelease, 2495).

Grimmia apocarpa rivularis Web. & Mohr, Taschenb., p. 129.

From Muir Glacier (Trelease, 2424, 2494); Yakutat Bay (Trelease, 2324).

Grimmia conferta Funck, Moostaschenb., p. 18, pl. 12.

From St. Paul Island (Trelease, 2470a); St. Matthew Island (Trelease, 2167).

Seems to belong to *G. conferta* by the short, hemispherical capsule, but the peristome is wanting.

Grimmia maritima Turn. Muscol. hib., p. 23, pl. 3, f. 2.

From Virgin Bay (Trelease, 2303); Port Wells (Trelease, 2279); Yakutat Bay (Trelease, 2325), Kodiak (Trelease, 2205, 2216); Agattu Island (U. S. S. *Albatross* Exped., 62). New to Alaska.

Grimmia torquata Grev. Scot. crypt fl., IV, p. 199.

From Kodiak (Trelease, 2203, 2204).

Grimmia elatior Br. eur., fasc. 25-28, p. 17, pl. 10, *forma?*

From Yukon River (W. H. Dall). New to Alaska.

We find only some stems of this moss, with a single capsule, mixed with *Polytrichum yukonense* Card. & Thér., and their determination remains rather doubtful.

Kindberg has recorded from Alaska *G. agassizii* Sulliv. and Lesq. and from Unalaska *G. crassinervis* C. Mull.

Rhacomitrium patens Hub. Muscol. germ., p. 198.

From Unalaska (J. M. Macoun).

Rhacomitrium sudeticum alaskanum var. nov.

Forma minor, habitu varietati *tenellum* Boul. similis, sed foliis subepiliferis vel apiculo hyalino omnino destitutis costaque validiore distincta.

Hidden Glacier Inlet, Yakutat Bay (Trelease, 2508 in part).

Rhacomitrium aciculare Brid. Mant., p. 80.

From Juneau (Coville and Kearney, 573); Kodiak (Trelease, 1849).

Rhacomitrium nevii Wats. Bot. Calif., II, p. 381.

From Juneau (Trelease, 2174); Atka Island (J. M. Macoun).

Rhacomitrium fasciculare Brid. Mant., p. 80.

From Portage Bay (U. S. S. *Albatross* Exped.); Yakutat Bay (Trelease, 1785, 2322); Cape Fox (Trelease, 2377); Muir Glacier (Trelease, 1781, 2455); Kodiak (Trelease, 1786, 2193); Sitka (U. S. S. *Albatross* Exped., 47); Hot Springs (Trelease, 1769, 2346, 2350).

Number 2322 is a forma *minor*.

Rhacomitrium tenuinerve Kindb. Rev. bryol., 1896, p. 19.

R. fasciculare var. *haplocladon* KINDB Not on Can. bryol., 1893
R. microcarpum var. *palmeri* KINDB. apud Macoun, Cat. Can. pl., VI, Musci, p. 267
R. palmeri KINDB. Rev. bryol., 1896, p. 19.

From St. Paul Island (J. M. Macoun); St. Matthew Island (Trelease, 1885, 2169); Pribilof Islands (Palmer, 1891).

R. tenuinerve and *palmeri* of Kindberg surely constitute but one species, which differs from *R. fasciculare* Brid. principally by its weak, flat costa, disappearing far from the point. Kindberg is mistaken in attributing to *R. palmeri* a percurrent or subexcurrent costa.

On the original specimen collected by Palmer, and which Kindberg himself formerly communicated to us, the costa has exactly the same length and the same structure as in *R. tenuinerve*. The latter is a form with long simple or hardly branched stems, whereas *R. palmeri* is a shorter and more ramulose form.

Rhacomitrium cyclodictyon sp. nov.

(Plate xv, fig 3^{a-g})

Dioicum? parvum, dense cespitosum, atrofuscum. Caulis depressus, ramosissimus, ramis confertis, erectis, brevibus, 3–5 millim. longis. Folia siccitate suberecta vix flexuosa, madore erecto-patentia, 1.25 millim longa, 0.5 lata, ovato-lanceolata, mutica, integerrima, inferne marginibus revoluta, costa sat tenui, 35–40 μ crassa, paulo sub apice evanida, rete subæquali, cellulis infimis juxta costam paucis rectangulis vel sublinearibus, haud sinuosis, omnibus cæteris rotundatis vel brevissime ovatis, 8–12 μ latis, parietibus incrassatis, levibus sed valde convexis, ita ut papillas maximas æmulent. Folia perichætialia multo majora, e basi subvaginante sensim et longe acuminata, madore erecta. Capsula in pedicello brevi, purpureo, demum nigricante, siccitate sinistrorsum torto, 5 millim. longo, erecta, anguste cylindrica, 1.5 millim. longa, 0.3 crassa. Sporæ minute granulosæ, diam. 16–17 μ. Cætera ignota.

From Muir Glacier (Trelease, 2431).

A most remarkable species, which cannot be mistaken for any other on account of its characteristic areolation very different from that of all known species of the genus *Rhacomitrium*.

Rhacomitrium heterostichum Brid. Mant., p. 79.

From Hot Springs (Trelease, 1773, 1774); Kodiak (Trelease, 1776); Orca (Trelease, 1961 in part).

Rhacomitrium heterostichum affine (Schleich.) Card. and Thér.

From Unalaska (Trelease, 2296).

Rhacomitrium lanuginosum Brid. Mant., p. 79.

From Juneau (Setchell, 1240); New Metlakatla (Trelease, 1949); Virgin Bay (Trelease, 1775); Sitka (Trelease, 1772); Kodiak (Brewer and Coe, 655); Hall Island (Trelease, 1777, 1778); St. Matthew Island (Trelease, 1856).

Number 1949 is the form *falcata* Boul. Numbers 1777, 1778 and 1856 belong to a form *stricta*. (Branches rigid when dry, subdistichous; leaves erect-appressed.)

Rhacomitrium canescens Brid. Mant., p. 78.

From Orca (Setchell, 1211); Muir Glacier (Trelease, 1764*b*, 1766, 1767, 1768, 2423, 2429, 2456); Hidden Glacier Inlet, Yakutat Bay (Trelease, 1780 in part), Disenchantment Bay (Trelease, 1779 in part); Unalaska (J. M. Macoun).

Rhacomitrium canescens ericoides Br. eur., fasc. 25-28, p. 12, pl 8, fig γ.

From Yakutat (Trelease, 1794); Disenchantment Bay (Trelease, 1065 in part, 1770, 1779 in part, 2505, 2506; Brewer and Coe, 639, 640); Hubbard Glacier (Coville and Kearney, 1071, 1073 in part, 1065 in part); Hidden Glacier Inlet (Trelease, 1771, 1780 in part); Russell Fiord (Coville and Kearney, 995); Muir Glacier (Trelease, 1764, 1765, 2418, 2430, 2464); Muir Inlet (Coville and Kearney, 636); Point Gustavus (Coville and Kearney, 776).

Numbers Trelease, 1780 in part, and Coville and Kearney, 1073 in part, constitute a form *epilosa* or *subepilosa*.

Coscinodon pulvinatus Spreng. has, teste M. W. Harrington, been recorded from Alaska by Lesquereux and James.

Family ORTHOTRICHACEÆ.

Amphoridium lapponicum Sch. Syn., ed. 1, p. 247.

From Orca, 1,200 ft. (Trelease, 2246), Port Wells (Brewer and Coe, 651); Yakutat Bay (Trelease, 2323).

Amphoridium mougeotii Sch. Syn., ed. 1, p. 248

From Juneau (Coville and Kearney, 577). New to Alaska.

Ulota drummondii Brid. Bryol. univ., 1, p 299.

From Kodiak (Trelease, 2209); Unga (Saunders, 2292).

Ulota phyllantha Brid. Mant., p 113.

From Bailey Harbor (U. S. S. *Albatross* Exped.), Cape Fox (Trelease, 2837); Yakutat Bay (Trelease, 2337*a*), Unalaska (Trelease, 2297); Kodiak (Trelease, 2210, 2227), Baranof Island (Trelease, 2348); St. Paul Island (Trelease, 2078, 2470 in part).

Numbers 2348 in part, 2470, 2337*a* and 2297 belong to the form called *U. maritima* by C. Muller and Kindberg.

Ulota alaskana sp nov

(Pl xv, fig 4^{a-g})

Ex affinitate *U. crispæ* Brid., a qua primo visu differt magnitudine, habitu robustiore (caule 2-4 centim. alto, valde ramoso), pedicello longiore (4-6 millim.), foliis inferne angustius hyalino-limbatis (4-5 seriebus cellularum), sporis majoribus, diam. 19-23 μ, et præsertim capsula siccitate ore dilatata, nunquam infra orificium constricta.

From Wrangell (Coville and Kearney, 407); Point Gustavus (Coville and Kearney, 774); New Metlakatla (Trelease, 2239); Yakutat Bay (Trelease, 2337); Virgin Bay (Trelease, 2499); Hot Springs (Trelease, 2347).

By the shape of its capsule, dilated at the mouth, this species is very distinct from *U. bruchii* Hornsch. and *U. intermedia* Sch. It cannot be, either, mistaken for *U. connectens* Kindb., which, according to the author, has a short, hardly emergent seta. *U. camptopoda* Kindb. would appear, according to the description, nearer to *U. alaskana*, but as Kindberg has recently joined it to his *U. connectens*, we need not take it into account. Besides, he gave it the aspect of *U. crispula* Bruch, which does not at all agree with our *U. alaskana*, characterized by its great size and the length of its seta.

Ulota crispa subcalvescens var. nov.

Capsula brevis, madida ut in *U. crispula*, sed sicca et vacua sub ore constricta ut in *U. crispa*. Calyptra tantum apice pilosa.

Baranof Island (Trelease, 2348 in part).

Two small tufts, mixed with *U. phyllantha* Brid.

Ulota barclayi Mitt. Journ. Linn. Soc., VIII, p. 26.

From Cape Fox (Trelease, 2384). First discovered at Sitka by Barclay.

Orthotrichum arcticum Sch. Br. eur. Suppl., pl. 5, et Syn., ed. 2, p. 310.

From St. Paul Island (Trelease, 2081, 2470). New to Alaska.

Orthotrichum fenestratum sp. nov.
(Pl. XVI, fig. 2^{a-n}.)

Monoicum, laxiuscule pulvinatum, atroviride, intus nigricans. Caulis pluries divisus, 1-1.5 centim. altus. Folia erecta, sicca imbricata, madida vix patentia, media 3.5 millim. longa, 0.75-1 lata, superiora majora, lanceolata vel ovato-lanceolata, acuta, marginibus integris usque apicem versus revolutis, costa angusta fuscescente sub apice evanida, cellulis inferioribus subhyalinis, rectangulis, 2-4 long quam lat., margines versus brevioribus, parietibus sinuosis, mediis et superioribus inæqualibus, rotundatis vel breviter ovatis, diam. 9-12 μ, parietibus incrassatis. Flos masculus sub femineo sessilis, foliis perigonialibus brevibus, apice rotundatis, ecostatis vel obsolete costatis, paraphysibus filiformibus. Capsula in pedicello brevi, 1–2 millim. longo exserta, pallide lutea, ovato-pyriformis, sicca subglobosa basi abrupte constricta, madida sensim collo longo in pedicello defluente attenuata, levis vel siccitate vix plicatula, cum collo 3 millim. longa, 1.5 crassa, stomatibus emersis, fasciis subindistinctis, cellulis paululum flavidioribus et magis inciassatis compositis, operculo depresso, longirostro. Calyptra conico-campanulata, plicatula, pilis paucis albidis ornata, apice brunnea. Vaginula nuda. Peristomium, ut videtur, simplex, dentibus 8 bigeminatis, pallide luteis, granulosis, siccitate erectis vel patentibus, in dimidio superiore cancellatis et cribroso-perforatis. Sporæ pro genero maximæ, diam. 24–28 μ, fuscæ, papillosæ.

From St. Paul Island (J. M. Macoun).

This moss was distributed as *O. anomalum* Hedw., but it bears no resemblance to that species. It is allied to *O. cribrosum* C. Müll. from the Chukchi peninsula, Siberia, chiefly by the shape of the capsule and the structure of the peristomial teeth, but it differs from it by its larger size and the leaf-areolation, composed of less incrassate and less papillose cells. In *O. cribrosum* the leaf-cells are strongly incrassate and coarsely papillose from the base.

Orthotrichum speciosum Nees v. Esenb. in Sturm, Deutsch. Fl., fasc. 17.

From Point Gustavus (Coville and Kearney, 791).

A doubtful specimen also from Wrangell (Trelease, 2314 in part).

Orthotrichum pulchellum Brunt. in Engl. bot., pl. 1787.

Prince of Wales Island (J. M. Macoun); Disenchantment Bay (Trelease, 2513); Wrangell (Trelease, 2314 in part); Sitka (Trelease, 2353).

Family ENCALYPTACEÆ.

Encalypta vulgaris Hedw. Sp. musc., p. 60.

From Juneau (Setchell, 1233 in part).

E. commutata Nees & Hornsch., *E. rhabdocarpa* Schw., *E. macounii* Aust. and *E. alaskana* Kindb. have been reported from Alaska.

Family TETRAPHIDACEÆ.

Tetraphis geniculata Girg. mss. Milde in Bot. Zeit., 1865, p. 155.

From Port Etches (J. M. Macoun), Sitka (J. M. Macoun, Trelease, 2352, 2362, 2363); Virgin Bay (Trelease, 2306); Orca (Trelease, 2263); Douglas Island (Trelease, 2394, 2401, 2413).

Tetraphis pellucida Hedw. has also been reported from Sitka.

Family SPLACHNACEÆ.

Dissodon splachnoides Grev. & Arn. in Mem. Wein. Soc., v, p. 468, pl. 15.

From Port Wells (Coville and Kearney, 1292, 1295).

Tayloria serrata Br. eur., fasc. 23–24, p. 6, pl. 1.

From St. Paul Island (J. M. Macoun).

Tayloria tenuis Sch. Syn., ed. 2, p. 360.

From Yakutat Bay (Trelease, 2321, 2474); Virgin Bay (Trelease, 2475), Douglas Island (Trelease, 2471, 2472). New to Alaska.

Tetraplodon mnioides Br. eur., fasc. 23–24, p. 5, pl. 2.

From Wrangell (Coville and Kearney, 432); Yakutat Bay (Trelease, 2473); New Metlakatla (Trelease, 2477); Kodiak (Trelease, 2502); Popof Island (Saunders, 2479); Hall Island (Trelease, 2481); St. Matthew Island (Trelease, 2482; Coville and Kearney, 2114); St. Paul Island (J. M. Macoun).

Tetraplodon mnioides cavifolius Sch. Syn., ed. 1, p. 304.

From Port Clarence (Trelease, 2480); St. Matthew Island (Brewer and Coe, 682, 683).

Tetraplodon urceolatus Br. eur., fasc. 23–24, p. 7, pl. 3.

From St. Matthew Island (J. M. Macoun).

Splachnum sphæricum Linn. fil. apud Swartz, Method. musc., p 33, pl. 1, f. 1.

From Wrangell (Coville and Kearney, 431); Sitka (Trelease, 2473, 2478); Yes Bay (Gorman, 129½); Unalaska (Trelease, 2298, 2476).

Splachnum wormskjoldii Hornem. in Fl. dan., x, fasc. 28, p. 8, pl. 1659.

From St. George Island (J. M. Macoun).

Splachnum luteum Linn. Fl. suec., p. 954.

From Koyukuk River (F. C. Schrader, 1899). New to Alaska.

S. vasculosum Linn. has, teste Bischoff, been reported from Sitka by Lesquereux and James.

Family FUNARIACEÆ.

Entosthodon spathulifolius sp. nov.

(Pl xvii, fig. 1ᵃ⁻ᵉ.)

Polygamus, densiuscule cespitosus, superne viridis, intus fuscescens. Caulis erectus, 10–15 millim. altus, radiculosus, ramosus, ramis gracilibus claviformibus, sub perichætiis nascentibus. Folia mollia, sicca erecto-appressa, interdum subcrispata, madida patula, inferiora minuta, ovata, superiora majora, 1.5-2 millim. longa, 1 lata, oblongo-spathulata, integra, obtusa subapiculatave, marginibus planis, basin versus interdum subrevolutis, costa tenui, attenuata, plus minus longe ab apice evanida, rete laxo, cellulis basilaribus subrectangulis, 60-80 μ longis, 30 μ latis, mediis superioribusque brevioribus, rectangulis, quadratis vel subhexagonis, long. 25-30 μ, lat. 20 μ, marginalibus sæpe longioribus angustioribusque, lutescentibus, 1-2-seriatis. Flores polygami, terminales, nunc unisexuales, nunc synoici; flores masculi in extremitate ramorum nascentes. Capsula in pedicello pallide luteo, 6-9 millim. longo, flexuoso, oblique erecta, pyriformis, collo distincto attenuata, operculo convexo, mamillato. Calyptra brevis, cucullata, haud vel vix inflata. Cætera ignota.

From St. Paul Island (Trelease, 2067, 2074)

A remarkable species, very distinct from all the *Entosthodon* of Europe and North America by its polygamous inflorescence, its leaves shortly spatulate, obtuse or subapiculate, and its calyptra hardly swelling. It is much to be regretted that the too immature capsules do not show the peristome, annulus and spores.

Funaria hygrometrica Sibth. Fl. oxon., p. 288.

From Alaska, sine loco (W. H. Evans), Douglas Island (Trelease, 2402).

Funaria hygrometrica calvescens Br. eur., fasc. 11, p. 8, pl. 3.

From Fort Yukon (F. C. Schrader).

Family BARTRAMIACEÆ.

Bartramia ithyphylla Brid. Muscol. recent., II, part III, p. 132, pl. 1, f. 6.

From Port Clarence (Trelease, without number); Disenchantment Bay (Trelease, 2520); Orca, 1,400 ft. (Trelease, 2242, 2483 in part), Kodiak (Trelease, 2488); Hall Island (Trelease, 2126); St. Paul Island (J. M. Macoun).

Bartramia ithyphylla strigosa Wahlenb. Fl. lapp., p. 362.

Bartramia ithyphylla var *rigidula* SCH Syn , ed 2, p 510
Bartramia ithyphylla subsp *rigidula* KINDB Eur. and N. Amer. Br., p. 323

From St. Matthew Island (Trelease, 2147, 2152, 2164; Coville and Kearney, 2181; Brewer and Coe, 679, 681)

Bartramia pomiformis Hedw. Sp. musc., p. 164

From Yes Bay (Gorman, 183); Juneau (Coville and Kearney, 574, 577 in part), Orca (Setchell, 1216, Trelease, 2243. 2483); Virgin Bay (Trelease, 2485); Douglas Island (Trelease, 2408).

Bartramia œderi Sw. in Schrad. Journ. bot., II, p. 181, pl. 3 B, f. 5.

From Juneau (Coville and Kearney, 572); Port Wells (Coville and Kearney, 1291).

B. menziesii Turn., *B. subulata* Br. eur., *B. breviseta* Lindb. and *B. circinnulata* C. Mull. & Kindb. have been reported to occur in Alaska and the islands of Bering Sea.

Conostomum boreale Sw. in Schrad. Journ. bot., I, III, p. 26, pl. 5.

From Port Wells (Trelease, 2281, 2486, 2487); Orca (Trelease, 2484); Hall Island (Trelease, 2137, 2138).

Philonotis macounii Lesq. & Jam. Man., p. 208.

From Juneau (Canby, 487; Coville and Kearney, 585); Muir Glacier (Trelease, 1783 in part; specimen in bad state, and rather doubtful). New to Alaska.

Philonotis fontana Brid. Bryol. univ., II, p. 18.

From Muir Glacier (Trelease, 1799, 1800, 1803, 1899, 1910, 2437, 2438, 2444, 2451; Coville and Kearney, 637 in part); Point Gustavus (Saunders, 1798; Coville and Kearney, 760); Hidden Glacier Inlet, Yakutat Bay (Trelease, 1811, 1812); Disenchantment Bay (Trelease, 1823, 1827, 2509, 2510; Coville and Kearney, 1073); head of Russell Fiord (Coville and Kearney, 961); Kukak Bay (Saunders, 1855); Kodiak (Trelease, 1789, 1843, 1852, 1928, 2190?; Brewer and Coe, 657); Unalaska (Coville and Kearney, 1743, 1744); Popof Island (Saunders, 1859; Trevor Kincaid); St. Matthew Island (Trelease, 1894); Attu Island (J. M. Macoun); St. Paul Island (J. M. Macoun).

A very variable plant. The numbers 1789, 1843, 1852, 1855 and 1928 of Trelease, as well as numbers 1743 and 1744 of Coville and Kearney, are forms more or less resembling var. *cæspitosa*. A specimen gathered on Unalaska Island by Mr. J. M. Macoun is a form remarkable by its subacute, distinctly nerved perigonial leaves, and by its stem-leaves, which are hardly revolute on the borders and possess a loose areolation, characters that place it near the var. *cæspitosa*, but it differs from the latter by its stems provided with much more numerous fasciculate branches. On the other hand, it is closely connected with the form that Kindberg named *P. acutiflora*, but in the latter the stem-leaves are strongly revolute. Number 1812 of Trelease, as well as the specimens from Kukak Bay and St. Paul Island, constitute a heterophyllous deformation, with upper leaves often obtuse or subobtuse. The var. *serrata* Kindb. (Attu Island, teste Macoun) does not appear to be distinguishable from the type.

Philonotis fontana cæspitosa Sch. Syn., ed. 2, p. 520.

Yakutat Bay (Trelease, 1819).

Philonotis capillaris Lindb. in Hedwigia, 1867, p. 40.

From Kodiak (Trelease, 1841). New to Alaska.

This sterile specimen has, it is true, the aspect, size and areolation of the European *P. capillaris*, but it differs from it by the leaves revolute on the borders from the base for two-thirds of their length. However, it seems impossible to ascribe it to another species. Moreover, according to Mr. Dixon (Handbook, p. 297), *P. capillaris* may have the leaves more or less revolute; this character would then be only more marked on the plant from Kodiak.

Kindberg has indicated from Alaska *P. vancouveriensis* Kindb and *P. seriata* Mitt.

Family MEESEACEÆ.

Meesea uliginosa Hedw., Descr., 1, p. 1, pl. 1, 2.

From Port Wells (Trelease, 2284, 2287); Popof Island (Saunders, without number); St. Matthew Island (Trelease, 1857, 2142).

Meesea tschuctschica C. Müll. in Bot. Centralbl., 1883, nos. 41–43.
(Pl xxiii, fig 3ᵃ⁻ᵉ.)

From St. Matthew Island (Trelease, 1893 in part). New to Alaska.

This specimen agrees exactly with a scrap of the type kindly communicated by the Royal botanical museum of Berlin, but in the latter the leaves are more crowded, giving to the plant a still more robust aspect. *M. tschutschica* differs from *M. triquetra* Angstr. by its larger size and broader leaf-cells.

Paludella squarrosa Brid-, Spec. musc, iii, p. 74.

From St. Matthew Island (Trelease, 1893 in part).

Family BRYACEÆ.

Leptobryum pyriforme Sch., Coroll, p. 64.

From Alaska, sine loco (A. Kellogg); Orca (Trelease, 2254, 2257); Bering Island (J. M. Macoun).

Webera cruda Bruch in Hüb. Musc. germ., p. 425.

From Juneau (Coville and Kearney, 578); White Pass, 3,000 ft. (Trelease, 2311, 2312); Orca (Trelease, 1840); Kodiak (Trelease, 2201); Unalaska (J. M. Macoun), St. Paul Island (J. M. Macoun).

Webera nutans Hedw. Descr., 1, p. 9, pl. 4.

From Juneau (Trelease, 2182, Brewer and Coe, 696); Port Clarence (Trelease, 2105); Cape Fox (Trelease, 2378); New Metlakatla (Trelease, 2241); Yakutat Bay (Trelease, 2318, 2333); Orca (Trelease, 2244); Sitka (Trelease, 2354, 2372); Kodiak (Trelease, 2208, 2223); Hall Island (Trelease, 2141); Douglas Island (Trelease, 2390, 2395, 2396, 2390, 2403); St. Lawrence Island (Trelease, 2122, 2123); St. Matthew Island (Coville and Kearney, 2124); Plover Bay, Siberia (Trelease, 2533, 2534, 2538; Brewer and Coe, 668; J. M. Macoun; L. J. Cole).

Webera nutans cæspitosa Hub., Musc. germ., p. 429.

From Virgin Bay (Trelease, 2307); Kodiak (Trelease, 2188); Douglas Island (Trelease, 2397, 2399, 2412).

Webera nutans bicolor Hub., loc. cit.

From St. Paul Island (Trelease, 2061); St. George Island (J. M. Macoun).

Webera nutans strangulata Sch. Coroll., p. 66.

From Yakutat Bay (Trelease, 2320).

Webera cucullata Sch. Coroll., p. 66.

From Egg Island in Disenchantment Bay (Coville and Kearney, 1016 in part); Port Wells (Trelease, 2269); St. Paul Island (J. M. Macoun).

Webera pseudogracilis sp. nov.
(Pl. XVII, fig. 2*a-g*.)

Dioica, laxe cespitosa, lutescenti-viridis. Caulis brevis, 4–5 millim. altus, simplex vel parce divisus. Folia æqualiter conferta, parva, sicca imbricata, madida erecto-patentia, 1–1.5 millim. longa, 0.4–0.6 lata, nec carinata, nec decurrentia, inferiora breviter ovata vel ovato-lanceolata, superiora lineari-lanceolata, acuta, apice denticulata, marginibus e basi usque ad ⅔ leniter reflexis, costa sat valida, 56 μ basi crassa, percurrente vel subpercurrente, demum rubente, rete denso, cellulis inferioribus rectangulis, rubellis, mediis linearibus, 48–64 μ longis, 8 μ latis, superioribus anguste linearibus, flexuosis, parietibus valde incrassatis, marginalibus angustioribus longioribusque. Folia perichætialia caulinis minora. Capsula in pedicello flexuoso, rubello, circa 2 centim. longo pendula, pallida, obovata, cum operculo convexo, mamillato, 3 millim. longa. Flos masculus terminalis subdiscoideus. Cætera ignota.

From Muir Glacier (Trelease, 2419, 2425, 2427, 2428, 2463.)

Aspect of *Webera gracilis* De Not., but the areolation is different and much closer; it is distinguished, on the other hand, from *Webera drummondii* Lesq. & Jam. by its leaves which are more crowded on the whole stem, and not carinate-concave, and its capsule hanging and with a mamillary lid.

Webera annotina Bruch in Hub. Muscol. germ., p. 431.

From New Metlakatla (Coville and Kearney, 370); Kodiak (Trelease, 2222), Unalaska (Trelease, 2300); Hall Island (Trelease, 2140). New to Alaska.

Webera proligera Kindb. Enum. br. dovr., Append., no. 309.

From Kodiak (Trelease, 2221).

This species has also recently been discovered in the Yukon territory by R. S. Williams, and in Minnesota by J. M. Holzinger.

Webera albicans Sch. Coroll., p. 67.

From Juneau (Trelease, 2172); Port Etches (J. M. Macoun); Sitka (Trelease, 1810); Muir Glacier (Trelease, 1783 in part, 2433, 2440, 2458; Coville and Kearney, 637 in part); Yakutat Bay (Trelease, 1822 in part).

Webera albicans glacialis Sch. loc. cit.

From Juneau (Coville and Kearney, 580); Hidden Glacier Inlet, Yakutat Bay (Trelease, 1813, 1817); Hall Island (Treloase, 1883 in part).

The following species have been recorded from Alaska and the islands of Bering Sea: *W. polymorpha* Sch., *W. crudoides* Sull. & Lesq., *W. cucullatiformis* Kindb., *W. drummondii* Lesq. & Jam.

Genus BRYUM.[1]

Subgenus CLADODIUM Sch.

Bryum ateleostomum Philibert sp. nov.

(Pl. xix, fig. 1*a*–*f*.)

Polygamum, viride, densissime cespitosum, radiculis numerosis arcte intertextum. Caulis ramosus, 1–1.5 centim. altus. Folia erecto-imbricata, ad extremitatem caulis et ramorum in comam congesta, 1.2–1.4 millim. longa, 0.5 lata, ovato-lanceolata, costa excurrente cuspidata, basi haud decurrentia, marginibus limbatis integris, nunc planis, nunc plus minus longe revolutis, costa tenui, 50–55 μ basi crassa, rete densiusculo, cellulis inferioribus quadratis vel rectangulis, 25–50 μ longis, 20–25 latis, cæteris oblongo- vel ovato-hexagonis, 28–45 μ longis, 12–13 latis. Capsula in pedicello rubello breviusculo, circa 1.5 centim. longo, nutans vel pendula, ovata, collo brevi instructa, 2 millim. longa, operculo depresse convexo, mamillato. Exostomii dentes pallide lutei, concolores, articulis 20, regularibus. Endostomium vix evolu-

---

[1] We are indebted to Mons. Philibert for the determinations of nearly all the species of this genus. He has himself described three of the new species in the *Revue bryologique* for 1900 and 1901.

tum, sæpius e membrana uniformi, tenui, fugaci compositum. Sporæ 18–20 μ crassæ.

From Kukak Bay (Coville and Kearney, 1516).

Bryum stenotrichum C. Müll. in Flora, 1887, p 219.

From Dyea Valley, Chilkoot and Taiyasanka (Krause brothers, 1882)

Bryum inclinatum Br. eur., fasc. 6–9, p 17, pl. 3.

From Juneau (Coville and Kearney, 571); Port Wells (Brewer and Coe, 652, Trelease, 2266, 2267); Cape Fox (Trelease, 2381), Yakutat Bay (Trelease, 2319), Disenchantment Bay (Trelease, 2522a); Egg Island (Coville and Kearney, 1016); Muir Glacier (Trelease, 2421), Kukak Bay (Coville and Kearney, 1536, 1590, 1602); Kodiak (Brewer and Coe, 656; Trelease, 2184, 2196, 2199, 2200, 2228; J. M. Macoun), Unalaska (B. W. Evermann), Agattu Island (U. S. S. *Albatross* Exped., 26, 30, 33); St. Paul Island (Trelease, 2065, 2068; J. M. Macoun), Hall Island (Coville and Kearney, 2056); Douglas Island (Trelease, 2400); St. Matthew Island (Trelease, 2144; Brewer and Coe, 680); Plover Bay, Siberia (Trelease, 2098, 2540, 2541; J. M. Macoun).

Very numerous forms, of which some are rather doubtful, on account of the imperfect state of the capsules.

Bryum treleasei Philib. sp. nov.

(Pl xx, fig. 1*a–g*.)

From St. Matthew Island (Trelease, 1890 in part, mixed with *Hypnum revolvens*).

We do no more than figure this species and the two following, which have been carefully described by Mons Philibert, in the *Revue bryologique*, 1901, pp 33–35, pl. VIII, fig. 1.

Bryum agattuense Philib. sp nov.

(Pl xx, fig. 2*a–h*.)

Described in Rev bryol, 1901, p. 35, pl. VIII, fig. 2.
From Agattu Island (U. S. S. *Albatross* Exped., 24, 27).

Bryum mucronigerum Philib. sp nov.

(Pl xvII, fig. 3*a–f*.)

Described in Rev. bryol., 1900, p. 91, pl v, fig. 3.

From Port Wells (Trelease, 2270; Coville and Kearney, 1296); Cape Fox (Trelease, 2379), St. Paul Island (Trelease, 2063, 2064, 2066).

Mons. Philibert describes the lid of this species as " convexe, peu saillant et obtus." We have seen it mamillate.

Subgenus EUBRYUM Lindb.

Bryum bimum Schreb. Spic. flor. lips., p. 83.

From Muir Glacier (Trelease, 2460). New to Alaska.

A short form.

Bryum pallescens Schleich. Crypt. exsicc. helv., no. 28.

From Indian Camp in Yakutat Bay (Brewer and Coe, 650); Disenchantment Bay (Brewer and Coe, 633); Hubbard Glacier (Coville and Kearney, 1070); Egg Island (Coville and Kearney, 1085); Muir Glacier (Trelease, 1791, 2420, 2435, 2436, 2439, 2457); Port Wells (Trelease, 2264); Douglas Island (Trelease, 2398); Agattu Island (U. S. S. *Albatross* Exped., 28, 32); St. Matthew Island (Trelease, 2145); St. Paul Island (Coville and Kearney, 1835; Trelease, 2068); Plover Bay, Siberia (Trelease, 2060, 2096, 2535).

Several forms Some specimens are rather doubtful because of the bad state of the capsules.

Bryum cylindrico-arcuatum Philib. sp. nov.

(Pl. XVIII, fig. 2^{a-g}.)

Monoicum (fide Philibert), viride, densiuscule cespitosum, radiculis numerosis intertextum. Caulis erectus, 1-2 centim. altus, superne ramos graciles emittens. Folia ad basin caulis et ramorum minuta, remota, superiora majora, in comam congesta, circa 2 millim. longa, 1-1.2 lata, sicca erecta subflexuosa, madida patentia patulave, e basi paululum decurrente ovato- vel oblongo-lanceolata, late breviterque acuminata, mucronata, marginibus integris haud limbatis parce revolutis, costa basi 80 μ crassa superne attenuata breviter excurrente, rete densiusculo, cellulis inferioribus laxioribus rectangulis, 55–85 μ longis, 22 latis, mediis oblongo-hexagonis, long. 28–56 μ, lat. 14, superioribus minoribus brevioribusque. Flos masculus terminalis, 25–30 antheridiis. Capsula in pedicello rubello flexuoso, 2 centim. longo, apice curvato, nutans vel pendula, anguste cylindrica, arcuata, longicollis, operculo obtuse conico. Peristomii dentes longissimi, basi rubri Endostomium valde perfectum, ciliis appendiculatis. Sporæ leves, diam. 12 μ.

From Kodiak (Trelease, 2186).

Bryum argenteum Linn. Sp. plant., p. 1120.

From Bogoslof volcano (Coville and Kearney, 2614 in part); St. Paul Island (Trelease, 1513, 2090; J. M. Macoun).

Number 2090 is a form near var. *majus* Br. eur.

Bryum laurentianum sp. nov.
(Pl. xix, fig 3*ᵃ⁻ᵍ*.)

Elatum, densissime cespitosum, lutescenti-viride. Caulis 3–4 centim. altus, radiculosus, laxiuscule foliosus, ramis numerosis erectis subclavatis. Folia sicca et madida erecto-imbricata, ovato- vel oblongo-lanceolata, circa 1.5 millim. longa, 0.75 lata, acute acuminata, marginibus planis inferne integris, superne distincte denticulatis, costa valida demum fuscescente, basi 80–100 μ crassa, sensim attenuata et sub apice evanida, cellulis basilaribus rectangulis, mediis superioribusque rectangulis vel oblongo-subhexagonis, long. 40–75 μ, lat. 14–17, marginalibus 4–5 seriatis, longioribus angustioribusque, linearibus, parietibus paululum crassioribus, limbum parum distinctum efformantibus. Cætera ignota.

From St. Lawrence Island (Trelease, 1871).

This species, which seems to belong to the group of *B. alpinum* Huds., is chiefly characterized by its more acuminate and distinctly denticulate leaves, and by its nerve disappearing below the apex.

Bryum leptodictyon Philib. sp. nov.
(Pl. xviii, fig 3*ᵃ⁻ᵍ*.)

Dioicum, gregarium, pallide vel lutescenti-viride. Caulis erectus, simplex, 4–6 millim. altus. Folia sicca imbricata, madida erecta, inferiora minora, ascendendo majora, anguste lanceolata, sublinearia, sensim longeque acuminata, 1–1.8 millim. longa, 0.35 lata, basi haud decurrente, marginibus planis inferne integris, superne minute denticulatis, costa angusta, basi 55 μ crassa, percurrente, rete perfecte weberaceo, cellulis uniformibus linearibus, mediis 45–60 μ longis, 5–6 latis. Capsula in pedicello rubello flexuoso, 1.5–2 centim. longo, abrupte pendula, oblonga, parva, 2 millim. longa, 0.8–0.9 crassa, pallida, collo brevi attenuata, operculo conico apiculato. Peristomium perfectum, dentibus basi rubris, ciliis appendiculatis. Sporæ leves, diam. 9–12 μ.

From Hidden Glacier in Russell Fiord (Coville and Kearney, 964).

Species very distinct, having quite the facies and areolation of a *Webera* with the peristome of *Bryum*.

Bryum heterogynum Philib. sp. nov.
(Pl. xix, fig. 2*ᵃ⁻ᵍ*)

Dioicum. Cespites humiles, intense rubri, ætate vinosi, basi terra obruti. Caulis erectus, radiculosus, ramosus, 5–12 mill. altus. Folia sicca erecta, madida erecto-patentia, ovato-lanceolata, 1.5 millim. longa,

0 5–0.6 lata, sat longe acuminata costaque excurrente cuspidata, apice parce et acute denticulata, marginibus sæpius limbatis, limbo inferne angusto, plano, superne crassiore, distincto, interdum subreflexo, rarius deficiente, costa angusta, basi 50–55 μ crassa, sensim attenuata, cellulis inferioribus rectangulis, 50–65 μ longis, 17–22 latis, mediis oblongo-hexagonis, 45–55 μ longis, 13 latis, marginalibus angustioribus linearibus. Capsula in pedicello rubello, 2 5–3 centim. longo, nutans vel pendula, ovato-pyriformis, collo attenuato instructa, 3–4 millim. longa, operculo convexo. Exostomii dentes pallide ferruginei. Endostomium perfectum, ciliis appendiculatis. Planta mascula brevis, gemmiformis, cespites distinctos efformans, foliis breviter ovato-cuspidatis.

From Muir Glacier (Trelease, 2426, 2434, 2441, 2461, 2462), Hidden Glacier Inlet in Yakutat Bay (Trelease, 2518).

Bryum acutiusculum C. Mull. in Flora, 1887, p. 220.

From Chilkoot (Krause brothers).

Bryum cæspiticium Linn. Sp. plant., p. 1121.

Alaska, sine loco (Frederick Funston, 26); Muir Glacier, (Trelease, 2427 in part).

Bryum pallens Sw. Musc. suec., pp. 47, 98, pl. 4, f. 12

From head of Russell Fiord (Coville and Kearney, 960); Disenchantment Bay (Trelease, 2522; forma *rubro-vinosa*). New to Alaska.

Bryum pseudostirtoni Philib. sp. nov.

(Pl. xviii, fig 4^{a-g}).

Sæpe synoicum, dense cespitosum, sordide vel lutescenti-viride. Caulis elongatus, filiformis, parce ramosus, 2 5–4 centim. altus. Folia mollia, laxiuscula, sicca erecto-imbricata, madida erecto-patentia, caulina ovato-lanceolata, acuminata costaque longe excurrente cuspidata, 2 millim. longa, o 7 lata, marginibus integris planis vel subreflexis, costa angusta, 60–70 μ basi lata, rete laxo, cellulis inferioribus rectangulis, mediis superioribusque ovato-hexagonis, long. 28–50 μ, lat. 14–17, marginalibus angustioribus. Folia ramea minora, inferiora ovata, subobtusa vel breviter cuspidata. Capsula in pedicello gracili, 1 5 centim. longo, nutans vel pendula, oblonga, parva, 2 millim. longa, collo brevi attenuata, sicca sub or econstricta, operculo conico-mamillato. Exostomii dentes pallidi, basi rubri. Endostomium perfectum, ciliis nunc longe appendiculatis, nunc simplicibus. Sporæ 12–18 μ crassæ.

From Muir Glacier (Trelease. 2448, 2459).

Bryum harrimani sp. nov.
(Pl. xxi, fig. 1ᵃ⁻ᵍ)

Sat robustum, densiuscule cespitosum, lutescenti-viride. Caulis erectus, 3–4 centim. altus, fragilis, radiculosus, laxe foliosus, ramosus, ramis erectis, obtusis. Folia mollia, sicca erecto-patentia, madida patula, 1.2–1.6 millim. longa, 0.8–0.9 lata, basi paululum decurrentia, integra, margine plana vel subreflexa, dimorpha, inferiora ovato-lanceolata, acuta, superiora et ramulina late ovata, valde concava, apice obtuso cucullato, costa tenui, 40–45 μ basi crassa, in foliis inferioribus acutis percurrente vel breviter excurrente, in superioribus obtusis sub apice evanida, rete laxissimo, parce chlorophylloso, cellulis inferioribus quadratis vel breviter rectangulis, long. 40–50 μ, lat. 25–35, cæteris ovato-hexagonis, marginalibus linearibus 1–2 seriatis. Cætera ignota.

From Yakutat Bay (Trelease, 1793); Hidden Glacier Inlet (Trelease, 1784 in part, 1815).

This moss can be placed near *B. obtusifolium* Lindb. from which it is easily distinguished by its dimorphous leaves, plane on the borders, and of a looser texture.

Bryum pseudotriquetrum Schw. Suppl., I, II, p. 110.

From Muir Glacier (Trelease, 1806, 2435a); Kodiak (Trelease, 1848a, 1850); Unalaska (Trelease, 2299); St. Paul Island (Trelease, 2068).

Bryum duvalii Voit, in Sturm, Deutsch. fl., II, Heft 12.

From Yakutat Bay (Trelease, 1817 in part, 1822 in part); Port Wells (Trelease, 2285); Kodiak (Trelease, 1842, 1846).

Bryum duvalii obtusatum var. nov.

A forma typica differt foliis obtusis, apice cucullato denticulato, basi paululum minus decurrentibus.

From Disenchantment Bay (Trelease, 2517).

Bryum drepanocarpum Philib. sp. nov.
(Pl. xviii, fig. 1ᵃ⁻ʰ.)

Ut videtur dioicum, laxiuscule cespitosum, fusco-viride vel rubrovinosum. Caulis erectus, 1–2 centim. altus, inferne radiculosus, superne ramosus, ramis erectis, numerosis, gracilibus. Folia sicca erecto-flexuosa, madida erecto-patentia, circa 2 millim. longa, 0.9 lata, e basi haud vel parum decurrente oblongo-lanceolata, acuminata, acuta vel costa excurrente brevissime cuspidata, marginibus integris, reflexis, anguste limbatis, costa tenui, attenuata, in foliis inferioribus percurrente, in superioribus breviter excedente, rete parce chlorophylloso, cellulis mediis subrectangularibus vel oblongo-hexagonis, long. 47–70 µ, lat. 16–22. Capsula in pedicello rubello, 1.5–2 cent. longo, nutans vel inclinata, ætate fusca, oblonga, collo longo attenuata, falcato-curvata, matura orificio dilatata, operculo conico. Peristomium perfectum; exostomii dentes basi rubri; endostomii membrana elata, ciliis appendiculatis.

From Juneau (Canby, 485; Coville and Kearney, 579); Disenchantment Bay (Trelease, 2515).

This species, which offers many points of resemblance to *B. meeseoides* Kindb., differs from it by the peristomial teeth which are firmer, stiffer, more scabrous and reddish at the base, the segments more acuminate and perforate from more irregular openings, and the higher membrane.

Subgenus ANOMOBRYUM Sch.

Bryum bullatum C. Mull. in Flora, 1887, p. 221.

From Takhin valley (Krause brothers).

Other species of the genus *Bryum* which have been recorded from Alaska and the islands of Bering Sea are the following. *B. alaskanum* Kindb., *B. brachyneuron* Kindb., *B. capillare* Linn., *B. erythrophyllum* Kindb., *B. fallax* Milde, *B. froudei* Kindb., *B. lacustre* Brid., *B. meeseoides* Kindb., *B. microstegioides* Kindb., *B. obtusifolium* Lindb., *B. pendulum* Sch., *B. wrightii* Sulliv.

Quite recently, the late Mr. Philibert has described in the Revue Bryologique, 1901, fasc. 2, two other new species, *B. submuticum* and *B. suborbiculare*, collected in the vicinity of Dawson by Mr. R. S. Williams.

Family MNIACEÆ.

Mnium medium Br. eur., fasc. 5, p. 32, pl. 10.

From Yakutat Bay (Trelease, 1720, 1721 in part); Disenchantment Bay (Trelease, 1718, 1719a; Coville and Kearney, 1075); Point Gustavus (Coville and Kearney, 785).

Mnium affine Bland. Musc. frond. exsic., fasc. III, no. 133. Schw. Suppl., 1, II, p. 134.

From Muir Glacier (Trelease, 1713); Kodiak (Trelease, 1725b); Agattu Island (U. S. S. *Albatross* Exped., 38).

Mnium affine elatum Br. eur., fasc. 5, p. 30, in part.

From Kodiak (Trelease, 1726); St. Paul Island (Trelease, 2093; a stunted form).

Mnium rugicum Laur. in Flora, 1827, p. 292.

From Kodiak (Trelease, 1725a); Plover Bay, Siberia (Trelease, 2100).

Mnium insigne Mitt. in Hook. Journ. of bot., 1856, p. 230.

From Alaska, sine loco (Evans, 1897); Wrangell (Trelease, 1711); Cape Fox (Trelease, 2380), Sitka (Trelease, 1714*b*, 1716), St. Paul Island (Trelease, 2069). New to Alaska.

Mnium spinulosum Br. eur., fasc. 31, Suppl. p. 4, pl. 4.

From Skagway (Canby, 480).

Mnium punctatum elatum Sch. Syn., ed. 1, p. 398.

From Port Wells (Trelease, 1723, 1724; Coville and Kearney, 1294); Indian camp, Yakutat Bay (Brewer and Coe, 642 in part); Disenchantment Bay (Trelease, 1717), Cape Karluk (Brewer and Coe, 687), Sitka (Trelease, 1715 in part); Kodiak (Trelease, 1725); St. George Island (C. Hart Merriam in 1891).

Mnium punctatum anceps var. nov.

A forma typica differt foliis sæpe cucullatis cellulisque superioribus multo minoribus, fere isodiametricis ut in *M. glabrescente*, sed ab illo limbo haud incrassato distincta.

From Unalaska (Trelease, 1727).

Mnium nudum Williams in Bryologist, 1900, p. 6.

From Yakutat Bay (Trelease, 1721). New to Alaska.

This specimen agrees exactly with *M. nudum* Williams, from Idaho and Montana. Mr Williams mentions as distinctive characters for his species, in comparison with *M. punctatum*, nothing but the unthickened margin of the leaf and the naked, not radiculose stems. Now, in the European specimens of *M. punctatum* var. *elatum*, it very often happens that the margin of the leaf is not thickened at all or only slightly towards the base; this character, therefore, is not valuable. But, besides the naked or hardly radiculose stems and the smaller height, *M. nudum* differs from *M. punctatum* var. *elatum* by a more regularly hexagonal areolation, the cells towards the margins being larger (45–55 μ instead of 28–35) and the ones near the costa of the same length as in the allied species (70–100 μ) but broader (50–60 μ, instead of 40–45); and the lid of *M. nudum* is shortly apiculate, while in *M. punctatum* it is rather long beaked. However, these distinctive characters are not of great importance, and it seems to us preferable to regard *M. nudum* as a subspecies of *M. punctatum*.

Mnium glabrescens Kindb. Notes on Canad. bryol., 1893.

From Alaska, sine loco (W. H. Evans, 1897); Farragut Bay (Trelease, 1712, 2417; Brewer and Coe, 611, 614); Orca (Trelease, 1722, 2248; Setchell, 1200), Port Wells (Trelease, 2265); Sitka

(Trelease, 1714, 1715; Canby, 461, Setchell, 1254; W. G. Wright, 1604); Prince of Wales Island (J. M. Macoun); St. George Island (J. M. Macoun); Yes Bay (Gorman, 184 in part); Wood Island (Brewer and Coe, 664).

This species is distinguished from *M. punctatum* by its cells which are nearly isodiametric and much smaller, by its larger and thicker margo, the axile fascicle of the nerve, which is colored in red and forms a line generally very distinct, the larger spores (44–55 μ, instead of 30–40) and the higher peristome (0.75 millim., instead of 0.60). Moreover the nerve is usually shorter than in *M. punctatum*.

Mnium subglobosum Br. eur., fasc. 31, Suppl., p. 3, pl. 3.

From Disenchantment Bay (Trelease, 1719), Port Wells (Coville and Kearney, 1293); St. Paul Island (J. M. Macoun).

Mnium cinclidioides Hub. Muscol. germ., p. 416

From Douglas Island (Trelease, 2410; a small form).

Leucolepis acanthoneura Lindb. Mniac. europ., p. 80.

From Alaska, sine loco (W. H. Evans, 1897); Sitka (J. M. Macoun).

Aulacomnium palustre Schw. Suppl., III, 1, 1, pl. CCXVI.

From Muir Glacier (Trelease, 1896); Wrangell (Trelease, 1907); Port Clarence (Trelease, 1900, 1901); Kodiak (Trelease, 1845, 1851, 1898, 1919, 1924), Popof Island (Saunders, 1858); St. Matthew Island (Trelease, 1905); St. Lawrence Island (Trelease, 1903); Plover Bay, Siberia (Trelease, 2547).

Aulacomnium turgidum Schw. Suppl., III, 1, 1.

From Port Clarence (Trelease, 1986); St. Matthew Island (Trelease, 1887 in part, 1904); St. Paul Island (J. M Macoun).

Aulacomnium androgynum Schw. Suppl., III, 1, 1, pl CCXV.

From Sitka (Trelease, 2371); Kodiak (Trelease, 2185). New to Alaska.

Timmia austriaca Hedw. Spec. musc., p. 176, pl. XLII, f. 1–7.

From White Pass (Trelease, 2310 in part).

A sterile and stunted form, with short leaves.

Family POLYTRICHACEÆ.

Bartramiopsis lescurii Card. & Ther. not Kindb.

(Pl. XXI, fig. 2^{a-i}.)

Atrichum lescurii James, Manual, p. 257.
Bartramiopsis sitkana Kindb. (ut subsp.) in Rev. bryol., 1894, p 35

From Virgin Bay (Trelease, 1733), Orca (Trelease, 1731); Douglas Island (Trelease, 1729, 1730).

The moss which was described by Mr. Kindberg under the name of *B. lescurii*, from sterile specimens collected in Japan, does not seem to be the true *Atrichum lescurii* James, because its leaves are only incurvate and not crispate when dry. On the contrary, it is probable that *B. sitkana* of Kindberg, equally described from sterile specimens, differs in nothing from the species of James. The latter was, after all, imperfectly known until now, the author having seen neither the calyptra nor the lid, and having been unable to ascertain the existence or absence of a peristome. Therefore, we here give a complete description with drawings of this interesting moss, which, by the absence of the peristome and chiefly by the structure of its leaves, which, except on the borders, consist of two layers of cells, seems to us to constitute a genus distinct from *Atrichum*.[1]

Dioicum, laxe cespitosum, atroviride. Caulis gracillimus, filiformis, flexuosus, simplex furcatusve, laxe foliosus, inferne longissime denudatus, 2–8 cent. altus. Folia sicca crispatissima, madida arcuato-patula, 4 millim. longa, basi subvaginantia, lineari-lanceolata, acuminata, marginibus basis inferne integris, superne utroque latere 3–5 ciliis longis ornatis, marginibus laminæ planis valde serratis, haud limbatis, costa lata, dorso levi, ventro lamellosa, lamellis 5–8, margine dentatis, in sectione transversali e 6–8 seriebus cellularum formatis; cellulis basilaribus areolationis rectangulis, hyalinis, 4–6 long quam lat., rete laminæ opaco, cellulis minutis hexagonis (diam. 8μ), bistratosis, tantum ad margines unistratosis ibique limbum translucentem fingentibus. Capsula in pedicello rubello brevi, 8–12 millim. longo, erecta, primum breviter ovato-cylindrica, ætate turbinata, gymnostoma, ore valde dilatato, epiphragmate columellæ adhærente clauso, operculo alte conico, longe acuminato, capsulam fere æquante. Calyptra nuda, glabra, breviter acuminata, operculum tantum obtegens. Sporæ ovatæ vel subtrigonæ, diam. 12–16 μ.

Atrichum parallelum Mitt. in Journ. Linn. Soc., VIII, p. 48, pl. 8.
A. leiophyllum KINDB. in Bull. Torr. Bot. Club, XVII, p 275.

From Douglas Island (Trelease, 1728, 2415); Port Etches (J. M. Macoun).

A. leiophyllum Kindb. cannot be specifically distinguished from *A. parallelum* Mitt., the characters put forward by Mr. Kindberg to justify the creation of his species being liable to vary on the same specimen. Such is more particularly the case with number 217 of the *Canadian Musci*, the leaves of which are sometimes destitute of dentate crests on the back and sometimes possess them well-developed.

[1] See Note 2, p 347.

On other specimens, coming from Vancouver Island, the crests are more generally wanting; however, they are sometimes found and the leaves often bear sparse teeth on the back toward the apex; moreover, the nerve is always lamelliferous on both sides, at least in the upper part.

Oligotrichum aligerum Mitt. in Journ. Linn. Soc., VIII, p. 48, pl. 8.

From Kodiak (Brewer and Coe, 658).

Oligotrichum integrifolium Kindb. in Rev. bryol., 1894, p. 40.

O. hercynicum var. *latifolium* C. MÜLL. & KINDB. in Macoun, Cat Can pl., VI, Musci, p 149.

From St. Lawrence Island (J. M. Macoun). New to Alaska.

Mr. Kindberg has attributed this moss to *O. hercynicum* typicum, but it certainly belongs to his *O. integrifolium*, characterized by its broader leaves, smooth and entire on the back, and by the cells of the leaf-areolation which are much larger; characters which appear to us sufficient to admit of a specific distinction.

Psilopilum arcticum Brid. Bryol. univ., II, p. 95.

From Port Clarence (Trelease, 2113, 2114, 2526); St. Paul Island (J. M. Macoun); St. Matthew Island (Coville and Kearney, 2125).

The specimens from St. Matthew Island have their stem-leaves a little longer than those of the European specimens, their basilar cells with thicker walls and their perichætial leaves hardly different from the comal ones, and thus almost exactly agree with *Catharinea* (*Psilopilum*) *tschuctschica* C. Mull., which does not appear to us a good species.

Pogonatum capillare dentatum Lindb. in Act. Soc. Sc. Fenn., 1872, p. 266.

Polytrichum dentatum MENZ. in Trans of the Linn. Soc., IV, p. 80, pl 7, f. 4.

From Juneau (Trelease, 1656; Brewer and Coe, 691*a*, 693, 695; Coville and Kearney, 583; Setchell, 1230; Canby, 435, 436 in part); Port Wells (Trelease, 1654); Kodiak (Trelease, 1653); Douglas Island (Trelease, 1657); St. Paul Island (J. M. Macoun).

Pogonatum dentatum (Menz.) Brid. is but a western race of *P. capillare*, characterized by having slenderer stems than those of the type, and by its pedicel which is not usually so flexuous.

Pogonatum contortum Lesq. in Mem. Calif. Acad. I, p. 27.

P. erythrodontium Kindb. in Macoun, Cat Can pl, VI, Musci, p 150.[1]

---

[1] As regards this synonymy, see Cardot, Étude sur la flore bryologique de l'Amérique du Nord. Revision des types d'Hedwig et de Schwægrichen; in Bull de l'herb. Boissier, VII, pp. 366-368

From Juneau (Canby, 436 in part), Wrangell (Trelease, 1652); Orca (Trelease, 1732; Coville and Kearney, 1306 in part), Kodiak (Trelease, 1847); Prince of Wales Island (J. M. Macoun), Yes Bay (Gorman, 182, with a slender, elongated male form of *Dicranella heteromalla*).

Pogonatum urnigerum Pal. Beauv. Prodr., p. 84.

From Hidden Glacier Inlet, Yakutat Bay (Trelease, without number); Disenchantment Bay (Trelease, 1655); Hubbard Glacier (Coville and Kearney, 1072); Muir Glacier (Trelease, 1660).

Pogonatum alpinum Rœhl. in Ann. Wett. Ges., III, p. 226.

From Alaska, sine loco (W. H. Evans in 1897), Juneau (Canby, without number, Trelease, 1680; Coville and Kearney, 560, 581), Yakutat Bay (Trelease, 1688; Brewer and Coe, 648); Point Gustavus (Coville and Kearney, 792); Port Wells (Trelease, 1658, 1690), Orca (Trelease, 1691, 1692), Kukak Bay (Coville and Kearney, 1605); Sitka (Trelease, 1685); Kodiak (Trelease, 1695); Douglas Island (Trelease, 1683*b*); Unalaska (J. M. Macoun); Attu Island (L. M. Turner); Kiska Island (U. S. S. *Albatross* Exped., 9); St. Paul Island (J. M. Macoun; L. J. Cole; Trelease, 1661, 1699, Coville and Kearney, 1821); Hall Island (Trelease, 1663; Brewer and Coe, 675); Plover Bay, Siberia (Trelease, 2545; Coville and Kearney, 1860).

Numerous forms, many of which pass to var. *macounii*.

Pogonatum alpinum macounii var. nov.

P. macounii KINDB. in Bull. Torr. Bot. Club, XVI, p. 96.

From Alaska, sine loco (W. H. Evans in 1897); Juneau (Setchell, 1237); Foggy Bay, near Cape Fox (Coville and Kearney, 2573); Prince of Wales Island (J. M. Macoun), Sitka (W. G. Wright, 1603).

No precise limits exist between *P. alpinum* and *P. macounii*. Kindberg attributes 60 lamellæ to the leaves of his species, but on the specimens which he sent to us we find only from 40 to 50 lamellæ; and, on the other hand, *P. alpinum*, to which he attributes only 30 lamellæ, often has 40. (Cfr. Barclay, Muscinées de la France, p. 198, and Limpricht, Laubmoose, II, p. 615.) There is no other more constant difference between the two mosses. *P. macounii* is therefore only a variety of *P. alpinum*, characterized by its greater dimensions, its longer leaves, more widely spreading when dry and usually provided with more numerous lamellæ (40 to 50). This var. *macounii* represents an extreme form of *P. alpinum*, of which the other extreme is var. *brevifolium*. In the specimens from Alaska we find all gradations of form between the two varieties.

Pogonatum alpinum septentrionale Brid. Bryol. univ., II, p. 131.

From Kodiak (Trelease, 1676); St. Paul Island (J. M. Macoun).

Pogonatum alpinum arcticum Brid. Bryol. univ., II, p. 131.

From Egg Island, Disenchantment Bay (Coville and Kearney, 1006).

Pogonatum alpinum brevifolium Brid. Bryol. univ., II, p. 131.

From St. Paul Island (Trelease, 1661 in part); St. Lawrence Island (Trelease, 1664); St. Matthew Island (Trelease, 1662); Plover Bay, Siberia (Trelease, 1670; Brewer and Coe, 667).

Pogonatum alpinum simplex Sch. Syn., ed. 2, p. 539.

From Port Clarence (Trelease, 1665). New to Alaska.

P. atrovirens Mitt. has been recorded from Alaska by Kindberg. *P. microdontium* Kindb., from St. Paul Island, seems to us not distinct from *P. alpinum* var. *septentrionale*.

Polytrichum formosum Hedw. Spec. musc., p. 92, pl. 19, figs. 1, *a*.

From Alaska, sine loco (W. H. Evans in 1897); Juneau (Trelease, 1681; Canby, 429); New Metlakatla (Trelease, 1678a, 1679), Wrangell (Trelease, 1679 bis; Canby, 434); Farragut Bay (Brewer and Coe, 610); Orca (Coville and Kearney, 1306; Setchell, 1204), Virgin Bay (Trelease, 1689); Sitka (Trelease, 1684, 1687, Coville and Kearney, 811); Hot Springs (Trelease, 1686); Kodiak (Trelease, 1694); Douglas Island (Trelease, 1682, 1683).

Polytrichum gracile Dicks. Menz. in Trans. Linn. Soc., IV, p. 73, pl. 6, fig. 3.

From Kodiak (Trelease, 1675). New to Alaska.

Polytrichum commune Linn. Spec. pl., II, p. 1109.

From Alaska, sine loco (W. H. Evans in 1897); between Cook Inlet and the Tanana River (Capt. E. F. Glenn in 1899); Kodiak (Trelease, 1693; L. J. Cole).

Polytrichum yukonense sp. nov.

(Pl. XXII, fig. 1*a–f*.)

Caulis 5–8 centim. altus, simplex vel parcissime ramosus, inferne longe denudatus, basi tomento albido obtectus. Folia rigida, sicca suberecta, madida erecto-patentia, 4–6 millim. longa, 1 lata, e basi appressa subvaginante lutescente breviter lineari-acuminata, in cuspidem fuscam integram attenuata, marginibus erectis integris, lamellis circiter 30, elatis, margine crenulatis, in sectione transversali e 8–12 cellulis compositis, cellula apicali majore, profunde emarginata. Cætera ignota.

From Yukon River (W. H. Dall, in 1867).

This species is easily distinguished from the smaller forms of *P. commune* by its short and entire leaves, its higher lamellæ with more deeply crenated borders and more strongly emarginated marginal cells.

A recently described species, *P. jensenii* Hagen (*P. fragilifolium* Lindb. fil. mss.), which has been found in Greenland, Spitzbergen, Lapland and Wyoming, comes very near our *P. yukonense* by its size and the height and structure of its lamellæ, but differs from it by its leaves being longer and dentate at the point, by the cells of the basilar and subvaginant part, which are wider, and by the much less emarginated apical cells of the lamellæ.

Polytrichum juniperinum Willd. Fl. berol. prodr., p 305

From New Metlakatla (Trelease, 1678*b*); Point Gustavus (Coville and Kearney, 772 in part); Kodiak (Trelease, 1674, 1696), Long Island (Trelease, 1697), Port Clarence (Trelease, 1666, 1667, 1668; Brewer and Coe, 670; L. J Cole).

Numbers 1667, 1668 of Trelease, and 670 of Brewer and Coe constitute a form near var. *alpinum* Sch.

Polytrichum strictum Banks apud. Menz. in Trans. Linn. Soc , IV, p. 77, pl. 7, f. 1.

From New Metlakatla (Trelease, 1659); Wrangell (Coville and Kearney, 414); Virgin Bay (Trelease, 1672, 1673; Coville and Kearney, 1237); Sitka (Trelease, 1671, 1687; Coville and Kearney, 893); Kodiak (Trelease, 1675).

Polytrichum hyperboreum R. Brown in Parry voyage, Suppl., p. 294

P boreale KINDB in Mac Cat Can pl , VI, Musci, p. 155.

From St. Paul Island (J. M. Macoun); Plover Bay, Siberia (Coville and Kearney, 1860 in part).

It is impossible to distinguish from *P. hyperboreum* R. Br. the *P. boreale* of Kindberg, the characters mentioned by the author for the latter having no stability, even on the original specimens he has communicated to us.

P. sexangulare Fl., *P. piliferum* Schreb and *P behringianum* Kindb. have been reported by Kindberg from Alaska and the islands of Bering Sea.

Family FONTINALACEÆ.

Fontinalis patula Card. in Rev. bryol., 1896, p. 67.

From Sitka (Trelease, 2368). New to Alaska.

Family NECKERACEÆ.

Neckera pennata Hedw. Descr., III, p. 17, pl. 19.

From Skagway (Canby, 428).

N menziesii Drumm , *N. douglasii* Hook. and *Alsia abietina* Sulliv , have been recorded from Alaska by Mr Kindberg

Family LEUCODONTACEÆ.

Antitrichia curtipendula Brid. Mant musc., p. 136.

From Wrangell (Trelease, 1992; Coville and Kearney, 404); Cape Fox (Trelease, 1964a, 2012); Yakutat Bay (Trelease, 1821 in part, 1916); Orca (Trelease, 2010); Kodiak (Trelease, 1920 in part); Unalaska (Trelease, 1983; J. M. Macoun); Popof Island (Saunders, 2293); Mist harbor, Nagai Island (U. S. S. *Albatross* Exped.).

Antitrichia curtipendula gigantea Sulliv. Lesq. Musci bor. amer. exsicc , ed. 2, no. 356. Sch. Syn., ed. 2, p. 577.

From Yakutat Bay (Trelease, 1917); Point Gustavus (Coville and Kearney, 572); Cape Fox (Trelease, 1964), Hot Springs (Trelease, 2003); Kodiak (Trelease, 1922, 1931); Popof Island (Saunders, 2037); Unalaska (Trelease, 1984).

This variety is not always larger than the type; it is specially characterized by its nerve being provided at the base with longer and more numerous fascicles (5–8 instead of 2–4); but doubtful forms are frequent.

A californica Sulliv has, teste Rothrock, been reported from Alaska by Kindberg.

Family HOOKERIACEÆ.

Pterygophyllum lucens Brid Mant musc., p. 149.

Sine loco (Brewer and Coe, 622). New to Alaska, if not collected in British Columbia.

Family LESKEACEÆ.

Myurella julacea Br eur., fasc. 46–47, p. 3, pl. 1.

From Port Wells (Trelease, 2286 in part).

Myurella julacea scabrifolia Lindb. Musc. scand., p. 37.

From Port Wells (Trelease, 1832 in part). New to Alaska.

Family ISOTHECIACEÆ.

Climacium dendroides Web. & Mohr, Reise in Schwed., p. 96.

From Alaska sine loco (U. S. S. *Albatross* Exped.); Disenchantment Bay (Trelease, 1703); Muir Glacier (Trelease, 1701); Head of Russell Fiord (Coville and Kearney, 949); Kodiak (Trelease,

1706); Hall Island (Trelease 1707); St. Paul Island (J. M. Macoun).

The specimens from St. Paul Island are remarkable by their leaves being entire or nearly so, and provided with rounded auricles, larger than in the type. In *C. americanum* Brid., the auricles are still more developed, and the areolation is chiefly formed of much shorter and wider cells. By its entire or subentire leaves, the form from St. Paul Island comes near var. *oregonense* Ren. & Card.

Climacium ruthenicum Lindb. Act. Soc. Fenn., x, p. 248.

From Juneau (Setchell, 1231; Coville and Kearney, 599); Yakutat Bay (Trelease, 1704); Virgin Bay (Trelease, 1705), Port Etches (J. M. Macoun); Sitka (Trelease, 1702; Canby, 407).

Orthothecium intricatum Br. eur., fasc. 48, p. 4, pl. 2, 3.

From Bailey Harbor (U. S. S. *Albatross* Exped., 1893)   New to Alaska.

A small form mixed with *Claopodium bolanderi* Best.

Orthothecium chryseum Br. eur., fasc. 48, p. 3, pl. 2.

From Port Wells (Trelease, 1897).

Family THUIDIACEÆ.

Pseudoleskea atrovirens Br. eur., fasc. 49–51, p. 2, pl. 1.

From Yakutat Bay (Trelease, 1746a). New to Alaska.

Pseudoleskea radicosa Best in Bull. Torr. Bot. Club, xxvii, p. 230.

P. rigescens REN & CARD. Musci Am. sept. exsicc., no. 93.

From Muir Glacier (Trelease, 1911).

A slender and somewhat etiolated form.

Pseudoleskea stenophylla Ren. & Card. in Bot. Centralbl., 1890, no. 51, p. 421.

P. rigescens BEST, loc. cit., p. 232.

Lescuræa imperfecta C. MULL. & KINDB. in Mac. Cat. Can. pl., vi, Musci, p. 170, fide Best.

From Yakutat Bay (Trelease, 1759, 2056). Muir Glacier (Trelease, 1782, 2442, 2452, 2453); Point Gustavus (Coville and Kearney, 753 in part). New to Alaska.

Numbers 2056 of Trelease, and 753 in part of Coville and Kearney, exactly agree with the type of Washington; the Muir Glacier plant has the leaves somewhat wider at the base, but the form of the segments of the endostome and the other characters leave no doubt as to its correct reference to *P. stenophylla*. Number 1759, from Yakutat Bay, is a stouter and sterile form, the determination of which is rather doubtful.

In his valuable *Revision of the North American species of Pseudo-leskea* (Bull. Torr. Bot. Club, xxvii), Dr. Best has substituted the name *P. rigescens* (Wils.) Lindb. for *P. stenophylla* Ren. & Card. It is impossible for us to admit any well grounded reason for this change; for, if Dr. Best saw, as he affirms, a specimen of *Leskea rigescens* Wils. identical with *P. stenophylla* Ren. & Card., on the other hand, we possess one which certainly belongs to *P. radicosa* (Drummond, Musci Americani, no. 225). Moreover, Dr. Best himself acknowledges that both species were mixed up under this number of Drummond's exsiccata and under the name *Hypnum congestum* Hook. & Wils. Now, as Wilson never described his *Leskea rigescens*, it is impossible to know to which of the two species he wished to give this name, and that must, therefore, be definitely abandoned. One of the two species should be called *P. radicosa* (Mitt.) Best, the other should preserve the name *P. stenophylla* Ren. & Card.

Thuidium abietinum Br. eur., fasc 49–51, p. 9, pl. 5.

From Port Clarence (Trelease, 2034, 2036).

Claopodium bolanderi Best, in Bull. Torr. Bot. Club, xxiv, p. 431.

From Bailey Harbor (U. S. S. *Albatross* Exped. in 1893); Kodiak (J. M. Macoun).

Kindberg mentions *C. crispifolium* and *C. laxifolium* as coming from Alaska. His specimens of *crispifolium* that we have seen belong to *C. bolanderi*. We have not seen any of the second one. Otherwise, it has been established that *Leskea laxifolia* Hook. is none other than *Brachythecium reflexum* Br. eur.

Family HYPNACEÆ.

Camptothecium nitens Sch. Syn., ed. 1, p. 530.

From Point Gustavus (Coville and Kearney, without number).

C. lutescens Br. eur. has also been reported from Alaska.

Brachythecium beringianum sp. nov.
(Pl. XXII, fig. 3^{a–e})

Dense cespitosum, habitu formis minoribus *B. albicantis* simile. Caulis erectus, 3–4 centim. altus, ramosissimus, ramis erectis, interdum fastigiatis, julaceis, acutis. Folia conferta, imbricata, caulina 1.5 millim. longa, 0.8 lata, ovato-lanceolata, basi paululum decurrentia, sat abrupte et breviuscule acuminata, concava, plicata, marginibus integris planis vel parce reflexis, ramea minora et angustiora, longius acuminata, costa tenui, basi 30–35 μ crassa, vix ad medium producta, sæpe furcata et interdum brevissima, cellulis alaribus numerosis, quadratis, in 5–6 seriebus secundum margines supeine productis, cæteris linearibus, 40–45 µ longis, 6–7 latis, parietibus incrassatis. Cætera ignota.

From St. Paul Island (Trelease, 1861, 2087), Agattu Island (U. S. S. *Albatross* Exped., 40)

Distinct from *B. acuminatum* Ren. & Card. by its habit, its more abruptly acuminate leaves, etc. It more closely resembles *B. albicans* Br. eur., from which it differs by its shorter and more abruptly acuminate leaves, its quadrate more numerous alar cells, its more chlorophyllose areolation, and by its narrower, short and often bifurcate costa.

Brachythecium albicans Br. eur., fasc. 52–54, p. 19, pl. 19.

From Yakutat Bay (Trelease, 2342); Muir Glacier (Trelease, 1909); Wrangell (Canby, 468, 472), Sturgeon River Bay, Kodiak (Trelease, 1930); St. Paul Island (Trelease, 1863); Agattu Island (U. S. S. *Albatross* Exped., 16 in part). Several forms.

Brachythecium salebrosum Br. eur., fasc. 52–54, p. 16, pl. 15, 16.

From Cape Fox (Trelease, 1762 in part, 1963); Skagway (Canby, 481 in part, forma *angustifolia*); Yukon River (W. H. Dall, in 1867); Sitka (Trelease, 2002); Agattu Island (U. S. S. *Albatross* Exped., 16 in part).

Brachythecium novæ-angliæ Jaeg. & Sauerb. Adumbr., II, p. 394.

From Kodiak (Trelease, 2057); St. Paul Island (Trelease, 2091). New to Alaska.

On these specimens nearly all the leaves are smooth on the back; however we have found a few branches with papillose leaves, which, added to the other characters, leaves no doubt as to their determination. Moreover, even on the specimens from New England, the leaves are sometimes quite smooth. This character is therefore variable, which prevents us from admitting the genus *Bryhnia*.

Mr. A. J. Grout has recently ascertained that *Hypnum chloropterum* C. Mull. & Kindb., from Canada, and *H. scabridum* Lindb., from Norway, should be reunited to *B. novæ-angliæ* (cf. Bull. Torr. Club, XXV, pp. 229–231). The distribution of this species, as it is now known, includes southern Norway, eastern Canada, Newfoundland, Miquelon Island, the Eastern States as far south as Maryland and as far west as Wisconsin, Alaska, the Bering Sea Islands and Japan.

Brachythecium rivulare Br. eur., fasc. 52–54, p. 13, pl. 12.

From Juneau (Trelease, 1796); Disenchantment Bay (Trelease, 1829); Orca (Trelease, 1840).

Number 1829 resembles *B. latifolium* (Lindb.) Philib. by its widely decurrent leaves; but the latter is a more slender plant, with a thinner costa and leaves hardly or not at all plicate.

Brachythecium reflexum pacificum Ren. & Card. in Bot. Centralbl. 1890, No. 51.

(Pl. xxiii, fig. 4^{a—e}.)

Eurhynchium pacificum KINDB. Eur. and N. Amer. br , p 101.

From Juneau (Trelease, 2173); Wrangell (Trelease, 1937); Cape Fox (Trelease, 1760a); Yakutat Bay (Trelease, 1746, 1758, 1826, 2339); Disenchantment Bay (Trelease, 2512; Brewer and Coe, 634); Muir Glacier (Trelease, 1753, 1754, 1755, 2469). New to Alaska.

This variety, which seems to occur along the Pacific Coast from Oregon to Alaska, differs from the type by its stouter aspect, its stem-leaves larger, less triangular, rather ovate-lanceolate, not so abruptly acuminate, and revolute on the borders in the lower part, by its costa thinner and generally vanishing at the base of the acumen, and by its leaf-areolation composed of cells of the same width (about $9\,\mu$) but at least twice longer (80–$90\,\mu$, instead of 30–35); those in the angles longer too, rectangular, seldom quadrate. These characters seem to be constant, and perhaps Mr. Kindberg is right in considering this moss as a species distinct from *B. reflexum*.

Brachythecium asperrimum Kindb. in Mac. Cat. Can. pl., vi, Musci, p. 200.

From Cape Fox (Trelease, 2382). New to Alaska.

Brachythecium lamprochryseum giganteum Grout in Mem. Torr. Bot. Club, vi, p. 181.

From Atka Island (U. S. S. *Albatross* Exped., 44).

Brachythecium plumosum Br. eur., fasc. 52–54, p. 4, pl. 3.

From Kodiak (Trelease, 2194). New to Alaska.

Kindberg has mentioned *B. turgidum* Hartm. as Alaskan. Four species of the genus *Scleropodium*, viz *S illecebrum* Br. eur., *S. cespitosum* Br. eur., *S. colpophyllum* (Sulliv) Grout, and *S kransei* (C Müll) Ren & Card , have also been recorded from Alaska We have not seen the first three, the last is a *Hypnum* of the section *Hygrohypnum*.

Eurhynchium myosuroides Sch. Syn., ed. 1, p. 549.

From Yakutat Bay (Trelease, 1820); Hot Springs (Trelease, 2003 in part); Unalaska (U. S. S. *Albatross* Exped., 41).

Forms approaching var. *spiculiferum* Card., or doubtful between this and var. *substoloniferum* Card.

Eurhynchium myosuroides spiculiferum Card. in Bull. de l'herb. Boissier, VII, p. 431.
From Prince of Wales Island (J. M. Macoun).

Eurhynchium myosuroides humile Grav. in Rev. bryol., 1883, p. 33.
From New Metlakatla (Trelease, 1751 in part). New to Alaska.

Eurhynchium strigosum fallax Ren & Card. in Bot. Gaz., 1889, p. 98.
From Skagway (Canby, 477, 481 in part, 482 in part).

Eurhynchium stokesii Br. eur., fasc. 57–61, p. 10, pl. 8.
From Cape Fox (Trelease, 1762a). New to Alaska.

Eurhynchium oreganum Jaeg. & Sauerb. Adumbr., II, p. 427.
From Hot Springs (Trelease, 2020). New to Alaska.

Eurhynchium cirrosum Husn. Muscol. gall., p. 338.
From Muir Glacier (Trelease, 1912).

E. myosuroides var. *stoloniferum* Auct., *E. strigosum* Br. eur. *typicum*, *E. vaucheri* Br. eur. and *E. stokesii* subsp. *pseudo-speciosum* Kindb. have been recorded by Kindberg from Alaska and the islands of Bering Sea.

Rhynchostegium serrulatum Jaeg. & Sauerb., Adumbr., II, p. 436.
From Alaska, sine loco (A. Kellogg). New to Alaska.
The presence of this species in Alaska is rather surprising; however, it is impossible not to refer to it the specimen we have had before our eyes.

Mr. Kindberg has recorded from Kodiak a *Raphidostegium subdemissum* Kindb. that we have not seen.

Plagiothecium undulatum Br. eur., fasc. 48, p. 17, pl. 13.
From Alaska, sine loco (W. H. Evans in 1897); Port Etches (J. M. Macoun); Point Gustavus (Coville and Kearney, 790); Orca (Trelease, 1739 in part, 1740; Setchell, 1214); Sitka (Trelease, 1736, 2497, Setchell, 1256; J. M. Macoun, W. G. Wright, 1609), Hot Springs (Trelease, 1735), Douglas Island (Trelease, 1737, 1743 in part).

Plagiothecium fallax sp. nov.

(Pl. XXII, fig. 4^{a-e}.)

Dioicum, robustum, lutescenti-viride, nitidum. Caulis prostratus vel decumbens, 5–8 centim. longus, flexuosus, parce ramosus, apice attenuato sæpius radiculosus. Folia laxe complanato-disticha, siccitate subundulato-crispatula, 2.5 millim. longa, 1–1.3 lata, e basi haud decurrente oblongo-lanceolata, asymmetrica, late breviterque acuminata, longitudinaliter plicatula, marginibus planis integris, costa gemella, inæquali, crure longiore ad ⅓ vel ½ producta, cellulis basilaribus paucis, quadratis vel breviter rectangulis, cæteris linearibus 125–225 μ longis, 9–14 latis Cætera ignota.

From Douglas Island (Trelease, 1743 in part)

Resembling in habit the species of the *denticulatum* group, but very distinct by its leaves being not decurrent.

Plagiothecium denticulatum Br. eur., fasc. 48, p. 12, pl. 8.

From Cape Fox (Trelease, 2376)'; Orca (Trelease, 1739 in part, 1741, 1942); Yakutat Bay (Trelease, 2330); Sitka (Trelease, 1431, 2356, 2357, 2496), Douglas Island (Trelease, 2406).

Plagiothecium denticulatum undulatum Ruthe in litt. 1873. Geheeb in Rev. bryol., 1877, p. 42, fide Limpricht.

P. ruthei LIMPR. Laubm., II, p 271.

From Yakutat Bay (Trelease, 2327). New to Alaska.

Plagiothecium denticulatum recurvum Warnst. Moosfl. d. Prov. Brandenb., p 73, fide Limpricht.

P. curvifolium SCHLIEPH mss Limpr Laubm., II, p 269.

From Douglas Island (Trelease, 1738). New to Alaska.

Plagiothecium denticulatum donii Lindb. in Not. Sallsk. fauna et fl. fenn., 1867.

From New Metlakatla (Trelease, 1751 in part). New to Alaska.

Plagiothecium sylvaticum Br eur., fasc. 48, p. 14, pl. 11.

From Juneau (Brewer and Coe, 691b); Kodiak (Trelease, 2192). New to Alaska.

Plagiothecium roeseanum Br. eur., fasc. 48, p. 15, pl. 10.

From Kodiak (Trelease, 1844, 2191). New to Alaska.

Plagiothecium muehlenbeckii Br. eur., fasc. 48, p. 11, pl. 6.

From Orca (Trelease, 2251), Kodiak (Trelease, 2207), Hot Springs (Trelease, 2349). New to Alaska.

Plagiothecium elegans Sulliv. Moss. of U S., p. 80.

From Farragut Bay (Coville and Kearney, 469); Hot Springs (Trelease, 1742, 1757); Douglas Island (Trelease, 2391). New to Alaska.

P. pulchellum Br eur has been recorded from the islands of Bering Sea by Mr Kindberg

Amblystegium serpens Br eur., fasc. 55–56, p. 9, pl. 3.

From Cape Fox (Trelease, 1760, 1761, 1762, 2375); St. Paul Island (Trelease, 2089 in part). New to Alaska.

Amblystegium serpens beringianum var. nov.

A forma typica differt foliis ovato-lanceolatis latioribus brevius acuminatis, costa validiore ad basin acuminis producta, cellulis basilaribus rectangulis, parietibus incrassatis

From St. Paul Island (Trelease, 2089 in part).

Under number 1760 we found some stems of a stouter species, much resembling *A. radicale* (Pal. Beauv.) Mitt.

Amblystegium varium alaskanum var. nov.

Robustius, dense ramosum, late depresso-cespitosum, folia breviora, late ovata, subito constricta, breviter et anguste acuminata, cellulis alaribus inflatis, multo majoribus.

From Muir Glacier (Trelease, 1752).

Genus Hypnum Dill

Section Chrysohypnum Hpe.

Hypnum treleasei Ren sp nov.

(Pl. xxii, fig 5^{a-e}.)

Dense cespitosum, fragile, lutescenti-viride. Caulis brevis, 2-3 centim. altus, erectus, inferne radiculosus, ramis erectis fastigiatis. Folia conferta, parva, subimbricata, interdum subhomomalla, 1.2 millim. longa, 0.6 lata, ovato-lanceolata, breviuscule acuminata, vix plicatula, plerumque magno augmento, praecipue basin versus, minute denticulata, costa gemella brevi, cellulis basilaribus quadratis vel breviter rectangulis, chlorophyllosis, externis elongatis decurrentibus, caeteris linearibus, 30-40 μ longis, 6-7 latis. Caetera ignota.

From Virgin Bay (Trelease, 2305); St. Matthew Island (Trelease, 2158, 2165).

The description here given, as also the drawing, is based on the St. Matthew Island specimens. The Virgin Bay specimen has the leaves longer, with a more elongated and narrower acumen, and a closer areolation, formed of longer and narrower cells. There is, however, no doubt of the specific identity of the two specimens. This species should be placed near *H stellatum* Schreb., from which it is distinguished by its much smaller dimensions, its short and fastigiate stems, its leaves which are small, imbricate, shortly acuminate and for the most part finely denticulate, and, finally, by its small, quadrate alar-cells, the median ones shorter.

Hypnum stellatum Schieb. Spic. fl. lips., p. 92.
From Port Wells (Trelease, 1836); Kodiak (Trelease, 1923)

Hypnum polygamum minus Sch. Syn., ed. 1, p. 604.
From Yakutat Bay (Trelease, 2341). New to Alaska.

Section DREPANOCLADUS C. Mull.[1]

Hypnum aduncum kneiffii Sch. Syn., ed. 2, p. 727.
From St. Paul Island (J. M. Macoun). New to Alaska.
This specimen was attributed by Mr. Kindberg to *H. conflatum* C. Mull. & Kindb. But, according to Renauld, it is impossible to separate it from *H. aduncum kneiffii*.

Hypnum fluitans Linn. Flor. suec., ed. 2, p. 899 in part.
From Yakutat Bay (Brewer and Coe, 690).
A form near var. *jeanbernati* Ren.

Hypnum fluitans alpinum Sch. Syn., ed. 1, p. 611.
From St. Lawrence Island (Trelease, 1981; Coville and Kearney, 1984; L. J. Cole). New to Alaska.

Hypnum fluitans exannulatum Ren. Rev. harpid., 1879.
From Yakutat Bay (Trelease, 1745). New to Alaska.

Hypnum revolvens Sw. Disp. musc. frond. suec., p. 101, pl. 7, f. 14.
From Kodiak (Trelease, 2030, 2031); St. Matthew Island (Trelease, 1890, 2163a); Hall Island (Trelease, 1663 in part, 2130 in part).

Hypnum uncinatum Hedw. Descr., iv, p. 65, pl. 25.
From Alaska, sine loco (F. Funston, 144); Juneau (Setchell, 1234, Canby, 486, 496; Coville and Kearney, 575); Skagway (Canby, 481 in part); Wrangell (Trelease, 2017); Head of Russell Fiord (Coville and Kearney, 950); Disenchantment Bay (Trelease, 1958, 2023, 2024); Orca (Trelease, 1961) Port Wells (Trelease, 1962, 2028), Muir Glacier (Trelease, 1951); Point Gustavus (Coville and Kearney, 753); Sitka (Trelease, 2005); Sturgeon River Bay, Kodiak (Trelease, 2225); Port Clarence (Trelease, 1971, 1973); St. Matthew Island (Coville and Kearney, 2129); St. Paul Island (Trelease, 1864).

With forms passing to varieties *plumulosum*, *subiulaceum* and *orthothecioides*.

---

[1] We are indebted to Mons. F. Renauld for the determinations of the species of this group.

Hypnum uncinatum forma **breviseta** Ren. in litt.

From Skagway (Canby, 842 in part), Sitka (Trelease, 1938; Coville and Kearney, 898); Kodiak (Trelease, 2058)

Hypnum uncinatum forma **plumosa** Ren in Husn., Muscol. gall., p 378.

Hypnum uncinatum plumosum Sch Syn., ed 1. p. 612.

From Indian Camp, Yakutat Bay (Brewer and Coe, 642); Disenchantment Bay (Trelease, 1957); Point Gustavus (Coville and Kearney, 753 in part); Yukon River (W. H. Dall, in 1867), Port Clarence (Brewer and Coe, 672; Trelease, 2014); St. Matthew Island (Trelease, 1887 in part, 1888 in part); Hall Island (Trelease, 2133).

Hypnum uncinatum plumulosum Br. eur., fasc. 57–61, p. 31, pl. 20, fig. 7, 1, 2.

From Orca (Trelease, 1943); Indian Camp, Yukutat Bay (Brewer and Coe, 643; forma *crassa* ad var. *polare* accedens); Port Clarence (Trelease, 1969, 1970, 1972), St Lawrence Island (Trelease, 1982); St Matthew Island (Trelease, 2163), Hall Island (Trelease, 1967); Plover Bay, Siberia (Trelease, 1977).

Hypnum uncinatum polare Ren. var. nov.

Habitu varietati *plumulosum* simile, sed rete basilari laxiore parenchymatoso, cellulis mediis brevioribus, magis chlorophyllosis.

From St. Matthew Island (Trelease, 2159), Plover Bay, Siberia (Trelease, 1978)

Hypnum uncinatum subjulaceum Br eur., loc cit., fig ε, 1, 2, forma **orthothecioides** Ren. in Husn. Muscol. gall., p 378

From Bailey Harbor (U. S. S. *Albatross* Exped.); Mist Harbor, Nagai Island (U. S. S. *Albatross* Exped.); Yakutat Bay (Trelease, 2026); Kodiak (Trelease, 1926, 1927); St. Paul Island (Trelease, 1975, 1985; J. M. Macoun); Hall Island (Trelease. 1966); Plover Bay, Siberia (Trelease, 1976; Coville and Kearney, 1851).

Section Cratoneuron Sulliv.

Hypnum filicinum Linn Spec. pl., p. 1125.

From Yakutat Bay (Trelease, 1818); Hidden Glacier Inlet (Trelease, 1814), Disenchantment Bay (Trelease, 1825, 1955, 2511); Head of Russell Fiord; (Coville and Kearney, 956); Muir Glacier (Trelease, 1756, 1792, 1807). Several forms.

Hypnum sulcatum stenodictyon Ren. var. nov.
Hypnum sulcatum Sch. Syn. ed., 1, p. 699.
A forma typica rete densiore cellulis angustioribus distincta.
From Muir Glacier (Trelease, 2019).

Section PTILIUM Sulliv.
Hypnum crista-castrensis Linn. Sp. pl., p. 1125.

From Virgin Bay (Trelease, 2027); Sitka (Trelease, 2022), Kodiak (Trelease, 2054; Coville and Kearney, 2339, 2261*a*), Mist Harbor, Nagai Island (U. S. S.*Albatross* Exped.).

Section STEREODON Brid.
Hypnum circinale Hook. Musci exot., pl. 107.

From Juneau (Brewer and Coe, 698); Yakutat Bay (Trelease, 2329); Fairagut Bay (Trelease, 1935, 1936; Brewer and Coe, 618, 623), Orca (Trelease 1748, 1941, 1943 in part, 1944, 2250, 2500; Setchell, 1210); Virgin Bay (Trelease, 2304); Sitka (Trelease, 1939, 1940; Coville and Kearney, 825; Setchell, 1257, 1267; Canby, 462, J. M. Macoun); Hot Springs (Trelease, 2345); Kodiak (Trelease, 1945, 2211; L. J. Cole); Wood Island (Brewer and Coe, 659, 660, 662); Prince of Wales Island (J. M. Macoun).

We do not distinguish from *H. circinale*, *H. sequoieti* C. Mull. in Flora, 1875, p. 91, the characters mentioned for the latter being inconstant and of little importance. We must equally refer to *H. circinale* the *Raphidostegium pseudorecurvans* Kindb. Not. on Canad. bryol., 1893, according to the specimens of the latter which were communicated to us by Mr. J. M. Macoun.

As we have said elsewhere (Revue bryologique, 1890, p. 18, and Hedwigia, 1893, p. 275) it was a mistake to describe *H circinale* as being monœcious, it is certainly diœcious, for on a hundred specimens that we have had the opportunity of examining, we have never found flowers of both sexes on the same stem.

Hypnum callichroum Br. eur., fasc. 57–61, p. 27, pl. 16.

From Port Wells (Trelease, 1747); Orca (Trelease, 1749, 2261); Yakutat Bay (Trelease, 1746); Head of Russell Fiord (Coville and Kearney, 948 in part); Wrangell (Trelease, 2018); Port Etches (J. M. Macoun); Sitka (Trelease 2021). New to Alaska.

Hypnum alaskæ Kindb. Not. on Canad. bryol., 1893.

From Port Etches (J. M. Macoun).

This species appears to be very close to the preceding, judging from the small specimen we received; however, it differs from it by its smaller dimensions, its creeping and radiculose stems and its much narrower leaves.

Hypnum dieckii Ren. & Card. in Bot Centralbl., 1890, no. 51. Hedwigia, 1893, p. 278.

From Orca (Trelease, 1960); Sitka (Trelease, 1744). New to Alaska.

Hypnum hamulosum Br eur., fasc. 57–61, p. 20, pl 10.

From Yakutat Bay (Trelease, 2025); Port Clarence (Trelease, 1968); Hall Island (Trelease, 2032).

The alar cells are here a little more numerous than on the European type; but we have specimens from the Pyrenees that are identical in this respect with those from Alaska.

Hypnum canadense Kindb. in Bull. Torr. Bot. Club, XVII, p. 280. Mac Cat. Can. pl., VI, Musci, p. 236

From Orca (Setchell, 1201), Prince of Wales Island (J M Macoun).

This species differs from *H. imponens* Hedw. by the auricles of the leaves being formed of one or two large outer hyaline cells, the inner cells being brown or yellowish.

Hypnum vaucheri Lesq. Cat. mouss. suisses, p. 48. Sch. Syn., ed. 1, p. 697.

From Bailey Harbor (U. S. S. *Albatross* Exped.).

Although the areolation is a little closer than usual, the alar cells, much more numerous than in *H. cupressiforme*, do not seem to leave any doubt on the determination of this moss.

Section HYGROHYPNUM Lindb.

Hypnum ochraceum Turn. in Wils. Bryol. brit., p. 400

From Disenchantment Bay (Trelease, 1820); Kodiak (Trelease, 2195).

Hypnum ochraceum flaccidum Milde, Bryol sil., p. 376.

From Disenchantment Bay (Trelease, 1828), Sitka (Trelease, 2366).

Hypnum subeugyrium occidentale var nov

Hypnum subeugyrium REN & CARD in Bot Gaz., XXII, p 52

A forma typica Terræ Novæ differt foliis pro more latioribus, mollioribus, magis concavis, apice integris, cellulisque alaribus paulo majoribus, auriculas interdum subinflatas sed semper multo minus distinctas quam in *H. eugyrio* efformantibus. Costa interdum subsimplex.

From Hidden Glacier Inlet, Yakutat Bay (Trelease, 1784), Muir Glacier (Trelease, 1805).

Hypnum krausei C Mull. in Flora, 1887, p. 224.

From Takhin valley (Dr Krause).

This moss, that C. Muller placed in his section *Illecebrina*, which corresponds to the genus *Scleropodium* Br. eur , is certainly a *Hygrohypnum* (*Limnobium* Sch), as appears from an examination of the original specimen, which was communicated to us by the Royal Botanical Museum in Berlin It comes near *H. subeugyrium occidentale* Card. & Thér., but differs from it by its longer leaves, its almost scarious and much less chlorophyllose areolation, and its thinner costa

Section CALLIERGON Sulliv.

Hypnum cordifolium Hedw. Descr , iv. p 97, pl 37.

From Yakutat Bay (Trelease, 1795); Kodiak (Trelease, 1842 in part); Sitka (Trelease, 2369).

Hypnum schreberi Willd. Prodr. fl berol., no. 955

From White Pass, 3,000 ft. (Trelease, 1950); Orca (Setchell, 1208), Sitka (Trelease, 2007), Port Clarence (Trelease, 1869, 2013, 2035); St. Matthew Island (Coville and Kearney, 2110); Hall Island (Trelease, 2033).

Hypnum sarmentosum Wahlenb. Fl. lapp., p. 380.

From Port Wells (Coville and Kearney, 1293 in part).

Hypnum sarmentosum beringianum var. nov.

Hypnum sarmentosum WAHLENB Fl lapp , p 380

A forma typica differt caulibus gracilioribus, laxius foliosis, costa latiore et præsertim cellulis alaribus multo minoribus, pro more quadratis, vix dilatatis.

From St. Matthew Island (Trelease, 1888 in part, 1889).

By the structure of the angles of the leaf, this moss comes near *H. brunneo-fuscum* C Mull. from the Chukchi peninsula, but the latter has a different facies, a closer areolation and a much thinner costa.

Hypnum stramineum Dicks. Fasc. pl. crypt., II, p 6, pl 1, f 9.

From Unalaska (U. S S. *Albatross* Exped., 11); Port Clarence (Trelease, 1866, 1870).

Section CALLIERGIDIUM Ren. in litt.

Pseudocalliergon REN. in Bryologist, IV, p. 63, non Limpr

Hypnum plesiostramineum Ren. sp. nov.[1]

(Pl XXIII, fig 2ᵃ⁻ʰ)

Cespites laxi, molles. Caulis gracilis, erectus, 4–6 centim. altus, simplex vel parce ramosus, ramis gracilibus. Folia sat conferta,

[1] See note 3, p 347

erecta, apice tantum paululum patentia, circa 1-4 millim. longa, 0.6 lata, diversiformia, inferiora ovato-oblonga vel subdeltoidea, acuminata, subobtusa, superiora elliptica, acumine latiore et obtusiore, ramea ovata, rotundato-obtusa, omnia plicatula, marginibus planis sinuolatis, costa tenui, ad ¾ vel ultra producta, basi 40–50 μ crassa, cellulis alaribus magnis, laxis, hyalinis, auriculas inflatas pulchre distinctas efformantibus, mediis anguste linearibus, flexuosis, extremitatibus obtusis, 40–60 μ longis, 5–6 latis, apicalibus brevibus, ovatis vel subhexagonis. Cætera ignota.

From Yukon River (W. H. Dall, in 1867).

This species resembles both *H. stramineum* Dicks. and *H. pseudostramineum* C. Müll.; but it is with the latter that it has the closest affinity. It differs from it by its leaves being shorter, subdeltoid, with a costa thicker (40–50 μ instead of 30–40), longer, usually exceeding the ¾, and finally by the firm areolation, formed of flexuous cells, rather obtuse (not truncate) at the ends, with thick walls, and resembling those of *Hygrohypnum*.

The comparative figures of *H. pseudo-stramineum* given on Plate XXIII, were supplied to us by Mons. Renauld, who drew them from an original collected by C. Müller at Halle-am-Saale.

Mr Kindberg has described a *H. pseudo-complexum* Kindb. from Alaska, of which we have not seen any specimen. *H. alaskanum* Lesq. & Jam. is also unknown to us.

Hylocomium splendens Br. eur. fasc., 49–52, p. 5, pl. 1.

From Alaska, sine loco (W. H. Evans, in 1897); Orca (Setchell, 1212; Trelease, 2050); Muir Glacier (Coville and Kearney, 673); Yakutat Bay (Trelease, 2049); Disenchantment Bay (Trelease, 2047); Head of Russell Fiord (Coville and Kearney, 957); New Metlakatla (Trelease, 2041); Farragut Bay (Trelease, 2042); Wrangell (Canby, 450); Karluk (Brewer and Coe, 686); Koyukuk River (F. C. Schrader, in 1899); Sitka (Setchell, 1260; Trelease, 2045, 2046; W. G. Wright, 1605); Kodiak (L. J. Cole, Trelease, 2029, 2052, 2053); Wood Island (Brewer and Coe, 663).

Hylocomium splendens gracilius Boul. Musc. de la France, p. 10.

H. alaskanum KINDB in Mac Cat Can pl., VI, Musci, p 248

From Muir Glacier (Trelease, 2043, 2044); Kodiak (Trelease, 2051); Unalaska (J. M. Macoun), Popof Island (Saunders, 2038); Hall Island (Trelease, 1989 in part, 2055, 2056).

This variety is *Hylocomium alaskanum* of Kindberg, but we much doubt whether it is the true *Hypnum alaskanum* of Lesquereux and James (Proced. Amer Acad, XIV, p. 139, and Manual, p. 405). These authors compare their plant to *Hypnum Schreberi*, to which this var. *gracilius* bears no resemblance, and attribute to it obtuse leaves, whereas they are apiculate on the moss of which we are speaking. Besides, it would be very surprising if such experienced bryologists as Lesquereux and James had not noticed the evident relations which would have existed between their species and *Hylocomium splendens*, if the identification proposed by Mr. Kindberg was exact. Until the contrary is proved, we think that *H. alaskanum* Lesq & Jam is a different species, much more resembling *H. schreberi* than *Hylocomium splendens*.

Hylocomium umbratum Br. eur., fasc. 49–52, p. 6, pl. 2.

From Yakutat Bay (Trelease, 1965 in part); Disenchantment Bay (Trelease, 2048). New to Alaska

Hylocomium squarrosum Br eur., fasc. 49–52, p. 9, pl. 6.

Yakutat Bay (Trelease, 1821 in part, 1959, 2328), Point Gustavus (Saunders, 2000); Cape Fox (Trelease, 1965); Sturgeon River Bay, Kodiak (Trelease, 1932), Unalaska (U. S. S. *Albatross* Exped., 19); St. Paul Island (Trelease, 1862, 1974), Hall Island (Trelease, 1883)

Numbers 1959, 1965 and 2000 are forms coming more or less near *H. calvescens* (Wils.) Jaeg., but on the plant from Finland the acumen is broader and shorter, which constitutes the chief character of this form, which, otherwise, it is impossible for us to specifically separate from *H. squarrosum*.

Hylocomium loreum Br. eur., fasc. 49–52, p. 7, pl. 4.

From Alaska, sine loco (W. H Evans, in 1897); Yakutat Bay (Brewer and Coe, 648a; Trelease, 1956, 2009); Disenchantment Bay (Trelease, 1954, 2008), Muir Glacier (Coville and Kearney, 674); Point Gustavus (Coville and Kearney, 783); Orca (Setchell, 1202, Trelease, 2011); Farragut Bay (Trelease, 1994), New Metlakatla (Trelease, 1993); Head of Russell Fiord (Coville and Kearney, 947 957a); Sitka (Setchell, 1261; Trelease, 2001, 2006· W. G. Wright, 1606, J. M. Macoun), Hot Springs (Trelease, 2004); Kodiak (L J. Cole); Wood Island (Brewer and Coe, 661).

Hylocomium triquetrum Br. eur., fasc. 49–52, p. 8, pl. 5.

From Skagway (Canby, 425), Disenchantment Bay (Trelease, 1915), Farragut Bay (Coville and Kearney, 467); Point Gustavus (Coville and Kearney, 789); Tongas Village (Brewer and Coe, 703), Kodiak (Trelease, 1920 in part, 1921, 1933); Sitka (Trelease, 1913;

Canby, 427, 448); Hall Island (Trelease, 1989), St. Paul Island (U. S. S. *Albatross* Exped.).

Hylocomium triquetrum beringianum var. nov.

Colore lutescente foliisque erecto-imbricatis, subhomomallis, minus papillosis distinctum

From Hall Island (Trelease, 1989 in part; Coville and Kearney, 2059).

Hylocomium rugosum De Not. Epil., 99.

From Skagway (Canby, 483 in part).

POSTSCRIPT.

NOTE 1.—Since the completion of this paper for the press, in March, 1901, a very important catalogue of the bryophytes of the Yukon, comprising 24 hepatics, 7 sphagna, and 222 mosses, has been published by Mr. R. S Williams, in the *Bulletin of the New York Botanical Garden*. Mr. Williams's list includes a large number of mosses that are here indicated as new to Alaska. The following species, however, to the number of fifty, are not found in Mr. Williams's list:

Rhabdoweisia fugax,
Aongstroemia longipes,
Dicranella grevilleana,
Dicranum anderssonii,
Hypnum callichroum,
H. dieckii,
H. subeugyrium,
D. starkei,
D. albicans,
D. groenlandicum,
D. neglectum,
D. howellii,
Dicranodontium longirostre,
D. aristatum,
Ditrichum homallum,
Barbula aciphylla,
Grimmia maritima,
G. elatior forma?,
Amphoridium mougeotii,
Orthotrichum arcticum,
Tayloria tenuis,
Splachnum luteum,
Philonotis macounii,
P. capillaris,
Meesea tschuctschica,

Webera annotina,
Bryum bimum,
B. pallens,
Mnium insigne,
M. nudum,
Aulacomnium androgynum,
Oligotrichum integrifolium,
Fontinalis patula,
Pterygophyllum lucens?,
Orthothecium intricatum,
Pseudoleskea atrovirens,
P. stenophylla,
Brachythecium novæ-angliæ,
B. asperrimum,
B. plumosum,
Eurhynchium stokesii,
E. oreganum,
Rhynchostegium serrulatum,
Plagiothecium sylvaticum,
P. roeseanum,
P. muehlenbeckii,
P. elegans,
Amblystegium serpens,
A. varium,
Hylocomium umbratum.

Of the species and varieties here described as new only one, *Hypnum plesiostramineum*, may possibly be identical with one of Mr. Williams's new species, *H. amblyphyllum*.

It should also be added that Mr. Williams's list contains 115 species not found in our list, so that at present the total number of mosses unquestionably shown to be Alaskan or of the Bering Sea islands is about 350.

NOTE 2 (p. 326).—In a recent paper in the Journal of Botany, vol. 39, pp. 339-341, Mr. E. S. Salmon points out that *Bartramiopsis lescurii* has the same leaf structure as *Lyellia crispa*, and he suggests placing it in this genus. But *Bartramiopsis* differs from *Lyellia* by its small, erect, symmetrical, not angular and macrostomate capsule, and it seems preferable to keep it as a distinct genus.

NOTE 3 (p. 343).—A preliminary diagnosis of this moss has been published by Mr. Renauld in Bryologist, IV, p. 65. It is perhaps the same species as *H. amblyphyllum* Williams, in Bull. N. Y. Bot. Garden, II, p. 139.

June, 1902.

PLATE XXX.

[Proc. Wash. Acad Sci., Vol. IV, Pl. XIII.]

NOTE.—Nachet's objectives 1, 3 and 5, oculars 1 and 2, with camera lucida. All drawings are reduced ¼ in photo-engraving. The magnification figures here printed are true for the drawings *as printed*.

FIGS. 1, a–i. *Cynodontium treleasei*.
   1, a. Entire plant, natural size.
   1, b. Leaf ($\times 34$).
   1, c. Apex of the leaf ($\times 135$).
   1, d. Perichætial leaf ($\times 34$).
   1, e. Capsule ($\times 13$).
   1, f. Lid ($\times 30$).
   1, g. Basal areolation of the leaf ($\times 135$).
   1, h. Marginal areolation in the middle ($\times 270$).
   1, i. Areolation in the upper part ($\times 270$).

2, a–b. *Dichodontium pellucidum kodiakanum*.
   2, a. Leaves ($\times 13$).
   2, b. Apex of the leaf ($\times 60$)

3, a–f. *Dicranum subflagellare*.
   3, a. Entire plant, natural size.
   3, b. Leaf ($\times 26$).
   3, c. Apex of the same ($\times 135$).
   3, d. Basal areolation ($\times 135$).
   3, e. Areolation in the middle of a leaf ($\times 270$).
   3, f. Areolation in the upper part ($\times 270$).

4, a–e. *Trichostomum cuspidatissimum*.
   4, a. Entire plant, natural size.
   4, b, b. Leaves ($\times 35$).
   4, c. Basal areolation ($\times 135$).
   4, d. Areolation in the middle of a leaf ($\times 135$).
   4, e. Areolation of the upper part ($\times 135$).

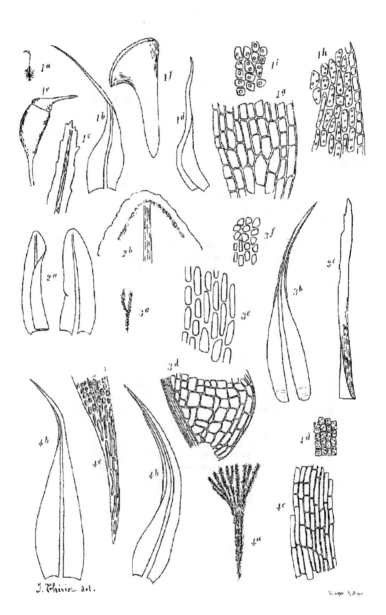

ALASKA MOSSES

PLATE XXXI.

[Proc. Wash Acad. Sci., Vol. IV, Pl. XIV.]

FIGS	1, a–e.	*Trichostomum sitkanum.*
	1, a.	Entire plant, natural size.
	1, b, b.	Leaves (× 13).
	1, c.	Basal areolation of a leaf (× 135).
	1, d.	Areolation in the middle (× 135).
	1, e.	Areolation in the upper part (× 135).
	2, a–i.	*Pottia heimii beringiana.*
	2, a.	Entire plant, natural size.
	2, b, b, b, b.	Leaves (× 13).
	2, c.	Transverse section of a leaf (× 60).
	2, d.	Part of the same (× 135).
	2, e.	Basal areolation of the leaf (× 135).
	2, f.	Areolation in the middle (× 135).
	2, g.	Areolation of the apex (× 135).
	2, h.	Capsule in moist state (× 13).
	2, i.	Capsule ripe, in dry state (× 13).
	3, a–i.	*Barbula brachypoda.*
	3, a.	Entire plant, natural size.
	3, b, b, b.	Lower leaves (× 13).
	3, c, c.	Upper leaves (× 13).
	3, d, d.	Perichætial leaves (× 13).
	3, e.	Basal areolation of the leaf (× 135).
	3, f.	Areolation in the middle (× 135).
	3, g.	Areolation of the upper part (× 135).
	3, h.	Capsule in moist state (× 13).
	3, i.	Portion of the annulus (× 60).

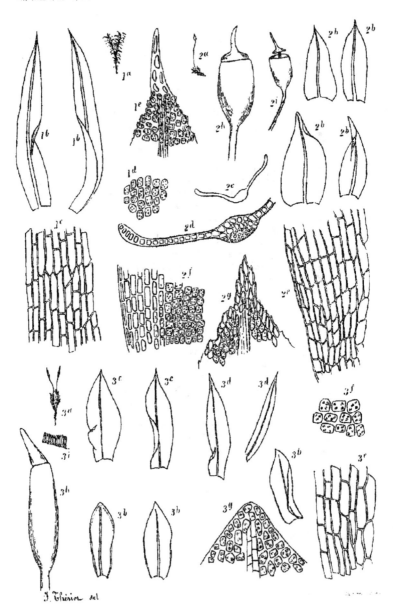

PLATE XXXII.

[Proc. Wash Acad Sci, Vol IV, Pl. XV]

FIGS 1, a–g	*Barbula rigens*	
1, a	Entire plant, natural size	
1, b, b.	Leaves ($\times 26$)	
1, c.	Apex of a leaf ($\times 135$).	
1, d.	Basal areolation ($\times 135$).	
1, e.	Cells in the middle of a leaf ($\times 135$).	
1, f.	Transverse section of the leaf in the lower part ($\times 135$).	
1, g.	Transverse section of the leaf in the upper part ($\times 180$)	
2, a–g	*Barbula treleasei.*	
2, a	Entire plant, natural size.	
2, b	Leaf ($\times 26$).	
2, c	Perichætial leaf ($\times 26$)	
2, d.	Apex of the stem leaf ($\times 60$)	
2, e.	Basal areolation of same ($\times 135$)	
2, f	Cells in middle of same ($\times 135$).	
2, g	Old capsule in dry state ($\times 13$).	
3, a–h	*Rhacomitrium cyclodictyon*	
3, a	Entire plant, natural size.	
3, b, b.	Leaves ($\times 26$).	
3, c.	Perichætial leaf ($\times 26$)	
3, d	Transverse section of a stem leaf ($\times 100$).	
3, e.	Basal areolation of same ($\times 270$)	
3, f.	Areolation in the middle ($\times 270$).	
3, g	Areolation of the apex ($\times 135$).	
3, h	Old capsule in moist state ($\times 13$).	
4, a–g.	*Ulota alaskana.*	
4, a	Entire plant, natural size.	
4, b, b, b	Leaves ($\times 13$).	
4, c	Marginal areolation in the lower part ($\times 135$).	
4, d	Capsule and calyptra ($\times 13$)	
4, e	Capsule and lid ($\times 13$)	
4, f.	Capsule ripe, in dry state ($\times 13$)	
4, g.	Same, in moist state ($\times 13$)	

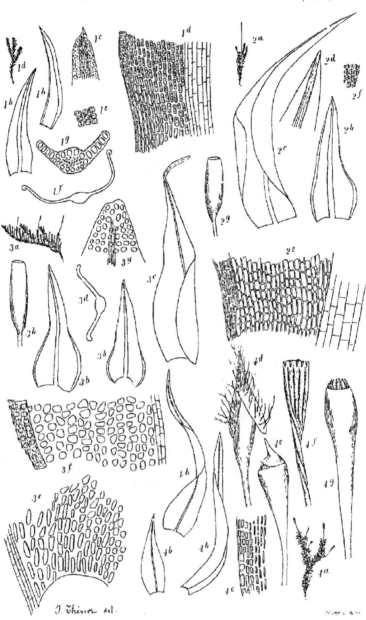

PLATE XXXIII.

[Proc. Wash. Acad Sci., Vol. IV, Pl. XVI.]

FIGS. 1, *a–i.* *Barbula saundersii.*
   1, *a.*   Entire plant, natural size.
   1, *b.*   Leaf ($\times 26$).
   1, *c.*   Apex of the same ($\times 60$).
   1, *d.*   Part of a transverse section of the same ($\times 100$).
   1, *e.*   Perichætial leaf ($\times 26$).
   1, *f.*   Basal areolation of a stem-leaf ($\times 135$).
   1, *g.*   Cells in the middle of the same ($\times 270$).
   1, *h.*   Capsule and lid ($\times 13$).
   1, *i.*   Capsule and peristome ($\times 13$).
   2, *a–n.* *Orthotrichum fenestratum.*
   2, *a.*   Entire plant, natural size.
   2, *b, b, b* Leaves ($\times 13$).
   2, *c.*   Transverse section of a leaf ($\times 60$).
   2, *d.*   Transverse section of the costa ($\times 270$).
   2, *e.*   Basal areolation of a leaf ($\times 135$).
   2, *f.*   Areolation in the middle ($\times 135$).
   2, *g.*   Areolation of the apex ($\times 135$).
   2, *h.*   Capsule and lid ($\times 13$).
   2, *i.*   Calyptra ($\times 13$).
   2, *j.*   Capsule, deoperculate, in moist state ($\times 13$).
   2, *k.*   The same split lengthwise ($\times 13$).
   2, *l.*   A stomate ($\times 135$).
   2, *m.*   A tooth of the peristome ($\times 135$).
   2, *n.*   Upper part of the same ($\times 270$).

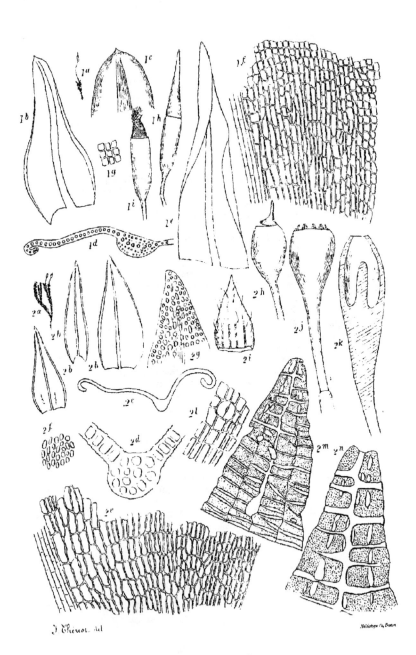

ALASKA MOSSES

PLATE XXXIV.

[Proc. Wash. Acad. Sci., Vol IV, Pl XVII.]

FIGS. 1, a–i.	*Entosthodon spathulifolius.*
1, a.	Entire plant, natural size
1, b, b, b, b	Leaves ($\times$ 13)
1, c.	Basal areolation of a leaf ($\times$ 135).
1, d	Areolation in the lower part ($\times$ 135).
1, e.	Areolation in the upper part ($\times$ 135)
1, f.	Areolation of the apex ($\times$ 135).
1, g	Capsule and calyptra ($\times$ 13)
1, h	Calyptra ($\times$ 13).
1, i	Capsule, unripe ($\times$ 13).
2, a–g.	*Webera pseudo-gracilis*
2, a	Female plant, natural size.
2, b.	Male plant, natural size
2, c, c	Lower leaves ($\times$ 26)
2, d, d	Upper leaves ($\times$ 26)
2, e	Basal areolation of a leaf ($\times$ 270).
2, f.	Areolation of the apex ($\times$ 270)
2, g	Capsule unripe ($\times$ 13).
3, a–f	*Bryum mucronigerum*
3, a	Entire plant, natural size
3, b, b	Leaves ($\times$ 13).
3, c	Basal areolation of a leaf ($\times$ 135).
3, d	Areolation in the middle ($\times$ 135).
3, e	Areolation of the apex ($\times$ 135)
3, f	Capsule unripe ($\times$ 13).

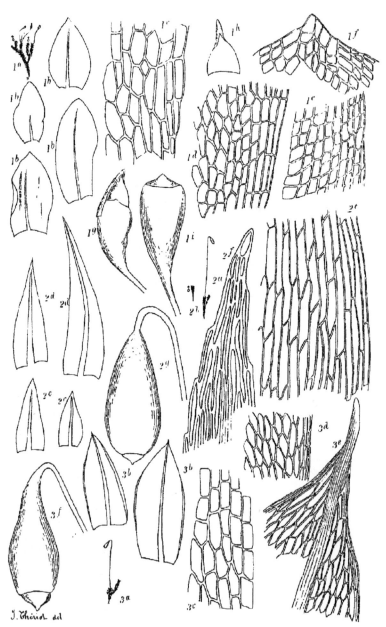

ALASKA MOSSES

PLATE XXXV.

[Proc. Wash. Acad. Sci., Vol. IV, Pl. XVIII.]

FIGS. 1, a–h.	*Bryum drepanocarpum.*
1, a.	Entire plant, natural size.
1, b, b.	Leaves ($\times 13$)
1, c.	Transverse section of a leaf ($\times 60$).
1, d.	Part of the same ($\times 135$).
1, e.	Marginal areolation in the middle of a leaf ($\times 135$).
1, f.	Areolation of the apex ($\times 135$).
1, g.	Young capsule ($\times 13$).
1, h.	Capsule ripe, in dry state ($\times 13$).
2, a–g.	*Bryum cylindrico-arcuatum.*
2, a.	Entire plant, natural size.
2, b, b.	Leaves ($\times 13$).
2, c.	Transverse section of a leaf ($\times 60$).
2, d.	Basal areolation ($\times 135$).
2, e.	Cells in the middle of a leaf ($\times 135$).
2, f.	Areolation of the apex ($\times 135$).
2, g.	Capsule in dry state ($\times 13$).
3, a–f.	*Bryum leptodictyon*
3, a	Entire plant, natural size.
3, b, b.	Leaves ($\times 13$).
3, c.	Basal areolation ($\times 135$).
3, d.	Cells in the middle of a leaf ($\times 135$).
3, e.	Areolation of the apex ($\times 135$).
3, f.	Capsule in moist state ($\times 13$).
4, a–g.	*Bryum pseudo-stirtoni*
4, a.	Entire plant, natural size.
4, b.	Stem-leaf ($\times 13$).
4, c, c, c.	Branch-leaves ($\times 13$).
4, d.	Basal areolation ($\times 135$).
4, e.	Cells in the middle of a leaf ($\times 135$).
4, f.	Capsule ripe, in moist state ($\times 13$).
4, g.	Capsule in dry state ($\times 13$).

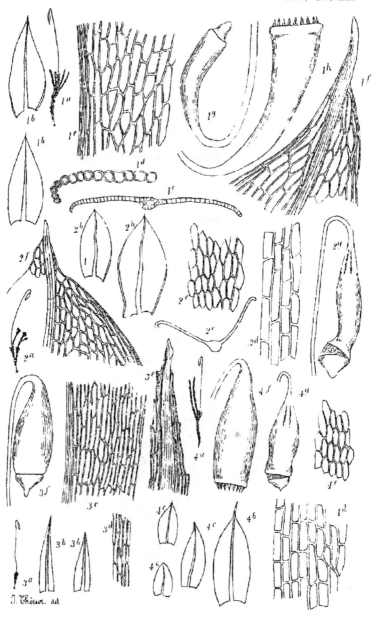

ALASKA MOSSES

PLATE XXXVI.

[Proc. Wash Acad Sci., Vol. IV, Pl XIX]

FIGS. 1, a–f. *Bryum atcleostomum*.
    1, a. Entire plant, natural size.
    1, b, b Leaves ($\times$ 13)
    1, c. Apex of a leaf ($\times$ 60).
    1, d Basal areolation of the same ($\times$ 135).
    1, e. Marginal areolation, in the middle ($\times$ 135).
    1, f Capsule ripe, in dry state ($\times$ 13).

2, a–g *Bryum heterogynum*
    2, a. Female plant, natural size
    2, b. Male plant, natural size
    2, c Leaf of the female plant ($\times$ 13).
    2, d. Apex of the same ($\times$ 60)
    2, e. Basal areolation ($\times$ 135).
    2, f Cells in the middle ($\times$ 135).
    2, g Young capsule in dry state ($\times$ 13).

3, a–g *Bryum laurentianum*
    3, a Entire plant, natural size.
    3, b, b Stem leaves ($\times$ 26).
    3, b'. Branch-leaf ($\times$ 26).
    3, c. Transverse section of a leaf ($\times$ 60).
    3, d Transverse section of the costa ($\times$ 270).
    3, e Basal areolation ($\times$ 135)
    3, f. Marginal areolation in the middle ($\times$ 135).
    3, g. Areolation of the apex ($\times$ 135).

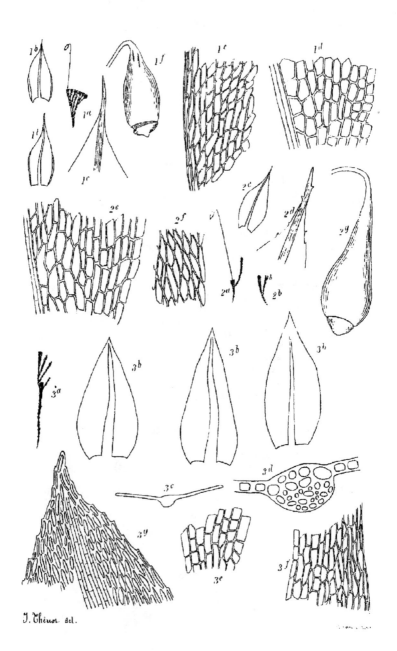

ALASKA MOSSES

PLATE XXXVII.

[Proc. Wash. Acad. Sci., Vol. IV, Pl. XX.]

FIGS. 1, a-g. *Bryum treleasei*
    1, a.   Entire plant, natural size.
    1, b, b   Leaves ($\times 13$)
    1, c, c.   Transverse section of a leaf ($\times 135$).
    1, d.   Basal areolation of the same ($\times 135$).
    1, e.   Marginal areolation in the lower part ($\times 135$).
    1, f.   Areolation of the apex ($\times 135$).
    1, g.   Young capsule, in moist state ($\times 13$).
    2, a-h   *Bryum aguttuense*
    2, a.   Entire plant, natural size.
    2, b, b.   Stem-leaves ($\times 13$).
    2, c.   Branch-leaf ($\times 13$).
    2, d.   Basal areolation ($\times 135$).
    2, e.   Areolation in the middle ($\times 135$).
    2, f.   Areolation of the apex ($\times 135$).
    2, g.   Capsule unripe, in dry state ($\times 13$).
    2, h.   Capsule ripe, in moist state ($\times 13$).

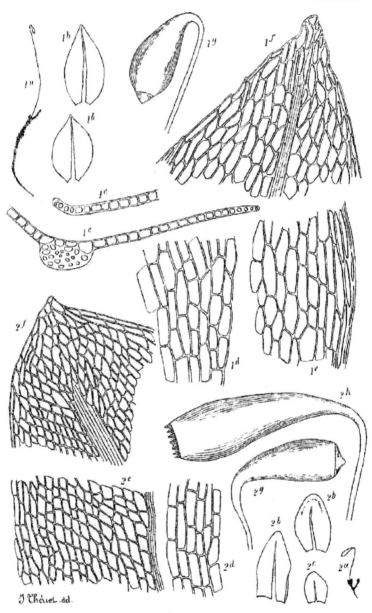

PLATE XXXVIII.

FIGS. 1, *a–g*   *Bryum harrimani*
  1, *a*   Entire plant, natural size
  1, *b, b*   Lower leaves ($\times 13$).
  1, *c, c*   Upper leaves ($\times 13$)
  1, *d*   Basal areolation ($\times 135$).
  1, *e*   Marginal areolation, in the middle ($\times 135$).
  1, *f*   Apex of a lower leaf ($\times 135$).
  1, *g*   Apex of an upper leaf ($\times 135$)
2, *a–l*   *Bartramiopsis lescurii*
  2, *a, a*   Entire plant, natural size, in dry state
  2, *b*   The same, in moist state.
  2, *c, c*   Lower leaves ($\times 13$).
  2, *d, d*   Upper leaves ($\times 13$).
  2, *e*   Cilium of a leaf ($\times 135$)
  2, *f*   Apex of a leaf, seen on the ventral side ($\times 60$).
  2, *g*   Transverse section of a leaf ($\times 135$)
  2, *h*   Basal areolation ($\times 135$)
  2, *i*   Cells in the lower part of the leaf ($\times 270$).
  2, *j*   Capsule and lid ($\times 13$).
  2, *k*   Capsule ripe, in dry state ($\times 13$).
  2, *l*   Calyptra ($\times 13$)

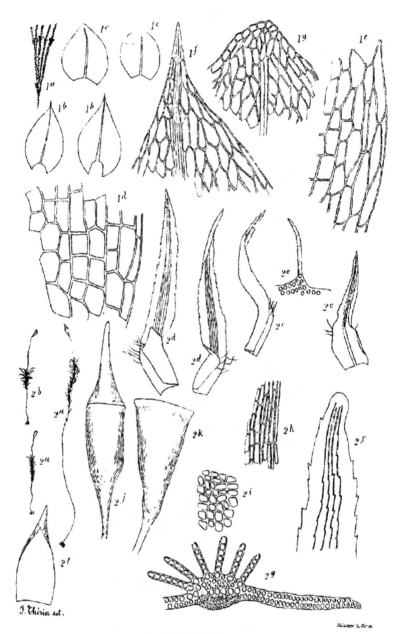

ALASKA MOSSES

PLATE XXXIX.

Figs 1 *a–f.* *Polytrichum yukonense*.
   1, *a*   Entire plant, natural size
   1, *b, b* Leaves ($\times 13$)
   1, *c*   Transverse section of a leaf ($\times 34$).
   1, *d*.   Transverse section of a lamella ($\times 135$).
   1, *e*.   Part of a lamella seen from side ($\times 270$).
   1, *f*.   Basal areolation of the leaf ($\times 135$).
   2, *a*   *Polytrichum jensenii*
   2, *a*   Basal areolation of the leaf ($\times 135$).
   3, *a–e* *Brachythecium beringianum*
   3, *a*.   Entire plant, natural size.
   3, *b*   Stem leaf ($\times 26$)
   3, *c, c*. Branch-leaves ($\times 26$).
   3, *d*.   Basal areolation ($\times 135$).
   3 *e*   Cells in the middle ($\times 270$).
   4, *a–e* *Plagiothecium fallax*
   4, *a*.   Entire plant, natural size
   4, *b*.   Leaf ($\times 13$)
   4, *c*   Perigonial leaf ($\times 26$)
   4, *d*.   Basal areolation of a leaf ($\times 135$)
   4, *e*.   Areolation in the middle ($\times 135$).
   5, *a–e* *Hypnum treleasei*.
   5, *a*   Entire plant, natural size.
   5, *b, b, b* Leaves ($\times 26$)
   5, *d*.   Basal areolation of a leaf ($\times 270$).
   5, *e*.   Cells in the middle ($\times 270$).

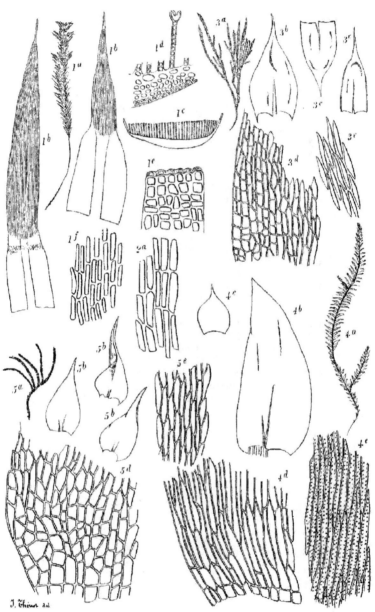

ALASKA MOSSES

PLATE XL.

[Proc. Wash. Acad. Sci., Vol. IV, Pl. XXIII.]

FIGS 1, *a–d.* *Hypnum pseudostramineum.*
- 1, *a, a* Leaves (×18)
- 1, *b* Lower part of the costa (×130).
- 1, *c* Areolation in the middle of a leaf (×225).
- 1, *d* Areolation of the apex of a leaf (×225).

2, *a–h* *Hypnum plesiostramineum.*
- 2, *a* Entire plant, natural size.
- 2, *b, b* Lower leaves (×18)
- 2, *c* Lower part of the costa (×130)
- 2, *d* Upper leaf (×18)
- 2, *e* Branch leaf (×18)
- 2, *f.* Auricle and basal areolation of a leaf (×225).
- 2, *g.* Cells in the middle (×225)
- 2, *h.* Areolation of the apex (×225).

3, *a–e* *Meesea tschuctschica.*
- 3, *a.* Entire plant, natural size.
- 3, *b* Part of a stem (×3)
- 3, *c, c* Leaves (×13).
- 3, *d* Marginal areolation in the middle (×135).
- 3, *e* Areolation of the apex (×135).

4, *a–c* *Brachythecium reflexum pacificum.*
- 4, *a* Stem-leaf (×13).
- 4, *b.* Basal areolation (×135).
- 4, *c.* Marginal areolation in the middle (×135)

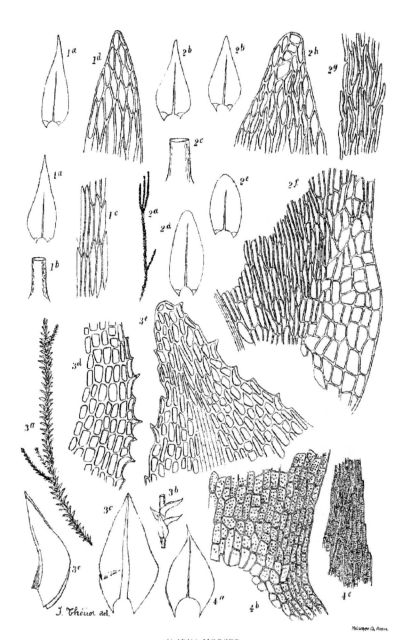

ALASKA MOSSES

ALASKAN SPECIES OF SPHAGNUM

BY WILLIAM TRELEASE

SINCE much of the Alaskan coast region is very humid, with frequent rainfall or mist, while in the north an almost continuous tundra exists, saturated with moisture when not frozen, the peat mosses or *Sphagna* are everywhere very abundantly represented in individuals, and, considering the genus as a whole, in species or the varieties into which specialists have divided what they regard as species. So far as I have been able to consult the publications referring to this region, eleven species and five additional varieties, not counting the forms of the latter that are sometimes distinguished, have thus far been reported as Alaskan. These, and the localities where they are said to occur, when the latter are more than 'Alaska,' have been incorporated in the following catalogue, the references being made clear by an appended list of the publications referred to.

Several members of the Harriman Expedition paid special attention to this obscure group of plants in collecting, and, though few of the specimens could be found in fruit, a large number were brought back. These, together with such other Alaskan material as could be found in the herbaria of the Missouri Botanical Garden and the United States National Museum, and a few specimens collected along Prince William Sound by Professor Setchell, were submitted to Dr. C. Warnstorf, the recognized authority on the group, whose determinations have been merely tabulated by the writer with reference to the geographical distribution of the species Dr. Warnstorf has further contributed two or three localities represented in his herbarium by specimens recently collected in the Yukon region by Mr. R. S. Williams.

The present list includes 22 species and 19 additional varieties, exclusive of minor forms of the latter, thus about doubling the number of species known to me as Alaskan, or trebling the number of distinguished forms. Of the forms listed, one only, *S. recurvum*, which may really refer to the listed variety of that species, rests solely upon published report. Two species, *S. ångstroemii* and *S. balticum*, are here for the first time recorded as American.

ALPHABETICAL CATALOGUE.

Sphagnum acutifolium (Ehrh.) Russ. & Warnst.
HOOKER & ARNOTT, 133.—ROTHROCK, 460.—TURNER, 82.

Sitka; Kotzebue Sound.

Dr. Warnstorf refers one specimen only to the typical form of the species (McGrath, June 3, 1890, without locality further than 'Alaska'). The localities cited on authority may pertain to one or other of the recognized varieties, rather than to the type.

Sphagnum acutifolium pallescens Warnst.

Sitka (Trelease, 1573).

Sphagnum acutifolium rubrum (Brid.) Warnst.
J. MACOUN, 253.

Sitka (Coville & Kearney, 895; Trelease, 1557); Hot Springs, Baranof Island (Trelease, 1556); Biorka Island (Brewer & Coe, 631); Orca (Coville & Kearney, 1342), Kadiak (Macoun, Sept. 22, 1891).

Sphagnum acutifolium versicolor Warnst.

Prince of Wales Island (Macoun, Sept. 30, 1891); Sitka (Coville & Kearney, 894; Trelease, 1567); Kadiak (Trelease, 1570); Virgin Bay (Trelease, 1558); Port Wells (Trelease, 1569).

Sphagnum ångstroemii Hartm.

Hall Island, Bering Sea (Trelease, 1621).
Not heretofore reported from America.

Sphagnum balticum Russ.

Port Wells (Trelease, 1584, 1614).
Not heretofore reported from America.

Sphagnum compactum imbricatum Warnst.

J. MACOUN, 255.

Wrangell (Trelease, 1551); Kadiak (Trelease, 1566); Attu Island; Nagai Island (Macoun, Sept 18, 1892).

Sphagnum cymbifolium (Ehrh.) Hedw.

J. MACOUN, 255.—ROTHROCK, 460 —TURNER, 82.

New Metlakatla (Trelease, 1604); Sitka (Coville & Kearney, 897); Unalaska (Macoun, July 25, 1891).

Sphagnum fimbriatum Wils.

J MACOUN, 251 —ROTHROCK, 460 —TURNER, 82.—WILSON, Bot. Herald, 44

Unalaska (Macoun, Aug. 18, 1891); Kotzebue Sound; St. George Island, Bering Sea (Townsend, distributed as Eaton & Faxon, NO. 16).

Sphagnum fimbriatum arcticum Jens.

J. MACOUN, 251 —J. M. MACOUN, 576 —MERRIAM, 149.
S. fimbriatum var. ROTHROCK, 460.—TURNER, 82.

Nagai Island (Macoun, Sept. 18, 1892); Norton Sound; Cape Vancouver; Port Clarence (Brewer & Coe, 673a; Cole, a; Coville & Kearney, 1881; Trelease, 1592, 1593, 1593b); Bering Sea St. George Island (Macoun, July 31, 1891); St. Paul Island (Macoun, Aug. 18, 1891); Hall Island (Trelease, 1596, 1621b, with *S. ångstroemii*); St. Matthew Island (Brewer & Coe, 685a, with *S. squarrosum;* Coville & Kearney, 2182; Trelease, 1562); St. Lawrence Island (Trelease, 1563, 1595).

A forma *fuscescens* is also reported, from the Pribilof Islands, by Merriam, *l. c.*

Sphagnum fuscum Klinggr.

New Metlakatla (Coville & Kearney, 351); Sitka (Trelease, 1559, 1568); Virgin Bay (Trelease, 1612); Kadiak (Macoun, Sept 22, 1891; Trelease, 1560, 1572); Kukak Bay (Saunders, 1561); Popof Island (Saunders, 1623); Yukon River (Williams, *fide* Warnstorf); Nagai Island (Macoun, Sept. 18, 1892); St. Lawrence Island, Bering Sea (Trelease, 1565).

Sphagnum fuscum pallescens Warnst.

J. MACOUN, 252.

Kukak Bay (Coville & Kearney, 1592); Kadiak.

Sphagnum fuscum robustum Warnst.

Wrangell (Coville & Kearney, 416).

Sphagnum girgensohnii Russ

J MACOUN, 251 — J M. MACOUN, 576

Farragut Bay (Brewer & Coe, 612; Coville & Kearney, 455; Trelease, 1598); Cape Fox (Cole, *b*; Coville & Kearney, 2579); New Metlakatla (Coville & Kearney, 367); Juncau (Brewer & Coe, 701); Sitka (Trelease, 1576); Hot Springs, Baranof Island (Trelease, 1574); Virgin Bay (Trelease, 1580, 1581, 1601); Port Wells (Trelease, 1583, 1613, 1615*a*); Orca (Coville & Kearney, 1205, 1206, 1207; Setchell, 1223, 1224, 1225; Trelease, 1585, 1586, 1600, 1610); Kadiak (Macoun, Sept. 22, 1891; Trelease, 1591*a*); Kukak Bay (Coville & Kearney, 1592*a*); Yukon River (Dall in 1867); Agattu Island (Townsend in 1894, distributed as Eaton & Faxon, no. 6, under the name var. *stachyodes*); Port Clarence (Trelease, 1593*a*, 1619); St. George Island, Bering Sea.

Also collected on Lowe Inlet, B. C. (Coville & Kearney, 349).

Sphagnum girgensohnii xerophilum Russ.

Port Wells (Coville & Kearney, 1298).

Sphagnum imbricatum cristatum Warnst.

J. MACOUN, 255

Sitka (Trelease, 1553); Virgin Bay (Coville & Kearney, 1257); Kadiak (Trelease, 1564); Attu Island (Macoun, Aug. 29, 1891)

Noted by Dr. Warnstorf as forma *fuscescens*.

Sphagnum lindbergii Schimp.

Wrangell (Trelease, 1599).

Sphagnum lindbergii immersum Limpr.

New Metlakatla (Trelease, 1602).

Sphagnum lindbergii microphyllum Warnst.

J M. MACOUN, 576 — MERRIAM, 149

Port Clarence (Brewer & Coe, 673*b*, with *S. fimbriatum arcticum*, Coville & Kearney, 1880); St. Paul Island, Bering Sea.

Noted by Dr. Warnstorf as forma *brachyclada*. The Merriam Pribilof Island reference is to forma *brachydasyclada*.

Sphagnum medium Limpr.

Prince of Wales Island (Macoun, Sept. 30, 1891); Sitka (Trelease, 1552); Port Etches (Macoun, June 18, 1892); Virgin Bay (Coville & Kearney, 1258); Attu Island (Macoun, Aug. 29, 1891).

Sphagnum medium pallescens Warnst.

Wrangell (Coville & Kearney, 411)

Sphagnum molluscum Bruch.

Virgin Bay (Coville & Kearney, 1257b, with *S. imbricatum cristatum*; Trelease, 1625).

Sphagnum papillosum normale Warnst.

Sitka (Trelease, 1554); Virgin Bay (Trelease, 1555); Nagai Island (Macoun, Sept 18, 1892)

Sphagnum parvifolium (Sendt.) Warnst.

Wrangell (Coville & Kearney, 418), Douglas Island (Trelease, 1624); Kadiak (Trelease, 1590).

Sphagnum recurvum (Beauv.) Russ. & Warnst.

J. MACOUN, 253

S. cuspidatum recurvum ROTHROCK, 460 — TURNER, 82.

Sitka; Kadiak

Perhaps referring to the next.

Sphagnum recurvum mucronatum (Russ.) Warnst.

New Metlakatla (Trelease, 1597, 1603), Wrangell (Coville & Kearney, 410, 417; Trelease, 1599a); Sitka (Coville & Kearney, 896; Trelease, 1578, 1579, 1608).

Also collected on Fraser Reach, B. C. (Coville & Kearney, 306).

Sphagnum riparium Ångstr.

J. MACOUN, 253 — J. M. MACOUN, 576 — MERRIAM, 149

Bering Sea. St. George Island; Hall Island (Trelease, 1621c, with *S. ångstroemii*); St. Matthew Island (Coville & Kearney, 2111).

Sphagnum rubellum Wils.

Virgin Bay (Coville & Kearney, 1257a, with *S. imbricatum cristatum*, Trelease, 1611a, with *S. subnitens*).

Sphagnum rubellum violascens Warnst.

Wrangell (Coville & Kearney, 415).

Sphagnum russowii Warnst.

Orca (Trelease, 1587); Port Wells (Trelease, 1582); Yes Bay (Gorman, 181[1]).

Sphagnum russowii rhodochroum Russ.

Sitka (Trelease, 1567a).

[1] Determined by M. Cardot.

Sphagnum squarrosum Pers.

KURTZ, 430.

Farragut Bay (Brewer & Coe, 612a, with *S girgensohnii*), Chilkat region; Douglas Island (Trelease, 1606); Sitka (Trelease, 1607); Yakutat (Trelease, 1609a); Kadiak (Coville & Kearney, 2340; Trelease, 1591, 1616, 1617); Nagai Island (Macoun, Sept. 18, 1892); Attu Island (Macoun, Aug. 29, 1891); Agattu Island (Townsend, 62), Bering Sea. Hall Island (Trelease, 1621a, with *S. ångstroemii*); St. Matthew Island (Brewer & Coe, 685).

Sphagnum squarrosum imbricatum Schimp.

J MACOUN, 254.—J M. MACOUN, 576.—MERRIAM, 149

Port Wells (Coville & Kearney, 1299; Trelease, 1615); Unalaska (Coville & Kearney, 1742), Atka Island, Cape Vancouver, Bering Sea: St. George Island (Macoun, July 16, 1891); Hall Island (Brewer & Coe. 677); St Matthew Island (Trelease, 1622).

The Merriam reference is to forma *brachyanoclada*.

Sphagnum squarrosum subsquarrosum Russ.

S squarrosum semisquarrosum COVILLE & FUNSTON, 350.—J MACOUN, 254 —J. M. MACOUN, 576.—MERRIAM, 149

Point Gustavus (Coville & Kearney, 759); Sitka (Trelease, 1575), Yakutat (Trelease, 1609); Khantaak Island; Cape Vancouver; Bering Sea: St. Paul Island; St. George Island; Hall Island (Coville & Kearney, 2057, 2058); St Lawrence Island (Trelease, 1620).

Also collected at Plover Bay, Siberia (Coville & Kearney, 1841; Trelease, 1618).

Sphagnum subnitens Russ. & Warnst.

Virgin Bay (Trelease, 1611); Orca (Trelease, 1610a).

Sphagnum subnitens pallescens Warnst.

Sitka (Trelease, 1577).

Sphagnum teres Ångstr.

J MACOUN, 254.—ROTHROCK, 460.—TURNER, 82.

Kadiak (Trelease, 1589, 1591b, with *S. squarrosum*); Kukak Bay (Saunders, 1594); Nulato; Attu Island.

Sphagnum teres subsquarrosum Warnst.

Kadiak (Trelease, 1588); Kukak Bay (Coville & Kearney, 1565).

Sphagnum warnstorfii Russ.

Popof Island (Saunders, 1623a, with *S. fuscum*).

Sphagnum warnstorfii purpurascens Russ.

Kadiak (Trelease, 1571); Lake Lindeman, Yukon River (Williams, *fide* Warnstorf).

Sphagnum warnstorfii violascens Warnst.

Port Etches (Macoun, June 18, 1892).

REFERENCES.

Coville and Funston.
 1896 Botany of Yakutat Bay. Contr. U. S. Nat. Herb. 3.

Hooker and Arnott.
 1841 Bot. Beechey. London.

Kurtz, F.
 1894 Flora des Chilcatgebietes. Bot. Jahrb. 19.

Macoun, J.
 1892 Catalogue of Canadian Plants. Part 6. Montreal.

Macoun, J. M.
 1899 List of the plants of the Pribilof Islands. Jordan, The Fur Seals and Fur-Seal Islands. Part 3. Washington.

Merriam, C. Hart.
 1892 Plants of the Pribilof Islands. Proc. Biol. Soc. Washington 7.

Rothrock, J. T.
 1872 Sketch of the Flora of Alaska. Smithsonian Rept. 1867. Washington. The mosses determined by T. P. James.

Turner, L. M.
 1886 Contributions to the Natural History of Alaska. Washington. The moss list based on Rothrock.

THE HEPATICÆ OF ALASKA

The following paper on the Liverworts (Hepaticæ) of Alaska, by Prof. Alexander W. Evans, of Yale University, was originally published in the Proceedings of the Washington Academy of Sciences, vol. II, pp. 287–314, Oct. 10, 1900. It is here reprinted from the same electrotype plates, so that it may be quoted exactly as if it were the original. The original pagination has been preserved and transferred to the inner or hinge side of the page, where it is enclosed in brackets, thus [288]; while the consecutive pagination of the present volume has been added in the usual place. In the plates the original numbers and running headline, slightly abbreviated, have been preserved [in brackets], while the volume designation and serial plate numbers have been added in the usual place. The original text references to the plates are unchanged. The present headpiece and title have been substituted for the running heading of the Academy's Proceedings and the original title, which was: *Papers from the Harriman Alaska Expedition V. Notes on the Hepaticæ collected in Alaska*. No other alterations have been made.

The author desires to record the following corrections:

Page 363 [309], ninth line from bottom, for 'Web & Mohr' read *Wahl*.

Pages 368–372 [314], explanation of plates, have been divided and corrected to face the plates to which they relate.

EDITOR.

HEPATICÆ OF ALASKA

BY ALEXANDER W. EVANS

OUR knowledge of the Hepaticæ occurring in Alaska, although doubtless still very incomplete, has been materially increased by the collections of the Harriman Expedition, the number of known species having been nearly doubled. The collections made by earlier visitors to the Territory were for the most part small and fragmentary, and it was upon these that our previous knowledge was based. Up to the close of 1899, forty-one species had been recorded as Alaskan; the determinations of several of these, however, must be looked upon with a certain degree of doubt. The first reference to Alaska Hepaticæ is found in the 'Synopsis Hepaticarum' of Gottsche, Lindenberg, and Nees von Esenbeck, published in 1844–47. In this volume, five species are quoted, the specimens mentioned (with one or two possible exceptions) being preserved in the herbarium of the Imperial Academy of Sciences at St. Petersburg. It is quite probable that certain of these plants would now be referred to different species. In 1867, Dr. J. T. Rothrock[1] pub-

[1] Sketch of the Flora of Alaska. Rept. Smithsonian Ins. for 1867: 462.

lished a list of six Alaska Hepaticæ. The specimens were apparently collected by himself, and the determinations were made by T P James. None of these species are given as Alaskan in the 'Synopsis,' but all are common northern forms with the exception of '*Fimbriaria tenella*,' to which one specimen is doubtfully referred. This determination is probably incorrect; but, as I am informed by Mr. W. R. Maxon, the specimen in question is no longer to be found among the collections of the Smithsonian Institution at Washington, so that the matter cannot be definitely settled. The next list to appear is that of Herr Stephani,[1] published in 1887. It is the longest yet given and includes twenty-two species collected by Drs Arthur and Aurel Krause in 1881–82. Of the plants mentioned in this list, only five had been previously recorded from Alaska, four are described as new, and several of the others are absent from all later collections.

Since the publication of Herr Stephani's enumeration, three very fragmentary lists by American authors have made their appearance. In the first[2] of these we find noted thirteen species, collected by Miss Grace E. Cooley, in southeastern Alaska and determined by Professor L. M. Underwood. Six of these species are here recorded for the first time. The second list[3] names three species from St. Paul Island, of the Pribilof group, collected by Dr. C. Hart Merriam and likewise determined by Professor Underwood. All of these species had been previously reported from Alaska. In the third list[4] are eight species collected by General Frederick Funston in the Yakutat Bay region and determined by the present writer. All except two of these were already known from the Territory. In addition to these three lists, which are parts of longer reports dealing pri-

[1] Hepaticæ von der Halbinsel Alaska Engler's Bot Jahrb. 8. 96–99. *pl. 3 figs 9–11* 1887

[2] Cooley, G E., Plants collected in Alaska and Nanaimo, B C., July and August, 1891 Bull Torr Bot Club, 19: 246, 247. 1892

[3] Merriam, C Hart, Plants of the Pribilof Islands, Bering Sea Proc Biol Soc. Wash 7 150 1892 The same 3 Hepaticæ are included by J M Macoun in his List of the Plants of the Pribilof Islands, Bering Sea, published in Jordan's Report on the Fur-Seals and Fur-Seal Islands of the North Pacific, 3: 587 1899

[4] Coville, F V., Botany of Yakutat Bay. Botanical Report. Contr. U S. Nat Herb 3 351 1895.

marily with Alaskan plants, the Hepaticæ of the region in question are included by Mr. W. H. Pearson in his 'List of Canadian Hepaticæ'[1] and by Professor Underwood in his 'Preliminary List of the Pacific Coast Hepaticæ.'[2] Attention is also called to several interesting species, including four not elsewhere recorded, by Dr. Marshall A. Howe[3] in two of his recent publications.

The brief survey just given considers those collections only of which published records have appeared. From time to time occasional specimens have been brought home by other visitors to the Territory, among whom Mr. C. H. Townsend, Mr. J. M. Macoun, and Mr. Thomas Howell should especially be mentioned. It is quite possible that some of the species reported in the present paper as new to Alaska may occur among their collections.

The hepatic flora of northern Alaska is essentially like that of other northern regions. A few of its species are known from Europe and America only, a still smaller number from Asia and America only, but the vast majority occur in a northern belt extending wholly around the earth. As we proceed southward, a few species characteristic of the Pacific Coast region of North America make their appearance and mingle with the more northern types. These include *Ptilidium californicum, Porella navicularis, Radula bolanderi, Frullania nisquallensis,* and *Frullania franciscana.* The number of endemic species is extremely small, and at present not one of them can be quoted with any degree of certainty. Of the species proposed as new by Herr Stephani, *Scapania albescens* is reduced to a synonym of *Scapania bolanderi* by Mr. Pearson, doubt is thrown upon the two species of *Radula* by Dr. Howe, while the fourth species, *Frullania chilcooticnsis,* is too incompletely known to be regarded as thoroughly established. As Dr. Howe has recently pointed out, *Lepidozia filamentosa* is

[1] Published in Montreal, 1890

[2] Zoe, 1: 361–367 1891. Two species are here noted as Alaskan for the first time.

[3] The North American Species of Porella. Bull. Torr. Bot. Club, 24: 512–527. 1897 The Hepaticæ and Anthocerotes of California. Mem. Torr. Bot. Club, 7: 1899.

now known with certainty from Alaska only, but it has been reported from Japan and from antarctic America, and it is extremely probable that its range extends into British America.

The Hepaticæ brought back by the members of the Harriman Expedition, which are in condition to be identified, number 63 species, of which 38 are here recorded from Alaska for the first time. Adding to these the 42 species previously known from the Territory, gives a total of 80 species. In addition to these there have been recently sent me specimens of *Nardia compressa*, collected on Atka Island by J. M. Macoun in 1891, and specimens of *Grimaldia fragrans*, collected in the Yukon River district by Funston in 1894. Both of these are new to Alaska and increase the number of known species to 82. Of these 82 species, 7 (or about 9%) are Marchantiaceæ, 8 (or about 10%) are Metzgeriaceæ, and 67 (or about 81%) are Jungermanniaceæ. No representatives of the Ricciaceæ or of the Anthocerotaceæ are as yet definitely known from the Territory.

In the following list the principal collectors are indicated by initials only. 'T.' referring to Dr. William Trelease, 'B. & C.' to Professor W. H. Brewer and Dr. W. R. Coe, and 'C. & K.' to Messrs. F. V. Coville and T. H. Kearney, Jr. The other collectors are named in full. A few specimens collected by Professor W. A. Setchell in 1899 are also included in the list, although he was not a member of the Harriman party.

MARCHANTIACEÆ.

1. **Conocephalum conicum** (L.) Dumort.

Sitka (T 1405); Juneau (B & C 694, in part, T 1403); Orca (C. & K. 1204, T. 1404, in great part); Disenchantment Bay (B. & C 636); Yakutat Bay (Saunders 1406); Farragut Bay (T. 1402). The species has also been collected in Alaska by Rothrock at Sitka and Iktigalik, by Miss Cooley at Salmon Creek, near Juneau, and by the Drs. Krause. It was also brought from Agattu Island by the Fish Commission in 1894.

2. **Preissia quadrata** (Scop.) Nees.

Juneau (Setchell 1241); Wrangell (C. & K. 408); Muir Glacier (T. 1410); Point Gustavus (Saunders 1411); Hooniah Village (C.

& K. 666), Port Wells (T. 1428). Also collected by the Drs. Krause, by Miss Cooley near Juneau, and by Funston at Coal Creek Hill, Yukon River district.

3. **Marchantia polymorpha** L.

Glacier Bay (T. 1409, C. & K. 757), Orca (T. 1408); St. Paul Island (T. 1413), St. Matthew Island (T. 1401); Hall Island (T. 1414). This cosmopolitan species has also been collected by Rothrock, by Bischoff, by the Drs. Krause, and by Miss Cooley.

Only 3 Marchantiaceæ occur in the collections. Of the other 4 species, already reported from Alaska, 2—the doubtful *Fimbriaria tenella* and *Grimaldia fragrans* (Balb.) Corda—have already been mentioned. The other 2 species are noted by Dr. Howe one of these is *Asterella fragrans* (Schleich.) Trevis.,[1] which is ascribed simply to Alaska; the other is a species of *Sauteria*, probably *S. alpina* (Nees & Bischoff) Nees,[2] which was collected by Mr. Kincaid on St. Paul Island in 1897.

METZGERIACEÆ.

4. **Aneura latifrons** Lindb.

Mt. Verstovia (C. & K. 927, in part); Fairagut Bay (C. & K. 454, in part, B. & C. 618, in part). New to Alaska.

5. **Pallavicinia hibernica** (Hook.) S. F. Gray, Nat. Ar. Brit. Pl. 2 684. 1821.[3]

Jungermannia hibernica HOOK. Brit. Jung. *pl. 78*. 1816.
Dilæna hibernica DUMORT. Comm. bot. 114. 1822.
Mærckia hibernica GOTTSCHE; Rabenhorst, Hep. eur. exsic. *no. 121*. 1860 (in obs. *Blyttia lyellii*).

Dioicous ♂ and ♀ plants mixed together, green: thallus prostrate, often creeping among other bryophytes, dichotomous, of about the same width throughout; midrib 15–20 cells thick in the middle on robust plants, strongly convex below, slightly concave above, narrowing rather abruptly on each side into a broad, translucent wing a single cell thick; margins of the wings more or less crispate-undulate; cells of the thallus everywhere with thin and colorless walls except in the postical part of the midrib, where they are slightly thicker and brownish: rhizoids numerous, white: archegonia in groups of 10 to 20 on the upper surface of the thallus near the apex, surrounded

[1] Mem. Torr. Bot. Club, 7 39. 1899.
[2] L. c., 56.
[3] A fuller synonymy is given by Lindberg, Not. ur Sallsk. pro F. et Fl. Fenn. 9 15. 1868.

by very irregular, more or less laciniate scales, connate with each other and with the base of the pseudoperianth; laciniæ of the scales variously dentate or ciliate; pseudoperianth cylindrical or obovate, mouth slightly contracted, irregularly lobed and finely denticulate from projecting cells; calyptra about half as long as pseudoperianth: ♂ scales sometimes distant and arranged in two distinct rows, one along each side of the midrib, sometimes more imbricated and less definitely arranged, variously connate with each other or free, margins irregularly lobed and toothed with sharp and often ciliate divisions; antheridia 1 to 3 in each axil, borne on short stalks; paraphyses few; capsule oval, on a long stalk, brown, valves several cells thick in the middle; spores brownish or greenish, the wall with fine, irregularly curved and angular ridge-like thickenings, scarcely forming a network; elaters rather broad in the middle tapering to each end, spiral bands 1 or 2, broad, brownish.

Thallus 3–3.5 mm. broad, wings 0.7–1 mm. broad on each side of midrib, cells of wing 24 μ in diameter, pseudoperianth 3–4 mm. long, 1–1.3 mm. in diameter, ♀ scales about 1.2 mm. long, antheridia 0.25 mm. in diameter, capsule 1.2 × 0.6 mm., spores 25 μ in diameter, elaters 0.1–0.2 mm. long, 12 μ wide in broadest part.

Yakutat (C. & K. 1145). New to Alaska.

Pallavicinia hibernica has already been recorded from British Columbia[1] and has a wide distribution in Europe. The Alaskan material includes both male and female specimens. The female plants are old and the pseudoperianths are mostly withered, but a few of them show the characteristic capsules. The male plants are robust and in excellent condition and show several indistinct rows of crowded antheridial scales on the upper surface of the midrib. According to Limpricht[2] and some of the older European writers, these scales should alternate with each other and be arranged in two longitudinal rows. Among the European material studied, the only male plants which I have been able to examine were collected in Ireland by Moore and distributed by Rabenhorst in Hep. eur. exsic. no. 295. These have old and empty antheridial scales, almost as crowded as in the Alaskan specimens, and certainly arranged in more than two ranks, and this irregularity of arrangement is also described by Leitgeb.[3] The scales in the Irish plant are a little more toothed than in the Alaskan, but the specimens agree so perfectly in all other respects that I have no hesitation in pronouncing them the same.

[1] Cf. Underwood, Zoe, 1: 365. 1891.
[2] Cohn, Kryptogamenfl. von Schlesien, 1: 326. 1876.
[3] Unters. uber die Leberm. 3: 87. 1877.

Pallavicinia hibernica differs from *P. lyellii*, which is rather common in eastern America, in having in the midrib no central strand composed of elongated thick-walled cells. This difference places it in the subgenus *Mœrckia*, which is regarded as a distinct genus by several European writers. Its closest ally is *P. blyttii* (Mörck) Lindb., a widely distributed European species, which may be expected also in northern America. *P. hibernica* differs from this species in its smaller size, in its white and not yellow rhizoids, in the comparatively broader unistratose wings of its thallus, in the sharper points on the divisions of its ♂ and ♀ scales, and in its spores, which are not tuberculate-spinose.

6. **Pellia endiviæfolia** (Dicks.) Dumort

Yakutat (Saunders). New to Alaska.

7. **Pellia neesiana** (Gottsche) Limpr.

Douglas Island (T. 1418, in part); Juneau (Saunders 1420); Port Wells (T. 1430, in part); Orca (T. 1425a); Yakutat (T. 1440). New to Alaska.

Many other sterile specimens of *Pellia* occur in the collection, but cannot be determined. It is probable that some of them are *P. epiphylla* (L.) Corda, which has been recorded by Miss Cooley from Salmon Creek, Sitka, and which is also mentioned by Professor Campbell[1] as abundant in Alaska.

8. Blasia pusilla L.

Juneau (T. 1421). New to Alaska.

Two species of *Metzgeria* have also been recorded from Alaska: *M. hamata* Lindb., collected by Miss Cooley at Gold Creek near Juneau, and *M. pubescens* (Schrad.) Raddi, collected by Miss Cooley in the same locality and also by the Drs. Krause at Chilcoot. Dr. Trelease's 2355 from Sitka, is a species of this genus, but is sterile and gemmiparous, and cannot be clearly identified.

JUNGERMANNIACEÆ.

9. **Gymnomitrium obtusum** (Lindb.) Pears. Journ. Bot. 18: 337. 1880

Cesia obtusa LINDB. Medd. Soc. F. et Fl. Fenn. 3: 190. 1878.

Dioicous densely cæspitose or scattered among other bryophytes, pale glaucous-green throughout, or at the tips of the stems and branches, brighter green and sometimes tinged with brownish or red-

[1] Amer. Nat. 33: 397. 1899.

dish: stems sparingly branched, canaliculate when dry along antical surface (between the rows of leaves), convex postically, on sterile plants of about the same width throughout, on sexual plants broadening clavately upward: leaves transversely inserted, densely imbricated, strongly concave and appressed symmetrically, broadly ovate or oval (when flattened), equally bilobed $\frac{1}{6}-\frac{1}{4}$ the length of the leaf with a very narrow sinus, broadening upward, and rounded or very obtuse lobes, sometimes overlapping slightly at the base; margins distinctly crenulate from projecting cells except in basal portions of leaf, green tissue of leaf limited to a patch extending from the base to, or considerably beyond, the middle, surrounded by a distinct hyaline border, except sometimes close to the antical base; marginal cells in crenulate portion of leaf with rather uniformly thickened walls, remaining hyaline cells with large and often confluent trigones, green cells with thin walls and distinct but sometimes very small trigones; cuticle densely and minutely verruculose, particularly in the hyaline portions of leaf ♀ inflorescence borne on a principal branch, outer bracts in three or four pairs, closely imbricated, similar in shape to the leaves, but larger, squarrose at the apex and more or less reflexed on margins of lobes; inner bracts much smaller and more delicate in texture, irregular in shape and variously lobed or cleft with subacute divisions, slightly crenulate on the margins from projecting cells and persistent papillæ; archegonia numerous (up to 10 or 12) : ♂ inflorescence on a principal branch, bracts in several pairs, closely imbricated, similar to the leaves in shape but more delicate in texture, subsquarrose at apex and often reflexed along margins of lobes; antheridia two in each axil, one on a much longer stalk than the other: capsule dark brown, globose, borne on a short stalk extending slightly beyond the cluster of ♀ bracts, capsule-wall composed of two layers of cells; thickenings in the partition-walls of outer layer very conspicuous, dark brown, rounded, extending $\frac{1}{8}-\frac{1}{3}$ across cell-cavity, more or less confluent at the base; similar thickenings of inner layer smaller and less distinct but deeply pigmented, half-ring thickenings of same layer much paler, often indistinct or wanting; spores brown, somewhat angular, with a thick, very minutely verruculose wall; elaters brown, mostly bispiral.

Leaves 0 8 × 0.75 mm., leaf-cells at edge of leaf 14 μ in diameter, in the middle 17 μ, at the base 30 × 22 μ, outer ♀ bracts 1 1 × 1 1 mm., ♂ bracts 0.85 × 0.85 mm., spores 13 μ in diameter, elaters 40–70 μ long, 7 μ wide.

Orca (T. 1512, in part, ♀ specimens with capsules). New to Alaska.

Gymnomitrium obtusum is probably as common in the northern parts of North America as in northern Europe, but is known with certainty from very few localities. So far it has been recorded from Greenland only, where it was collected many years ago by Vahl. It has, however, been found by Holzinger in northwestern Montana and by J. Macoun on Vancouver Island. The specimens of the latter were distributed as *Cesia concinnata*, in 'Canadian Hepaticæ,' no. 63.

Although *Gymnomitrium obtusum* is the only member of the genus occurring in the Harriman collections, two other species have been reported from Alaska: *G. concinnatum* (Lightf.) Corda, which was collected at 'Tahiti' by the Drs. Krause, and *G. coralloides* Nees, which the same collectors found in the 'Dejathal.' The latter species has also been found on St. Paul Island by Merriam and by J M. Macoun. *G. coralloides* is rather closely related to *G. obtusum*, but can readily be distinguished even in sterile condition. In *G. coralloides*, the very young leaves are shortly but distinctly bilobed at the apex with rounded or obtuse lobes and narrow sinus. On the margin is a single row of thin-walled projecting cells, making the leaf distinctly crenulate, at least in the upper part. As the leaf becomes older, the walls of these marginal cells remain thin, except where they bound the next inner cells; the cells themselves become perfectly hyaline and lifeless, the projecting outer walls collapse and are sometimes entirely worn away, so that the outlines of the cells become very indistinct. On account of these changes, the shallow sinus of the leaves grows less and less marked, and in mature leaves cannot always be distinguished. The cells just within the empty marginal cells acquire thick walls very early. The thickenings first appear as small but distinct trigones; these increase in size very rapidly and soon become confluent, so that the cell-cavities are oval or circular in outline. Several rows of these cells also become empty and hyaline, but their thick walls prevent them from collapsing. The green cells, which are found in the middle and toward the base of the leaf, have thin walls and small, sometimes very minute, trigones. They pass by gradations into the thick-walled submarginal cells. The cuticle of the leaves is smooth throughout.

10. **Marsupella emarginata** (Ehrh.) Dumort.

Port Wells (T. 2273); Columbia Fiord (C. & K. 1383, in part, 1384*a*, 1386); Juneau (Setchell 1232). New to Alaska.

The closely related *Marsupella sphacelata* (Gieseke) Dumort. has already been collected in Alaska by the Drs. Krause.

11. **Nardia scalaris** (Schrad.) S. F. Gray.

Juneau (B. & C. 694*a*)

Although this species is rather common in Europe, it has been very rarely collected in America. In addition to the station mentioned above, it was found at Yes Bay, Alaska, by Howell, in 1895, and was also collected by Professor Farlow on Campobello Island, New Brunswick, close to the Maine boundary, in 1898. It was first recorded as American by Pearson, on the strength of specimens collected by J. Macoun on Vancouver Island.

On account of its strongly concave and closely imbricated leaves, *Nardia scalaris* bears some resemblance to large forms of *N. crenulata*, except that it grows in more compact tufts and is likely to be greener. Even without its characteristic fructification, the species is readily recognized by its lanceolate underleaves, which are persistent and much more conspicuous than in any of our other hepatics with undivided leaves. The large and glistening 'fat-bodies' are also a striking feature in many cases; they are oval in form, though sometimes with an irregular contour, and 2 or 3 of them are usually present in each cell. The trigones of the cells are always distinct but are sometimes small. The species has been well represented by Hooker,[1] and the cell-structure is figured by Gottsche.[2]

12. **Nardia hæmatosticta** (Nees) Lindb. Musc. scand. 8. 1879.

Jungermannia scalaris β minor NEES, Naturg. der europ. Leberm. 1 : 281. 1833.
Jungermannia hæmatosticta NEES, l. c. 2 : 453. 1836.
Alicularia geoscypha DE NOT. Mem. Acc. Tor. II. 18 : 486. 1859.
Alicularia scalaris β minor NEES ; G. L. & N. Syn. Hep. II. 1844.
Nardia geoscypha LINDB., Carr. Brit. Hep. 27. 1874.
Alicularia minor LIMPR., Cohn, Kryptogamenfl. von Schlesien. 251. 1877.
Nardia minor ARNELL, Lebermosstudien im nordl. Norwegen, 39. 1892.

Paroicous: densely and intricately cæspitose, green, sometimes tinged with reddish; stems prostrate, ascending at the tips, attached by a thick felt of whitish rhizoids: leaves on slender and sterile branches distant, on robust and fertile axes imbricated, obliquely inserted or, sometimes, almost transverse, broadly orbicular, rounded or broadly emarginate at the apex, entire or slightly sinuate: cell-walls rather thin, with small but very distinct trigones, cuticle smooth or verruculose: underleaves lanceolate, minute, fugacious except in the inflorescence. ♀ inflorescence borne on a principal branch; stem-apex hollowed out into a rudimentary, radiculose sac, extending downward at right angles to axis; bracts in 3 or 4 pairs, gradually increasing in size

[1] Brit. Jung. *pl. 61.* 1816.
[2] Gottsche & Rabenhorst, Hep. eur. exsic. no. 223.

toward perianth, similar to the leaves but broader, irregularly lobed or simply crispate-sinuate on the margins; innermost bracteole large, irregularly bilobed or trilobed, the lobes mostly rounded, second bracteole much smaller, other bracteoles indistinct; perianth extending scarcely if at all beyond the bracts, delicate in texture, contracted at the denticulate or subentire mouth; archegonia about 10: antheridia borne in the axils of the ♀ bracts: capsule on a long and slender stalk, spherical or slightly longer than broad; spores very minutely verruculose.

Leaves 0.7×0.9 mm., underleaves $70 \times 25\ \mu$, leaf-cells in the middle and at the edge of leaf $20\ \mu$ in diameter, at the base $32 \times 23\ \mu$, ♀ bracts 0.7×1.2 mm., spores $16\ \mu$ in diameter.

Disenchantment Bay (B & C $637a$, in part, 641, $641a$, T. 1504); Hidden Glacier Inlet (T. 1505, in part); St Lawrence Island (T. 1517, C. & K 2007, in part). New to Alaska

Nardia hæmatosticta is apparently also new to the American continent, but has recently been reported from Greenland.[1] It seems to be much rarer in Europe than *N. scalaris*, but has a wide distribution there in northern and mountainous regions. By many of the earlier writers it was included under this latter species as a variety; it is, however, well distinguished by its smaller size, its less concave and sometimes emarginate leaves, its paroicous inflorescence, and by the early disappearance of its underleaves. These are, in fact, very difficult to demonstrate except in connection with the inflorescence and in very young apical regions, where the leaves are still undeveloped. The curious 'fat bodies,' so characteristic of *N. scalaris*, are either absent from the smaller species or are inconspicuous. The rudimentary sac of *N. hæmatosticta* is a most interesting feature and indicates, as has already been pointed out by other writers, an approach to such typically saccate genera as *Arnellia* and *Gyrothyra*. The species has been well figured by Schiffner[2] and by Massalongo and Carestia.[3]

13. **Nardia obovata** (Nees) Lindb.

Farragut Bay (T. 1464, in part); Kadiak (T. 1416, in part). New to Alaska.

The present species was first recorded for the United States by Dr. Howe,[4] who based his determination upon sterile California specimens.

---

[1] Jensen, Medd. om Grønland, 15. 381. 1898.
[2] Engler & Prantl, Nat Pflanzenfam 1³ 78. 1893.
[3] Nuovo Gior Bot Ital 14 *pl. 12 fig. 2* and *pl. 13* 1882.
[4] Mem Torr Bot Club, 7· 96. 1899.

It had previously been reported from Greenland[1] and from tropical America (New Granada).[2] The plant is probably much less rare in America than might be inferred from these meager published notices, and has in fact already been twice distributed under different names in 'Hepaticæ Americanæ' (no. 83, as *N. crenuliformis*, and no. 113, as *Jungermannia cordifolia*). In both instances the specimens were collected by the writer in the White Mountain region. The Alaskan plants referred to *Nardia obovata* agree perfectly with authentic European specimens, except that it is impossible to demonstrate the paroicous inflorescence in a wholly satisfactory manner. Some of the Farragut Bay specimens have ripe capsules and these show, below the adnate perichætial bracts, a few slightly saccate leaves, which may well be the perigonial bracts. Other specimens show young antheridia, but no archegonia; some of the antheridia, however, are extremely immature, and it is possible that the female organs have not yet begun to develop. It should be noted also that European authors are not unanimous in ascribing a paroicous inflorescence to this species; Herr C. Muller, of Freiburg, in fact, says in a recent paper that it is dioicous.[3] The delicate striations in the cuticle of the leaves are sometimes either transitory or poorly developed; it is usually possible to find them, however, even where they are otherwise indistinct, in the somewhat elongated cells near the base of a leaf.

The fourth Alaskan species of this genus, *Nardia compressa* (Hook.) S. F. Gray, from Atka Island (J. M. Macoun), was collected many years ago in Greenland, but has not since been recorded from America. It is our largest species, and, when well developed, grows in compact tufts, the individual stems being erect or nearly so. The leaves are broadly orbicular or reniform, closely imbricated and appressed to the stem. The underleaves are small and fugacious and the rhizoids are very scanty. In many cases the plants give off flagella, which are particularly well seen on young and prostrate stems. On such plants also the leaves are less appressed than on older specimens

14. **Jungermannia sphærocarpa** Hook.

Hooniah Village (C. & K. 664); Disenchantment Bay (B. & C. 637a, in part); Port Clarence (T. 1514, 2116, Fernow 1515, in great part). New to Alaska.

[1] Jensen, Medd om Grønland, 15 381 1898.
[2] Gottsche, Ann des Sc. Nat. V. 1· 119. 1864.
[3] Mitteil des Bad. bot. Vereins. 1899: 8 (reprint).

15. **Jungermannia atrovirens** Dumort. Syll. Jung. 51. 1831.

Aplozia atrovirens DUMORT. Hep. Europ. 63. 1874.

Virgin Bay (Saunders 1427, in small part). New to Alaska.

The specimens referred to this species, although very scanty, show both male plants and female plants with perianths. They are mixed with sterile specimens of an *Aneura* and a *Lophozia*, both of which are indeterminable. *J. atrovirens* was first described by Dumortier, but his description was so incomplete that the plant remained unrecognized by European hepaticologists until the type-specimens were discovered by Dr. Henri Bernet in the Schleicher Herbarium. Bernet described the species more fully and gave an excellent figure of it, citing numerous Swiss localities where it had been found.[1] The plant has since been recorded from Scandinavia, from Styria, and from Greenland. *J. atrovirens* differs from *J. pumila* With. mainly in its dioicous inflorescence and more plicate perianth. Some of the Alaskan specimens show distinct but often minute trigones in the younger leaves. These seem to become indistinct with age, and are not to be clearly made out in the European material which I have studied.

16. **Jungermannia lanceolata** L.

Juneau (B. & C. 699). New to Alaska.

Jungermannia cordifolia Hook., collected by the Drs. Krause at 'Tlehini,' does not appear in the Harriman collections.

17. **Anastrophyllum reichardtii** (Gottsche) Steph. Hedwigia, 32: 140. 1893.

Jungermannia reichardtii GOTTSCHE, Juratzka, Verh. zool.-bot. Gesellschaft zu Wien, 20: 168. *pl. 3 B.* 1868.

Jungermannia nardioides LINDB. Musc. Scand. 8 1879.

Dioicous: caespitose or scattered among other bryophytes, blackish-purple varying to brownish or brownish-green, glossy; stems dark, firm and rigid, prostrate or usually ascending, simple or very sparingly branched, in ♀ plants often repeatedly innovant, more or less radiculose below with whitish or brownish rhizoids, mostly eradiculose above: leaves more or less imbricated, ovate to rotund-quadrate when explanate, complicate-bilobed about one-third with more or less incurved, mostly acute lobes and acute or obtuse sinus, antical lobe slightly smaller than the postical, arching across stem at the rounded or subcordate base, margin of leaves entire: leaf-cells with thick walls and large, irregular, and often confluent trigones, but no intermediate thickenings, cell-lumen distinctly stellate except near the edges and

[1] Cat. des Hépat du Sud-Ouest de la Suisse, 60 *pl. 2. figs 2, 3.* 1888.

toward the base of the leaf; cuticle smooth: ♀ bracts a little larger and paler than the leaves but otherwise scarcely distinguishable from them, lobes a little more acute, with entire or very obscurely angular-dentate margins, bracteoles wanting; perianth ovate-cylindrical, gradually contracted and deeply 4- to 5-plicate in the upper part, the mouth lacerate with ciliate divisions, the cilia slender, variously curved and contorted; color of the perianth pale at the base, hyaline at the mouth, reddish or brownish in a broad median zone; cells in a single layer except at the very base, thick-walled, some of the cells in the upper part projecting outward and upward as obtuse or subacute papillae, one or two cells long; archegonia 10–12; ♂ spike intercalary, bracts in 6–10 pairs, imbricated, smaller than the leaves and more delicate but similar in shape, strongly concave, arching across axis and sometimes bearing a small lanceolate or ovate lobe-like tooth at antical base, antheridia mostly in pairs, paraphyses sometimes present, minute and very variable in shape, from subulate to oblong and from acuminate to obtuse at the apex; sporophyte unknown.

Stem 0.2 mm. in diameter, leaves 0.9 × 0.8 mm., leaf-cells at edge of leaf 14 μ in diameter, in the middle 19 × 17 μ, at the base 35 × 17 μ, ♀ bracts 1.05 × 0.95 mm., perianth 2.2 × 1 mm., ♂ bracts 0.7 × 0.75 mm.

Columbia Fiord (C. & K. 1389), Orca (T. 1512, in part), Port Wells (T.). New to America.

The discovery of this local European species in America is a matter of much interest, more particularly as the specimens are more complete than any that have yet been described. The plant is known in Europe from various parts of Austro-Hungary, from Italy, and from the mountainous regions of southeastern Norway, where, according to Kaalaas, it is not especially uncommon.

It will be noticed that my description of the perichaetial bracts and perianths does not agree in all respects with the published descriptions of European authors. Upon consulting these descriptions, however, it will be found that they are at variance with one another and that all are drawn from specimens with undeveloped perianths. The earliest account of the floral organs is that given by Limpricht,[1] and is as follows: bracts smaller and more tender [than the leaves], hollow, sharply incised, sparingly toothed; bracteole almost rectangular, many times irregularly incised; perianth immersed, very tender, plicate, deeply and irregularly laciniate-ciliate; archegonia about 12, always unfertilized. He states also that scattered cells of the perianth some-

[1] Cohn, Kryptogamenfl. von Schlesien, 1: 279. 1876.

times grow out into long papillæ. According to Stephani,[1] the bracts are much larger than the leaves, orbicular, with a shorter sinus and incurved lobes, forming a terminal incurved bunch; the perianth is immersed, small, almost hyaline, oval, strongly plicate, ciliate-laciniate at the mouth. Massalongo[2] describes the parts as follows: bracts bifid to quadrifid, perianth erect, oval, immersed in the involucre, plicate, mouth ciliate-laciniate, the laciniæ on the external surface subechinate from projecting cells. The description given by Kaalaas[3] agrees closely with that of Limpricht.

Of European material, I have studied Styrian specimens collected by Herr Breidler and Norwegian specimens collected by Dr. Bryhn. I find in these that the plants are either sterile or female, and that the latter are repeatedly floriferous by means of innovations. The bracts are similar to the leaves except that they are a little larger, and in no case have I been able to find more than two lobes. The perianth is always small and rudimentary, and closely agrees with the descriptions of the European authors. I have, however, been quite unable to find any trace of a bracteole. The Alaskan specimens agree perfectly with this European material, some of them in fact showing the peculiar rudimentary perianths with their innovations. The specimens with fully developed perianths, however, are often destitute of such innovations.

The genus *Anastrophyllum* is most luxuriant in the mountainous regions of the Tropics, where it is represented by numerous species. *A. reichardtii* is not a typical member of the genus, being intermediate between *Anastrophyllum* and the *Sphenolobus* section of *Lophozia*. In fact it was the existence of this species (and of one or two others) that deterred Spruce from elevating his group *Anastrophyllum* to generic rank, as was afterwards done by Stephani. The present species has, in common with the genus, the reddish color, the very thick-walled leaf-cells with stellate cavities, and the lacerate perianth with ciliate divisions. The plants described by Lindberg as *Jungermannia nardioides* do not show the cell-characters of *A. reichardtii* in a very marked degree and are probably to be looked upon as poorly developed individuals [4]

18. **Lophozia ventricosa** (Dicks.) Dumort.

Juneau (B. & C. 702, in part); Sitka (C. & K. 927, in small part); Douglas Island (T. 1498, in part); Virgin Bay (T. 1457, in small

[1] Ber. des bot. Vereins zu Landshut, 7: 35. 1879.
[2] Atti Soc. Veneto-Trent. II, 2: (37) 1895.
[3] Nyt Mag. for Naturvidensk, 33: 371. 1893.
[4] Cf. Kaalaas, Vidensk. Skrifter I. Math.-nat. Klasse, no. 9: 18. 1898.

part); Columbia Fiord (C. & K. 1396, 1400, in part); Port Wells (T. 1530, 1475, in part); Orca (T. 1529, in part); Yakutat (Saunders 1438, T.); Kadiak (C. & K. 2321, in part); Port Clarence (Fernow 1515, in small part). This common and widely distributed species occurs in the Krause collections; it has also been found on Popof Island by Townsend, and on St. George and Nagai islands by J. M. Macoun.

19. **Lophozia guttulata** (Lindb. & Arnell).

Jungermannia guttulata LINDB. & ARNELL, Kongl. Sv. Vet. Akad. Handl. 23, No. 5: 51 1889.

Dioicous: depressed-caespitose, green, varying to brownish, stems reddish-brown to black, densely radiculose, sparingly branched; leaves distant to imbricated, obliquely inserted, spreading or the upper ones often complicate, slightly decurrent, bifid one-third to one-half with triangular, acute or acuminate, slightly divergent lobes and acute to obtuse, often gibbous, sinus, margin entire: underleaves wanting: leaf-cells with thin walls but distinct and very large, sometimes confluent trigones, projecting out into the stellate cell-cavities; cuticle smooth: innermost ♀ bracts erect-spreading, bifid to quadrifid about two-fifths with triangular, obtuse to short-acuminate, often unequal lobes, margins otherwise subentire; bracteole very variable, lanceolate or bifid, connate on one or on both sides; perianth cylindrical or obovate-clavate, contracted at the ciliolate mouth (the cilia mostly two to four cells long), terete below, plicate in upper fourth: ♂ plants mixed with the ♀, bracts in several pairs, strongly saccate at base, cells in saccate portion often with slightly and uniformly thickened walls, other cells normal.

Leaf-cells at edge of leaf 22 μ in diameter, in the middle 28 μ, and at the base 35 μ.

Point Gustavus, Glacier Bay (C. & K. 758); Columbia Fiord (C. & K. 1397, 1400, in part); Kadiak (C. & K 2321, in part). New to America.

Lophozia guttulata was first described from Siberian specimens, but is now known also from various parts of Scandinavia, from Austria, and from Italy. Professor Massalongo[1] looks upon it as a variety of *Lophozia ventricosa*, and it approaches somewhat certain forms which were formerly included under *Jungermannia porphyroleuca*. When well developed, however, it is very easily distinguished and is probably entitled to specific rank. The most important differences between it and *L. ventricosa* are the following: the plants are smaller;

[1] Atti Soc. Veneto-Trent. II, 2: (14) 1895.

the leaves are more deeply lobed with more sharply pointed divisions and gibbous sinus; the leaf-cells have very large and conspicuous trigones, which are sometimes confluent; gemmæ are either entirely absent or are extremely rare. The innermost ♀ bracts and bracteole are more variable than the original description represents, and this variability affects not only the Alaskan specimens but European specimens as well. The species is apparently confined to rotten logs.

20. **Lophozia incisa** (Schrad.) Dumort.

Hot Spring, near Sitka (T.); Juneau (B. & C. mixed with 641, 691, 699, and 702, Setchell 1229, in part); Columbia Fiord (C. & K 1391, in part, 1403); Orca (T. 1444, 1491, in part, 2249), Kadiak (C. & K. 2321, in great part); Hall Island (T. 1442). New to Alaska.

21. **Lophozia obtusa** (Lindb.).

Jungermannia obtusa LINDB. Musc Scand. 7. 1879.

Juneau (B. & C. mixed with 693). New to America.

There are only a few sterile stems of the present plant in the collection, but there is little doubt that they should be referred to this rare European species. The Alaskan specimens have been carefully compared with authentic plants from Norway, kindly sent me by Dr. Bryhn, and I find that they agree in all essential respects. The species was first described by Lindberg from specimens collected near Stockholm, and has since been found in various other parts of Scandinavia. It is known also from Styria, from Switzerland, and from Italy, but has not been reported either from America or from Asia. The plant is well figured by Bernet[1] and is so fully described by Arnell,[2] that I add here simply a short account of the stem and leaf characters: Creeping among other bryophytes or rarely cæspitose, green; stems mostly simple, becoming more or less pigmented with age, and bearing numerous short, whitish rhizoids: leaves distant or, more rarely, subimbricated, very obliquely inserted, plane or slightly concave, rotund, bifid about one-third with broad, mostly rounded lobes, separated by a narrow, obtuse and gibbous sinus; antical lobe subequal to the postical or a little smaller, in some cases varying from rounded to obtuse, apiculate or even acute on the same stem; margins slightly decurrent, entire, or bearing a small tooth-like lobe near the antical base: underleaves rudimentary and apparently often fugacious, simple or deeply bifid with subulate divisions, sometimes irregularly and

[1] Cat. des Hépat. du Sud-Ouest de la Suisse, *pl 4*. 1888.
[2] Lebermoosstudien im nördl. Norwegen, 30. 1892.

sparingly toothed: leaf-cells with thin walls and minute but distinct trigones; cuticle delicately striate-verruculose.

22. **Lophozia inflata** (Huds.) M. A. Howe.

Kadiak (C. & K. 1426). New to Alaska.

23. **Lophozia heterocolpa** (Thed.) M. A. Howe.

Port Wells (B. & C. mixed with 652 and 654). New to Alaska.

24. **Lophozia attenuata** (Lindb.) Dumort.

Virgin Bay (T. 1474, in part). New to Alaska.

25. **Lophozia quinquedentata** (Huds.) Schiffn.

St. Matthew Island (T. 1480, 1519, in part, 2161, in part). New to Alaska.

26. **Lophozia floerkii** (Web. & Mohr) Schiffn.

Orca (T. 1529, in part), Port Wells (T.). New to Alaska.

27. **Lophozia quadriloba** (Lindb.).

Jungermannia quadriloba LINDB., Lindb. & Arnell, Kongl. Sv. Vet. Akad. Handl. 23, no. 5. 55. 1889.

Hoonıah Village (C. & K. 665). New to Alaska.

This distinctly arctic and alpine species has not before been recorded from the American continent: it is now known from various parts of northern Europe including the island of Spitzbergen, from Styria, from Siberia, and from Greenland. The Alaskan plants agree closely with Norwegian specimens collected by Dr. Arnell. Lindberg's description is so full that I give here simply an account of the leaves and underleaves, drawn from the sterile Alaskan material: leaves remote or imbricated, almost transversely inserted, widely spreading from the base, almost erect in the upper half, lobed to about the middle with 3 or 4 (rarely only 2) acute or obtuse, triangular lobes separated by narrow sinuses; margins mostly entire, but bearing at the base, both antically and postically, a very few (usually only one or two) small, variously curved cilia, mostly 6-10 cells long and 1-3 cells wide at the base: underleaves deeply bifid with triangular-subulate, long-acuminate lobes separated by a narrow sinus; basilar cilia similar to those of the leaves: leaf-cells with thick walls and distinct, slightly bulging trigones: cuticle densely covered with coarse verrucæ, circular or oval in outline or, near the base of the leaf, tending to be elongated; cells at the edge of the leaf $14\,\mu$ in diameter, in the middle $17\,\mu$ and at the base $30\times 17\,\mu$.

The nearest relative of *Lophozia quadriloba* is perhaps *L. floerkii*, which differs in its larger size, in its obliquely inserted and less deeply lobed leaves, and in its thinner walled leaf-cells with smooth or nearly smooth cuticle and smaller trigones. In *L. kunzeana* (Huben), which is also a close ally, the leaves are more distinctly complicate, so that the plant appears flattened rather than terete-foliate as in *L. quadriloba;* the leaves moreover are usually only bilobed, they lack basal cilia, and their cells have a smooth or minutely striate-verruculose cuticle.

28. **Lophozia minuta** (Crantz) Schiffn

Columbia Fiord (C. & K. 1388, in part), Orca (T. 1511, in part); Hall Island (T. 1518, in part); St. Lawrence Island (T. 2125, in great part). The species was first collected in Alaska by the Drs Krause at Chilcoot; it has also been found at Sitka (U. S. Fish Commission, 1894), and on Popof Island (Townsend).

29. **Lophozia ovata** (Dicks.) M. A. Howe.

Yakutat (T. in very small amount, mixed with 1527). New to Alaska

The generic position of this little species is still a matter for discussion: by certain authors it is placed in the genus *Diplophylleia* Trevis (*Diplophyllum* Dumort.), by others it is considered a species of the *Sphenolobus* section of *Lophozia*.[1] It forms, in fact, a connecting link between these two groups of Hepaticæ. The closely related *Diplophyllum argenteum* Spruce,[2] a species apparently confined to the northwestern coast regions of our continent, is also recorded as Alaskan by Professor Underwood.[3]

Lophozia saxicola (Schrad) Schiffn , which was collected by the Krause brothers in Alaska, does not appear in the Harriman collections

30. **Plagiochila asplenioides** (L) Dumort

Farragut Bay (T 1469, a single sterile stem). The species is known also from Sitka (U. S. Fish Commission, 1894) and from near Yakutat (Funston), and ought to be widely distributed in Alaska

31. **Mylia taylori** (Hook.) S F. Gray.

Hot Spring (T. 1470); Juneau (Setchell 1229, in part); Douglas Island (T. mixed with 1495, 1496, and 1498), Virgin Bay (T. 1474, in part); Farragut Bay (T 1485, in part); Orca (T. 1490,

---

[1] The synonymy of this species, together with a full description, is given by Dr Howe, Mem Torr Bot Club, 7 111 1899

[2] Hep Amaz et And. 417 1885 (footnote)

[3] Zoe, 1. 366 1891.

also mixed with 1492 and 1508, Setchell 1205); Columbia Fiord (C. & K. 1388, in part); Port Wells (C. & K. 1297, T. 1475, in part). This species has not before been recorded from Alaska, but I have a few sterile scraps of it collected at Sitka, by the Fish Commission in 1894.

32. **Lophocolea cuspidata** (Nees) Limpr.

Cape Fox (T. 2383). New to Alaska.

33. **Chiloscyphus polyanthos** (L.) Corda

Juneau (B. & C. mixed with 699); Point Gustavus, Glacier Bay (C. & K. mixed with 758); Yakutat (Saunders, 1437, in part). The var. *rivularis* of this species is reported by Miss Cooley from Salmon Creek, near Juneau.

34. **Harpanthus flotowianus** Nees.

Hot Spring (T. 1435, in part); Orca (T. 2247, also mixed with 1424); Port Wells (T. 1430); Yakutat (B. & C. mixed with 689). New to Alaska.

35. **Cephalozia bicuspidata** (L.) Dumort.

Sitka (T. 1501, in part, Setchell 1258, in part, 1269); Mt. Verstovia (C. & K. 927, in part); Juneau (B. & C. mixed with 691); Hidden Glacier Inlet (T. 1505, in part); Orca (T. 1507, also mixed with 1491 and 1510); Columbia Fiord (C. & K. 1394); Farragut Bay (C. & K. 453, also mixed with 454); Yakutat (B. & C. mixed with 689); Kadiak (C. & K. mixed with 2321). This species, which has not before been reported from Alaska, has also been collected on Attu Island (U. S. Fish Commission, 1894).

36. **Cephalozia media** Lindb.

Sitka (T. 1502); Douglas Island (T. mixed with 1495); Orca (T. 1508, 1510, Setchell, 1203); Columbia Fiord (C. & K. 1393, in part); Farragut Bay (B. & C. 621, in part). The species has also been collected by Miss Cooley, at Salmon Creek, near Juneau, and by Funston, near Yakutat.

37. **Cephalozia leucantha** Spruce, on *Cephalozia*, 68. 1882.

Dioicous: depressed-cæspitose, pale green: stems not pigmented, sparingly branched from the postical aspect but never bearing true flagella, about 6 cells in diameter, interior cells with uniformly thickened walls, cortical cells (in about 12 longitudinal rows) a little larger than the interior cells and with slightly thinner walls: rhizoids whitish, mostly scattered: leaves distant (except in the apical region), transversely or slightly obliquely inserted, somewhat spreading, plane or slightly concave, ovate, equally bifid to or beyond the middle with triangular, acute, spreading or connivent lobes, separated by an obtuse or subacute sinus, each lobe about 4 cells wide at the base and 5 cells long, ending in a row of 2 cells underleaves wanting: leaf-cells with uniformly thickened walls: ♀ inflorescence borne on a usually very short postical branch; bracts in 2 or 3 pairs, innermost bracts broadly orbicular, bifid about one-third with acuminate, spreading divisions and broad sinus, margins slightly and irregularly denticulate, cell-walls thin; innermost bracteole connate on one side, sometimes undivided and acuminate, sometimes bifid, margins denticulate; bracts of second row similar to the innermost, but smaller and with subentire margins, corresponding bracteole undivided and blunt; perianth ovate-cylindrical, one cell thick, terete below, obtusely 3- (or 4-) keeled above, somewhat contracted at the irregularly lobed mouth, the lobes ciliate (each cilium 1 or 2 cells long) ♂ spike occupying the whole or a part of a short postical branch, sometimes intercalary on a longer branch; bracts in 2 to 5 pairs, imbricated, strongly concave, bifid about one-third; bracteoles small, linear-subulate to ovate, antheridia borne singly: capsule purple-brown, borne on a rather long stalk; spores yellowish-brown, with a thickened, very minutely verruculose wall; elaters rather blunt, bispiral.

Stems 0.08 mm. in diameter, leaves 0.17 × 0.14 mm., leaf-cells at edge of leaf 23 × 14 μ, in the middle and at the base 18 μ in diameter, innermost bracts 0.6 × 0.6 mm., innermost bracteole 0.6 × 0.5 mm., bract of second row 0.4 × 0.4 mm., bracteole of second row 0.35 × 0.25 mm., perianth 1.4 × 0.5 mm., spores 9 μ in diameter, elaters 250 × 9 μ. These measurements are taken from the Alaskan specimens and run a little lower than those given by Spruce.

Columbia Fiord (C. & K. 1393, in part). New to America.

Since the original publication of this species, it has been found to have a wide distribution in Europe, being particularly plentiful in northern regions. It has not yet, however, been reported from northern Asia. The species is intermediate in some respects between Spruce's subgenera *Eucephalozia* and *Cephaloziella*. Spruce himself placed it, with some hesitation, in *Cephaloziella*, but to the writer it seems to fit a little better in the other subgenus. *C. leucantha* resembles *C. divaricata* in size, but differs more particularly in its pale color and in its cladogenous inflorescence. From *C. catenulata*, it differs in its color, in its narrower and more distant leaves, and in its smaller leaf-cells *C media*, which is likewise a pale green plant, differs in its decurrent and differently shaped leaves with lunulate sinus and in the larger cells of its leaves and stems.

Cephalozia divaricata has not yet been found fruiting in Alaska Sterile specimens collected by Dr. Trelease at Hot Spring (mixed with 1526) probably belong here, as do also similar specimens collected by Funston at Yakutat

38. **Kantia trichomanis** (L.) S. F. Gray.

Douglas Island (T. mixed with 1408 and 1495), Orca (T. mixed with 1508); Columbia Fiord (C. & K. 1399); Fairagut Bay (B. & C. 621, in part). Previously collected by Miss Cooley, at Sitka, and by Funston, near Yakutat.

39. **Bazzania deflexa** (Mart.) S. F. Gray.

Hot Spring (T. mixed with 1488 and 1489); Wrangell (C. & K. 407a), Juneau (B. & C. 691, in part, Setchell mixed with 1228); Port Wells (T. 1531); Fairagut Bay (B. & C. 620 and 623, in part). Known also from Loring (Miss Cooley), from Chlowak (Krause), and from Sitka (Townsend 66, Canby 459)

40. **Lepidozia filamentosa** (Lehm. & Lindb.) Lindb.

Douglas Island (T. 1497); Columbia Fiord (C. & K. 1384), Fairagut Bay (B. & C. mixed with 620) Reported by Dr. Howe from Prince of Wales Sound (J. M. Macoun) and from Sumdum (Miss Jessie Trowbridge).

41. **Lepidozia reptans** (L.) Dumort.

Sitka (T. 1501, in part), Douglas Island (T. 1495, 1498, in part), Orca (T. 1491). The species has also been found at Sitka by Miss Cooley and at Yakutat by Funston.

42. **Lepidozia setacea** (Web.) Mitt.

Orca (T. 1511, in part); Columbia Fiord (C. & K. 1319, in part). New to Alaska.

43. **Blepharostoma trichophyllum** (L.) Dumort.

Juneau (B. & C. mixed with 691, 699, and 702, Setchell mixed with 1229), Orca (T. mixed with 1477, 1491, 1508, and 1510); Yakutat (B. & C. mixed with 689), Hall Island (T. mixed with 1518). Previously collected in Alaska by Rothrock and by Funston.

44. **Blepharostoma setiforme** (Ehrh.) Lindb.

St. Matthew Island (T. 2529). First collected in Alaska by the Drs. Krause.

45. Anthelia julacea (L.) Dumort

Virgin Bay (Kincaid 1534); St. Matthew Island (T. 2073, 2161, in part, C. & K. 2130); St. Lawrence Island (T. 1516, C. & K 2007, in part); Hall Island (T. 1518, in part). New to Alaska.

46. Anthelia juratzkana (Limpr.) Trevis.

St. Matthew Island (T. 1519, in part); Hall Island (T. 1445). New to Alaska.

47. Herberta adunca (Dicks.) S. F. Gray.

Hot Spring (T 1525a, also mixed with 1471). This species is reported from St. Paul Island by Merriam and by J. M. Macoun; it has also been collected at Yes Bay by Howell.

48. Ptilidium californicum (Aust.) Underw. & Cook.

Sitka (T. 1453, Setchell, 1268); Virgin Bay (T. 1456, 1458); Port Wells (T 1416a); Orca (T. 1459, 1460, also mixed with 1491 and 1529, Setchell 1209); Columbia Fiord (C. & K. 1344, 1390). Although this species has not before been recorded as Alaskan, a few fragmentary specimens were collected by J. M. Macoun, in 1891, on Prince of Wales Island.

49. Ptilidium ciliare (L.) Nees.

Juneau (Setchell 1239); Virgin Bay (T. 1457); Port Wells (T. 1461); Kadiak (T. 1454, 1455); St. Matthew Island (T. 1463); Port Clarence (Fernow 1462) First collected in Alaska by the Drs. Krause.

50. Diplophylleia albicans (L.) Trevis.

Hot Spring (T. 1488); Mt. Verstovia (C. & K. 927, also mixed with 926); Orca (T. 1508, 1511, 1512, 1529, in part); Columbia Fiord (C. & K. 1392); Port Wells (T. 1475, in part, 1833); Farragut Bay (C. & K. 471). This species occurs in Rothrock's list I have also seen Alaskan specimens from Barlow Cove (Kellogg) and from St. Paul Island (J. M. Macoun).

51. Diplophylleia taxifolia (Web. & Mohr) Trevis.

St. Matthew Island (T. 1519, in part). In the 'Synopsis Hepaticarum' this species is accredited to Unalaska Island. In has also been reported from St. Paul Island (Merriam & J. M. Macoun), and has likewise been collected at Sitka (Townsend).

52. Diplophylleia plicata (Lindb.).

Diplophyllum plicatum LINDB. Acta Soc. Sci. Fenn 10 235. 1872.

Dioicous plants loosely tufted, green, varying to brownish or yellowish: stems prostrate or ascending, simple or sparingly branched, the branches apparently arising in the axils of ordinary leaves: rhizoids sometimes numerous, sometimes few or none: leaves distant or subimbricated, closely appressed at the base, widely spreading above, complicate-bilobed with a distinct strongly arched keel less than half the length of the postical lobe; antical lobe erect-spreading, arching across the axis and sometimes beyond, ligulate, rounded at the apex, subentire or sometimes sharply and irregularly dentate at the apex, and more rarely at the decurrent base; postical lobe longer and broader, widely spreading, oblong or obovate, obtuse or rounded at the sharply and irregularly dentate apex, margins otherwise subentire though sometimes sharply ciliate-dentate at the short-decurrent base; apical teeth mostly one or two cells long; basal teeth, when present, each consisting usually of a single pointed cell: median leaf-cells with thin walls and very distinct trigones sometimes becoming confluent, marginal and submarginal cells with more uniformly thickened walls; cuticle varying from strongly verruculose to nearly smooth: ♀ inflorescence borne on a principal branch, sometimes with one or two innovations; bracts in a single pair, similar to the leaves but more erect and smaller, clasping the base of the perianth, postical margin varying from entire to finely seriate; perianth ovoid-cylindrical, gradually narrowed toward the mouth, deeply plicate throughout with about 16 sharp folds separated by narrow grooves, terete or slightly flattened, mouth irregularly lacerate, the divisions variously curved and contorted, finely ciliate, each slender cilium ending in a long row of cells: androecium intercalary, bracts imbricated, in many pairs, similar to the leaves but saccate at the base and with more erect antical lobes, antheridia 2–6 in each axil; paraphyses numerous, variable in shape but most frequently linear, entire, often variously curved, one to three cells wide in the middle: gemmæ broadly fusiform, mostly two-celled, occasionally produced both by sterile and sexual plants at and near the apices of the leaves: mature sporophyte unknown.

Stems 0.4–0.5 mm. in diameter, postical lobes of leaves 2–2.5 mm. long, 0.8 mm. wide, antical lobes 1.2–1.7 mm. long, 0.4–0.5 mm. wide, leaf-cells at apex of leaf 14 μ in diameter, in the middle 16–23 μ long, 16 μ wide, at the base 45 × 16 μ, perianth 3.5–4.2 mm. long, 9–1.4 mm. in diameter, gemmæ 18 × 14 μ.

Orca (T. 1492, in part); Farragut Bay (B & C. 619); Hall Island (T. 1478). New to America.

D. plicata was described by Lindberg from specimens collected on the island of Sachalin in eastern Siberia and was also reported by him from two stations in Amur. Quite recently Herr Stephani has accredited it to Japan.[1] Its discovery in Alaska makes a most interesting addition to our hepatic flora. The specimens collected by the Harriman Expedition would seem to indicate that the species is somewhat more variable than Lindberg supposed. The Hall Island specimens agree best with his description and with the type specimens, kindly loaned me by Dr. Harald Lindberg; the Orca specimens are likewise very similar but have a nearly smooth cuticle; the Farragut Bay specimens, which have a distinctly roughened cuticle, differ in having teeth at the base of both antical and postical lobes and in having cells with less pronounced trigones. It is possible that these last specimens represent a distinct, undescribed species, but it seems wisest not to try to separate them until a more complete series has been obtained.

D. plicata is the largest known member of the genus. It is distinguished from both *D. albicans* and *D. taxifolia* by its robustness and by its leaf-cells, which, with the exception of those near the edge, have thin walls and distinct trigones instead of being uniformly thickened. The absence of the false nerve would, of course, also distinguish it from *D. albicans*.

53. Scapania bolanderi Aust.

Scapania albescens Steph Engler's Bot. Jahrb **8** 96 1886.

Sitka (T. 1486, 1487, 1500, 1503, Setchell 1258, in part); Hot Spring (T. 1489, also mixed with 1471); Mt. Verstovia (C. & K. 926, 927, in part), Juneau (B. & C. 702, in part, T. 1484, Setchell 1228, in part), Douglas Island (T. 1483, also mixed with 1495), Orca (T. 1491, 1509, also 1477 and 1510, in part, Setchell 1207, in part); Columbia Fiord (C. & K. 1385, 1395), Farragut Bay (B & C mixed with 620, 621, 623*b*, T. 1485, in part); Kadiak (C. & K. 2321, in part) This species, which seems to be very abundant in Alaska, was collected by Kellogg in 1867, and has also been found by J. M. Macoun on Prince of Wales Island, by Townsend at Sitka, and by the Drs. Krause at Chlowak and Chilcoot.

54. Scapania undulata (L.) Dumort.

Sitka (T. 1432); Juneau (B. & C. 691, in part), Virgin Bay (T. 1473), Orca (T. 1476); Columbia Fiord (C. & K. 1359, 1383, a large purple form), Farragut Bay (T. 1464); Yakutat Bay (Saunders 1437, in part, 1472); Popof Island (Saunders 1479). Not before reported from Alaska, but collected by J. M. Macoun on St. Paul Island in 1892.

[1] Bull de l'Herb Boissier, **5** 78 1897.

55. **Scapania irrigua** (Nees) Dumort.

Poit Clarence (B. & C. 673). New to Alaska.

56. **Scapania umbrosa** (Schrad.) Dumort.

Sitka (Setchell 1258, in part); Mt. Verstovia (C. & K. 927, in part), Juneau (B. & C. 691, in part, Setchell 1236); Orca (T. 1477, Setchell 1207, in part); Columbia Fiord (C. & K. 1398); Yakutat (T., B. & C. mixed with 689). New to Alaska.

57. **Scapania curta** (Mart.) Dumort.

Yakutat Bay (B. & C. 645, in part). In the 'Synopsis,' this species is quoted from Unalaska Island.

Scapania nemorosa is included in Rothrock's and Stephani's lists, but does not occur in the Harriman collections.

58. **Radula bolanderi** Gottsche.

Hot Spring (T. mixed with 1471); Sitka (Setchell 1266). Also collected by Townsend at Sitka. *Radula arctica* Steph., collected at Chlowak and at Chilcoot by the Dis. Krause, is doubtfully referred to this species by Dr. Howe.[1]

59. **Radula complanata** (L.) Dumort.

Sitka (T. 1501, in part). *Radula krausei* Steph, from Chilcoot, is referred by Dr. Howe[2] to this species, which has also been collected by Funston near Yakutat.

60. **Porella rivularis** (Nees) Trevis

Sitka (T. 1465); Yakutat (Saunders 1466). Also collected by Miss Cooley, according to Dr. Howe.[3]

61. **Porella navicularis** (Lehm. & Lindb.) Lindb.

Hot Spring (T. 1471, in part, also mixed with 1525). This species is noted in the 'Synopsis' as occurring near Sitka. Kellogg collected it also in the same locality, and it has been found at Chilcoot by the Krause brothers.

Porella platyphylla (L.) Lindb has been reported from Unalaska (Syn. Hep.) and from Guissen (Krause). It does not occur in the present collection.

62. **Frullania nisquallensis** Sulliv.

Cape Fox (T. 1532); New Metlakahtla (T. 1523); Sitka, (Setchell, 1252); Hot Spring (T. 1471, in part, 1525); Wrangell (C. & K

---

[1] Mem. Torr. Bot. Club, 7: 159. 1899 (footnote).
[2] L. c. 160.
[3] Bull. Torr. Bot. Club, 24: 520. 1897.

401, 407a); Orca (T. 1528); Yakutat (T. 1527). Also known from Chilcoot (Krause).

63. **Frullania franciscana** M. A. Howe.

Sitka (T. 1524, Setchell 1253); Hot Spring (T. 1526). New to Alaska.

Two other species of *Frullania* have been recorded from Alaska: *F. tamarisci* (L.) Dumort., from Sitka (Syn. Hep.), and the imperfectly known *F. chilcootiensis* Steph., from Chilcoot (Krause).

YALE UNIVERSITY, June, 1900.

PLATE XLI.

Gymnomitrium obtusum (Lindb.) Pearson.

FIG. 1 Leaf, ×32.
    2 Cells from middle of leaf, ×290
    3 Cells from apex of leaf, ×290

The figures are all drawn from Dr Trelease's No 1512, collected at Orca

Anastrophyllum reichardtii (Gottsche) Steph.

FIG. 4. Part of stem with perianth, antical view, ×18.
    5 Part of stem with androecium, antical view, ×18.
    6–8. Leaves, ×18
    9 Cells from apex of leaf, ×290
    10 Cells from middle of leaf, ×290
    11 Cells from near base of leaf, ×290
    12, 13 ♀ bracts, ×18
    14 A part of the perianth-mouth, ×230.
    15 Transverse section of perianth in upper third, ×32.
    16 ♂ bract, ×16
    17 Antical base of ♂ bract, ×32

The figures are all drawn from specimens collected by Messrs Coville and Kearney at Columbia Fiord (No. 1389).

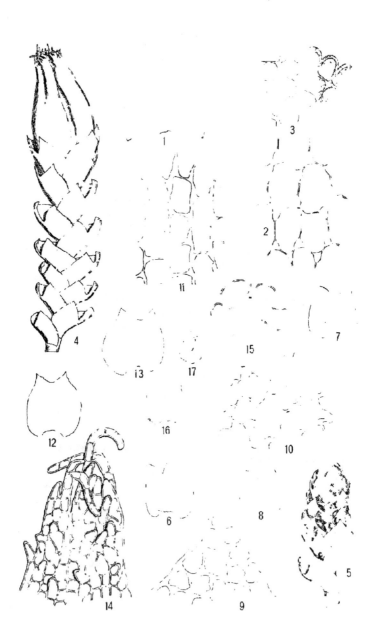

ALASKA HEPATICAE

PLATE XLII.

Cephalozia leucantha Spruce.

FIG. 18 Part of stem with ♀ branch and perianth, × 32
19 Leaf, × 230
20 Bract with connate bracteolate of innermost row, × 32.
21. Remaining bract of the same row, × 32.
22–24 Bracts and bracteole of second row, × 32.
25. A part of the perianth-mouth, × 230
26 Transverse section of perianth above middle, × 32

The figures are all drawn from No. 1393, collected at Columbia Fiord by Messrs Coville and Kearney

Diplophylleia plicata (Lindb.) Evans.

FIG. 27 Part of stem with perianth, antical view, × 15

Fig 27 is drawn from the type-specimen, collected in 1861 by Glehn, at Dui, on the island of Sachalin, Siberia.

PLATE XLIII

[Proc. Wash. Acad. Sci., Vol. II, Pl. XVIII.]

Diplophylleia plicata (continued).

FIG. 28 Part of sterile stem, antical view, some of the upper leaves gemmiparous, × 14
29 Postical base of leaf, × 28
30 Cells from apex of leaf, × 270
31 Cells from middle of leaf, × 270
32 Teeth and cells from postical base of leaf, × 270
33 Part of sterile stem, postical view, × 14.
34 ♂ bract with antheridia, × 14
35 Cells from middle of leaf, × 270

Figs. 28–32 are from specimens collected by Messrs. Brewer and Coe at Farragut Bay (No. 619), and figs. 33–35, from specimens collected by Dr. Trelease at Orca (No. 1192).

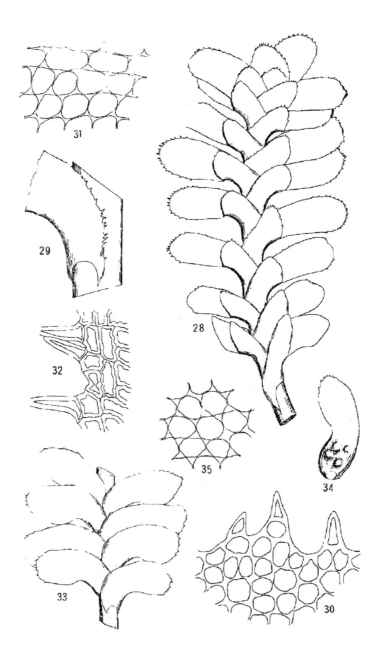

THE FERNS AND FERN ALLIES OF ALASKA

BY WILLIAM TRELEASE

No plants attract more general attention than the ferns and club-mosses, and as a rule none are earlier or more fully collected and studied in any region, partly because of this general interest and partly because identifiable fragments of most of them are more easily dried and brought in than of most of the higher plants, even in the absence of proper appliances for that purpose. Hence the publications on this group and on the Alaskan flora, though widely scattered, contain an unusually full record of the Pteridophytes occurring in that region, though details as to their distribution are not plentiful.

The members of the Harriman Expedition collected a large number of representatives of each of the families of Pteridophytes, their collections representing thirty-three species and thirteen additional varieties. This material, as well as that contained in the herbaria of the Missouri Botanical Garden and the United States National Museum, has been passed in review, and the results are embodied in the following catalogue, which admits 74 forms, comprising 58 species and 16 additional varieties, distributed by families as follows: Ophioglossaceæ, 7 species and 1 variety; Filices, 29 species and 5 varieties; Equisetaceæ, 8 species and 8 varieties, Lycopodiaceæ, 8 species and 1 variety; Selaginellaceæ, 3 species and 1 variety, and Isoetaceæ, 2 species. Where the name of a collector is not given, the localities mentioned rest upon published report in one or another of the papers cited after the name of the species, the works not fully cited being brought together in a bibliographic list which follows the catalogue.

For a reexamination of the Ophioglossaceæ I am indebted to Professor L. M. Underwood, who has also done me the favor to look through the entire catalogue. Mr. B. D. Gilbert has examined the specimens of *Athyrium*, and Mr. A. A. Eaton has examined and furnished some descriptions for the Isoetaceæ and Equisetaceæ, the varieties of the latter now for the first time recorded as Alaskan being no doubt more properly attributable to his acumen in recognizing the more trivial forms in the genus Equisetum than to the paucity of forms observed or brought in by earlier botanists.

CATALOGUE

Family OPHIOGLOSSACEÆ.

1 **Ophioglossum alaskanum** E. G. Britton.

E. G. BRITTON, Bull Torr. Bot Cl **24** 556, Fern Bull **6** 2.—MAXON, List 624.—UNDERWOOD, 67

Ophioglossum vulgatum DAVENPORT, 607.—EATON, **2** : 261.—LEDEBOUR, **4** 504.—MILDE, Fil 189.—ROTHROCK, 459.—TURNER, 81.—UNDERWOOD, 128

Ophioglossum vulgatum alaskanum GILBERT, 12

Unalaska (Turner in 1879). Mr. Turner notes that it grows in abundance among the rankest patches of ferns and weeds

2. **Botrychium boreale** Milde.

DAVENPORT, 607.—EATON, 1 37.—FLETT, Fern Bull **9** 32.—GILBERT, 12.—GRAVES et al., Linnean Fern Bull **3** 17.—MAXON, 637 ; List 625.—MILDE, Botrych 119 ; Fil 195.—OSTENFELD, 2.—TURNER, 81.— UNDERWOOD, 70 ; Bull Torr. Bot Cl. **30** : 44

? *Botrychium simplex* DAVENPORT, 606.

Unalaska (Turner in 1881).

3. **Botrychium lanceolatum** (Gmel.) Ångstroem.

BRITTON, 3.—DAVENPORT, 606.—EATON, 1 34.—GILBERT, 12.—KURTZ, 426.—MILDE, Botrych. 133 ; Fil 197.—OSTENFELD, 5.—RUPRECHT, Mél. Biol **3** : 23 ; Beitr. **11** 38.—TURNER, 81.—UNDERWOOD, 71 ; Bull. Torr. Bot. Cl. **30** . 46.

Botrychium rutaceum lanceolatum MOORE, Index 211.
Botrychium rutaceum tripartitum LEDEBOUR, 4: 505.—MOORE, Index 211.

Chilkat region; Popof Island (Kincaid; Saunders, 2644); Unalaska (Turner in 1881).

4. Botrychium lunaria (L.) Swartz.

BRITTON, 3.—CLUTE, 54.—DAVENPORT, 607.—EATON, 2: 274.—GILBERT, 12.—KAULFUSS, 25, 279.—LEDEBOUR, 4: 505.—J. M. MACOUN, 575.—MAXON, List 625.—MILDE, Botrych. 103.—MOORE, Index 208.—PRESL, Suppl. 43.—ROTHROCK, 459.—RUPRECHT, Symb. 101.—TURNER, 81.—UNDERWOOD, 70; Bull. Torr. Bot. Cl. 30 : 46.

Glacier Bay (Coville & Kearney, 679; Kincaid; Saunders, 2643); Yakutat Bay (Coville & Kearney, 1126); Popof Island (Kincaid); Unalaska (Evermann, 128; Turner in 1881); Attu; St. Paul Island, Bering Sea; Bering Strait.

5. Botrychium lunaria incisum Milde.

Glacier Bay (Saunders, 2643*a*, with the type). New to Alaska.

Professor Saunders collected on Popof Island, with *B. lanceolatum*, a coarser plant (2644*a*) resembling, but broader than, *B. matricariæfolium* as figured by Roeper, Zur Flora Mecklenburgs, fig. 7, which may be an extreme form of the present variety. (Fig. 1.)

6. Botrychium robustum (Rupr.) Underwood.

UNDERWOOD, Bull. Torr. Bot. Cl. 30 : 51.
Botrychium rutaceum robustum RUPRECHT, Beitr. 11 : 40.
Botrychium rutæfolium robustum MILDE, Nova Acta 26² : 763. *pl. 55. fig. 9.*
Botrychium rutaceum ROTHROCK, 459.—RUPRECHT, Mél. Biol. 3 : 23 ; Symb. 101.
Botrychium ternatum DAVENPORT, 607.—EATON, 1 : 150, 154.—TURNER, 82.

Unalaska (Harrington in 1871-2; Turner in 1881).

7. Botrychium neglectum Wood.

MAXON, List 625.—UNDERWOOD, Bull. Torr. Bot. Cl. 30 : 47.
Botrychium matricariæfolium DAVENPORT, 607.—EATON, 1 : 130.—J. M. COUN, 254.—MILDE, Botrych. 125 ; Fil. 196.
Botrychium crassinervium RUPRECHT, Mél. Biol. 3 : 24 ; Beitr. 11 : 42. *pl.*

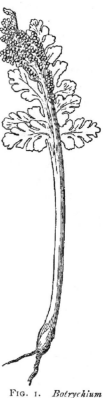

FIG. 1. *Botrychium lunaria incisum.*

Botrychium crassinervium obtusilobum RUPRECHT, Beitr. 11: 43.
Botrychium ramosum KURTZ, 426
Botrychium rutaceum HOOKER & BAKER, 447.—LEDEBOUR, 4: 505.—MOORE, Index 211.—TURNER, 82.

Chilkat region, Unalaska.

8. **Botrychium virginianum** (L.) Swartz.
DAVENPORT, 612.—TURNER, 82.

Unalaska (Turner in 1881—the *gracile* form, fide Davenport in litt.).

Family FILICES.

9. **Polypodium vulgare** Linnæus.
COOLEY, 182, 246.—COVILLE & FUNSTON, 349.—DAVENPORT, 607.—EATON, 1: 238.—HOOKER, 2: 258.—HOOKER & BAKER, 334.—KAULFUSS, 101, 279.—KURTZ, 426.—LEDEBOUR, 4: 508.—LYELL, 128.—J. M. MACOUN, 575.—MERRIAM, 147.—ROTHROCK, 459.—RUPRECHT, Symb. 119.—TURNER, 82.—UNDERWOOD, Bull. N. Y. Bot. Gard. 2: 148.
Polypodium vulgare cambricum MILDE, Fil. 20.
Polypodium vulgare occidentale MAXON, 637; List 628.

Juneau (Brewer & Coe, 718); Skagway, Chilkat Inlet; Sitka; Yakutat (Funston, 13), Kadiak (Brewer & Coe, 709, Evans, 369); Bailey Harbor (Townsend in 1893); Unalaska (Coville & Kearney, 1766, Evans, 513; Evermann, 7, Kincaid in 1897, Trelease, 2699); Iliuliuk (Harrington in 1871-2); Killisnoo; St. Paul Island, Bering Sea (Thompson in 1885). In the Yukon Territory it has been collected 50 miles above Stewart River (Tarleton, 154).

10. **Polypodium vulgare occidentale** Hooker.
FLETT, Fern Bull. 9: 31.—HOOKER, 2: 258.—LEDEBOUR, 4: 508.—MILDE, Fil. 19.—RUPRECHT, Symb. 119.
? *Polypodium falcatum* CAMPBELL, 399.
Polypodium vulgare, var. BONGARD, 175.

Cape Fox (Coville & Kearney, 2548); New Metlakatla (Coville & Kearney, 362); Wrangell (Evans, 59); Sitka (Evermann, 193, 256; W. G. Wright, 1611), Hot Springs, Baranof Island (Trelease, 2696); Yakutat (Brewer & Coe, 714, Saunders, 2698, Trelease, 2697), Atka (Evermann, 9). One specimen from Cape Fox (Coville & Kearney, 2548a) brings this far too close to the next species, though ordinarily it stands apart from the latter and from the type of *P. vulgare.*

11. **Polypodium falcatum** Kellogg
KURTZ, 426.—MAXON, List 628.

Cape Fox (Trelease, 2704); Farragut Bay (Coville & Kearney, 468; Trelease, 2702), New Metlakatla (Trelease, 2701), Killisnoo.

12. **Gymnopteris triangularis** (Kaulf.) Underwood.

EASTWOOD, Bot. Gaz 33 : 129.
Ceropteris triangularis UNDERWOOD, Bull Torr. Bot. Cl **29** 630

Cape Nome.

13. **Adiantum pedatum** Linnæus.

BRITTON, 8.—BRITTON & BROWN, 1 : 27.—CHRIST, 140.—CLUTE, 245.—
    COOLEY, 182.—DAVENPORT, 607.—EATON, 1 ; 136, 139.—HOOKER &
    BAKER, 126.—KAULFUSS, 202, 279.—KURTZ, 426.—MAXON, List 631.—
    MILDE, Fil 31.—ROTHROCK, 460.—TURNER, 82.—VASEY, 218.
Adiantum pedatum aleuticum LEDEBOUR, 4 526.—MOORE, Index 33.—
    RUPRECHT, Symb 117
Adiantum boreale PRESL, Tent. Pterid 158.
? *Adiantum capillus veneris* BESSEY, Science, n s **13** 833.

Glacier Bay (Trelease, 2694); Chilkat region; Sitka (Evans, 201; Evermann, 234); Kadiak; Unalaska (Harrington in 1871-2; Kincaid, 100); Attu.

14 **Pteridium aquilinum pubescens** Underwood.

UNDERWOOD, 91.
Pteridium lanuginosum CLUTE, Fern Bull. **8** : 38.
Pteris aquilina CAMPBELL, 399.—LEDEBOUR, 4 524.—MILDE, Fil. 45.—
    ROTHROCK, 460.—RUPRECHT, Symb. 114.—TURNER, 82
Pteris aquilina lanuginosa BONGARD, 176.—COOLEY, 182, 246.—EATON, 1.
    264.—KURTZ, 426.
Pteris lanuginosa CLUTE, Fern Bull **8** 37.

Juneau, Chilkat region; Sitka (Evans, 784); Hot Springs, Baranof Island (Trelease, 2688). Abundant from the Puget Sound region to about Sitka, but developing late, and hence not commonly collected. Professor Underwood calls my attention to the fact that this form does not depart in pubescence very far from the common form of the brake in Europe.

CHEILANTHES ARGENTEA (Gmel.) Kuntze.

DAVENPORT, 607.—GILBERT, 15.—GRAVES et al., Linn. Fern Bull **3** 7.—
    MAXON, List 633.—UNDERWOOD, 97.
Pteris argentea LEDEBOUR, **4** : 524.—ROTHROCK, 460.—TURNER, 82

Apparently first ascribed to Russian America by Pallas, as collected by Steller, and copied by recent writers, of whom, however, Davenport questions it, and Turner states that it evidently rests on error.

15. **Cryptogramma acrostichoides** Robert Brown.

BRITTON, 8.—BRITTON & BROWN, **1** : 28.—BONGARD, 176.—COOLEY, 182,
    246.—COVILLE & FUNSTON, 349.—DAVENPORT, 607.—EATON, **2** : 100.
    —FLETT, Fern Bull. **9** : 33.—MAXON, 637; List 633.—MOORE, Index
    263
Cryptogramma acrostichoides foveolata GILBERT, 16, 252.
Cryptogramma crispa HOOKER, **2** 264.—LYELL, 126.

Cryptogramma crispa acrostichoides HOOKER & BAKER, 144
Cryptogramma sitchensis MOORE, Index lxvi, 263.
Allosorus acrostichoides KURTZ, 426
Allosorus crispus KAULFUSS, 143, 279 —MOORE, Index 44.
Allosorus crispus acrostichoides MILDE, Fil 24
Allosorus foveolatus LEDEBOUR, 4: 525 —ROTHROCK, 460.—RUPRECHT, Symb 114 —TURNER, 82
Allosorus sitchensis LEDEBOUR, 4: 525 —MILDE, Fil. 26 —ROTHROCK, 460 —RUPRECHT, Symb 115 —TURNER. 82,

Glacier Bay (Trelease, 2689), Juneau; Lynn Canal, Sitka (Evermann, 235, on Mount Verstovia); Port Wells (Coville & Kearney, 1273; Trelease, 2691); Russell Fiord (Coville & Kearney, 982), Yakutat Bay (Coville & Kearney, 1142; Funston, 129); Disenchantment Bay (Brewer & Coe, 707, Coville & Kearney, 1087; Trelease, 2690); Kadiak (Evans, 370, 588; Kincaid, 99, Trelease. 2692), Unga (Saunders, 2693); Popof Island (Kincaid); Unalaska (Turner in 1880 and 1881), Cape Nome.

16 **Cryptogramma stelleri** (Gmel.) Prantl.

MAXON, List 633.
Allosorus stelleri KURTZ, 426.

Klehini, Lynn Canal region.

PELLÆA DENSA (Brack.) Hooker.

CLUTE, 87.

Doubtfully Alaskan.

17. **Asplenium viride** Hudson.

EATON, 2: 276 —LEDEBOUR, 4: 521 —LYELL, 127 —MAXON, List 636 — MILDE, Fil. 60 —MOORE, Index 177

Sitka; Yes Bay (Howell, 1727), Orca (Trelease, 2759).

18. **Athyrium cyclosorum** Ruprecht

GILBERT, 14, 31 —MAXON, 637, List 637
Athyrium filix-fæmina cyclosorum RUPRECHT, Symb 109 —MOORE, Index 183.
Athyrium filix-femina MILDE, Fil 52
Athyrium filix-femina sitchense MILDE, Fil 50 —RUPRECHT, Symb 109
Asplenium filix-fæmina BRITTON, 13 —BRITTON & BROWN, 1: 26 —CAMPBELL, 399 —DAVENPORT, 612 —HOOKER & BAKER, 228 —KNOWLTON, 221 —KURTZ, 427 —J M. MACOUN, 575 —ROTHROCK, 460 —TURNER, 82 —VASEY, 218
Asplenium filix-femina cyclosorum EATON, 2: 228 —LEDEBOUR, 4: 519
Asplenium filix-femina sitchense LEDEBOUR, 4: 519
Asplenium cyclosorum FLETT, Fern Bull. 9: 31

Cape Fox (Trelease, 2735), Glacier Bay (Coville & Kearney, 648a); Sitka (Evans, 163, 162—an aberrant form with round, deeply-cut pinnules, Evermann, 201; Trelease, 2749), Hot Springs,

Baranof Island (Trelease, 2750); Juneau (Coville & Kearney, 2503); Portage Bay; Orca (Trelease, 2756); Disenchantment Bay (Trelease, 2755); Kadiak (Brewer & Coe, 708; Cole; Coville & Kearney, 2366; Evans, 395; Kincaid; Trelease, 2751, 2752, 2753, 2753*a*, 2754); Wood Island (Evans, 452); Kukak Bay (Coville & Kearney, 1606); Nushagak; Unalaska (Evans, 520; Trelease, 2757, 2758); Afognak, Akun (Townsend in 1893); Adak (Townsend in 1893); St. Paul Island, Bering Sea (True & Prentiss, 63).

Probably the most striking of Alaskan ferns, growing in great abundance in many localities, where, as, for instance, on Kadiak Island, it covers entire mountain sides.

19. Athyrium cyclosorum strictum Gilbert.
GILBERT, 14, 32.

Sitka (Evermann, 199); Kadiak (Coville & Kearney, 2242); Unalaska.

20. Athyrium cyclosorum hillii Gilbert.
GILBERT, 14, 32.

Sitka (Evermann, 202); Unalaska (True & Prentiss, 127), Keechatno River (Herron in 1899).

PHYLLITIS SCOLOPENDRIUM (L.) Newman.
MAXON, List 637.

Very questionably ascribed to Alaska.

PHEGOPTERIS ALPESTRIS (Hoppe) Mettenius.
DAVENPORT, 607
Polypodium alpestre HOOKER, Brit. Ferns, with *pl. 6* —LYELL, 128.

Sitka.

22. Phegopteris dryopteris (L.) Fée.
BRITTON, 17.—BRITTON & BROWN, 1 : 19 —COOLEY, 182, 246.—COVILLE & FUNSTON, 349.—DAVENPORT, 607 —EATON, 1 158.—FLETT, Fern Bull. 9 33 —GILBERT, 19 —KNOWLTON, 221 —KURTZ, 427 —MAXON, 638; List 637.—MILDE, Fil 98 —TURNER, 82 —UNDERWOOD, 109
Polypodium dryopteris HOOKER & BAKER, 309 —KAULFUSS, 123, 279.— LEDEBOUR, 4 : 509 —LYELL, 128 —ROTHROCK, 459 —RUPRECHT, Symb 120
Polypodium calcareum BONGARD, 175

Wrangell (Evans, 77; Trelease, 2718), Douglas Island (Trelease, 2721, 2721*a*—an abnormal frond with round, deeply cut pinnules); Juneau (Brewer & Coe, 717; Coville & Kearney, 2514); Chilkat region; Sitka (Coville & Kearney, 818, Evans, 225; Evermann, 200, 241; Trelease, 2719), Orca (Trelease, 2726), Yakutat (Brewer & Coe, 713; Trelease, 2724, 2725 toward the variety); Disenchantment

Bay (Trelease, 2724); Kadiak (Trelease, 2722, 2723); Cook Inlet to Tanana River (Glenn in 1899); Nushagak, Kasilof (Evans, 626), Shumagin Islands (Harrington in 1871-2), Unalaska (Turner in 1881); Atka, Afognak, Attu; Cape Nome In the Yukon territory this species has been collected on Coal Creek Hill (Funston, 145) and 50 miles above Stewart River (Tarleton, 152a).

23 **Phegopteris dryopteris disjuncta** (Rupr.) Ledebour
LEDEBOUR, 4 509.
Polypodium dryopteris disjunctum RUPRECHT, Symb. 120.

Wrangell (Coville & Kearney, 400); Juneau (Trelease, 2720); Sitka (W. G. Wright, 1614), Yakutat (Brewer & Coe, 713a).

24. **Phegopteris phegopteris** (L.) Underwood.
BRITTON 16.—BRITTON & BROWN, 1 19.—FLETT, Fern Bull 9 32-33.—MAXON, 637, List 637
Phegopteris polypodioides COOLEY, 182, 246.—DAVENPORT, 607.—EATON, 2 218.—KURTZ, 427.—MILDE, Fil. 101.—TURNER, 82.
Phegopteris connectilis LAWSON, Fern Fl. Canada 247.
Polypodium phegopteris HOOKER & BAKER, 308.—ROTHROCK, 459.—RUPRECHT, Symb. 119.

Farragut Bay (Trelease, 2710), Chilkoot Inlet, Juneau (Trelease, 2711), Sitka, Yes Bay (Howell, 1726); Orca (Trelease, 2713, 2714); Kadiak (Cole), Unalaska (Trelease, 2716), Afognak; Attu; Cape Nome, St. George Island, Bering Sea (True & Prentiss, 62).

25. **Phegopteris phegopteris intermedia** (Hook.).
Phegopteris polypodioides J. M. MACOUN, 575
Polypodium phegopteris intermedium LEDEBOUR, 4 509

Wrangell (Evans, 83), Sitka (Trelease, 2712), Yes Bay (Howell, 1726 in part); Cook Inlet to Tanana River (Glenn in 1899); Kadiak (Evans 433, Trelease, 2715, 2772); Nagai (Townsend in 1893); Unalaska; St. Paul Island, Bering Sea.

26. **Polystichum braunii** (Spenn.) Lawson.
BRITTON, 14.—MAXON, List 641.
Polystichum aculeatum lobatum GILBERT, 19.
Polystichum aculeatum vestitum RUPRECHT, Symb. 107
Dryopteris braunii BRITTON & BROWN, 1 15.
Aspidium aculeatum COOLEY, 246.—DAVENPORT, 607.—HOOKER, 2: 261.—LYELL, 127.—ROTHROCK, 459.—TURNER, 82
Aspidium aculeatum braunii EATON, 2 125.—KURTZ, 427.—MILDE, Fil. 109.
Aspidium vestitum BONGARD, 175.

Glacier Bay (Coville & Kearney, 724), Juneau, Sitka (Evans, 164), Russell Fiord (Coville & Kearney, 942); Yes Bay (Howell,

1728), Yakutat (Saunders, 2731); Disenchantment Bay (Trelease, 2730)

27. **Polystichum lemmoni** Underwood.

GILBERT, 20.—MAXON, List 641.

Ascribed to the Alaskan region in the checklists referred to.

28. **Polystichum lonchitis** (L.) Roth.

BRITTON, 14.—FLETT, Fern Bull. 9: 32.—MAXON, 639.—RUPRECHT, Symb. 106
Dryopteris lonchitis BRITTON & BROWN, 1: 14.—COVILLE & FUNSION, 350
Aspidium lonchitis COOLEY, 246.—DAVENPORT, 612.—EATON, 1: 162.—
KAULFUSS, 235, 279.—KURTZ, 427.—LEDEBOUR, 4: 512.—J. M. MACOUN, 575.—MERRIAM, 147.—MILDE, Fil. 104.—ROTHROCK, 459.—TURNER, 82.
? *Aspidium acrostichoides* VASEY, 218.

Juneau, Chilkat region, Disenchantment Bay (Coville & Kearney, 1032); Unalaska (Evermann, 6; Harrington in 1871–2, Kincaid in 1897; Turner in 1881), St. Michael; St. Paul Island, Bering Sea (Thompson in 1885).

29. **Polystichum munitum** (Kaulf.) Underwood.

GILBERT, 20.—MAXON, List 640.
Aspidium munitum Kurtz, 427.

Prince of Wales Sound (W. G. Wright, 1615), Howkan (Evans, 135).

A fern very abundant in the British Columbia region, but barely reaching up into Alaska along the coast.

33. **Dryopteris fragrans** (L.) Schott

BRITTON, 15.—COLLIER, 167.—EASTWOOD, Bot. Gaz. 33: 129.—FLETT, Fern Bull. 9: 33.—MAXON, 638, List 639.
Aspidium fragrans CLUTE, 148.—EATON, 1: 76.—KURTZ, 427.—MILDE, Fil. 118.—MUIR, 49.—OSTENFELD, 5.—ROTHROCK, 460.—RUPRECHT, Symb. 103.—TURNER, 82.
Lastrea fragrans LAWSON, Fern Fl. Canada 243
Nephrodium fragrans GILBERT, 17.—HOOKER & ARNOTT, 132
Polystichum fragrans BRITTON & BROWN, 1: 16.—LEDEBOUR, 4: 514

Sitka, Chilkat region, Unalaska (Harrington in 1871–2); Iliuliuk; Norton Sound; Kotzebue Sound; Cape Nome; Cape Prince of Wales; Port Clarence (Brewer & Coe, 711; Coville & Kearney, 1899—a very dwarf compact form); St. Michael (Muir in 1881); Gens de Large and Koyukuk rivers (Schrader in 1899); branch of Koyukuk River (Mendenhall in 1901, Kobusk River (Mendenhall in 1901); Alatna River (Mendenhall in 1901); Neukluk River (Collier in 1900); Upper Kowak River (Thompson in 1885). Also collected in the Yukon territory: 50 miles above Stewart River (Tarleton, 153); 20 miles below Dawson (Osgood in 1899); and at Red Mountain (Gorman, 975).

31 **Dryopteris aquilonaris** Maxon. (pl. xliv)

MAXON, 638; List 639.
Nephrodium fragrans aquilonaris GILBERT, 17 —FLETT, Fern Bull. 9 : 33

Cape Nome.

32 **Dryopteris montana** (Vogler) Kuntze

UNDERWOOD, 110.
Dryopteris oreopteris MAXON, List 638
Lastrea montana LAWSON, Fern Fl Canada 243
Aspidium oreopteris DAVENPORT, 607 —EATON, 2 273 —TURNER, 82 — UNDERWOOD, 3 ed 114.
Nephrodium oreopteris GILBERT, 17

Short Bay (Howell, 1729); Unalaska (Turner in 1881), Attu.

33. **Dryopteris rigida arguta** (Kaulf.) Underwood.

MAXON, List 640.
Aspidium rigidum argutum KURTZ, 427.

Portage Bay, in the Chilkat region.

34. **Dryopteris dilatata** (Hoffm.)

Dryopteris spinulosa dilatata BRITTON, 16 —BRITTON & BROWN, 1 : 18 — MAXON, 639; List 640.
Dryopteris spinulosa BRITTON, 16 —COVILLE & FUNSTON, 349.—FLETT, Fern Bull. 9 : 32 —MAXON, List 640
Aspidium spinulosum BONGARD, 175 —COOLEY, 182 —DAVENPORT, 607.— KNOWLTON, 221 —KURTZ, 427 —J MACOUN, 275 —MERRIAM, 147 —MUIR, 50 —ROTHROCK, 460.
Aspidium spinulosum dilatatum CLUTE, 146 —COOLEY, 246 —EATON, 2 166 —GORMAN, 78, Fern Bull. 5 : 9 — KURTZ, 427 —J. M. MACOUN, 575 —MILDE, Fil 137 —OSTENFELD, 6 —TURNER, 82.
Aspidium dilatatum BONGARD, 175.—RUPRECHT, Symb 106
Polystichum spinulosum LEDEBOUR, 4 : 516.

Cape Fox (Trelease, 2734), New Metlakatla (Trelease, 2733); Wrangell (Evans, 57), Douglas Island (Trelease, 2738), Juneau (Brewer & Coe, 716; Cole, Coville & Kearney, 2507; Trelease, 2739); Glacier Bay (Coville & Kearney, 723); Chilkat region; White Pass (Trelease, 2740); Sitka (Coville & Kearney, 797; Evermann, 196; W. G. Wright, 1612); Orca (Coville & Kearney, 1307, Kincaid, Trelease, 2748), Kadiak (Trelease, 2742, 2744, 2745) Wood Island (Brewer & Coe, 710, Evans, 453), Cook Inlet (Coville & Kearney, 2436); Cape Karluk (Brewer & Coe, 712), Yakutat Bay (Funston, 33; Trelease, 2747), Disenchantment Bay (Trelease, 2746): Russell Fiord (Coville & Kearney, 955); Kasilof (Evans,

656), Nagai (Townsend in 1893); ? Unalaska (Harrington in 1871-2, as *Aspidium fragrans*); Afognak; Attu; Golofnin Bay; Cape Nome; Nushagak; Kotzebue Sound; Oogluk Bay (Walpole, 1733—toward the following form), Bering Sea: St. George Island; St. Paul Island.

A thicker-leaved, more compact small form, typically deltoid-ovate, the forma *nana*, which is very near the so-called variety *dumetorum*, also occurs abundantly, as follows: Cape Fox (Cole); Douglas Island (Trelease, 2737); Juneau (Brewer & Coe, 715); Sitka (Trelease, 2741); Kadiak (Coville & Kearney, 2243; Trelease, 2743); Cook Inlet to Tanana River (Glenn in 1899); Nagai (Harrington in 1872); Bering Sea: St. George Island (Evermann, 96); St. Paul Island (Townsend in 1893; True & Prentiss, 45; Townsend, June 24, 1893—growing into the larger form).

DRYOPTERIS SPINULOSA INTERMEDIA (Willd.) Underwood.
BRITTON, 16.—BRITTON & BROWN, 1 18.—MAXON, List 640.
Aspidium spinulosum intermedium COOLEY, 246.
Nephrodium spinulosum intermedium GILBERT, 17.

Wrangell.

DRYOPTERIS BOOTTII (Tuckerm.) Underwood.
Aspidium boottii CLUTE, 143 —COOLEY, 246.

Loring.

This and the preceding probably refer rather to *D. dilatata*, the indusial characters and form of which are found in all of the specimens I have been able to examine, though I have not seen Miss Cooley's material.

35. **Dryopteris filix-mas** (L.) Schott.
BRITTON, 16.—BRITTON & BROWN, 1 171.—J. M. MACOUN, 575 —MAXON, List 639.

St. George Island, Bering Sea.

36. **Cystopteris bulbifera** (L.) Bernhardi.
CLUTE, 214.—KURTZ, 428.
Filix bulbifera MAXON, List 642.

Pyramid Harbor.

37. **Cystopteris fragilis** (L.) Bernhardi.
BRITTON & BROWN, 1 · 13.—COOLEY, 182, 246.—COVILLE & FUNSTON, 350 —
  DAVENPORT, 607 —FLETT, Fern Bull 9 32, 33.—HOOKER & ARNOTT,
  132 —KURTZ, 428.—LEDEBOUR, 4: 516.—LYELL, 126 —J. M. MACOUN,
  575.—MOORE, Index 280.—MUIR, 51.—OSTENFELD, 7 —ROTHROCK,
  460.—RUPRECHT, Symb. 108.—TURNER, 82.

Cystopteris fragilis huteri MILDE, Fil 150
Aspidium fragile KAULFUSS, 243, 279
Filix fragilis BRITTON, 17 —COLLIER, 167 —EASTWOOD, Bot Gaz 33 129.—
    FLETT, 68 —MAXON, 639, List 642

Chilkat region; Juneau (Brewer & Coe, 721, Cole; Coville & Kearney, 2508, Trelease, 2762); Glacier Bay (Saunders, 2766, Trelease, 2763, 2764, 2765), Sitka (Evermann, 255, 233—with unusually broad pinnules); Orca (Kincaid; Trelease, 2769, 2770); Columbia Fiord (Coville & Kearney, 1367), Disenchantment Bay (Funston, 120); Cook Inlet (Coville & Kearney, 2437); Loring (Howell, 1730); Kadiak (Trelease, 2767), Kukak Bay (Coville & Kearney, 1600; Saunders, 2768); Red Hump Mountain (Collier in 1900); Unalaska (Harrington in 1871, Turner in 1880), Svenoi; Atka; Attu, St Michael, Cape Nome, Cape Thompson, Kotzebue Sound; Kobuk River (Mendenhall in 1901), near Port Clarence (Walpole, 2047, 1750, 1609, 1530), Bering Sea St. George Island (True & Prentiss, 61); St Paul Island (Townsend in 1893; True & Prentiss, 41). Also in the Yukon Territory Red Mountain (Gorman, 1098); Coal Creek Hill (Funston, 71, 146), above Stewart River (Tarleton, 151).

38. Cystopteris montana (Lam) Link.

DAVENPORT, 607, 611 —FLETT, Fern Bull. 9 32 —GILBERT, 16 —UNDERWOOD, 3 ed. 114
Filix montana COLLIER, 167 —EASTWOOD, Bot Gaz 33 129 —FLETT, 67 —MAXON, 639 —UNDERWOOD, 119

Cape Nome, Kruzgamepa River; Seward Peninsula (Collier in 1900); Reindeer Station near Port Clarence (Walpole, 1956) Also in the Yukon Territory Klondike-Indian Divide (Tarleton, 152c).

The restoration of the generic name *Filix* for *Cystopteris*, as proposed by Underwood (Mem. Torrey Bot. Club 6 278), would cause these species to be known respectively as *Filix bulbifera* (L) Underw., *F. fragilis* (L) Underw., and *F montana* (Lam) Underwood.

WOODSIA ALPINA (Bolt.) S. F. Gray.

BRITTON, 18 —BRITTON & BROWN, 1 10 —MAXON, List 643.
Woodsia hyperborea, CLUTE, 99

Perhaps referring to the next.

39 Woodsia glabella R. Brown.

BRITTON, 18 —BRITTON & BROWN, 1 10 —FLETT, Fern Bull 9 33 —GILBERT, 21 —MAXON, 639, List 643
Woodsia alpina glabella D C. EATON, Can Naturalist 1865 89

Near Port Clarence (Walpole, 1454); Cape Nome; Bering Strait; Kobuk River (Mendenhall in 1901).

40. **Woodsia ilvensis** (L.) R. Brown

FLETT, Fern Bull 9 33.—MAXON, 639; List 643.—MUIR, 49.
Woodsia hyperborea rufidula MILDE, Fil 165

Sitka, Unalaska, St. Michael; Cape Nome; Alatna River (Mendenhall in 1901—a linear-lanceolate form).

41. **Woodsia obtusa** (Spreng.) Torrey.

CIUTE, 97.—MAXON, List 643
Physematium obtusum KURTZ, 428

Portage Bay, in the Chilcat region. Specimens marked "American arctic flora" also in Hb. Field Columbian Museum, 15451-2.

42. **Woodsia scopulina** D. C. Eaton

KURTZ, 428.—MAXON, List 643

Chilcat region.

43. **Blechnum spicant** (L.) Smith.

CAMPBELL, 399.—CHRIST, 180.—LEDEBOUR, 4 523.—MILDE, Fil 47.—MOORE, Index 205.—ROTHROCK, 460.—TURNER, 82
Blechnum MERTENS, Linnæa 4 69.—HOOK. Bot. Misc 3 20
Blechnum spicant crenatum MOORE, Index 205
Blechnum boreale BONGARD, 176.—HOOKER, 2: 263
Struthiopteris spicant MAXON, List 634

Observatory Inlet; Cape Fox (Brewer & Coe, 719); New Metlakatla (Trelease, 2706); Wrangell (Evans, 12); Sitka (Coville & Kearney, 860, Evermann, 197, 237; Evans, 224, 580; W G. Wright, 1613), Hot Springs, Baranof Island (Trelease, 2707); Orca (Trelease, 2708).

Professor Underwood's recent studies may cause this to be called *Struthiopteris spicant* (L.) Scopoli.—See Mem. Torr. Bot. Club **6**: 282, and Our Native Ferns, 6 ed. 101.

Family EQUISETACEÆ.

44. **Equisetum arvense alpestre** Wahlenberg.

GILBERT, 8

Glacier Bay (Trelease, 2627, 2628a); Disenchantment Bay (Trelease, 2631); Bering Sea: Hall Island (Trelease, 2636), St. Matthew Island (Coville & Kearney, 2119).

45. **Equisetum arvense boreale** (Bong.) Ruprecht.

GILBERT, 8.—MILDE, Monogr 221.—RUPRECHT, Symb. 87.
E arvense BRITTON, 22.—BRITTON & BROWN, 1: 36.—CAMPBELL, 399.—

COOLEY, 246 —FLETT, Fern Bull. 9 : 32.—GILBERT, 8.—HOOKER & ARNOTT, 132—KAULFUSS, 2, 279.—KURTZ, 429 —LEDEBOUR, 4 : 487.—J. MACOUN, 249 —J. M. MACOUN, 575.—MAXON, 640, List 645.— MILDE, Fil. 217.—OSTENFELD, 11 —ROTHROCK, 459 —TURNER, 81.
E. boreale BONGARD, 174.

Farragut Bay (Trelease, 2615), Wrangell (Coville & Kearney, 422; Evans, 72; Trelease, 2614); Taku Harbor (Saunders, 2773); Douglas Island (Trelease, 2616); Juneau (Coville & Kearney, 550); Chilkat region; Glacier Bay (Coville & Kearney, 728—with short recurved branches; Trelease, 2617, 2628); Sitka (Trelease, 2620); Virgin Bay (Trelease, 2623, 2634); Orca (Trelease, 2622, 2635), Disenchantment Bay (Brewer & Coe, 638, Trelease, 2621, 2630); Kadiak (Brewer & Coe, 688; Cole; Coville & Kearney, 2291, 2370—toward *nemorosum;* Evans, 390; Trelease, 2618, 2619, 2629); Cook Inlet to Tanana River (Glenn in 1899); Kussilof (Evans, 610*a*); Fort Yukon (Schrader), "Camp 29" (Schrader); Gens de Large and Koyukuk Rivers (Schrader in 1899); Echeatnu River (Herron in 1899); Popof Island (Harrington in 1872; Saunders, 2625); Unalaska (Coville & Kearney, 1729; Evermann, 127; Trelease, 2626); Akun (Townsend in 1893); Adak (Townsend in 1893); Amaknak (Evermann, 162); Attu (Jacobs in 1894); Cape Nome; Bering Sea St. Paul Island (Coville & Kearney, 1839; Kincaid, 107; Townsend in 1893; Trelease, 2639); St. George Island. Also in the Yukon Valley: Ingersoll Islands (Gorman, 989); Forty Mile Creek (Funston, 45).

This is the most abundant *Equisetum* of Alaska, varying extremely according to exposure, soil, latitude, and altitude, and to my eye represents the prototype of all of the other Alaskan forms of *E. arvense*, though Mr Eaton finds that the latter are readily arranged under European varieties derived directly from the type.

46. **Equisetum arvense campestre** (Schultz) Milde.

Popof Island (Harrington in 1872). Not before reported as Alaskan.

47. **Equisetum arvense decumbens** Meyer.

Wrangell (Coville & Kearney, 422*a*; Trelease, 2614*a*); Juneau (Trelease, 2610); Glacier Bay (Kincaid, 104), Yakutat (Trelease, 2612); Kadiak (Trelease, 2611), Reindeer Station, Port Clarence (Walpole, 1942); Bering Sea: St. Paul Island (Trelease, 2638); St. Matthew Island (Coville & Kearney, 2119; Trelease, 2613).

48. **Equisetum arvense diffusum** A. A. Eaton.

GILBERT, 8, 25.

Kuzitrin River near Port Clarence (Walpole, 1638); St. Paul Island, Bering Sea (Kincaid, 100).

49. **Equisetum arvense nemorosum** (Bell) A. Braun.

Farragut Bay (Coville & Kearney, 478—peculiar in having the branches recurved); Glacier Bay (Trelease, 2617a), Cook Inlet to Tanana River (Glenn) Not before reported as Alaskan.

50 **Equisetum arvense riparium** (Fries) Milde.

Yakutat (Saunders, 2632, 2633). Not before reported as Alaskan

51 **Equisetum fluviatile** Linnæus.
BRITTON, 23 —BRITTON & BROWN 1. 37 —MAXON, List 645.

Glacier Bay (Coville & Kearney, 711).

52. **Equisetum fluviatile limosum** Linnæus
GILBERT, 8
E limosum Milde, Monogr 351

Sitka, Kukak Bay (Saunders, 2601), Kussilof (Evans, 610), Shumagin Islands (Harrington in 1871-2); Kuzitrin River near Port Clarence (Walpole, 1661).

53. **Equisetum hyemale** Linnæus
COOLEY, 246

Juneau (Coville & Kearney, 552).

54. **Equisetum palustre** Linnæus.
BRITTON, 22 —BRITTON & BROWN, 1: 37.—A. A. EATON, Fern Bull. **9**: 62 —MAXON, List 645
Equisetum palustre nanum GILBERT, 9

Popof Island (Saunders, 2609), "Camp 29" (Schrader); Reindeer Station, Port Clarence (Walpole, 1420, 1581, 1815).

55. **Equisetum pratense** Ehrhart.
BRITTON, 22 —BRITTON & BROWN, **1**: 36.—A. A. EATON, Fern Bull **9** 4 — EASTWOOD, Bot. Gaz **33**: 129 —MAXON, List 645.

Popof Island (Saunders, 2624), Gens de Large and Koyukuk Rivers (Schrader in 1899); Reindeer Station, Port Clarence (Walpole, 1419a, 1814).

56. **Equisetum pratense nanum** Milde.
A A. EATON, Fern Bull **9**: 4

St. Paul Island, Bering Sea (Coville & Kearney, 1840).

57. **Equisetum scirpoides** Michaux
BRITTON, 23 —BRITTON & BROWN, 1. 39 —J. M MACOUN, 575 —MAXON, List 646 —OSTENFELD, 9

Bering Sea St. George Island; St. Paul Island; Hall Island (Coville & Kearney, 2010a; Trelease, 2607); St. Matthew Island (Trelease, 2608). Also collected on Ingersoll Islands, Yukon Valley (Gorman, 988).

58. **Equisetum sylvaticum** Linnæus.

BRITTON, 22.—BRITTON & BROWN, 1: 36.—A. A. EATON, Fern Bull. 9: 33 —FLETT, 67, Fern Bull. 9: 32 —KNOWLTON, 220.—J. MACOUN, 250.— MAXON, 640; List 645 —MILDE, Monogr. 298 — ROTHROCK, 459 — TURNER, 81.

Equisetum sylvaticum squarrosum A. A. EATON, Fern Bull. 9: 36 — GILBERT, 9.

Nushagak; Kotzebue Sound; Cape Nome.

EQUISETUM VARIEGATUM Schlich.

COVILLE & FUNSTON, 349 —EASTWOOD, Bot. Gaz. 33: 129 —FLETT, 67; Fern Bull. 9: 32 —KURTZ, 429 —J. MACOUN, 252 —J. M. MACOUN, 575.—MAXON, 640.—MILDE, Monogr. 589.—UNDERWOOD, 129.

Chilcat region; Bartlett Bay; Khantaak Island; Unalaska; Bering Sea: St. George Island; St. Paul Island.

Probably all referring to the next.

59. **Equisetum variegatum alaskanum** A. A. Eaton, var. nov.

GILBERT, 9—name only.

Glacier Bay (Brewer & Coe, 629, Coville & Kearney, 620, 635, 733; Kincaid, 108; Trelease, 2602, 2603, 2604); Yakutat Bay (Trelease, 2606, 2606a); Disenchantment Bay (Brewer & Coe, 632; Coville & Kearney, 1040, 1084, Trelease, 2605); Russell Fiord (Coville & Kearney, 932); Gens de Large and Koyukuk Rivers (Schrader in 1899), Reindeer Station near Port Clarence (Walpole, 1420); Unalaska (Evans, 541). Also collected on Coal Creek Hill, on the Yukon (Funston, 82).

Aspect of small *hyemale*. Rootstocks black: roots densely brown felted. stems tufted, 1.5–4.5 dm. tall, 2–4 mm. wide, usually erect, but decumbent or assurgent in small cespitose forms, often branched after the first year when the tip of the main stem has been destroyed; branches up to 1.5 dm. long if unfruited, internodes 25–40 cm. long, dark green or with a reddish tinge, 8–12-angled, deeply and broadly grooved; ridges with a deep carinal groove, each resulting angle bearing a row of flint points; stomata in a single regular row on each side of the ridge, each stoma connected with its opposite by two rows of close-set rosulæ. Sheaths short, rigid, very slightly or not at all widened upwards, the leaves 4- or in very large specimens often 6-angled, black at base of teeth at first, this band extending downward over one-third or one-half of the sheaths or completely covering the lower ones, a cinereous band usually developing near the top in the second year; the uppermost sheath subtending the fruit, broadly campanulate, black, with about ten very broad 6–8-ridged teeth. teeth broad, rigid, erect or incurved, persistent, black, with a narrow white often deciduous border above, abruptly pointed, tipped with a rough black deciduous awn, deeply 3-grooved the whole length. Fruit-spike on a short stalk about 12 cm. long, apiculate.—Coville & Kearney, no 1084, from Hubbard Glacier, Disenchantment Bay, is taken as the type.—*A. A. Eaton*

The anatomical characters of this variety are those of *variegatum*. The vallecular bast traverses the walls to the holes, thus separating the parenchyma, a character said by Milde never to occur, but shown in some specimens from Hungary. By its external characters, it might well be taken for a variety of *hyemale*, the dark green rigid stems and appressed sheaths, becoming ashen above, being distinctly those of that species; but the latter has more numerous ridges which, in American specimens, bear no carinal grooves, while these are very evident in the present variety, and the teeth of *hyemale* are thin and evanescent, usually twisted together at top and articulated with the sheath below so as to become mechanically detached by the growth of the stem and hence coming off like a candle-extinguisher, leaving very blunt sheath-tips behind, while in the present plant the teeth do not disarticulate but are rigid, persistent, and deeply grooved centrally, with a short deciduous awn. From *variegatum* it differs in being taller and stouter, and, principally, in the short appressed sheaths and broad black narrow-bordered incurved teeth. The appressed sheaths would place it with the European *trachyodon*, which differs from *variegatum* principally in this character.—*A. A. Eaton.*

Family LYCOPODIACEÆ.

60. Lycopodium alpinum Linnæus.

BRITTON, 25.—BRITTON & BROWN, 1 42.—COVILLE & FUNSTON, 349.— EASTWOOD, Bot Gaz 33 : 129.—FLETT, Fern Bull. 9 : 32.—GILBERT, 11.—KAULFUSS, 11, 279.—LLOYD & UNDERWOOD, 165.—J. M. MACOUN, 575.—MACOUN, 641 ; List 647.—ROTHROCK, 459.—RUPRECHT, Symb 98.—SPRING, Monogr 1 : 104.—TURNER, 81.—UNDERWOOD, 136

Juneau (Saunders, 2646); White Pass (Coville & Kearney, 507), Orca (Coville & Kearney, 1197; Trelease, 2649); Yakutat Bay (Funston, 13), Disenchantment Bay; Kadiak (Evans, 587; Trelease, 2647); Kukak Bay (Coville & Kearney, 1522); Popof Island (Kincaid), Unalaska (Coville & Kearney, 2198, Harrington in 1871–2); Amaknak (Evermann, 161); Akun (Townsend, Aug 31, 1893);

Cape Nome, Oogluk Bay (Walpole, 1729 in part); St Paul Island, Bering Sea. Also collected in the Yukon Valley (Gorman, 1137), and at the Klondike-Indian divide (Tarleton, 184).

61. Lycopodium sitchense Ruprecht.

BONGARD, 175 —FLETT, Fern Bull 9: 32—GILBERT, 11—KURTZ, 428—LEDEBOUR, 4: 499—LLOYD & UNDERWOOD, 162.—MAXON, 640, List 647.—ROTHROCK, 459—RUPRECHT, Beitr 3: 30, Symb 98—TURNER, 81.—UNDERWOOD, 135.
Lycopodium alpinum, var. SPRING, Monogr. 2: 48.
Lycopodium alpinum sitchense MILDE, Fil. 258.

Chilcat region; Sitka (W. G. Wright, 1608); Orca (Coville & Kearney, 1198), Virgin Bay (Saunders, 2648), Yes Bay (Howell, 1732); Back Bay, Unalaska (Evermann, 4), Atka.

62. Lycopodium complanatum Linnæus.

BRITTON, 26.—BRITTON & BROWN, 1: 43—COOLEY, 246—GILBERT, 11.—KURTZ, 429—LEDEBOUR, 4: 499.—LLOYD & UNDERWOOD, 164—ROTHROCK, 459—RUPRECHT, Symb. 97.—TURNER, 81.—UNDERWOOD, 136.

Sitka, Juneau, Chilcat region, Lake Lindeman.

63. Lycopodium inundatum Linnæus.

LLOYD & UNDERWOOD, 152.—MAXON, List 646.—UNDERWOOD, 132.

Wrangell (Coville & Kearney, 392); Short Bay; Yes Bay (Howell, 1731).

64. Lycopodium clavatum Linnæus.

BRITTON, 26.—BRITTON & BROWN, 1: 43—FLETT, Fern Bull. 9: 32—GORMAN, 80, 81.—KAULFUSS, 9: 279.—KURTZ, 429—LEDEBOUR, 4: 500.—LLOYD & UNDERWOOD, 159—MAXON, 640, List 647—MERTENS, Linnæa, 5: 68—ROTHROCK, 459—RUPRECHT, Symb 97—SPRING, 1: 90; 2: 42—TURNER, 81.—VASEY, 218
Lycopodium clavatum δ HOOKER, 2: 267—J. MACOUN, 290.
Lycopodium clavatum pauci-divisum SPRING, 1: 91; 2: 42.
Lycopodium clavatum sitchense SPRING, Flora 21: 173—RUPRECHT, Symb 97.
Lycopodium aristatum robustius BONGARD, 175.

Observatory Inlet; Stikine; Chilcat region; Sitka; Kadiak; Unalaska (Coville & Kearney, 1789, 2213; Evermann, 3; Harrington in 1871-2; Trelease, 2685), Atka, Bering Strait.

65. Lycopodium annotinum Linnæus.

BRITTON, 25.—BRITTON & BROWN, 1: 42—BONGARD, 174.—CAMPBELL, 399.—COOLEY, 246—COVILLE & FUNSTON, 349.—GILBERT, 11—GORMAN, 80, 81.—HOOKER, 2: 266.—HOOKER & ARNOTT, 132—KAULFUSS, 12, 279.—KNOWLTON, 220.—KURTZ, 428.—LEDEBOUR, 4: 498—LLOYD & UNDERWOOD, 159.—J. MACOUN, 289—J. M MACOUN, 575—MAXON, 640, List 647.—OSTENFELD, 12.—ROTHROCK, 459—RUPRECHT, Symb. 96.—SPRING, 1: 78; 2: 36.—TURNER, 81.—UNDERWOOD, 134

Observatory Inlet; Millbank Sound; New Metlakatla (Kincaid); Wrangell (Coville & Kearney, 420, Evans, 16); Glacier Bay (Coville & Kearney, 672); Juneau (Saunders, 2670); Chilcat region; Sitka (Evans, 198a); Hot Springs, Baranof Island (Brewer & Coe, 630). Prince William Sound (Evans, 279); Orca (Coville & Kearney, 1201; Trelease, 2671); Columbia Fiord (Coville & Kearney, 1347); Yakutat (Trelease, 2669); Agua Dulce River (Brewer & Coe, 649); Killisno; Unalaska; Akun (Townsend, Aug. 31, 1893); Nushagak; Kotzebue Sound; Kuzitrin River (Walpole, 1652); Bering Strait; St Paul Island, Bering Sea. It has also been collected in the Yukon Territory at Upper Porcupine River (Funston, 170), and 50 miles above Stewart River (Tarleton, 155).

The following numbers approach var. *pungens*:

New Metlakatla (Coville & Kearney, 357; Trelease, 2674); Wrangell (Coville & Kearney, 409; Trelease, 2675); White Pass (Trelease, 2672); Orca (Trelease, 2687); Kadiak (Evans, 430; Trelease, 2679); Kasilof (Evans, 628); Oogluk Bay (Walpole, 1729).

66. Lycopodium annotinum pungens Linnæus.

MILDE, Fil. 253.—EASTWOOD, Bot. Gaz. **33**: 129. FLETT,—Fern Bull. **9**: 32.—OSTENFELD, 12.

Glacier Bay (Coville & Kearney, 746); Sitka (Coville & Kearney, 865; Trelease, 2676); White Pass (Osgood in 1899; Trelease, 2680); Orca (Coville & Kearney, 1200; Trelease, 2677); Port Wells (Coville & Kearney, 1289; Trelease, 2673); Virgin Bay (Coville & Kearney, 1252; Saunders, 2683; Trelease, 2682), Yakutat (Trelease, 2684); Kukak Bay (Coville & Kearney, 1525); Popof Island (Saunders, 2678); Unalaska (Coville & Kearney, 1790; Harrington in 1871–2; Trelease, 2686); Kussilof (Evans, 696); Nagai (Townsend, June 24, 1893); Atka; Amaknak (Evermann, 160); Cape Nome; Kotzebue Sound; St. Matthew Island, Bering Sea (Coville & Kearney, 2175; Trelease, 2681).

67. Lycopodium obscurum Linnæus.

BRITTON, 25.—BRITTON & BROWN, **1**: 41.—GILBERT, 11.—LLOYD & UNDERWOOD, 161.—MAXON, List 647.—UNDERWOOD, 134.
Lycopodium dendroideum GORMAN, 80, 81.—LEDEBOUR, 4. 498.—ROTHROCK, 459.—TURNER, 81.
Lycopodium juniperoideum RUPRECHT, Symb. 96.

New Metlakatla (Kincaid); Wrangell (Brewer & Coe, 624; Coville & Kearney, 421; Trelease, 2645); Sitka; Yes Bay (Howell, 1734).

68 Lycopodium selago Linnæus.

BONGARD, 75.—BRITTON, 24 —BRITTON & BROWN, 1 : 40 —EASTWOOD, Bot. Gaz. 33 : 129 —FLETT, 67 ; Fern Bull. 9 : 32.—GILBERT, 11 —GORMAN, 80.—HOOKER & ARNOTT, 132.—KAULFUSS, 21, 279 —KURTZ, 428.—LEDEBOUR, 4 : 497.—LLOYD & UNDERWOOD, 149.—J. MACOUN, 287 —J. M. MACOUN, 575 —MAXON, 640 , List 646 —MERRIAM, 147 —OSTENFELD, 12 —ROTHROCK, 459 —RUPRECHT, Symb. 96.—TURNER, 81 —UNDERWOOD, 131.

Lycopodium selago β HOOKER, 2 : 266 —J. MACOUN, 287.
Lycopodium selago patens MILDE, Fil. 252.

Observatory Inlet; Millbank Sound; New Metlakatla (Trelease, 2650); Glacier Bay (Coville & Kearney, 715); Taku Harbor (Saunders, 2653); Douglas Island (Trelease, 2651); Juneau (Brewer & Coe, 697; Coville & Kearney, 541; Evans, 154; Saunders, 2652); Chilkat region; White Pass (Brewer & Coe, 627); Sitka (Evans, 198; W. G. Wright, 1610); Hot Springs, Baranof Island (Trelease, 2667, 2668); Virgin Bay (Saunders, 2656); Orca (Coville & Kearney, 1199; Trelease, 2658, 2660); Columbia Fiord (Coville & Kearney, 1358); Port Wells (Coville & Kearney, 1290; Trelease, 2661); Yes Bay (Howell, 1733); Russell Fiord (Coville & Kearney, 993); Disenchantment Bay (Brewer & Coe, 83; Coville & Kearney, 1007; Trelease, 2662); Kadiak (Evans, 586; Trelease, 2654, 2655); Kukak Bay (Coville & Kearney, 1697); Popof Island (Saunders, 2663); Unga (Harrington in 1872); Unalaska; Akun Island (Townsend, Aug. 31, 1893); Nagai Island (Townsend, June 22, 1893), Port Clarence (Coville & Kearney, 1968; Trelease, 2665), Kotzebue Sound, Cape Nome; Bering Sea : St. Paul Island; St. George Island; St. Matthew Island (Coville & Kearney, 2112; Trelease, 2664), Hall Island (Coville & Kearney, 2016; Trelease, 2666). It has also been collected on the Klondike-Indian divide, in the Yukon Territory (Tarleton, 183).

Specimens very suggestive of *S. lucidulum*, and to which the varietal names above cited may refer, were collected as follows : Hot Springs, Baranof Island (Trelease); Orca (Trelease, 2657, 2659).

Family SELAGINELLACEÆ.

69. Selaginella schmidtii Hieronymus.

HIERONYMUS, Hedwigia 39 : 292
Selaginella rupestris LEDEBOUR, 4 : 500 —MAXON, 641.—MILDE, Fil. 261.—RUPRECHT, Symb. 99 —SPRING, 2 : 56
Selaginella rupestris sibirica GILBERT, 22.
Lycopodium rupestre KAULFUSS, 15, 279.

Unalaska; Cape Nome; Port Clarence (Trelease). Also collected at Dawson, in the Yukon Territory (Tarleton, 188).

70. **Selaginella schmidtii krauseorum** Hieronymus

HIERONYMUS, Hedwigia 39 293.
Selaginella rupestris KURTZ, 428

Klehini River, Chilcat region

71. **Selaginella selaginoides** (L.) Link.

BRITTON, 26.—BRITTON & BROWN, 1 44.—GORMAN, 81.—MAXON, List 647.
Selaginella spinosa LEDEBOUR, 4 501 —J MACOUN, 291.—ROTHROCK, 459 — TURNER, 81

Yes Bay (Howell, 1735); Unalaska (Harrington in 1871-2).

72 **Selaginella struthioloides** (Presl) Underwood.

UNDERWOOD, Bull. Torr. Bot. Club 25 132
Selaginella rupestris SPRING, 2 56.
Lycopodium rupestre HOOKER, 2 267

Observatory Inlet

Family ISOETACEÆ.

73. **Isoetes echinospora truncata** A A Eaton.

Isoetes echinospora BRITTON, 28.—BRITTON & BROWN, 1 46.
Isoetes echinospora braunii MAXON, List 650.

New Metlakatla (Coville & Kearney, 386), Kadiak (Coville & Kearney, 2336, 2337)

All the specimens collected were under-ripe, and those from New Metlakatla are placed here only from their general appearance, but mature macrospores were found among the roots of the Kadiak Island specimens.

74 **Isoetes macounii** A. A Eaton.

GILBERT, 10.—UNDERWOOD, 143

Atka.

BIBLIOGRAPHY [1]

Bongard, H G.
  1832 Observations sur la végétation de l'île de Sitcha Mém. Acad Sci St Petersb VI 2.

Britton, N. L
  1901 Manual of the flora of the Northern States and Canada New York

Britton, N. L., & A. Brown.
  1896 An illustrated flora of the Northern United States, etc , I New York.

Campbell, D H
  1899 Vacation Notes, II , The Northern Pacific Coast Amer Nat 33 391.

Christ, H.
  1897 Die Farnkrauter der Erde Jena.

[1] A few scattering references, fully cited in the text, are omitted from this list.

Clute, W. N.
　1901　Our ferns in their haunts　New York.
Collier, A. J., in Brooks,
　1901　Reconnaissance of Seward Peninsula.　U S Geol Survey
Cooley, Grace E
　1892　Impressions of Alaska. Plants Collected in Alaska and Nanaimo B C., July and August, 1891.　Bull Torrey Bot. Club 19
Coville, F. V., & F. Funston.
　1895　Botany of Yakutat Bay, Alaska.　Contr U S Nat Herb 3
Davenport, G. E
　1883　Some comparative tables showing the distribution of ferns in the United States of North America.　Proc. Amer. Phil. Soc. 20.
Eaton, D. C.
　1879–80　The Ferns of North America, 1, 2.　Boston.
Flett, J. B
　1901　Notes on the flora about Nome City　Pl World 4.
　1901　Ferns and allies at Unalaska and Nome City　Fern Bull 9.
Gilbert, B. D.
　1901　Working list of North American Pteridophytes　Utica, N. Y.
Gorman, W. J.
　1896　Economic botany of Southeastern Alaska　Pittonia 3
Hooker, W. J
　1840　Flora Boreali-Americana 2　London.
Kaulfuss, G. F.
　1824　Enumeratio filicum quas in itinere circa terram legit Cl. Adalbertus de Chamisso.　Lipsiæ
Knowlton, F H.
　1886　List of plants collected by Mr Charles L McKay at Nushagak, Alaska, in 1881, for the United States National Museum.　Proc U. S. Nat Mus 8
Kurtz, F.
　1894　Die Flora des Chilcatgebietes im südostlichen Alaska.　Bot Jahrb 19.
a Ledebour, C. F.
　1853　Flora Rossica 4　Stuttgartiæ
Lloyd, F E., & L. M. Underwood
　1900　A revision of the species of *Lycopodium* of North America　Bull. Torrey Bot. Club 27
Lyell, K. M.
　1870.　A geographical handbook of all the known ferns　London.
Macoun, J.
　1890　Catalogue of Canadian plants, pt. 5　Montreal
Macoun, J. M
　1899　A list of the plants of the Pribilof Islands, Bering Sea, with notes on their distribution.　Jordan, Fur seals and fur-seal islands of the North Pacific Ocean, pt. 3.　Washington

Maxon, W R
- 1900 A list of the Pteridophyta collected in Alaska in 1900 by Mr. J. B. Flett. Bull. Torrey Bot. Club 27
- 1901 List of the ferns and fern allies of North America. Proc. U. S. Nat. Mus. 23. Cited as "List."

Merriam, C Hart
- 1892 Plants of the Pribilof Islands, Bering Sea. Proc. Biol. Soc. Wash. 7. (The ferns listed after Vasey.)

Milde, J.
- 1869 Botrychiorum monographia. Verhandl. zool.-bot. Gesellsch. in Wien 19
- 1867 Filices Europæ et Atlantidis. Lipsiæ.
- 1865 Monographia Equisetorum. Dresden. Verhandl. K. Leop. Carol. deutsch. Akad. 32^2

Moore, T.
- 1857 Index filicum. London.

Muir, J.
- 1883 Botanical notes. Cruise of the revenue steamer Corwin in Alaska and the N. W. Arctic Ocean in 1881. Washington.

Ostenfeld, C. H.
- 1902 Flora Arctica. Copenhagen.

Presl, C. B.
- 1845 Supplementum tentaminis pteridographiæ. Pragae. Acta Soc. Reg. Bohem. Scient. V. 4.
- 1836 Tentamen pteridographiæ. Pragae.

Rothrock, J. T.
- 1872 Sketch of the flora of Alaska. Ann. Rept. Smithsonian Inst. 1867. Washington

Ruprecht, F. J.
- 1857 Bemerkungen uber einige Arten der Gattung *Botrychium*. Mélanges Biol. 3.—Beitrage zur Pflanzenkunde des Russischen Reiches, 11. 31. 1859
- 1846 Symbolæ ad historiam et geographiam plantarum Rossicarum. Petropoli. (Part 2 of this, "Distributio cryptogamarum vascularium in imperio Rossico," pp. 69–124, is frequently cited apart, under a repagination.)

Spring, A.
- 1842, 1849 Monographie de la famille des Lycopodiacées. Bruxelles (1) 1842, (2) 1849. Mém. Acad. roy. de Bruxelles, **15, 24.**

Underwood, L. M.
- 1900 Our native ferns and their allies. 6th ed. New York

Vasey, G.
- 1890 Scientific results of explorations by the U. S. Fish Commission steamer Albatross, VI. List of the plants collected in Alaska in 1889. Proc. U. S. Nat. Mus. 12

PLATE XLIV.

Dryopteris aquilonaris Maxon.
Cape Nome, Alaska

(398)

FERNS OF ALASKA
PTERIS AQUILONARIS Maxon

INDEX

New species in black-face type, synonyms in parenthesis.

Absorbents 7
Achnanthes glabrata 209
   lanceolata 209
   subsessilis 209
Adiantum boreale (379)
   capillus-veneris (379)
   pedatum 379
      aleuticum (379)
Aecidium alaskanum 37
   asterum 37
   astragali-alpini 38
   circinans aconiti-delphinifolii 38
   claytonianum 38
   epilobii 37
   fraseræ 36
   geranii 37
   grossulariæ 36
   orchidearum 37
   parnassiæ 37, 40
   ranunculacearum 36
   violascens 37, 39
Agaricus campester 45
   mutabilis 6
Agarum gmelini 159, 194, 248, Pl. XXVIII
   turneri 157, 159, 195
Ahk 8
Ahnfeldtia plicata 159, 199
Alaria 5, 181
   cordata 158, 190, 238, Pl. XXIII
   esculenta (190)
   fistulosa 158, 190, 193, 240, Pl. XXIV
   fragilis 158, 189, 234, Pl. XXI
      bullata 189
   lanceolata 158, 190, 232, Pl. XX
   laticosta 158, 189, 236, Pl. XXII
   pylaii 189

Alectoria 140
   divergens 132, 139, 144
   fremontii 140
   jubata 137, 138, 140
      bicolor 139
      chalybeiformis 139
      nigricans 138
   ochroleuca 137
      circinata 138
      rigida 137
      sarmentosa 138
      thulensis (138)
Algæ 4, 153
Alicularia geoscypha (350)
   minor (350)
   scalaris minor (350)
Allosorus 4
   acrostichoides (380)
   crispus (380)
      acrostichoides (380)
   foveolatus (380)
   sitchensis (380)
   stelleri (380)
Alsia abietina 291
Amblystegium radicale 298
   serpens 297, 306
      beringianum 298
   varium 306
      alaskanum 298
Amphiroa epiphlegmoides 160, 205, 206
   planiuscula 160, 206
   tuberculosa 160, 206
Amphisphæria applanata 30
Amphora elliptica 211
   ovalis 211
Amphoridium lapponicum 269
   mougeotii 269, 306

Anastrophyllum reichardtii 353, 368,
  pl XLI, f 4-17
Andreæa papillosa 254
  parvifolia 254
  petrophila 254
    sylvicola 254
Aneura 353
  latifrons 345
Anœctangium compactum 254, 265
  compactum alaskanum 254
Antennaria 35
  rectangularis 34, 56, pl III, f 9
  robinsonii 34
Anthelia julacea 363
  juratzkana 363
Antithamnion boreale 160, 203
  boreale corallina 203
Antitrichia californica 291
  curtipendula 291
  gigantea 291
Aongstrœmia longipes 257, 306
Aphanothece microspora 161
Aplozia atrovirens (353)
Arctoa anderssonii (258)
Arcyria cinerea 21
  denudata 21
Arnellia 351
Arthonia mediella alnicola 74
  punctiformis 74
Arthrodesmus convergens 167, 214, pl.
  XI, f. 14
Ashes for tobacco 6, 44
Aspidium acrostichoides (383)
  aculeatum (382)
    braunii (382)
  boottii (385)
  dilatatum (384)
  fragile (386)
  fragrans (383, 385)
  lonchitis (383)
  munitum (383)
  oreopteris (384)
  rigidum argutum (384)
  spinulosum (384)
    dilatatum (8, 384)
      intermedium (385)
  vestitum (382)
Asplenium cyclosorum (380)
  filix-femina cyclosorum (380)

Asplenium filix-femina sitchense (380)
  filix-fœmina (380)
  viride 380
Asterella fragrans 345
Athyrium cyclosorum 3, 8, 380
  cyclosorum hillii 381
    strictum 381
  filix-femina (380)
    sitchense (380)
  filix-fœmina cyclosorum (380)
Atrichum leiophyllum (286)
  lescurii (285)
  parallelum 286
Aulacomnium androgynum 285, 306
  palustre 285
  turgidum 285

Bæomyces acicularis (97)
  æruginosus 86
  degenerans (94)
  icmadophilus (86)
  spinosus palamæus (92)
Bangia atropurpurea pacifica 159, 196
Barbula aciphylla 266, 306
  brachyphylla 264
  brachypoda 262, 263, 310, pl XXXI,
    f 3
  cuneifolia 264
  cylindrica 265
  fallax 265
  fragilis 265
  muelleri 266
  rigens 265, 312, pl XXXII, f 1
  rigidula 265
  ruralis 266
    alaskana 266
  saundersii 264, 314, pl XXXIII, f 1
  subcuneifolia 264, 266
  tortuosa 263
  treleasei 265, 312, pl XXXII, f 2
  unguiculata 264
  vinealis 265
Bartramia breviseta 274
  circinnulata 274
  ithyphylla 273
    rigidula (273)
    strigosa 273
  menziesii 274
  œderi 274

Bartramia pomiformis 273
  subulata 274
Bartramiopsis lescurii 285, 307, 324,
  pl. XXXVIII, f. 2
  sitkana (285)
Basket materials 7, 8
Batrachospermum vagum 156, 163
  vagum flagelliforme 197
Bazzania deflexa 362
Beds 7
Beverages 5, 8
Biatora 81
  apochroeiza 85
  artyta 85
  cinnabarina 75, 84
  cuprea 85
  granulosa 85
  hypnophila 84, 102, 112
  laureri 85
  lucida 84
  milliaria 85
  sanguineo-atra 85
  sphaeroides 85
  varians 85
  vernalis 84
  viridescens 85
Bibliographies 147, 337, 395
Biddulphia aurita 207
Blasia pusilla 347
Blechnum boreale (387)
  spicant 4, 387
  crenatum (387)
Blepharostoma setiforme 362
  trichophyllum 362
Blindia acuta 260
  acuta flexipes 260
Bogs 3
Bostrichonema alpestre 17
Botrychium 4
  boreale 376
  crassinervium (377)
    obtusilobum (378)
  lanceolatum 376, 377
  lunaria 377
    incisum 377, f. 1
  matricariæfolium (377)
  neglectum 377
  ramosum (378)
  robustum 377

Botrychium rutaceum (377, 378)
  rutaceum lanceolatum (377)
    robustum (377)
    tripartitum (377)
  rutæfolium robustum (377)
  simplex (376)
  ternatum (377)
  virginianum gracile 378
Botrytis vulgaris 17, 26
Brachythecium acuminatum 294
  albicans 293, 294
  asperrimum 295, 306
  beringianum 293, 326, pl XXXIX,
    f. 3
  lamprochryseum giganteum 295
  latifolium 295
  novæ-angliæ 294, 306
  plumosum 295, 306
  reflexum 293
    pacificum 295, 328, pl XL, f. 4
  rivulare 294
  salebrosum 294
    angustifolia 294
  turgidum 295
Bryophytes 4, 9, 251, 329, 339
Bryhnia (294)
Bryum 262
  acutiusculum 281
  agattuense 278, 322, pl XXXVII, f. 2
  alaskanum 283
  alpinum 280
  argenteum 279
    majus 279
  ateleostomum 277, 320, pl. XXXVI,
    f. 1
  bimum 279, 306
  brachyneuron 283
  bullatum 283
  cæspiticium 281
  capillare 283
  cylindricoarcuatum 279, 318, pl.
    XXXV, f. 2
  drepanocarpum 282, 318, pl XXXV,
    f. 1
  duvalii 282
    obtusatum 282
  erythrophyllum 283
  fallax 283
  froudei 283

Bryum hammani 282, 324, pl. XXXVIII,
　　f. 1
　　heterogynum 280, 320, pl. XXXVI,
　　　f. 2
　　inclinatum 278
　　lacustre 283
　　laurentianum 280, 320, pl. XXXVI,
　　　f. 3
　　leptodictyon 280, 318, pl. XXXV, f. 3
　　meeseoides 283
　　microstegioides 283
　　mucronigerum 278, 316, pl. XXXIV,
　　　f. 3
　　obtusifolium 282, 283
　　pallens 281, 306
　　　rubro-vinosa 281
　　pallescens 279
　　pendulum 283
　　pseudo-stirtoni 281, 318, pl. XXXV,
　　　f. 4
　　pseudotriquetrum 282
　　stenotrichum 278
　　submuticum 283
　　suborbiculare 283
　　treleasei 278, 322, pl. XXXVII, f. 1
　　wrightii 283
Buellia 70, 80, 100, 107
　　albo-atra 78
　　alpicola 78
　　atro-alba (78)
　　　chlorospora (78)
　　colludens 78
　　geographica 75, 81, 104, 105, 106,
　　　109, 131
　　　atrovirens 76, 105
　　　contigua 76
　　myriocarpa 77, 106
　　　chloropolia 77, 136
　　papillata 77
　　　albo-cincta 77
　　parasema 77, (83), 107, 108, 113
　　　triphragmia 78
　　parmeliarum 78
　　petræa 76, (82)
　　　grandis 76
　　　montagnæi 77
Bulbochæte brebissonii 176
　　insignis 177
　　intermedia 177

Bulbochæte monile 177
　　nana 177
　　nordstedtii 177

Cæoma saxifragarum 36
Callithamnion floccosum pacificum 159,
　　203
　　pikeanum 159
　　plumula 159, 203
Calothrix æruginosa 163
　　fusca 163
　　scopulorum 163
Calvatia (41)
Camptothecium lutescens 293
　　nitens 293
Campylopus schimperi 260
　　virginicus (260)
Cantharellus bryophilus 46
Capitularia amaurocræa (91)
　　gracilis chordalis (94)
Catharinea tschuctschica (287)
Cenomyce ailotropa crispata (93)
　　coccocephala (89)
　　ecmocyna (96)
　　pungens (96)
　　radiata (96)
　　rangiferina (92)
　　squamosa muricella (93)
　　uncialis (90)
Cephalozia bicuspidata 360
　　catenulata 361
　　divaricata 361, 362
　　leucantha 360, 370, pl. XLII, f. 18–
　　　26
　　media 360, 362
Ceramium codicola 160, 203
　　rubrum 160, 203
Ceratiomyxa fruticulosa 21
Ceratodon heterophyllus 261
　　purpureus 261
Ceratothamnion pikeanum 203
Cercospora apii angelicæ 16
　　apii selini-gmelini 16
　　polytæniæ 16
Ceropteris triangularis (379)
Cesia concinnata (349)
　　obtusa (347)
Cetraria 92, 113, 134
　　aculeata 146

Cetraria aleurites 146
    arctica 145
    chrysantha 146
    ciliaris 142
    crispa 146
    cucullata 132, 139, 143
    delisei 145
        submedia 146
    fahlunensis 78, 143
        major (143)
        minor (143)
    glauca 139, 140, 142
        stenophylla 146
        substraminea 146
    islandica 7, 139, 144, 145
        delisei 145
        gracilis 144
        leucomeloides 144
        platyna 144, 145
        robustus 144
    juniperina 146
        pinastri 141
    lacunosa 142
    nigricans 146
    nivalis 143
    platyna (145)
    ramulosa 146
    sæpincola chlorophylla 142
Chætoceras hispidum 207
Chætomorpha 178
    cannabina 177
    melagonium rupincola 177
Chara contraria 180
    fragilis 180
Cheilanthes argentea 379
Chichiyulkutha 8
Childbirth 7
Chiloscyphus polyanthos 360
    polyanthos rivularis 360
Chorda filum 158, 188
Chordaria abietina 158, 187, 188
    attenuata 184
    flagelliformis 158, 188
Choreocolax polysiphoniæ 159, 197
Chroococcus rufescens 160, 163
    turgidus 160, 161
Chrysomyxa pirolæ 38
Ciboria rufo-fusca 26
Cladina lepidiota (96)

Cladonia 122, 132, 144
    acuminata 96
    alcicornis (96)
    alpestris 91
    amaurocræa 91
    bellidiflora 88
    coccocephala 89
        gracilenta (89)
        hookeri 89
        ramulosa 89
    cariosa corticata 95
    carneola 91
    cenotea 96
    coccifera 90
        pleurota 90
        stemmatina 95
    cornuta 93
    crispata 93
        cetrariæformis (96)
        divulsa 96
    cyanipes 96
    decorticata 96
    deformis 88
    degenerans 94
        trachyna (94)
    digitata 95
    dilatata (94)
    fimbriata 95, 96
        radiata 96
        simplex 94
        tubæformis (95)
    foliacea alcicornis 96
    furcata 96
        palamæa 92
        racemosa 92
    gracilescens 96
    gracilis 96
        chordalis 94
        dilatata 94
        elongata 93
            macroceras (94)
        hybrida (94)
    hookeri (89)
    lacunosa (95)
    macilenta 88
    mitrula 96
    papillaria 95, 134
    pleurota (90)
    pyxidata 95

Cladonia pyxidata pocillum 96
    pyxidata cervina (96)
    racemosa (92)
    rangiferina 7, 92, 139, 143
        alpestris (91)
        sylvatica (92)
    rangiformis 96
    reticulata 95
    squamosa 93
        muricella 93
    subsquamosa 96
    sylvatica 92
        sylvestris 91
    uncialis 90
        adunca (90)
    verticillata 93
Cladophora arcta 178
    flexuosa 178
    scopæformis 178
Claopodium bolanderi 292, 293
    crispifolium (293)
    laxifolium (293)
Clathromorphum circumscriptum 160, 206
Climacium americanum 292
    dendroides 291
        oregonense 292
    ruthenicum 292
Clithris 24
Clitocybe cyathiformis 48
    diatreta 48
    laccata 48
Closterium acerosum 165, 212, Pl x, f. 27
    acutum 165
    angustatum reticulatum 165
    brebissonii 165
    dianæ 165
    juncidum 165
    lunula 165
    parvulum 165, 212 Pl x, f 14
    striolatum 165
    venus 165, 212, Pl x, f 15
Cocconeis placentula 209
    scutellum 209
Cocconema lanceolatum 209
Codium adhærens 180
    mucronatum californicum 180, 203
Coilodesme bulligera 158, 186

Coilodesme californica 158, 186
    linearis 158, 185, 222, Pl xv
Collema furvum subhirsutulum 115
    melænum 115
        polycarpum 115
    pulposum 115
    tenax 115
    triptodes 115
Collemopsis flotoviana 115
Collybia dryophila 48
    velutipes spongiosa 48
Colpomenia sinuosa 158, 185
Condiments 5
Coniosporium atratum 16
Conocephalum conicum 344
Conostomum boreale 274
Constantinea rosa-marina 157, 160, 205
Coprinus plicatilis 44
Corallina arbuscula 160, 206
    pilulifera filiformis 160, 206
Cordyceps militaris 27
Cornicularia divergens (139)
    ochroleuca (137)
        nigricans (138)
Corticium incarnatum 43
Cortinarius 45
Coscinodiscus argus 207
    lineatus 207
Coscinodon pulvinatus 269
Cosmarium bioculatum 167, 212, Pl x, f. 28
    blyttii 214, Pl xi, f 15
    botrytis 169, 212, Pl x f. 11
    broomei 170, 212, Pl x, f 26, 35, 36
    cælatum 169, 212, Pl. x, f. 2
    conspersum 169, 212, Pl x, f 1
    constrictum 167, 212, Pl. x, f 33, 34
    contractum 168, 214, Pl xi, f 16
    costatum 169
    depressum 167, 212, Pl x, f 17
    granatum 167, 212. Pl x, f 8
    hammeri 167, 212, Pl x, f 7
        subangustatum 167
    holmiense 167, 214, Pl xi, f 28
    intermedium 169, 214, Pl xi, f 1
    kitchelii 168, 214, Pl xi, f. 17
    latum 168 214, Pl xi, f 4

Cosmarium meneghinii braunii 214, pl XI, f 19
    ochtodes 169, 212, pl X, f 10
    ornatum 170, 213, pl X, f 3
    pachydermum 168, 214, pl XI, f 12
    parvulum 168, 212, pl X, f 6
    phaseolus 169, 214, pl XI, f 8
    portianum nephroideum 169, 212, pl X, f 12, 13
    pseudogranatum 169, 212, pl X, f 21
    pseudotaxichondrum 170, 212, pl X, f 5
    pulcherrimum 169, 212, pl X, f 18, 19
    pyramidatum 168, 212, pl X, f 40
    quadrifarium 169, 212, pl X, f 22
    ralfsii 214, pl XI, f 22
    sexangulare 168, 212, pl X, f 39
    sphalerostichum 170, 214, pl XI, f 6
    subcrenatum 169, 212, pl X, f. 20
    tumidum 168, 214, pl XI, f 21
        subtile 168
    undulatum 168, 214, pl XI, f 9
    venustum 167
        induratum 168
Cosmetics 6
Costaria mertensii 159
    turneri 195
Cough medicines 5, 8
Cryptogramma acrostichoides 379
    acrostichoides foveolata (379)
    crispa (379)
        acrostichoides (380)
    sitchensis (380)
    stelleri (380)
Cryptonemia obovata 160, 204
Cryptosiphonia grayana 160, 205
Cudonia circinans 26
Cymathera triplicata 157, 158, 194
Cymbella ehrenbergii 211
    inæqualis 211
Cynodontium polycarpum 255
    polycarpum alaskanum 256
    laxirete 256
    torquescens 255
    treleasei 255, 308, pl XXX, f 1

Cynodontium virens 256
    seriatum 256
    wahlenbergii 256
    brevifolia 256
Cyphella 16
Cystophyllum lepidium 154, 159, 185, 186, 196
Cystopteris bulbifera 385
    fragilis 385
        huteri (386)
    montana 386

Dactyomyces deliquescens 42
    palmatus 42
Dactylina arctica (145)
Dasyscypha bicolor 24
Delesseria alata 159, 201, 202
    baerii 159, 201
    crassifolia 159, 201
    decipiens 201
    quercifolia 201
    serrata 159, 202
    sinuosa 159, 201
Derbesia marina 179
    vaucheriæformis 179
Dermocarpa biscayensis 161
    fucicola 161, 218, pl XIII, f 4, 5
    prasina 161
Desmarestia aculeata 158, 182, 186, 194
    viridis 158, 186
Desmatodon latifolius 263
    systylioides (262)
Desmidium swartzii 172
Desmonema wrangelii 162
Diaporthe 29
    anisomera 16, 30, 60, pl V, f 10
    pungens 31
    strumella oligocarpa 30
Diatoma hyemale 208
    pectinale 208
Dichodontium pellucidum kodiakanum 257, 308, pl XXX, f 2
Dicranella crispa 257
    grevilleana 257, 306
    heteromalla 257, 288
    latinervis 257
    orthophylla 257
    polaris 257
    rufescens 257

Dicranella squarrosa 257
    subulata (257)
Dicranodontium aristatum 260, 306
    longirostre 260, 306
Dichodontium flavescens (257)
    pellucidum 256
        fagimontanum 256
        kodiakanum 257
    serratum 257
Dicranoweisia contermina (254)
    crispula 254
    obliqua (255)
    roellii (254)
Dicranum (122)
    albicans 258, 306
    anderssonii 257, 306
    angustifolium 260
    bergeri 260
    bonjeani 260
        schlotthaueri 260
    congestum (259)
    dipteroneuron 259
    elongatum 258
    flagellare 258
    fuscescens 259
    grœnlandicum 258, 306
    howellii 260, 306
    hyperboreum 258
    majus 260
    miguelonense 258
    molle 260
    muehlenbeckii 260
        brevifolium 259
    neglectum 259, 306
    scoparium 259
    spadiceum (259)
    starkei 258, 306
    strictum 258
    subflagellare 258, 308, Pl. XXX, f. 3
    virginicum 260
Dictyoneuron 157
Dictyosiphon fœniculaceus 157, 158, 186
Diderma niveum 22
Didymodon baden-powelli 262
    rubellus 262
Didymosphæria arenaria macrospora 30, 58, Pl. IV, f. 9
    nana 30, 32

Dilæna hibernica (345)
Dillesk 5
Dilsea arctica 160, 205
    californica 160, 205
Diplophylleia 359
    albicans 363, 365
    plicata 363, 370, 372, Pl. XLII, f. 27, XLIII. f. 28–35
    taxifolia 363, 365
Diplophyllum argenteum 359
    plicatum (363)
Disphinctium connatum 166, 212, Pl. X, f. 30
    cucurbita 166
Dissodon splachnoides 272
Distichium capillaceum 261, 265
Distilled beverages 8
Ditrichum flexicaule densum 261
    glaucescens 261
    homallum 261, 306
Docidium baculum 166
    coronulatum 166
    dilatatum 166
    gracile 166
    minutum 167
Dothidea betulina 13, 27
Dothidella betulina 27, 32
    betulina **yakutatiana** 27, 60, Pl. V, f. 15[1]
Dryopteris aquilonaris 384, 398, Pl. XLIV
    boottii 385
    braunii (382)
    dilatata 384
        dumetorum 385
        nana 385
    filix-mas 385
    fragrans 383
    lonchitis (383)
    montana 384
    oreopteris (384)
    rigida arguta 384
    spinulosa (384)
        dilatata (384)
        intermedia 385
Dufourea arctica (145)
Dulse 5
Dumontia filiformis 160, 204
Dye stuffs 7

Eccilia conchina 46
Economic uses of plants 4
Ectocarpus confervoides 158, 182
    confervoides corticulatus 182
        pygmæus 182
    corticulatus (182)
    tomentosus 158, 181
Eggs of fish 5
Eisenia arborea 159, 195
Elachista lubrica 158, 187
Encalypta alaskana 271
    commutata 271
    macounii 271
    rhabdocarpa 271
    vulgaris 271
Endocladia muricata 159, 198
Enteromorpha 174
    crinita 176
    intestinalis 175
        cylindrica 175, 176
        maxima 175
    linza 174
        crispata 175
        lanceolata 175
    micrococca 175
    prolifera 175
Entoloma clypeatum 46
Entosthodon spathulifolius 272, 316, pl. XXXIV, f. 1
Ephebe pubescens 115
Epithemia gibba 211
    jurgensii 211
    westermannii 211
Equisetum arvense (4, 387)
    arvense alpestre 387
        boreale 387
        campestre 388
        decumbens 388
        diffusum 388
        nemorosum 389
        riparium 389
    boreale (388)
    fluviatile 389
        limosum 389
    hyemale 389, 390, 391
    limosum (389)
    palustre 8, 389
        nanum (389)
    pratense 389

Equisetum pratense nanum 389
    scirpoides 389
    sylvaticum 8, 390
        squarrosum (390)
        trachyodon 391
    variegatum (4, 390)
        alaskanum 390
Erineum 13
    alneum 49
    aucupariæ 49
    pyrinum 49
    roseum 49
Euastrum affine 172, 212, pl. x, f. 32
    ansatum 171
    crassum 171, 212, pl. x, f. 4
    didelta 171, 214, pl. xi, f. 2
    elegans 172, 214, pl. xi, f. 2, 25, 26, 30
    gemmatum 171
    oblongum 171, 212, pl. x, f. 37
    pokornyanum 171
    verrucosum 171, 212, pl. x, f. 9
Eudesme 158
    flavescens 187
    virescens 187
Eunotia gracilis 209
    lunaris 209
    robusta 209
Eurhynchium cirrosum 296
    myosuroides 295
        humile 296
        spiculiferum 295, 296
        stoloniferum 296
        substoloniferum 295
    oreganum 296, 306
    pacificum (295)
    stokesii 296, 306
        pseudo-speciosum 296
    strigosum 296
        fallax 296
    vaucheri 296
Eurotium herbariorum 35
Euthora cristata 157, 159, 199
Evernia divergens (139)
    ochroleuca (137)
        circinnata (138)
    thamnodes 147
    vulpina 7
Exobasidium vaccinii 13, 42

Fabræa cincta 23, 60, pl v, f 16
Fermented beverages, 5, 8
Ferns 3, 4, 8, 373
Filix bulbifera (385, 386)
    fragilis (386)
    montana (386)
Fimbriaria tenella 342, 345
Fisk 5, 6, 9
Flammula fulvella 45
Fomes applanatus 44
    fomentarius 43
    igniarius 6, 44
    lucidus 44
    pinicola 43
    tinctorius 6
Fontinalis patula 290, 306
Food plants 5, 6 7, 8, 200
Forests 2
Fragilaria construens 208
    exilis 208
    striatula 208
    virescens 208
Frullania chilcootiensis 343, 367
    franciscana 343, 367
    nisquallensis 343 366
    tamarisci 367
Fucus 183, 197
    edulis 5
    esculentus 5
    evanescens 5, 159, 181
        cornuta 196, 250, pl xxix, f. 2
        macrocephala 5, 182, 183, 196, 250, pl xxix, f 1
        megacephala (157, 161)
        harveyanus 157
        lutkeanus (6)
        platycarpus (196)
        saccharinus (5)
        vesiculosus (5)
Funaria hygrometrica 273
    calvescens 273
Fungi 3, 4, 6, 11, 13
    host-list 49
Fusarium illosporioides 15, 56, pl. iii, f 10

Galera sphagnorum 45
Galls 13, 49
Gigartina pacifica 159, 199

Gigartina papillata 159, 198
    papillata cristata 199
    subsimplex 198
Gloiopeltis 154
    furcata 160, 204
Gloiosiphonia (154)
    californica 160, 204
    furcata (160)
Glomerularia corni 17
Gnomoniella tubiformis 32, 34
Godronia 29
    urceolus 24
Gomontia polyrhiza 179
Gomphonema affine 211
    geminatum 211
    subtile 211
Grammatophora marina 208
Graphis scripta 74
Grimaldia fragrans 344, 345
Grimmia agassizii 267
    apocarpa 266
        alpicola 266
        gracilis 266
        rivularis 266
    conferta 266
    crassinervis 267
    elatior 267, 306
    maritima 266, 306
    torquata 267
Guepinia lutea 42
    merulina 42
Guignardia alaskana 34, 64, pl vii, f 1-5
Gyalecta convarians 147
    rhexoblephara 147
Gymnomitrium concinnatum 349
    coralloides 349
    obtusum 347, 368, pl xli, f 1-3
Gymnopteris triangularis 379
Gymnostomum curvirostre scabrum 254
Gymnozyga longata 173
Gyrophora proboscidea (127)
Gyrothyra 351

Halosaccion firmum 159, 200
    fucicola 159, 200
    macrosporum 159, 200
    ramentaceum 159, 200

Halosaccion ramentaceum densa 200
    tilesii 159, 200
Haplosiphon pumilus 163
Harpanthus flotowianus 360
Hedophyllum sessile 158, 193, 228, pl
    XVIII
    subsessile 158, 194
Helotium alaskæ 25, 54, pl II, f 3
    fumigatum 26
    lenticulare 26
Hepaticæ 339
Herberta adunca 363
Heterosphæria patella 22
Heterothecium 85
    pezizoideum 83
    sanguinarium 83
        affine 75, 83
Hildenbrandtia rosea 160, 205
Homeostroma latifolium 158, 184
    lobatum 158, 184, 218, pl XIII, f. 6
    undulatum 158, 183, 218, pl XIII, f 3
Hoochinoo 8
Hormidium parietinum 176
Hormiscium altum 35
Hosts of fungi 49
Hot-water algæ 161
Hyalospora polypodii-dryopteridis 40
Hydrurus penicillatus 164
Hygrophorus limacinus 47
Hylocomium alaskanum (304)
    calvescens 305
    loreum 3, 305
    rugosum 306
    splendens 3, 304
        gracilius 304
    squarrosum 305
    triquetrum 305
        beringianum 306
    umbratum 305, 306
Hymenochæte tabacina 43
Hypnum 295
    aduncum kneiffii 299
    alaskæ 301
    alaskanum 304
    amblyphyllum 307
    brunneo-fuscum 303
    callichroum 301, 306
    canadense 302

Hypnum chloropterum (294)
    circinale 301
    conflatum (299)
    congestum (293)
    cordifolium 303
    crista-castrensis (301)
    cupressiforme 302
    dieckii 302, 306
    eugyrium 302
    filicinum 300
    fluitans 299
        alpinum 299
        exannulatum 299
        jeanbernati 299
    hamulosum 302
    imponens 302
    krausei 303
    ochraceum 302
        flaccidum 302
    polygamum minus 299
    plesiostramineum 303, 307, 328, pl. XL, f 2
    pseudo-complexum 304
    pseudostramineum 304, 328, pl. XL, f 1
    revolvens 299
    sarmentosum 252, 303
        beringianum 252, 303
    scabridum (294)
    schreberi 303, 305
    sequoieti (301)
    stellatum 298, 299
    stramineum 303, 304
    subeugyrium (302, 306)
        occidentale 302, 303
    sulcatum (301)
        stenodictyon 301
    treleasei 298, 326, pl XXXIX, f. 5
    uncinatum 299
        breviseta 300
        orthothecioides 299
        plumosa 300
        plumosum, 299, 300
        polare 300
        subjulaceum 299
            orthothecioides 300
    vaucheri 302
Hypoxylon majusculum 34
    ohiense 34, 58, pl IV, f. 2

Iceland moss 7
Injury to trees 3, 140
Intoxicants 5, 8
Iridæa heterocarpa (198)
    laminarioides 159, 198
    membranacea 159, 198
Isoetes echinospora (395)
    echinospora braunii (395)
        truncata 395
    macounii 395
Isthmia obliquata 207

Jungermannia atrovirens 353
    cordifolia (352) 353
    guttulata (356)
    hæmatosticta (350)
    hibernica (345)
    lanceolata 353
    nardioides (353, 355)
    obtusa (357)
    porphyroleuca (356)
    pumila 353
    quadriloba (358)
    reichardtii (353)
    scalaris minor (350)
    sphærocarpa 352

Kalymenia californica 159, 199
Kantia trichomanis 362

Laboulbenia nebriæ 22
Lachnea scutellata 26
Lady fern 3
Laestadia alaskana (34)
    saxifragæ 33, 58, pl iv, f. 3
Lagenidium entophytum 35
Laminaria andersonii 157
    bongardiana 157, 158, 193
        subsessilis (194)
    bullata 157, 158, 192
    cuneata 158
    cuneifolia 193, 226, pl. xvii, f. 1
    saccharina 5, 158, 193
    sessilis (193)
    sinclairii 157
    solidungula 158, 193
Lamp wicks 7, 8
Lastrea fragrans (383)
    montana (384)
Laver 5

Leathesia difformis 187
Lecanora 76, 78, 80, 100, 107
    adglutinata (128)
    atra 107
    atrosulphurea 81, 106, 107
    atrynea 110
    cenisia 110
    belonioides 110
    cæsiorufa 110, 112
    cæsiorufella 110
    cervina 110
        discreta 110
    chlarona 110
    chrysoleuca opaca (109)
    cinerea 77, 104
        gibbosa 76, 105
    contractula 110
    crenata 110
    disceptans 110
    epibrya 110
    epiglypta 110
    elatina 110
    frustulosa 108
    fuscoatra 110 (112)
    fuscolutea 110
    gelida 109
    glaucomela 110
    gyalectina 110
    hageni 107
    hypnorum deaurata 110
    inæquatula 110
    intricata (106)
    irrubata 110
    lacustris 110
    lævata candida 110
    lobulata 110
    mniaræa 110
        pachnea 110
    muralis 109
    occulata 105
        gonatodes 111
    ochromicra 110
    pacifica 107
    pallescens 106
        rosella 110
    pallida 108
    privigna revertens 104, 106
    pyracea 110
        ramulicola 110

Lecanora quadruplans 110
  rubina 109
    opaca 109
  saxicola 111
  smaragdula 110
  stillicidiorum 110
    chloroleuca 110
  straminea 109, 131
  suaveolens 110
  subfusca 107
    allophana 108
    argentata 108
    coilocarpa 108 (113)
    hypnorum 110
  subintricata 110
  subradians 110
  subradiosa 110
  tartarea 105, 106
    frigida 105
    pterulina 106
    upsaliensis (110)
  tetraspora 110
  thamnitis 110
  tribacea (120)
  turfacea (102)
  umbrina 110
  upsaliensis 110
  varia 77, 106, 107
    intricata 77, 106
    symmicta 107, 135
  ventosa 110
  verrucosa 110
  vitellina (111)
Lecidea 76, 100, 107, 113
  affinis (82, 83)
  alaskensis 83
  albocærulescens 80
    flavocærulescens 80
  albohyalina 81
  alpicola 82
  apochroeiza (85)
  arctica 81
  assimilata 81
  associata 82
  atroalbens 82
  atrocæsia 82
  atrorufa 82
  brachyspora 82
  candida 82

Lecidea carneo-pallida (100)
  chionea 82
  chloropolia (77)
  cinnabarina (84)
  confervoides 82
  confluens 80
    steriza (80)
  contigua 80
    meiospora 82
    speirea 81
  crustulata 82
  denotata 81
  disciformis insignis 82
  dovrensis 82
  enteroleuca 74, 79, 111, 112
    flavida 79
    latypea 81
    muscorum 81
  enteroleucodes 82
  epiphæa 82
  excentrica 82
  fecunda 82
  fuscoatra 81
  geminata (77) 82
  geographica contigua (76)
  hypnophila (84)
  hypopodia subassimilata 82
  incongrua 82
  insperabilis 81
  internectens 81
  jemtlandica 82
  laurentiana 82
  limosa 82
  meiobola 81
  meiocarpa 81
  melanchelma 79, 112
  montagnæi (77)
  muscorum 82
  nigrocinerea 81
  pallidella 82
  panæola 81
  papillata (77)
  paraphanella 82
  parasema (77)
    euphora 82
  petræa (76)
    fuscoatra grandis (76)
  pezizoidea 82
  plana 82

Lecidea platycarpa 79, 109, 131
   platycarpa steriza 80
   ramulosa 82
   rhexoblephara 82
   sabuletorum 81
   sanguinaria 82
   sanguineoatra 82
   scabrosa 82
   sphæroides (85)
   spilota (82)
   suballinita 74, 82
   subduplex 81
   subfuscula 82
   subnegans 82
   syncomista 81
   tenebrosa subsparsa 82
   ternaria 82
   tessellata 81
   tornoensis 82
   triphragmia (78)
   triplicans 81
   vernalis (84)
Lepidomorphum yendoi 160, 206
Lepidozia filamentosa 343, 362
   reptans 362
   setacea 362
Leptobryum pyriforme 275
Leptogium 118, 122
   albociliatum 114
   muscicolum 115
   myochroum 114
      saturninum 114
      tomentosum 115
   parculum 115
   saturninum (114)
   scoticum 115
   tenuissimum 115
   tremelloides 115
Leptosphæria agnita labens 30, 60, pl. v, f. 11
   doliolum 18, 29
   fœniculacea lupina 29, 60, pl. v, f. 12
   juncicola 30
   leersiana 29, 32
   marginata 30
   ophiopogonis graminum 29
   silenes-acaulis 30
Leptothyrium clypeosphærioides 18

Leptothyrium vulgare 18
   vulgare parryæ 18
Leptotrichum tomentosum 261
Lescuræa imperfecta (292)
Leskea laxifolia (293)
   rigescens (293)
Leucolepis acanthoneura 285
Lichens 3, 4, 7, 9, 65
Lichen æruginosus (86)
   albo-cærulescens (80)
   ambiguus (131)
   anthracinus (127)
   apthosus (120)
   arcticus (122)
   ater (107)
   atrocinereus (102)
   atrosulphureus (107)
   atrovirens (76)
   aurantiacus (113)
   bellidiflorus (88)
   bicolor (139)
   brunneus (116)
   cæsius (128)
   caninus (118)
   cerinus (112)
   chalybeiformis (139)
   chlorophyllus (142)
   cinereus (104)
   cocciferus (90)
   confluens (80)
   conspersus (131)
   cornutus (93)
   crocatus (123)
   croceus (117)
   cucullatus (143)
   cylindricus (128)
   dactylinus (100)
   deformis (88)
   elænius (128)
   elegans (113)
   elongatus (93)
   erosus (127)
   fahlunensis (142)
   ferrugineus (112)
   fimbriatus simplex (94)
   floridus (140)
   fragilis (73)
   frigidus (105)
   frustulosus (108)

Lichen fuscellus (71)
    gelidus (109)
    geographicus (75)
    glaucus (142)
    granulosus (85)
    grœnlandicus (122)
    horizontalis (120)
    hypnorum (116)
    islandicus (144)
    jubatus (138)
    jungermanniæ (112)
    lanatus (131)
    lucidus (84)
    muralis (109)
    murorum (113)
        crenulatus (111)
    myochrous (114)
    nivalis (143)
    occulatus (105)
    ochroleucus (137)
    olivaceus (132)
    omphalodes (135)
    pallescens (106)
    pallidus (108)
    paschalis (98)
    pertusa (100)
    physodes (132)
    plicatus (140)
    polycarpus (136)
    polydactylus (120)
    proboscideus (127)
    pulmonarius (124)
    pyxidatus (95)
    quercizans (123)
    rangiferinus (92)
        alpestris (91)
    resupinatus (122)
    rigidus (137)
    rubinus (109)
    rufescens (108)
    sanguinarius (83)
    sarmentosus (138)
    scriptus (74)
    squarrosus (93)
    stellaris (129)
    stygius (131)
    subfuscus (107)
    tartareus (105)
    turfaceus (102)

Lichen uncialis (90)
    varius (106)
    venosus (121)
    vernalis (84)
    viridescens (85)
    vitellinus (111)
Licmophora cuneata 208
    granulata 208
    pennatula 208
Liebmannia 158, 181, 188, 224 pl XVI
Limacinia alaskensis 34, 58, pl IV, f. 1
Lithophyllum compactum 160
    farlowii 160, 206
    glaciale 160
Lithothamnion compactum 206
    glaciale 206
    læve 160, 206
Liverworts 8, 339
Lobaria linita (124)
Lophocolea cuspidata 360
Lophodermium maculare 26
    oxycocci 26
Lophozia 353
    attenuata 358
    floerkii 358
    guttulata 356
    heterocolpa 358
    incisa 357
    inflata 358
    kunzeana 359
    minuta 359
    obtusa 357
    ovata 359
    quadriloba 358
    quinquedentata 358
    saxicola 359
    ventricosa 355, 356
Lycoperdon puriforme 41
    saccatum 41
Lycopodium alpinum 391
    alpinum sitchense (392)
    annotinum 8, 392
        pungens 393
    aristatum robustius (392)
    clavatum 392
        pauci-divisum (392)
        sitchense (392)
    complanatum 392
    dendroideum (393)

Lycopodium inundatum 392
    juniperoideum (393)
    lucidulum 394
    obscurum 393
    rupestre (394, 395)
    selago 8, 394
        patens (394)
    sitchense 392
Lyellia crispa 307
Lyngbya ærugineo-cœrulea 162

Macrocystis pyrifera 159, 195, 246, pl. XXVII
Marasmius androsaceus 46
    filipes 46
    perforans 46
Marchantia polymorpha 345
Marsupella emarginata 349
    sphacelata 349
Massarina dryadis 29
Medicines 5, 8
Meesea triquetra 275
    tschuctschica 275, 306, 328, pl. XL, f. 3
    uliginosa 275
Melampsora alpina 40
    farinosa 40
    reticulata 40
Melobesia patena 154, 160, 205
Melosira granulata 206
    nummuloides 207
    sol 207
    sulcata 207
Meridion circulare 208
Mesogloia 188
    simplex 158, 187, 226, pl. XVII, f. 2-4
Mesotænium braunii 164, 212, pl. X, f. 29
Metasphæria empetri 29
Metzgeria hamata 347
    pubescens 347
Micrasterias denticulata 172, 214, pl. XI, f. 11
    fimbriata elephanta 172, 214, pl. XI, f. 31
    kitchelii 172, 214, pl. XI, f. 23
    oscitans pinnatifida 172, 214, pl. XI, f. 27

Micrasterias rotata 172, 212, pl. X, f. 25
    truncata 172, 214, pl. XI, f. 7
Microcera brachyspora 15, 28, 62, pl. VI, f. 28
Microcladia borealis 160, 204
Microcoleus vaginatus 161, 162
Microcystis marginata 160, 161
Microthyrium abietis 27
    harrimani 26, 54, pl. II f. 1
Mnium affine 283
    affine elatum 283
    cinclidioides 285
    glabrescens 259, 284
    insigne 284, 306
    medium 283
    nudum 284, 306
    punctatum anceps 284
        elatum 284
    rugicum 283
    spinulosum 284
    subglobosum 285
Moerckia hibernica (345)
Monostroma fuscum 173
    grœnlandicum 174
    splendens 174
    vahlii 174
Mosses 3, 4, 7, 251, 329
Munk 7
Mushrooms 6
Mycena atrocyanea 48
    atrocyanea minor 48
    debilis 48
    stannea 48
Myelophycus cæspitosa 184, 185
    intestinalis 157, 158, 184, 220, pl. XIV
Mylia taylori 359
Myrionema strangulans 158, 187, 218, pl. XIII, f. 1, 2
Myurella julacea 291
    julacea scabrifolia 291

Nardia compressa 344, 352
    crenulata 350
    crenuliformis (352)
    geoscypha (350)
    hæmatosticta 350
    minor (350)
    obovata 351

Nardia scalaris 350
Naucoria badipes 45
    camerina 45
    vernalis 45
Navicula apis 210
    cyprinus 209
    elliptica 209
    legumen 210
    major 209
    pupula 210
    radiosa 209
    silicula 209
Neckera menziesii 291
    pennata 291
Nectria episphæria 28
    sanguinea 15, 28
Nemastoma californica (204)
Nephrodium fragrans (383)
    fragrans aquilonaris (384)
    oreopteris (384)
    spinulosum intermedium (385)
Nephroma 118
    arcticum 122
    expallidum 122
    lætevirens 122
    lævigatum 121, 123, 129
        parile 122
    polaris (122)
    tomentosum 122
Nephromium parile (122)
Nereocystis giganteus 157
    lutkeanus (195)
    priapus 6, 159, 181, 195, 203, 242, 244, pl. xxv, xxvi
Nidularia candida 41
Nitella acuminata subglomerata 180
    opaca 180
Nitophyllum fryeanum 201
    latissimum 201
    ruthenicum 159, 201
Nitschia angularis 210
    closterium 210
    diadema 210
    sigmoidea 210
    vermicularis 210
Nolanea juncea 46
Nolaviea (46)
Normandina lætevirens (122)
Nostoc commune 161

Nostoc sphæroides 162

Odonthalia aleutica 157, 159, 202
    kamtschatica 159, 202
Œdipodium griffithsianum 252
Œdogonium concatenatum 176
Oligotrichum aligerum 287
    hercynicum latifolium (287)
    integrifolium 287, 306
Omphalia campanella 45, 47
    gracillima 48
    montana 47
    pseudo-androsacea 48
    pyxidata hepatica 48
    semivestipes 47
    sphagnophila 47
    umbellifera 47
Oncophora suecica 256
Oocystis solitaria crassa 173
Opegrapha 85
    varia 75
Ophioglossum 4
    alaskanum 376
    vulgatum (376)
        alaskanum (376)
Oreoweisia serrulata 255
Orthothecium chryseum 292
    intricatum 292, 306
Orthotrichum anomalum (271)
    arcticum 270, 306
    cribrosum 271
    fenestratum 270, 314, pl. xxxiii, f 2
    pulchellum 271
    speciosum 271
Oscillatoria amœna 161
Ovularia bulbigera 17
    sommeri 17
    trientalis (17, 35)

Pallavicinia blyttii 347
    hibernica 345
    lyellii 347
Paludella squarrosa 275
Pannaria brunnea 116
    hypnorum 116
    lanuginosa 116
    lepidiota coralliphora 116
    nigra 117
Pannularia nigra (117)

Parmelia 76, 113, 146
  ambigua 131
    albescens 131
  apiola (129)
  austerodes 135
  confragosa (102)
  conspersa 131
    stenophylla 131
  diatrypa (135)
  enteromorpha (133)
  lanata 131
  lanuginosa (116)
  olivacea 128, 132
  omphalodes (135)
  parietina (136)
    pygmæa (136)
  perforata 135
  perlata 135
  pertusa 135
  physodes 132, 139, 140, 144
    enteromorpha 133
    obscurata 132
    vittata 132, 133
  saxatilis 111, 132, 133, 139, 144
    omphalodes 77, 106, 107, 134, 135, 142
    panniformis 135
    sphærophoroidea 134
    sulcata 135
  straminea (109)
  stygia 109, 131
  sulcata (135)
  tartarea frigida (106)
  tiliacea 135
Parmeliopsis aleurites (135)
  ambigua (131)
Patellaria myriocarpa (77)
Patinella aloysii-sabaudiæ 22, 49, 54, pl II, f. 6
Peat 7, 331
Pediastrum angulosum 173
  boryanum 173
Pellæa densa 380
Pellia endiviæfolia 347
  epiphylla 347
  neesiana 347
Peltidea apthosa (121)
  canina membranacea (118)
    spuria (118)

Peltidea polydactyla scutata (121)
  pulverulenta (119)
Peltigera 122
  apthosa 120
  canina 118
    membranacea 119
    sorediata 121
    spongiosa 118
    spuria 119
  horizontalis 120
  polydactyla 120
    scutata 121
  pulverulenta 119
  rufescens 119
  scabrosa 121
  tomentosa (122)
  venosa 121
Peniophora disciformis borealis 43
Penium closterioides 164
  digitus 164, 214, pl XI, f 3
  interruptum 164
  margaritaceum 164
  oblongum 164
  polymorphum 164
Peridermium cerebrum 36
Peronospora ficariæ 35
  parasitica 35
Pertusaria 76, 107, 112
  bryontha 101
  carneo-pallida 100
  communis 100, (102), 106
    isidioidea 100
  dactylina 100
  glomerata 99
    corniculata 101
  multipuncta 100
  occulata (105)
  panyrga 101
  pocillaria 101, 152, pl. IX, f 1-5
  pustulata 99
  rhodocarpa 100
  rhodoleuca 101, 102
  sommerfeldtii 101
  subdactylina 101
  subobducens 101
  subplicans 101
  trochiscea 101
  velata 101
  xanthostoma 101

Phacidium diminuens 23
Phegopteris alpestris 381
    connectilis (382)
    dryopteris 381
        disjuncta 382
    phegopteris 382
        intermedia 382
    polypodioides (382)
Phialea albida 25
    broomei 25
    carneala 25, 54, Pl. II, f. 2
    cyathoidea 25
Philonotis acutiflora 274
    capillaris 275, 306
    fontana 274
        cæspitosa 274, 275
        serrata 274
    macounii 274, 306
    seriata 275
    vancouveriensis 275
Pholiota marginata 46
    præcox sylvestris 46
    unicolor 46
Phoma 30
    complanata 21
    oleracea 21
    ruborum 18
Phormidium autumnale 162
    laminosum 162
Phragmidium rubi 38
    rubi-idæi 38
    subcorticium 38
Phycocelis baltica 158, 180
Phyllachora filicina 27, 60, Pl. V, f. 15
    heraclei 27
Phyllitis fascia 158, 185
    scolopendrium 381
Phyllosticta caricicola 21, 62, Pl. VI, f. 18
    caricis 21
    helleboricola coptidis 21, 62, Pl. VI, f. 19
Physalospora alpina crepiniana (33)
    borealis 33, 58, Pl. IV, f. 4
    crepiniana 33
Physcia 78, 113
    adglutinata 128
    cæsia 109, 128
    leucomela 144
    lychnea (136)

Physcia melops 129
    melops ossicola 130
    muscigena 130
    obscura 130
        sciastra 130
    parietina lychnea (136)
    pulverulenta 129
    stellaris 129
        apiola 129
    tribacea 122, 123, 129
Physematium obtusum (387)
Physoderma menyanthis 35
Pilophoron polycarpum (97)
Pilophorus cereolus acicularis 97
    cereolus hallii 96
    robustus 97
Pirottæa yakutatiana 25, 30, 54, Pl. II, f. 4
Placodium 78, 79
    aurantiacum 113
    cerinum 108, 112
    coralloides 113
    crenulatum 111
    elegans 113
        tenue 114
    ferrugineum 74, 112
    fuscoatrum 112
    granulosum 114
    jungermanniæ 102, 112
    miniatum (114)
    murorum 108, 113
    nivale 114
    sinapispermum 114
    variabile 114
    vitellinum 111
Plagiochila asplenioides 359
Plagiothecium curvifolium (297)
    denticulatum 297
        donii 297
        recurvum 297
        undulatum 297
    elegans 297, 306
    fallax 296, 326, Pl. XXXIX, f. 4
    muehlenbeckii 297, 306
    pulchellum 297
    roeseanum 297, 306
    sylvaticum 297, 306
    undulatum 296
Platysma cucullata (144)

Platysma nivale (143)
　sæpincola minuta (146)
　septentrionale (146)
　tilesii (146)
Pleospora herbarum 29
　infectoria 28
　media 28
　　limonum 28
　pentamera 28
Pleurophycus 191
　gardneri 159, 191, 230, pl XIX
Pleurosigma angulata 210
　attenuata 210
　fasciola 210
Pleurotæniopsis debaryi 170, 214, pl. XI f. 20
　debaryi spitzbergensis 170
　pseudoconnata 170
　ralfsii 170
Pleurotænium minutum (167)
　nodosum 166
　truncatum 166
Plocamium coccineum uncinatum 159, 200
Pogonatum alpinum 288
　alpinum arcticum 289
　　brevifolium 289
　　macounii 288
　　septentrionale 289
　　simplex 289
　atrovirens 289
　capillare dentatum 287
　contortum 287
　dentatum (287)
　erythrodontium (287)
　macounii (288)
　microdontium (289)
　urnigerum 288
Polypodium alpestre (381)
　calcareum (381)
　dryopteris (381)
　　disjunctum (382)
　falcatum 8, 378
　phegopteris (382)
　　intermedium (382)
　vulgare 378
　　cambricum (378)
　　occidentale 378
Polyporus melanopus 44

Polyporus pubescens 44
Polysiphonia 197
　arctica 159, 202
　bipinnata 157, 159, 202
Polystichum aculeatum lobatum (382)
　aculeatum vestitum (382)
　braunii 382
　fragrans (383)
　lemmoni 383
　lonchitis 383
　munitum 383
　spinulosum (384)
Polystictus abietinus 43
　radiatus 43
　versicolor 43
Polytrichum behringianum 290
　boreale (290)
　commune 289, 290
　dentatum (287)
　formosum 289
　fragilifolium (290)
　gracile 289
　hyperboreum 290
　jensenii 290, 326, pl XXXIX, f. 2
　juniperinum 290
　　alpinum 290
　piliferum 290
　sexangulare 290
　strictum 290
　yukonense 267, 289, 326, pl XXXIX, f 1
Porella navicularis 343, 366
　platyphylla 366
　rivularis 366
Poria crassa 43
Porina glomerata (99)
　pustulata (99)
Porphyra amplissima 159, 197
　laciniata 159, 197
　miniata cuneiformis 159, 197
　perforata 5, 159, 197
　pertusa 200
　tenuissima 159, 197
Postelsia 157
Pottia heimii 262
　heimii arctica 262
　　beringiana 261, 310, pl XXXI, f 2
　　obtusifolia (262)

Prasiola crispa (176)
Preissia quadrata 344
Psathyrella atomaria 44
    disseminata 44
Pseudoleskea atrovirens 292, 306
    radicosa 292
    rigescens (292)
    stenophylla 292, 306
Pseudopeziza bistortæ 23
    cerastiorum arenariæ 23
Pseudovalsa ribesia 29, 60, pl. v, f. 14
Psilocybe polytrichi 44
Psilopilum arcticum 287
Pteridium aquilinum pubescens 379
    lanuginosum (379)
Pteridophytes 4, 8, 9, 373
Pteris aquilina (379)
    aquilina lanuginosa (379)
    argentea (379)
    lanuginosa (379)
Pterygophyllum lucens 291, 306
Ptilidium californicum 343, 363
    ciliare 363
Ptilota asplenoides 159, 203
    plumosa 159, 203
    serrata 160, 203
Puccinia asteris 39
    bullata 38
    caricis 37, 40
    circææ 38
    fergussoni 39
    gentianæ 37
    geranii silvatici 37, 39
    heucheræ 39
    laurentiana 38
    moliniæ 37
    porphyrogenita 39
    prenanthis 39
    procera 39
    saxifragæ 39
    saxifragæ-ciliatæ 38
    thlaspeos 39
    tiarellæ 39
    uliginosa 40
    valerianæ 39
Punctaria plantaginea 158, 184
    plantaginea linearis 184
Pycnothalia cladinoides 147
Pylaiella littoralis 158, 196

Pylaiella littoralis acuta 182
    densa 183
    macrocarpa 183
    opposita 182
    varia 183
Pyrenophora chrysospora 28
    connata 28
    phæospora 28
    polyphragmia 28
    polyphragmoides 28, 60, pl. i, f 13
Pyrenula 78
    gemmata 70
Pythium gracile 35

Radula arctica (366)
    bolanderi 343, 366
    complanata 366
    krausei (366)
Ralfsia clavata 158, 188
    deusta 158, 180, 188
Ramalina 3
    calicaris farinosa 147
    cuspidata 147
    geniculata (147)
    minuscula 147
    polymorpha 146
        emplecta 146
    pusilla geniculata 147
Ramularia æquivoca 17
    anserina 16
    arnicalis 17
    cercosporoides 16
    heraclei 17
    macrospora 17
    pratensis 17
    punctiformis 16, 56, pl. III, f. 8
Raphidostegium pseudorecurvans (301)
    subdemissum 296
Red snow 173
Reindeer 7
Remedies 5
Rhabdonema arcuata 207
    biquadratum 207
    elegans 207
    fauriæ 207
    japonica 207
    striatula 207
Rhabdospora camptospora 18, 62, pl. VI, f. 26

Rhabdoweisia fugax 255, 306
    fugax subdenticulata 255
Rhacomitrium aciculare 267
    canescens 269
        ericoides 269
            epilosa 269
            subepilosa 269
    cyclodictyon 268, 312, pl. XXXII, f. 3
    fasciculare 267
        haplocladon (267)
        minor 267
    heterostichum 268
        affine 268
    lanuginosum 268
        falcata 268
        stricta 268
    microcarpum palmeri (267)
    nevii 267
    palmeri (267)
    patens 267
    sudeticum alaskanum 267
    tenuinerve 267
Rhizoclonium riparium implexum 178
Rhodamea floccosa (154, 186)
Rhodochorton rothii 160, 204
Rhodomela 154
    floccosa 154, 159, 186, 202
    larix 159, 186, 200, 202
Rhodymenia palmata 5, 159, 187, 200
    pertusa 157, 159, 200
Rhoicosphenia curvata 211
Rhynchophoma 29, 31
    radula 21
    raduloides 20, 24, 60, pl. V, f. 17
Rhynchostegium serrulatum 296, 306
Rhytisma rhododendri 23
    salicinum 23, 32
Rinodina sophodes 102
    sophodes atrocinerea 102
    confragosa 102
    nimbosa 102
    turfacea 102, 112
        miniarea 102
        roscida 102
Rivularia biasolettiana 163
Rock tripe 7
Russula nigrodisca 47

Sagedia macrospora 101

Salix 7
Salt 5
Sargassum agardianum 157
Sauteria alpina 345
Scapania 259
    albescens (343, 365)
    bolanderi 343, 365
    curta 366
    irrigua 366
    nemorosa 366
    umbrosa 366
    undulata 365
Schizothrix lacustris 161
    lardacea 160
Scleroderris treleasei 24, 56, pl. III, f. 7
Scleropodium 303
    cespitosum 295
    colpophyllum 295
    illecebrum 295
    krausei (295)
Sclerotium durum 49
    varium 49
Scolecotrichum graminis 16
Scyphophorus bellidiflorus (88)
Scytonema figuratum 162
    mirabile 161, 162
    myochrous 162
    varium 162
Scytosiphon 184, 186
    bullosus 158, 185
    lomentarius 158, 184, 185
    complanatus 185
Selaginella rupestris (394, 395)
    rupestris sibirica (394)
    schmidtii 394
    krauseorum 395
    selaginoides 395
    spinosa (395)
    struthioloides 395
Septoria canadensis 18
    chamissonis 19, 62, pl. VI, f. 25
    dearnesii 19
    eriophorella 19, 62, pl. VI, f. 24
    eriophori 19
    grylli 19
    petroselini treleaseana 19, 62, pl. VI, f. 23
    rubi 18
    scirpi 19

Siphon 6
Siphula ceratites 74
   dactyliza 74
Skeletons 3
Smothering of trees 3, 140
Snow, red 173
Soil formers 9
Solorina crocea 117
   saccata 117
      spongiosa 117
   spongiosa (117)
Soranthera ulvoides 158, 186
Speira effusa 16
   minor 16
Sphacelaria cirrhosa 158, 161, 183
   racemosa arctica 158, 161, 183
Sphærella adusta 33
   alni-viridis 32
   californica 29, 32
   crus-galli 32
   eriophila 31
   graminum 32, 58, pl. IV, f. 5
   grossulariæ salicella 32, 58, pl. IV, f. 6
   harthensis 27, 32
   ignobilis 33
   lacustris 173
   leptospora 31, 58, pl. IV, f. 7
   octopetilæ 32
   ootheca 32
   pachyasca 33
   perexigua 31
   rumicis 33
   stellarinearum 32
   wichuriana 32
Sphærographium abditum 18, 29, 62, pl. VI, f. 27
Sphærophoron coralloides 73, 134
   fragile 73
   globiferus (73)
Sphærophorus 137
Sphærozosma excavatum spinulosum 172
Sphagnum 3, 7, 122, 331
   acutifolium 332
      pallescens 332
      rubrum 332
      versicolor 332
   aongstrœmii 332, 333, 335, 336

Sphagnum balticum 332
   compactum imbricatum 333
   cuspidatum recurvum (335)
   cymbifolium 333
   fimbriatum 333
      arcticum 333, 334
         fuscescens 333
   fuscum 333, 336
      pallescens 333
      robustum 333
   girgensohnii 334
      stachyodes (334)
      xerophilum 334
   imbricatum cristatum 334, 335
   lindbergii 334
      immersum 334
      microphyllum 334
         brachyclada (334)
         brachydasyclada (334)
   medium 334
      pallescens 335
   molluscum 335
   papillosum normale 335
   parvifolium 335
   recurvum 332, 335
      mucronatum 335
   riparium 335
   rubellum 335
      violascens 335
   russowii 335
      rhodochroum 335
   squarrosum 333, 336
      imbricatum 336
         brachyanoclada (336)
      semisquarrosum (336)
      subsquarrosum 336
   subnitens 335, 336
      pallescens 336
   teres 336
      subsquarrosum 336
   warnstorfii 336
      purpurascens 337
      violascens 337
Sphinctrina turbinata 147
Spirogyra 14
   porticalis 173
   varians 173
Splachnum luteum 272, 306
   sphæricum 272

Splachnum vasculosum 272
  wormskjoldii 272
Sporonema strobilinum 18
Sporormia ambigua 29
Stagonospora anemones 19
  aquatica lacustris 20
    luzulicola 20, 62, Pl. VI, f. 20
  graminum 20, 62, Pl VI, f. 22
  heleocharidis caricina 20, 62, Pl. VI, f. 21
  pulsatillæ 18, 19, 33
Staurastrum arctiscon 171
  calyxoides 170, 212, Pl. X, f. 31
  dejectum 170, 214, Pl XI, f. 5
    mucronatum 170
  echinatum 171, 212, Pl X, f 16
  furcigerum 171
  polymorphum 171, 212, Pl X, f. 23, 24
  pygmæum 170
  ravenelii 170, 214, Pl XI, f. 29
Stauroneis phœnicentron 210
Stemonitis smithii 22
Stereocaulon alpinum (98)
  coralloides 99
  denudatum 97
  paschale 98
  tomentosum 98
    alpinum 98
  wrightii 99
Sticta anthraspis 123
  crocata 122, 123, 129
  limbata 125
  linita (124, 125)
  oregana 124, 125
  pulmonacea (124)
  pulmonaria 124
    linita 125
  quercizans 123
  scrobiculata 125
Stigonema 160, 161
  ocellatum 163
Streblonema irregularis 158, 181, 216, Pl XII, f. 2
  minutissima 158, 180, 216, Pl. XII, f. 3
  minutulum 181
  pacifica 158, 181, 216, Pl. XII, f. 1
Stilophoræ 181

Stropharia magnivelaris 44
Struthiopteris spicant (387)
Sunburn 6
Surirella elegans 210
Synedra crotonensis 208
  fasciculata 208
  prolongata 208
  ulna 208
Systophyllum lepidum (154, 186)

Tabellaria flocculosa 208
Tænia lennebackeræ 157
Tayloria serrata 272
  tenuis 272, 306
Tetmemorus brebissonii 166, 214, Pl. XI, f. 13
  lævis 166
Tetraphis geniculata 271
  pellucida 271
Tetraplodon 3
  mnioides 272
    cavifolius 272
  urceolatus 272
Thalassiophyllum clathrus 159
Thalassosira cleve 207
Thamnolia 92, 122
  vermicularis subuliformis 86
    taurica 86
Thecopsora vacciniorum 38
Thelephora laciniata 43
Theloschistes lychneus 77, 109, 136
  lychneus pygmæus 108, 109, 136
  parietinus 136
    polycarpus (136)
  polycarpus 129, 136
Thermal algæ 161
Thuidium abietinum 293
Tillandsia 3
Timmia austriaca 285
Tiyeti 5
Tobacco 6, 44
Tolypothrix tenuis 162
Trees smothered 3, 140
Tremella atro-virens 42
  phyllachoroidea 42, 56, Pl. III, f. 11
Trentepohlia iolithus 177
Triceratium wilkesii 207
Trichia scabra 21
Tricholoma melaleucum 49

Trichopeziza earoleuca 24, 54, pl. II,
  f. 5
  hamata 24
  relicina 24
Trichostomum bambergeri 263
  cuspidatissimum 262, 263, 308, pl.
    xxx, f. 4
  cuspidatum (262)
  mutabile 262
    cuspidatum 262
  sitkanum 263, 310, pl. XXXI, f. 1
Triploceras gracile (166)
Trochiscia moniliformis 207
Tsakwat 6
Tubaria brevipes 45
Tubifera ferruginosa 22
Tuburcinia trientalis 17, 35
Tundra 3, 331
Turnerella mertensiana 159, 199

Uhtonah 8
Ulota alaskana 269, 312, pl. XXXII, f. 4
  barclayi 270
  bruchii 270
  camptopoda 270
  connectens 270
  crispa 269
    subclavescens 270
  crispula 270
  drummondii 269
  intermedia 270
  maritima (269)
  phyllantha 269, 270
Ulothrix flaccida 176
  parietina (176)
Ulva lactuca 187
  lactuca myriotrema 174
    rigida 174
  priapus (195)
Umbilicaria 7
  anthracina 127
  cylindrica 128
  erosa 127
    subradicans 127
  flocculosa 128
  hirsuta 126
    papyria 126
  hyperborea 127
  muhlenbergii alpina 126

Umbilicaria proboscidea 127
  rugifera 128
  vellea tylorrhiza 126
Urceolaria gibbosa (105)
  scruposa 147
Uredo aspidiotus 41
  ledicola 36
  nootkatensis 36
Uromyces dactylidis 36
  erythronii 41
  lapponicus 41
Urospora penicilliformis 177
Uroveet 7
Uses of cryptogams 4
Usnea 3
  barbata 140
    dasypoga 141
  florida 140
  plicata 140, 141
  longissima 132, 139, 140
  ochroleuca (137)
Ustilago bistortarum 35
  bistortarum glabra 36
    inflorescentiæ 35
  vinosa 35

Vampyrella spirogyræ 22
Vanheurckia rhomboides 210
Varicellaria microstica 147
Variolaria multipuncta (100)
Vaucheria 162
  sessilis 179
Venturia circinans 31
  kunzei 31
    ramicola 31, 58, pl. IV, f. 8
Verrucaria acrotella 72
  aurantii 72
  bryophila 72
  bryospila 72
  ceuthocarpa 72
  chlorotica 72
  discedens 72
  exalbida 72
  fallax 72
  fulva 71, 150, pl. VIII, f. 1-3
  fuscella 71
  gemmata (70)
  hymenogonia 72
  integra 72

Verrucaria intercedens 72
    intermedia 72
    lævata 72
    leptaleoides 72
    maura 71
    maurioides 72
        conyzoides 72
    mucosa 71
    muralis dolosula 72
    nigrata 72
    obnigrescens 72
    obtenata 72
    pernigrata 72
    prominula 72
    punctiformis 72
    pyrenophora 72
    sublectissima 72
    subumbrina 72
    terrestris 72
    thelodes 71, 72
    verrucosa-areolata 72
Vibrissea truncorum 26

Webera 280
    albicans 277
        glacialis 277
    annotina 277, 306
    cruda 275
    crudoides 277
    cucullata 276
    cucullatiformis 277
    drummondii 276, 277

Webera gracilis 276
    nutans 275
        bicolor 276
        cæspitosa 276
        strangulata 276
    polimorpha 277
    proligera 277
    pseudo-gracilis 276, 316, pl. xxxiv, f. 2
Wicks 7, 8
Woodsia alpina 386
    alpina glabella (386)
    glabella 386
    hyperborea (386)
        rufidula (387)
    ilvensis 387
    obtusa 387
    scopulina 387

Xanthidium antilopæum 167, 212, pl. x, f. 38
    armatum 167, 214, pl. xi, f. 18
Xylographa 79
    opegraphella 74
    parallela pallens 75

Zonaria tournefortii 157
Zoostera (154)
Zostera 154
    marina 183, 184, 187
Zygnema 162, 173

CPSIA information can be obtained
at www.ICGtesting.com
Printed in the USA
LVHW080856250922
729223LV00003B/22